ACHIEVING YOUR DIPLOMA
in EDUCATION *and* TRAINING

2nd Edition

Jim Gould and Jodi Roffey-Barentsen

Los Angeles | London | New Delhi
Singapore | Washington DC | Melbourne

Los Angeles | London | New Delhi
Singapore | Washington DC | Melbourne

SAGE Publications Ltd
1 Oliver's Yard
55 City Road
London EC1Y 1SP

SAGE Publications Inc.
2455 Teller Road
Thousand Oaks, California 91320

SAGE Publications India Pvt Ltd
B 1/I 1 Mohan Cooperative Industrial Area
Mathura Road
New Delhi 110 044

SAGE Publications Asia-Pacific Pte Ltd
3 Church Street
#10-04 Samsung Hub
Singapore 049483

Editor: James Clark
Assistant editor: Robert Patterson
Production editor: Nicola Carrier
Copyeditor: Jill Birch
Proofreader: Derek Markham
Indexer: Author
Marketing manager: Dilhara Attygalle
Cover design: Sheila Tong
Typeset by: C&M Digitals (P) Ltd, Chennai, India
Printed in the UK

Library of Congress Control Number: 2017946071

British Library Cataloguing in Publication data

A catalogue record for this book is available from the British Library

ISBN 978-1-5264-1132-7
ISBN 978-1-5264-1133-4 (pbk)

At SAGE we take sustainability seriously. Most of our products are printed in the UK using FSC papers and boards. When we print overseas we ensure sustainable papers are used as measured by the PREPS grading system. We undertake an annual audit to monitor our sustainability.

ACHIEVING YOUR DIPLOMA
in EDUCATION *and* TRAINING

Sara Miller McCune founded SAGE Publishing in 1965 to support the dissemination of usable knowledge and educate a global community. SAGE publishes more than 1000 journals and over 800 new books each year, spanning a wide range of subject areas. Our growing selection of library products includes archives, data, case studies and video. SAGE remains majority owned by our founder and after her lifetime will become owned by a charitable trust that secures the company's continued independence.

Los Angeles | London | New Delhi | Singapore | Washington DC | Melbourne

CONTENTS

LIST OF FIGURES

ABOUT THE AUTHORS

Jim Gould has over 40 years of experience in teaching within the schools, Adult Education and Further Education sectors. He has managed Teacher Education departments in colleges in Surrey and Hampshire, and, although now semi-retired, remains active in the delivery of Diploma, Professional Graduate Certificate in Education and BA (Hons) Education programmes. Jim has extensive experience in curriculum development and has acted in a consultancy role in a variety of course planning and validation events. Despite everything, he still supports Blackpool Football Club.

Jodi Roffey-Barentsen is Senior Lecturer and Programme Leader at the School of Education at the University of Brighton. She has extensive experience in teaching and learning in a range of educational settings, including Further and Higher Education. Her research interests are in the fields of Reflective Practice, Learning Support and Widening Participation. Jodi works as a consultant for an international exam board and is a Senior Fellow of the Higher Education Academy.

NEW TO
SECOND EDITION

The primary updates to this new edition of *Achieving your Diploma in Education and Training* include new reflective activities placed throughout each chapter, these tasks challenge you to engage critically with the topics and points raised in the text and will help to develop your thinking on key issues.

Also new to this edition is new content on employability skills, which has been incorporated into Chapter 1 as well as a Further Reading feature which has been added to each chapter in order to direct you toward other literature in the field.

Alongside these updates, the book has been revised more generally to reflect major developments in Further Education and Skills Sector education and training that have taken place since the publication of the first edition.

ACKNOWLEDGEMENTS

The authors are grateful to Richard Bicknell and Esther Hewson for allowing us to adapt planning documents they use. Particular thanks are due to Dr Michael Johnson for the sharing of his expertise in quality assurance and his significant contribution to Chapter 10 of this book – 'Thanks for the bits he did'.

A debt of gratitude is also due to Iain Wolloff for his considerable contribution to this second edition in updating the sections on policy and quality. Matters move on quickly in these areas and Iain's depth of knowledge coupled with his experience in the sector have proved invaluable.

1
EDUCATION AND TRAINING: THE TEACHER'S ROLE AND RESPONSIBILITIES

This chapter sets the scene for those who are working, or are intending to work, within Education and Training. It looks at what teachers actually do and what is expected of them by examining the different aspects of the teaching role, the associated responsibilities and boundaries of practice. Issues of diversity, inclusion, differentiation and equality figure largely in this mix and the different terms are defined and their implications for practice explained. Ways of setting ground rules which contribute to an inclusive approach to teaching are explored before the chapter finishes with a discussion of the importance of functional skills and the part that teachers play in supporting the needs of learners in this respect.

When you have completed this chapter you will be able to:

- categorise the different roles fulfilled by the teacher in the Further Education and Skills sector and give examples of these roles
- describe the specific responsibilities associated with the teaching role
- define the following terms: diversity, inclusion, differentiation, equality
- state the different aspects of diversity exhibited by learners within Education and Training

(Continued)

- recognise that different learners have different preferences in learning style
- list different strategies employed in providing a differentiated learning environment
- identify different aspects of equality and how these impact on practice
- evaluate different approaches to the setting of ground rules, identifying which would be appropriate within your own teaching context
- define the terms 'minimum core' and 'functional skills'
- describe what is meant by the term 'embedding functional skills'
- identify when employability skills are embedded within the session
- differentiate between activities that fall within and outside of the role of the teacher.

TEACHING IN EDUCATION AND TRAINING

Teaching qualifications within the Further Education and Skills sector have undergone several changes in the last few years. The Level 5 Diploma in Education and Training was introduced in 2013 replacing the previous Diploma in Teaching in the Lifelong Learning Sector (DTLLS), as a consequence of the findings of the 2012 Lingfield report (BIS, 2012) into professionalisation within the sector. The new diploma is part of a suite of qualifications (including the Level 3 Award and the Level 4 Certificate in Education and Training) introduced with the intention of simplifying the overall qualification structure and bringing it into line with the Qualifications and Credit Framework (QCF). The diploma is built up by combining a number of units. These are divided into two groups. Group A contains a number of mandatory units at Levels 4 and 5, which will be taken by everyone who is enrolled for the diploma. They are:

Teaching, learning and assessment in education and training (20 credits, Level 4)

Developing teaching, learning and assessment in education and training (20 credits, Level 5)

Theories, principles and models in education and training (20 credits, Level 5)

Wider professional practice and development in education and training (15 credits, Level 5)

The remaining 45 credits at Levels 4 and 5 required to complete the diploma are taken from a list of optional units contained in Group B.

Although there is some overlap with various optional units, the chapters in this book primarily address the requirements of the mandatory units. The 'fit' between chapters and units can be found in the mapping document in Appendix 1 at the end of the book.

ROLE OF THE TEACHER IN EDUCATION AND TRAINING

When we think about a 'role', we consider the duties or activities we associate with a given job or position. If you take on the role of a lorry driver, for instance, your role is to drive a lorry. If you are a dancer, you dance; if you are a cleaner, you clean. Logically then, if you are a teacher, you teach. Is this the full story of the role of the teacher though? Certainly, teaching will constitute a large proportion of what you do, but unlike the other examples above, being a teacher involves much more than the 'core' role that the name of the occupation suggests.

ACTIVITY 1.1

Take a moment to reflect on everything that you do in a working day. Keep a brief log for a week of all the activities in which you engage during your working day to get an idea of the scope of the job that you are doing. For example:

Monday

9.00 Answer emails – two course enquiries.................

Activity 1.1 illustrates that although it is reasonable to assume that passing on knowledge or skills to learners is the main activity in which teachers are involved, a good proportion of the working day is spent on other pursuits. Your analysis of your daily work pattern will have identified a number of sub-roles, many of which will appear in Figure 1.1. The initial impression given by the results of this exercise is that the list is scarily long and one is tempted to wonder how we can possibly fulfil all of these functions within the hours allocated – but somehow we do!

An analysis of the overall role that we fulfil helps in coming to a conscious recognition of all that we do. This recognition can help us in managing and organising our time. For this purpose, it can be helpful to consider the various roles as falling into discrete categories. For example:

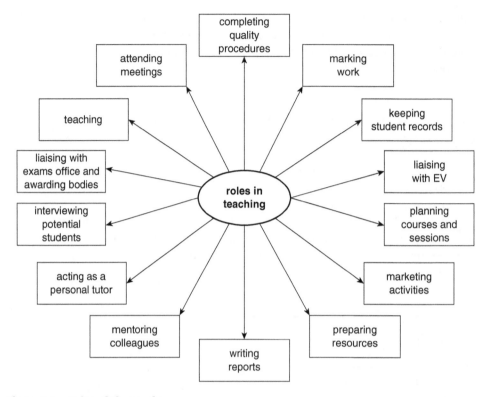

Figure 1.1   Roles of the teacher

TEACHING-RELATED ROLES

Writing schemes of work and session plans; preparing resources; preparing and delivering teaching sessions; marking work; giving feedback to learners; acting as an internal verifier; taking part in course development.

ADMINISTRATIVE ROLES

Writing reports; marking registers; keeping learners' records; implementing quality procedures; corresponding with parents, employers and examining bodies.

INSTITUTIONAL ROLES

Attending parents'/open evenings; preparing prospectus entries; dealing with course enquiries; acting as a mentor to new colleagues; attending meetings; providing data.

PASTORAL ROLES

Acting as a personal tutor; chasing absences; dealing with lateness or discipline problems.

Once identified, the various sub-roles can be prioritised, enabling them to be more effectively and efficiently managed. Tensions can still arise, however, as various roles compete for our time and difficult decisions often have to be made. A further complication arises in that considerations of what constitutes a priority can depend on the viewpoint taken. Others may put pressure on us to engage in what we consider to be less important tasks at the expense of what we see as more important tasks. Your view and your line manager's view, for instance, may differ as to whether thorough preparation of tomorrow's teaching session is more important than completing those employer feedback forms that have been lying around for some time now. If both have to be completed for the next day and there is only sufficient time to tackle one properly, which will it be?

An awareness of all that is asked of us also means that we are better able to identify which aspects of our role we feel uncertain about so we can plan our CPD opportunities accordingly. Whilst we may feel reasonably confident in the performance of the main duties we have to carry out, we sometimes have to take on a role with which we feel less comfortable. You may have been asked to take on a tutoring role, although you feel you do not have the necessary experience or preparation, especially if having to teach aspects of social and personal education are included in this. This could be raised as a developmental issue at appraisal or you could enquire at an earlier stage about the possibilities of shadowing a more experienced colleague who was in this role.

REFLECTIVE TASK 1.1

Take a moment to consider the different sub-roles that you are expected to fulfil during your everyday working life. Which of these do you consider to be your core 'professional roles'? Can you identify any tensions between any of these roles – if so, how can you resolve these?

RESPONSIBILITIES

As we have seen, a lorry driver has a narrower and more easily definable role than a teacher. Within that narrower role, however, there are a number of responsibilities. There is an expectation that the lorry will be driven in a safe manner showing due respect for other road users and with regard to any speed restrictions that might apply. The lorry driver will be expected to keep up to date with relevant legislation, such as the number of hours that can be spent driving in a 24-hour time period; to check the roadworthiness of their vehicle and ensure that it is securely loaded before venturing onto the road. Lorry drivers are not unique in this respect, and, over and above the defining of tasks or duties associated with the specific role to be filled, *all* jobs are accompanied by an associated set of responsibilities. As well as carrying out all of the duties associated with the teaching role we are to fulfil, there is also an expectation that we do a 'proper job', subscribing to what is considered 'good practice', carrying out the role in a professional manner. But what exactly does this mean?

For a start, we are expected, like our lorry driver, to be aware of and keep up to date with the various bits of legislation that apply to our role.

ACTIVITY 1.2

Whilst some legislation is at least in part subject-related, there is a considerable body of legislation that applies within the Further Education and Skills sector as a whole. List as many examples as you can of legislation which must be adhered to in the performance of the teaching role.

You may be surprised by the amount of legislation you have identified and by the range of activity it covers. To help make sense of it all, we can consider it as falling into the following categories:

- Legislation relating to health and safety – the responsibility to provide a safe environment, both physical and psychological:
  - Health & Safety at Work Act (1974)
  - Manual Handling Operations Regulations (1992)
  - RIDDOR – Reporting of Injuries, Diseases and Dangerous Occurrences Regulations (1995)
  - Management of the Health & Safety at Work Act (1999)
  - COSHH – Control of Substances Hazardous to Health Regulations (2002).

- Legislation relating to equality – the responsibility to treat others with due respect and ensure equality of opportunity for all:
  - DDA – Disability & Discrimination Act (1995)
  - SENDA – Special Educational Needs and Disability Act (2001)
  - Sex Discrimination Act (1975)
  - Race Relations Act (1976, amended 2000)
  - Human Rights Act (1998)
  - Equal Opportunities Act (2004)
  - Most of the above have now been subsumed into and replaced by the Equality Act of 2010.
- Legislation of a more general nature – including the responsibility to safe-guard learners and their rights:
  - Safeguarding Vulnerable Groups Act (2006)
  - Data Protection Act (1998)
  - Copyright Designs and Patents Act (1998)
  - Computer Misuse Act (1990)
  - Protection from Harassment Act (1997).

The range of legislation is vast and is subject to periodic change. Fortunately, the institution that you work in will have responded to the vast majority of the legislation listed above and will have translated it, through a variety of different committees, into institutional policy. You will, for example, have to undergo a DBS (Disclosure and Barring Service – formed through a merging of the Criminal Records Bureau [CRB] and the Independent Safeguarding Authority [ISA]) check before you can take up a place-ment or enter into employment in most institutions in the sector. New staff will be informed of institutional policy as part of their induction programme and all staff will be informed of policy updates and changes. By following institutional policy, you will therefore generally be complying with the appropriate legislation. You still need to be aware of any particular legislative requirements related to your subject specialism, however, and follow the procedures these demand (e.g. filling in risk assessments before taking students off-site or wearing appropriate personal protection equipment in workshop environments) in a responsible manner.

There is also a more general responsibility to comply with a Code of Conduct. A new professional body for the sector – The Education and Training Foundation (originally proposed as the Further Education Guild) – came into being in 2013 and part of its remit was to promote professionalism in the sector, which included the set-ting of professional standards and code of conduct. This replaced the Code of Conduct originally provided by the Institute for Learning (IfL) which covered Integrity, Respect,

Care, Practice, Disclosure and Responsibility. The current professional standards can be found at www.et-foundation.co.uk/supporting/support-practitioners/professional-standards/

Alongside this runs the 'doing a good job' or 'exemplifying good practice' element and this is more difficult to pin down. Sometimes, it can be difficult to identify 'good practice' as it leads to a smooth-running process. It is often better to start with a consideration of 'bad practice', which is easier to identify as its results are more easily recognisable.

REFLECTIVE TASK 1.2

Drawing on your own experiences of being taught, make a list of what you consider to be 'bad practice' in teaching and use it to construct a 'good practice' list. What does this list tell you about the responsibilities associated with the teacher's role? Use this list as a framework to reflect upon your own practice – how does it compare?

You might like to check your list against the points made in the following chapters, but in the meantime use it as a checklist against which to compare your own 'good practice'.

The next section looks at another major responsibility associated with teaching within the sector and relates to differences in learners and their implications for the way we go about teaching.

DIVERSITY AND INCLUSION

ACTIVITY 1.3

You will come across the terms diversity, inclusion, equality and differentiation frequently in your reading around practice in the sector and in your conversations with colleagues. Before you read the next section, think about what these terms mean to you. When you have finished this chapter, you may want to come back and revisit these thoughts. Imagine you are at a social gathering and are taking part in a conversation with a reasonably large group of friends and acquaintances. The topic of conversation is quite contentious but involves something that everyone in the group has some familiarity with, although the level of knowledge is quite varied. You know quite a lot about the topic and know most of the group but not all of them. How would you participate in the conversation? Would you talk to everyone in the same way? Would you use the same tone of familiarity and the same level of vocabulary with everyone? Would you talk to some of the group and not to others? Would you treat all contributions to the conversation with the same respect?

The above is quite a common situation and we normally call on a variety of social skills when engaging in such a conversation. We may explain a point or express a view in a different way depending on who we are talking to; we would probably smile encouragingly or ask a straightforward question of someone who seemed to be struggling to take part in the conversation so that they wouldn't feel left out. Although we disagreed with some of the points made, we would still acknowledge the right of others to hold and express their own opinions. We would probably do all of these things intuitively without even thinking about them. In short, we would recognise the differences in the various people in the group and respond accordingly, allowing effective communication with everyone and making them all feel part of the conversation.

When we teach, we are faced with a similar situation. Any group that we meet will contain a rich mix of learners with their own particular backgrounds, capabilities, previous experience and confidence levels. The term we use for this variety in learner characteristics is *diversity*. We will, however, want to ensure that, regardless of difference, all learners participate fully in and feel part of the sessions we deliver. We will want our sessions to be *inclusive* of all learners in the same way that we would want everyone to feel part of the conversation described above. We would want to demonstrate 'inclusive practice', engaging in 'an approach to teaching and learning that endeavours to encourage the fullest participation of learners and that recognises and respects equality and diversity' (Duckworth and Tummons, 2010: 21).

In conversation, we achieve this through tailoring our exchanges with others in a way that we think is appropriate to that particular individual. To achieve this in a teaching situation, we would need to recognise the differences in our learners and respond to these through the use of *differentiation* strategies, an approach which 'both recognises the individuality of learners and also informs ways of planning for learning and teaching that take these individualities into consideration' (Duckworth and Tummons, 2010: 21).

Just as we would be respectful of others and their views in a social setting, we would also have to ensure that all learners felt their contributions would be valued and opinions respected, encouraging them to participate fully in the teaching session. This would form part of the *equality* policy that operated during our sessions.

In normal life, we deal with all of these quite naturally, using the social skills we have built up over the years. In our teaching life, we need to develop an equivalent set of teaching skills to manage the same issues when we meet them within the learning environment.

We will consider the issue of diversity first.

REFLECTIVE TASK 1.3

We have defined diversity as the range of different characteristics displayed by learners. What differences have you noticed in learners you have met? Do you think you have responded to these and if so, in what way?

When we are born, we have no experience of the outside world – we are essentially a blank page waiting to be written on, and so early on in life the diversity within a group is relatively limited. As we progress through life, we begin to form a sense of our own identity which is shaped by the experiences we have. As we grow older and gain further experience, this sense of identity, or who we are, gradually becomes more clearly defined but also more complex. By the time learners reach the stage of young adults, this process is fairly well advanced and so groups of learners within the sector tend to exhibit a far greater range of diversity than, for instance, the schools sector. Diversity in learners is thus more prevalent in the Further Education and Skills sector and needs to be recognised and taken account of.

Diversity can be viewed in different ways. It can be considered as a further complication to be taken account of in teaching – a problem to be solved. Alternatively, it can be regarded as a characteristic which enriches, rather than complicates, the learning environment. Diversity can be thought of as introducing new ideas and ways of looking at things – it can broaden horizons and become a resource for learning. It is this latter view of valuing or 'celebrating' diversity that leads to the positive inclusive learning environment that we would wish to create.

ASPECTS OF DIVERSITY

What form does this diversity take?

The 2010 Equality Act describes diversity in terms of nine protected characteristics:

- age
- disability

- gender reassignment
- marriage and civil partnership
- pregnancy and maternity
- race
- religion and belief
- sex
- sexual orientation.

Definitions of these can be found at www.equalityhumanrights.com/en/equality-act/protected-characteristics

The issues raised by these characteristics will largely be addressed through institutional policy, and our view of diversity needs to be wider ranging and consider all aspects of diversity which have a direct impact on learning. When we first meet a group of learners, some aspects of diversity are fairly evident, others less so. The analogy that is often used to illustrate this point is that of an iceberg. When we see an iceberg, what is visible to us is that part of the iceberg which protrudes above the surface of the sea. The vast bulk of the iceberg, however, lies beneath the surface. To obtain an accurate picture of the whole of it, we would have to explore beneath the surface as well as above it; similarly with the learners we meet. They display a physical presence that we can see, but if we wish to understand them as a whole, we need to probe beneath the surface to see what is hidden there. Some of the characteristics we might come across are illustrated in Figure 1.2, along with their relative visibilities.

How do we get to know our learners? How do we begin to find out what lies beneath their various surfaces? The first steps in this process may be taken before the course itself actually commences. *Initial assessment* can provide a preliminary picture, and has two principle functions:

1. To ensure that learners are placed on the appropriate course or programme of study.
2. To identify any form of additional support that will be required in order for learners to be successful on their chosen course.

The first of these functions is normally met through some form of interview process and we may make contact with our prospective learners at this point. The interview process should answer questions such as:

- Does the learner fulfil any entry requirements that exist?
- Is this course a natural progression from qualifications already held?
- Is the course pitched at an appropriate level?
- Is the course compatible with learner aspirations and career goals?

Its purpose lies in ensuring that learners are placed on the most appropriate course in the first place. Retention has a major impact on funding and we wish to ensure that

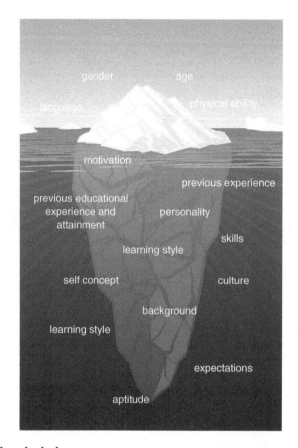

gender   age

language   physical ability

motivation

previous experience

previous educational
experience and   personality
attainment

skills

learning style

self concept   culture

background

learning style

expectations

aptitude

Figure 1.2   The diversity iceberg

Source: © istockphoto.com/ultra_generic

once accepted onto a course learners will 'stay the distance'. Having arrived at an appropriate choice of course, will learners require any additional support in order to ensure a successful outcome? We would not want to set anyone up to fail, and wish to avoid the consequences for funding of lack of achievement on the part of learners. Initial assessment normally includes, therefore, a number of tests relating to capability in numeracy, literacy and ICT, as well as a possible identification of learning styles. So it is possible, depending on our level of involvement and the rigour of the initial assessment process, that we will have some advance knowledge of our learners, but at a minimum we should be aware of the results of the tests they have taken as part of the initial assessment process.

Once we meet learners as a group in the learning environment, we gradually get what is colloquially termed 'a feel for' both the group and the individual learners within it through the work they produce, the comments they make and the conversations we have with them, either on an informal basis or as part of a tutorial function; in short, by doing all of the things we normally do in the process of getting to know people.

DIVERSITY AND LEARNING

Given that any mature group we meet in everyday life will exhibit a range of individual differences, why is it of particular concern to us as a teacher within the sector? The simple answer is that the differences identified above have an effect on the way in which people engage in the learning process.

ACTIVITY 1.4

Look at the characteristics in the 'diversity iceberg'. Pick out three characteristics and identify the effect each might have on a person's learning. How might you respond to each characteristic in your teaching? Use a grid like the one below to structure your response. An example entry has been provided.

Table 1.1

Aspect of diversity	Effect on learning	Teaching response
Self-concept	If poor, might lead to lack of confidence	Set work which results in successful outcomes, increasing confidence

---

LEARNING STYLES: AN EXAMPLE OF DIVERSITY

Ginnis (2002: 23) suggests that teachers may feel overwhelmed when faced with the diversity referred to above, but suggests that models of learning styles provide some relief in that they 'simplify the complexity and enable us to manage the territory'.

Many definitions of learning styles have been put forward but, for our purposes, we will turn to that suggested by Tennant (2006: 81), who defines learning style as 'an individual's characteristic and consistent approach to organising and processing information'. Similarly, there are numerous models which try and explain this process by identifying what the different 'approach(es) to organising and processing information' are. Perhaps the most well-known models are those of Kolb (Converger, Diverger,

Assimilator, Accommodator) and Honey and Mumford (Activist, Theorist, Pragmatist and Reflector), but this section focuses on the model proposed by Gregorc, as described in Ginnis (2002), which suggests that a learning style has two parts to it:

1. Taking information in.
2. Processing the information.

Taking information in

Before you can use a piece of furniture you have bought in the form of a flat pack, your first job, on arriving home, is to assemble it. How do you approach this task?

Some people will start by tipping all of the bits onto the floor and picking out various parts and starting to put them together in a fairly experimental manner until finally all the bits are used (hopefully) and the piece of furniture is fully assembled. Others will take the pieces out and lay them out on the floor in a systematic manner, first checking what they have against the parts list before following the instructions in a step-by-step manner until the job is completed. Others will start off by looking at the diagrams which are included as part of the instructions and identify the appropriate pieces and assemble them as the diagram suggests. Each approach will work but different individuals may well have a preference for one or the other – they will feel more at home tackling the task in one particular way. What happens, however, if someone's preference is the 'get on with it' approach, but half way through they find they have more bits left than they thought and can't work out where they go? One solution is to just throw it all out and resolve never to buy flat-pack furniture again. A cheaper option, however, is to either look at the diagrams and try to make sense of where they have got to, or start reading the instructions on the recommended method of assembly and see if that can resolve the dilemma. The point is that although individually we have a preference for one approach, it does not mean we are incapable of doing it any other way. We can adopt any of the three approaches described above but have a preference for one. Similarly, with accessing information in a learning situation, we are capable of using all approaches but have a preference for one or another. We can all take in information by listening, looking or engaging with it in a more practical manner but have our own particular preferences. For some of us these preferences are strong, for others less so.

Whatever approach we finally take, initially information is taken in through the five senses – sight, hearing, touch, taste and smell. Sonbuchner (2008: 3) suggests that the use of different combinations of the senses, equates to the use of different 'learning channels'. These are the visual channel, the auditory channel and the kinaesthetic channel and relate principally to seeing, hearing and doing respectively. This approach to categorising learning styles has its roots in neuro-linguistic programming (NLP) and is commonly referred to as the VAK model. Learners' preferences in these areas are often identified as part of the initial assessment process. Ginnis (2002: 40) suggests that, statistically, the combination of learners found in any group we encounter will span the VAK range and so, as far as possible, the 'minimum requirement is to check that all lessons have sufficient elements of all three modalities'. So, the way in which we prefer to take in information when we learn is an aspect of diversity, and Ginnis suggests that when we teach we should include elements of listening, looking and doing within a session to take account of this.

Gregorc uses the terms 'concrete' and 'abstract' to describe how we take in and make sense of information. Concrete refers to things which are 'real' and can be accessed through the senses – not unlike the kinaesthetic or 'doing' approach described above. 'Abstract' refers to information presented in a more intangible or conceptual form such as words, which would suit an auditory or 'hearing' approach. The VAK model can be related to Gregorc's categories of concrete and abstract, as shown in Figure 1.3. The visual approach can be thought of as occupying a central position as a picture or a diagram, for instance, whilst not real (concrete) is less conceptual than a verbal description (abstract).

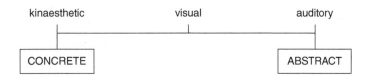

Figure 1.3   VAK and Gregorc

Processing the information

Gregorc next considers the way in which this information is organised and arranged. He suggests that some learners like to organise (and therefore receive) information in a linear, step-by-step manner following a logical train of thought. He called this a 'sequential' approach. Others prefer to take a 'random' approach, organising information in chunks in no particular order and then making their own particular sense out of it.

GREGORC'S MODEL OF LEARNING STYLES

The different combinations of these four characteristics lead to four different learning styles, as demonstrated in Figure 1.4. You can identify your own preferred 'Gregorc style' at www.thelearningweb.net/personalthink.html

As in the VAK model, learners can access all of the different styles, but will have their own particular preferences to some degree or another. The table in Figure 1.5 shows how the different styles might influence approaches to learning.

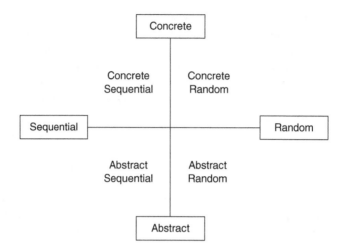

Figure 1.4   Gregorc's learning styles

Style	Like	Learn best from
Concrete Sequential	An ordered, structured, practical hands-on approach	Practical activities, structured workshops, using checklists
Concrete Random	An independent, experimental, investigative approach	Games and simulations, practical problem-solving activities
Abstract Sequential	A logical, academic, intellectual, structured approach	Lectures, independent research, reading
Abstract Random	An imaginative, flexible, deep, sensitive approach	Group discussion, role play, short lectures

Figure 1.5   Learning styles and learning preferences

Although it should not be taken too literally, Gregorc's model gives us some ideas about an appropriate range and mix of teaching strategies which can be used to accommodate the diverse ways in which people learn. Coffield et al. (2004) suggest that this should probably be the limit of our use of learning styles as serious question marks exist over the accuracy of the tests used to identify them. A systematic matching of teaching styles and learning styles is, he suggests, unrealistic and, in any case, the tendency to label people with one learning style or another is unhelpful. Generally, however, the view taken is that different people learn best in different ways, and Coffield et al. agree that the concept of learning styles gives teachers and learners a language with which to discuss these. A copy of Coffield et al.'s report can be found at http://sxills.nl/lerenlerennu/bronnen/Learning%20styles%20by%20 Coffield%20e.a.pdf

This particular aspect of diversity suggests, therefore, that learners have different preferences in the way in which they access and process information, and learn best from particular activities. We would respond to this by trying to include a balance of learning activities in the sessions we deliver to accommodate the mix of different learning styles, thus creating an inclusive learning environment.

REFLECTIVE TASK 1.4

What is your own preferred approach to learning? At a simple level, are you more visual, aural or kinaesthetic? If you do not know, try the exercise at: www. personal.psu.edu/bxb11/LSI/LSI.htm. Often, we teach in a way that is similar to our preferred style of learning. Do you think your teaching style is determined by your preferred learning style or is it sufficiently varied to accommodate all the preferences for learning exhibited by your learners?

DIFFERENTIATION IN LEARNING

The approach outlined above, where the diverse learning styles within a group are taken account of when teaching, is an example of a *differentiated* approach. As teachers, we are aware of this aspect of diversity and try to respond to it in our teaching. Petty (2009: 587) defines differentiation as 'adopting strategies that ensure success in learning for all, by accommodating individual differences of any kind'. In your response to Activity 1.4, you identified first an area of diversity and then by considering its effect on learning, arrived at a way of responding to it in your teaching. You identified a differentiation strategy appropriate to that particular aspect of diversity.

One of the most common aspects of diversity encountered in the groups we teach is the difference in previous knowledge and experience learners may bring with them and the aptitude they possess for the subject. Put simply, some learners may pick up on the ideas and concepts within the subject we teach more easily and quickly than others or engage with the subject matter at a deeper level. This can result in situations where, for instance, some learners or groups finish an exercise that has been set whilst others are still some way off completing it. How can a differentiated approach be used to take account of this particular aspect of diversity, whilst still maintaining the momentum of the group as a whole? Some possibilities include:

- Having an extra task ready for those that complete early. This task should be slightly more difficult to stretch learners that bit further as it is evident they can complete tasks of the original level of difficulty. For this reason, it is known as an 'extension' task as it extends learners that bit more.

- Using worksheets in which the questions or exercises gradually increase in complexity and difficulty. Each person completes as many of the questions or exercises as they can.
- Having stronger learners 'buddy up' with and help weaker learners. This is beneficial to both parties as one is receiving extra support whilst the other has to think hard and deep about the subject in order to provide that support.
- When questioning, nominating who is to answer and matching the difficulty of the question to the level at which the learner is working.
- Within reason, spending extra one-to-one time with those that need it most.
- Setting individualised objectives which demand different levels of achievement around the same learning, thus stretching stronger learners whilst providing a more achievable goal for weaker learners. Typically, this might involve three levels of objective. An 'all will' basic objective, a 'some will' objective and 'a few might' objective. This approach needs to be managed carefully, however, and Ginnis (2002: 234–45) gives an excellent explanation of how to go about this.

Generally, the more open an activity, the more control learners have. Learning becomes self-regulated and is therefore more likely to occur at a level which is manageable but challenging for each individual. It can be argued that, given the opportunity, learners themselves manage differentiation more effectively than teachers.

EQUALITY

Consider the following extract from a conversation between Jeremy Paxman and Tony Blair from the BBC programme *Newsnight* (BBC, 2002):

> By definition, a meritocracy is not the same as equality in our economic circumstances. (Jeremy Paxman)

> It depends how you define 'equality'. If you want to define 'equality' as equality of outcome then I agree. If you don't define 'equality' as a quality of an outcome, if you define it, well I call it equal worth actually, because I think it is more than just equality of opportunity, but certainly it includes equality of opportunity, then that's exactly what a meritocracy is. (Tony Blair) (BBC, 2002)

As long ago as 1952, Tawney (p. 35) suggested that 'equality possesses more than one meaning'. What does equality mean to you? Try Activity 1.5 before reading on.

ACTIVITY 1.5

Does equality mean we should treat all learners in the same manner or differently? What examples can you provide to support your answer?

Perhaps the way we treat learners depends on the type of equality we are thinking of but, generally, within a learning context, equality is considered to embody:

- an expectation of fair treatment
- an opportunity to participate on equal terms.

In your response to Activity 1.5, you will probably have cited examples of treating learners with equal respect. In this sense, we would treat learners in the same way and they would expect to be treated fairly and consistently, 'without fear or favour'. This requires us to be non-judgemental and accept that others see the world differently to us, recognising others have a right to their own viewpoint. We would doubtless all claim to do this, but it is inevitable that our views of learners will be subject to some bias – we are only human after all. Recognition that learners have a right to their own point of view, however, does not mean that we have to agree with all of the opinions they express, and we may well wish to challenge and debate some of them. We would certainly wish to challenge attitudes, behaviour or language exhibited by learners that is at odds with this particular view of equality.

Recognising diversity means that we may have to treat learners differently, however, if they are all to 'participate on equal terms'. Some learners may have issues relating to access or opportunity due to their personal circumstances. For this reason, institutions may provide additional support such as crèche facilities for learners with a need for childcare, bursaries for those for whom finance represents a barrier to access, and ramps and lifts for learners with a physical disability. Within a teaching session, other barriers may exist – access to resources, access to the teacher's time and support, for instance – and we need to be aware of these.

Initial assessment may have identified learners who require additional support with areas such as literacy or numeracy. Most institutions will provide such support either on an individual or group basis, as well as offering a number of other kinds of support designed to allow all learners to participate on equal terms. It can be seen that issues of diversity, equality and inclusion permeate the teaching and learning process and operate at different levels, and addressing these is another responsibility inherent in the role of the teacher.

INCLUSION

Inclusion operates at many different levels and in many different contexts. Tomlinson (1996: 26) defined inclusion as 'the greatest degree of match or fit between individual learning requirements and provision'. His main concern was the inclusion of students with learning difficulties and disabilities into mainstream college provision, but from a more general viewpoint we can consider inclusive teaching as that which allows *all* learners to potentially benefit and learn from any aspect of a teaching session. Inclusion is both about planning so that all learners are included and about learners *feeling* included. Taking account of the issues outlined above relating to diversity, differentiation and equality help us to create a truly inclusive learning environment.

SETTING GROUND RULES

When a group comes together for the first time, it enters an initial period of uncertainty when its new members are unsure both of each other and of what is expected of them. To help overcome this, we would normally establish some ground rules which provide a structure within which the group can function effectively, setting the scene for the ways of working and the relationships which are to follow. Establishing a climate for learning in this manner is another of the responsibilities associated with the teaching role. Figure 1.6 illustrates a number of ways in which this can be achieved.

Which of these approaches is adopted will depend on a number of practical considerations such as:

- the nature of your subject
- the level of maturity displayed by your learners
- the confidence that you have in yourself and your ability to control or influence the group.

Normally, rules will be in place at an institutional level which cover areas such as mobile phones, eating and drinking in class. Similarly, rules which cover health and safety legislation within various learning environments such as workshops will exist. Ground rules are more to do with the day-to-day organisation and practices and procedures within the group which will lead to the best environment in which to learn. Whichever of the ways below of establishing ground rules is adopted, the process should begin with a reminder of the existing institutional and safety rules and an explanation of the purpose of and necessity for ground rules.

Generally, ground rules would be set by the teacher if the group was not considered mature enough to either take the process seriously or contribute sensibly, although despite impressions to the contrary, such groups can respond well to being given some responsibility. The sector is often viewed as a 'second chance' for many and taking this more authoritarian route can serve to reinforce some of the messages received by learners as part of their previous educational experience. Nonetheless, it may well be appropriate to adopt this approach in some situations and it leads to a clear and precise understanding of expectations. It should be recognised, however, that ground rules are 'owned' by those that set them and who are therefore responsible for ensuring they are followed. If, on the other hand, the rules are set by the learners, ownership passes to them and it is their responsibility to ensure that they are adhered to. Responsibility for formulating ground rules should not be given to learners, however, unless the teacher is prepared to accept the conclusions reached. A certain level of trust has been placed in the group to carry out this task and this trust must be maintained. Perhaps for this reason, the approach most often adopted is one which is nearer to the middle of the diagram in Figure 1.6. If so, ground rules become an agreed and shared responsibility, although this may lie more heavily with one party than the other, depending on the exact position chosen on the continuum.

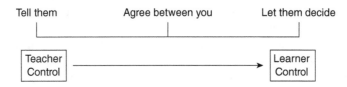

Figure 1.6 Approaches to setting ground rules

Source: Francis and Gould, 2013: 19

Do you have a set of ground rules that has been established within your diploma group? Adult groups will sometimes feel that they are sufficiently mature to operate without the benefit of ground rules. Experience suggests that this is not necessarily the case. In some circumstances, however, it can be agreed that ground rules are not established at the outset but are agreed on and built up during the course in response to events as they occur.

ACTIVITY 1.6

Ground rules need to be as few in number as possible but it is always a good idea to have in mind those that are important to you before entering into any negotiation or agreement. Identify THREE ground rules that you think are essential to the orderly running of a group of learners.

FUNCTIONAL SKILLS AND MINIMUM CORE: THE BACKGROUND

There has been a longstanding concern in this country with the standards of literacy and numeracy of the population. The 1992 DES discussion paper on 'Curriculum Organisation and Classroom Practice in Primary Schools' stated that 'to function effectively in the 21st century, our children will need higher standards of literacy and numeracy than ever before' (DES, 1992: 11), and led to the introduction of the 'literacy hour' and the 'numeracy hour' in schools in 1998 and the establishment of the teaching assistant role in an attempt to raise standards of literacy and numeracy.

In 1998, a working group looking at the basic skills of the post-school population was set up under Sir Claus Moser and concluded that 'Something like one adult in five in this country is not functionally literate and far more people have problems with numeracy' (Moser, 1999: 1). It identified the consequences of this situation as low economic productivity at a national level and potential social exclusion at an individual level, and resulted in the setting up of the Adult Basic Skills Strategy Unit and subsequent launch of the Skills for Life programme (the national strategy for improving adult literacy and numeracy) in 2001.

This focus on adult literacy and numeracy skills didn't, however, include the population of younger learners who were engaged in full- or part-time education on both vocational and academic routes within the Further Education (FE) system. Concerns had been expressed by employers concerning the literacy and numeracy capabilities of this group, and on the recommendation of the Dearing Review of 1996 Key Skills qualifications were introduced with the intention of equipping learners with the skills regarded as essential to succeed not only in education and employment but also their own lifelong learning and personal development.

The Key Skills programme received a mixed reception, however, and was not as successful as perhaps the government had hoped and anticipated, suffering from 'an image and publicity problem from the day it was introduced' (Peart in Wallace, 2010: 46–7).

A number of different approaches existed then to the raising of literacy and numeracy levels amongst the population at large. In 2010, these began to be brought together under the generic title of 'functional skills'. Functional skills are now defined as those skills required for competence in the use of English, maths and ICT and it is considered essential that young people and adults possess these in order to participate in life, learning and work. Functional skills are not just about knowledge in English, maths and ICT, however; they are also about knowing when and how to use that knowledge in real-life situations. Functional skills are therefore considered to include:

- identifying a problem or engaging in a task
- selecting the appropriate skills required
- using these skills, or knowing where to access them if we don't already possess them, to arrive at a solution.

Functional skills now form a core part of all four of the different qualification routes open to young people – GCSE/A-Level, Foundation, Diploma and Apprenticeship, as well as being stand-alone qualifications in their own right at Entry Level, Level 1 and Level 2.

As with most things in the sector, the role and nature of functional skills is currently under review and liable to change. There has been an increased emphasis on maths and English in recent government thinking and the Education Funding Agency (EFA) introduced new funding rules in 2014 (updated 2016) for post 16 education with respect to maths and English, stating that:

> All students aged 16 to 18 starting or who have already started a new study programme of 150 hours or more on or after 1 August 2014 and who do not hold a GCSE grade A* to C, new GCSE 9 to 4 or equivalent qualification in maths and/or in English, are required to be studying these subjects as part of their study programme in each academic year. (EFA, 2016)

Compulsory maths and English thus became part of the study programme of post 16 students in the 2014/15 academic year and alongside the new numerical grading systems introduced for GCSE qualifications, which places a 'good pass' at a more challenging level than the current grade C, placed FE colleges under some considerable strain in staffing and managing this extra load. There has subsequently been some debate concerning the relationship between English/maths, functional skills and the appropriateness of each to the workplace prompting the government to commission a review of the issue in 2014, carried out by the Education and Training Foundation (ETF) and entitled 'Making maths and English work for all: The review of what employers and learners need from the maths and English qualifications taken by young people and adults'. This review, published in 2015, found that functional skills qualifications were favoured by employers who were aware of their nature, whilst accepting that steps could still be taken to improve the relevance and content of Functional Skills, as well as improve their recognition and credibility in the eyes of employers in general.

The ETF's recommendations are currently being considered by the government, and it is expected that new Functional Skills qualifications will be introduced in 2019 (ETF, 2017) which will be more robust and greater credibility when placed alongside GCSE Maths and English qualifications.

Whilst the exact form that functional skills will take in the future is currently under debate, it is evident that the sector is being required to take on considerable responsibility in the upskilling of students in this area and we as teachers within the sector are expected to share heavily in that responsibility.

A related concept is that of the Minimum Core. The Minimum Core identifies two requirements placed on teachers working within the sector. The first of these requires teachers to recognise the ways in which low levels of literacy, numeracy and ICT skills might constitute a barrier to the learning of their students. Within the teaching of their own particular subject specialism, teachers should be able to support learners in these areas, which leads to the second requirement that they themselves must possess a minimum level of personal skills in these areas, currently set at Level 2.

DELIVERING FUNCTIONAL SKILLS AS PART OF THE MINIMUM CORE

The proposals for reform in the 14–19 sector suggest that the teaching and learning of functional skills can be achieved through a number of different approaches ranging from discrete lessons through to fully embedding them within subject delivery. The Excellence Gateway (n.d.) defines embedding as 'teaching and learning [which] combines the development of literacy, language, numeracy with vocational and other skills' and suggests that 'the skills acquired provide learners with the confidence, competence and motivation necessary for them to succeed in qualifications, in life and at work'. Embedding, then, seeks to integrate the teaching of subject and functional skills, taking advantage of naturally occurring circumstances in which the two come together. A study conducted by Casey et al. (2006) into the embedding of literacy and numeracy into vocational courses, in which literacy and numeracy specialists worked alongside subject teachers, found that the approach produced extensive benefits for learners:

- increased retention and success rates, particularly on Level 2 programmes
- learners more likely to achieve literacy, language and numeracy qualifications
- learners' belief that they were better prepared for work in the future.

This type of approach is quite resource-intensive, however, and although it is expected that in the long-term functional skills will remain the responsibility of specialists in this area, it is anticipated that they will be reinforced throughout the rest of the curriculum in all sessions (DCSF, 2009: 6).

The issue was felt sufficiently important for the LLUK to suggest, in 2007, that all initial teacher training courses 'must prepare trainee teachers to teach their own learning programmes in ways that take account of the language, literacy, numeracy and ICT needs of their learners' and that 'all teachers need to be confident in working with colleagues to ensure the development of the language, literacy, numeracy and ICT needs of their learners' (LLUK, 2007: 2).

It is evident that, at some level, there is a responsibility on teachers within the sector to be alert to and address the functional skills needs that learners experience within the subject they are studying. This does not mean that as teachers of history, hairdressing or whatever our subject specialism is, we also become functional skills teachers. For one thing, we lack the necessary expertise and, for another, as a participant in the Casey study remarked, 'You wouldn't expect a maths teacher to teach plastering'. What *is* required is the following:

- We should be able to provide support for individual learners we teach, when a lack of some aspect of a functional skill proves a stumbling block to further progress.
- On the basis that functional skills are developed through practice, we should identify opportunities that may exist within our teaching where such practice can be accommodated without distracting from the main purpose of the session.

Naturally, this entails our own functional skills being at a level sufficient to allow us to do this, hence the second requirement of the Minimum Core.

REFLECTIVE TASK 1.5

Reflecting upon your own practice, how successful do you think you are in embedding functional skills within your planning and teaching? Identify at least three specific examples of ways in which you can improve upon this area of your practice.

EMPLOYABILITY SKILLS

Embedding employability remains a key priority of the Government, universities and colleges, and of employers, as it will 'bring both significant private and public benefit, demonstrating higher education's broader role in contributing to economic growth as well as its vital role in social and cultural development' (HEFCE, 2011: 5). Defining employability, however, is a challenging task as it is seen as a 'contentious concept, with a plethora of micro-interpretations' (Harvey, 2003: 3). Even so, many definitions do exist, such as:

> Employability concerns the extent to which people possess the skills and other attributes to find and stay in work of the kind they want. It is thought by many to be a key goal for individuals to aim for in managing their careers, and for organisations to foster in workforces. (Rothwell and Arnold, 2007, abstract)

> Employability is not just about getting a job. Conversely, just because a student is on a vocational course does not mean that somehow employability is automatic. Employability is more than about developing attributes, techniques or experience just to enable a student to get a job, or to progress within a current career. It is about learning and the emphasis is less on 'employ' and more on 'ability'. In essence, the emphasis is on developing critical, reflective abilities, with a view to empowering and enhancing the learner. (Harvey, 2003: 3)

Employability, then, is more than finding employment; it is something to continue to develop throughout one's career. Bridgstock (2009) has created a model of career management for maximum employability, which she sees as:

> an ongoing process of engaging in reflective, evaluative and decision-making processes using skills for self-management and career building, based on certain underlying traits and dispositional factors, to effectively acquire, exhibit and use generic and discipline-specific skills in the world of work. (Bridgstock, 2009: 35)

From the above, it appears that the emphasis is on the 'softer' skills of an applicant or employee. In collaboration with British businesses, the Confederation of British Industry (CBI) (2009: 8) have defined employability skills as 'a set of attributes, skills and knowledge that all labour market participants should possess to ensure they have the capability of being effective in the workplace – to the benefit of themselves, their employer and the wider economy'. Employability skills, therefore, identified by the CBI (ibid.) include the softer skills as well as some more specific ones such as functional skills:

- Self-management – readiness to accept responsibility, flexibility, resilience, self-starting, appropriate assertiveness, time management, readiness to improve own performance based on feedback/reflective learning.
- Teamworking – respecting others, co-operating, negotiating/ persuading, contributing to discussions, and awareness of interdependence with others.
- Business and customer awareness – basic understanding of the key drivers for business success – including the importance of innovation and taking calculated risks – and the need to provide customer satisfaction and build customer loyalty.
- Problem solving – analysing facts and situations and applying creative thinking to develop appropriate solutions.
- Communication and literacy – application of literacy, ability to produce clear, structured written work and oral literacy – including listening and questioning.
- Application of numeracy – manipulation of numbers, general mathematical awareness and its application in practical contexts (e.g. measuring, weighing, estimating and applying formulae).
- Application of information technology – basic IT skills, including familiarity with word processing, spreadsheets, file management and use of internet search engines.

> They continue that 'underpinning all these attributes, the key foundation, must be a positive attitude: a "can-do" approach, a readiness to take part and contribute, openness to new ideas and a drive to make these happen' (ibid.). So, how can you ensure your students acquire all those skills? How can you 'integrate and balance different ways of teaching and learning that promote both effective learning and employability for students?' (Pegg, et al., 2012: 4)

Fortunately, you do not have to do this all by yourself….it is important to collaborate, thus using your own employability skills (!), with other Schools or departments. Most educational institutions will have a Careers Department or equivalent, where students can seek advice on making the best career choice. It may be helpful for them to complete a SWOT analysis to identify their strengths, weaknesses, opportunities and threats to gain employment. Once they have identified their best career option they then need to put a plan together to make it happen. This may include designing a Gantt chart, in which activities are mapped within a timeframe. Having an effective solid career plan is crucial to achieving their ambitions. It may also be helpful for students to engage in mentoring, volunteering or work experience. This can be as part of their programme of study or in their free/spare time. These activities need to be captured and recorded. Therefore, students may need guidance on how to build a good CV. The next step is advice on job hunting. Students need to understand different job search methods and also understand the importance of networking to aid job hunting. There may also be opportunities for students to engage in mock interviews, introducing different types of interviews, such as: competency, motivational and scenario based.

Some of the employability skills, however, are likely to be embedded within your teaching. It is important to highlight these skills within the planning of your sessions and share this with the students. For instance, if you are planning for students to do a presentation as part of an assessment, it should be noted that by presenting, students also develop employability skills, such as self- and time management. If it is a group presentation, they need to engage in teamwork, communication and maybe problem solving skills as well. Not all students like doing a presentation, however, but if they are aware of the other skills they develop alongside, they may be more willing to engage. Further, allow students to be reflective and evaluative; again, they may already do this in the form of a 'reflective journal or log' as part of your programme. Remember to differentiate your sessions appropriately and to support students where necessary. A 'can-do' attitude, after all, may be easily damaged by consistent failure. Finally, as a teacher, you are a role model; therefore, your own attitude is highly important. Try to be enthusiastic, positive and professional in your attitude.

BOUNDARIES OF PRACTICE

The list of responsibilities discussed so far is extensive and rather daunting, but in reality it does not take long for many of these responsibilities to become second nature. As well as knowing the extent of the job in which we engage, however, it is equally important to know its limits, and it is these boundaries of practice that we turn to next.

In many jobs which involve contact with other people, particularly if in a caring or supportive role, it is considered important to preserve a degree of 'professional distance'. There is a need to remember the relationship such jobs involve, what it is intended to achieve and act accordingly. Take nursing as an example. Without the maintenance of professional distance, an attachment to a patient can be formed, making it difficult to remain objective about their condition and their treatment. Similarly, it is important to maintain objectivity in teaching.

A second aspect of boundaries of practice relates to the limits of our expertise. Most people come into teaching because they have an enthusiasm for their subject that they wish to pass on to others. This is generally accompanied by a desire to be supportive and helpful to those they teach. Learners sometimes feel we are the only ones they can come to for help and advice about a particular issue, but no matter how well intentioned, being supportive and helpful can cause more problems than it solves if it concerns matters outside of our knowledge, skills and expertise.

ACTIVITY 1.7

Which of the following issues do you consider to fall within the role and responsibilities of a teacher in the Further Education and Skills sector?

1   Bereavement
2   Study skills
3   Family problems
4   Depression
5   Prolonged absence
6   Consistently low test marks
7   Bullying
8   Stress

Items 2, 5 and 6 are directly related to learning and 7, if taking place on the premises, contravenes an institutional policy. All of these would fall within the remit of the job and we would address them accordingly. However, 1, 3, 4 and 8 fall outside of the boundaries of our practice. Whilst we might concern ourselves with the ways in which they affected learning, we do not have the necessary expertise to deal with the root causes. Rather than leave learners 'hanging' though, we need to be aware of the different internal and external agencies that are equipped to deal with such issues so we can refer learners on.

ACTIVITY 1.8

Make a list of the different points of referral that exist within your own institution for future reference.

This chapter has set the scene for teaching within the sector by outlining what the job involves and the context within which it is carried out. The next chapters concern the 'how' of teaching and look at the knowledge and skills that guide our practice.

SUMMARY OF KEY POINTS

In this chapter, we have looked at the context of teaching within the Further Education and Skills sector, identifying the different roles taken on by teachers and the responsibilities associated with these. The notion of diversity within learners in the sector was explored, along with a consideration of the issues of differentiation, equality and inclusion this raises. An inclusive environment is encouraged by the setting of appropriate ground rules and the different ways of going about this were explored. Functional skills are an important issue at both a national and individual level and the notion of embedding these within the teaching we do was explored next. Finally, the extent and limits of the teaching role were investigated.

The key points in this chapter are:

- Teaching in the sector involves a number of roles such as teaching, administration, institutional and pastoral duties.
- Diversity refers to the individual differences that are evident in learners.
- An aspect of diversity likely to be met in most groups is that different learners have different preferred styles of learning.
- Differentiation strategies are used by teachers to accommodate the differences in their learners.
- Equality can be interpreted in different ways. All learners are treated the same in that they are afforded equal respect, but are treated differently, dependent on their individual needs, so they can participate on equal terms.

(Continued)

- Inclusion means that all learners participate in and feel part of a teaching session.
- Ground rules establish the ways in which a group can work most effectively and can be established by the teacher, the group, or jointly between the two. The approach used determines the responsibility of each party in ensuring compliance.
- Functional skills and the Minimum Core are important at both a national and individual level and are best delivered by being embedded within the subject matter being taught.
- It is important to recognise the limits of our responsibilities and expertise and to refer learners on to the appropriate people or agencies when the issues they bring to us fall outside the boundaries of our practice.

REFERENCES

BBC (2002) *Newsnight.* Available online at: http://news.bbc.co.uk/1/hi/programmes/news night/1988874.stm (accessed 24/04/17).

BIS (2012) *Professionalism in Further Education.* Available online at: www.gov.uk/government/ uploads/system/uploads/attachment_data/file/34641/12-1198-professionalism-in-further-education-final.pdf (accessed 24/04/17).

Bridgstock, R. (2009) The graduate attributes we've overlooked: enhancing graduate employability through career management skills. *Higher Education Research & Development.* 28 (1): 31–44. Available online at: www.tandfonline.com/doi/abs/10.1080/07294360802444347 (accessed 28/04/2017).

Casey, H., Cara, O., Eldred, J., Grief, S., Hodge, R., Ivanic, R., et al. (2006) 'You wouldn't expect a maths teacher to teach plastering': Embedding literacy, language and numeracy in post-16 vocational programmes – the impact on learning and achievement. Available online at: http://dera.ioe.ac.uk/22311/1/doc_3188.pdf (accessed 24/04/17).

CBI (2009) Future fit: preparing graduates for the world of work. Available online at: www. universitiesuk.ac.uk/policy-and-analysis/reports/Documents/2009/future-fit-preparing-grad uates-for-the-world-of-work.PDF (Accessed 04/05/2017).

Coffield, F., Moseley, D., Hall, E. and Ecclestone, C. (2004) *Learning Styles for Post 16 Learners: What Do We Know?* London: Learning & Skills Research Centre.

Dearing Review (1996) Review of qualifications for 16-19 year olds. Available online at: www.edu cationengland.org.uk/documents/dearing1996/dearing1996.html (accessed 24/10/2017).

Department for Education and Science (DES) (1992) 'Curriculum organisation and classroom practice in primary schools: a discussion paper'. Available online at: www.educationengland. org.uk/documents/threewisemen/threewisemen.html (accessed 24/04/17).

Department for Children, Schools and Families (DCSF) (2009) *Nuts and Bolts Guide: Functional Skills.* London: DCSF.

Duckworth, V. and Tummons, J. (2010) *Contemporary Issues in Lifelong Learning*. Maidenhead: Open University Press.

EFA (2016) *16 to 19 funding: maths and English condition of funding*. Available online at: www.gov.uk/guidance/16-to-19-funding-maths-and-english-condition-of-funding (accessed 14/05/2017).

ETF (2015) *Making maths and English work for all: The review of what employers and learners need from the maths and English qualifications taken by young people and adults*. Available online at: www.et-foundation.co.uk/wp-content/uploads/2015/04/Making-maths-and-English-work-for-all-25_03_2015002.pdf (accessed 14/05/2017).

ETF (2017) *Maths and English Functional Skills Reform Programme*. Available online at: www.et-foundation.co.uk/research/maths-and-english-functional-skills-reform-programme/ (accessed 14/05/2017).

Excellence Gateway. Available at: http://rwp.excellencegateway.org.uk/Embedded%20Learning/ (accessed 24/04/17).

Francis, M. and Gould, J. (2013) *Achieving Your PTLLS Award: A Practical Guide to Teaching in the Lifelong Learning Sector* (2nd edn). London: Sage.

Ginnis, P. (2002) *The Teacher's Toolkit*. Carmarthen: Crown House Publishing.

Harvey, L. (2003) *Transitions from Higher Education to Work: A briefing paper prepared by Lee Harvey (Centre for Research and Evaluation, Sheffield Hallam University), with advice from ESECT and LTSN Generic Centre colleagues*. Available online at: http://bit.ly/oeCgqW (accessed 28/04/ 2017).

HEFCE (2011) *Opportunity, Choice and Excellence in Higher Education*. Bristol: HEFCE. Available online at: www.hefce.ac.uk/news/hefce/2011/strategy.htm (accessed 28/04/2017).

Lifelong Learning UK (LLUK) (2007) *Addressing Literacy, Language, Numeracy and ICT Needs in Education and Training: Defining the Minimum Core of Teachers' Knowledge, Understanding and Personal Skills*. London: LLUK.

Moser, C. (1999) *A Fresh Start*. London: DfEE.

Pegg, A., Waldock, J., Hendy-Isaac, S. and Lawton, R. (2012) *Pedagogy for Employability*. York: Higher Education Academy.

Petty, G. (2009) *Teaching Today: A Practical Guide* (4th edn). Cheltenham: Nelson Thornes.

Rothwell, A. and Arnold, J. (2007) 'Self-perceived employability: development and validation of a scale', *Personnel Review*, 36(1): 23–41.

Sonbuchner, G.M. (2008) *The Learning Styles Handbook for Teachers and Tutors*. Bloomington, IN: Author House.

Tawney, R.H. (1952) *Equality*. London: Allen & Unwin.

Tennant, M. (2006) *Psychology and Adult Learning* (3rd edn). Abingdon, Oxon: Routledge.

Tomlinson, J. (1996) *Report of the Further Education Funding Council Learning Difficulties and/ or Disabilities Committee*. Coventry: FEFC.

Wallace, S. (ed.) (2010) *The Lifelong Learning Sector Reflective Reader*. Exeter: Learning Matters.

FURTHER READING

Sharrock, T. (2016) Embedding English and Maths: Practical strategies for FE and Post-16 tutors. Northwich: Critical Publishing.

This book starts off with a discussion around the meaning of embedding, the importance of English and maths skills before exploring the barriers to learning that might be encountered within these subjects. The remainder of the book is devoted to practical activities that can be used, mainly within vocational subjects, to achieve embedding. Each activity includes explanatory notes as well as ways in which to make links to employability skills.

Spenceley, L. (2014) *Inclusion in Further Education.* **Northwich: Critical Publishing.**
A thought provoking book, looks at inclusion from the perspectives of theory, policy and practice before discussing implementation in a variety of different contexts and settings. An excellent read if you wish to think more deeply about inclusion and your own attitudes and practice.

2
PLANNING FOR TEACHING AND LEARNING

Planning is about making decisions. In this chapter, we look at the planning decisions which teachers in the Further Education and Skills sector are asked to make on a regular basis. The main purpose of the chapter is to present a general picture of the factors that influence the planning process. Many of these factors will be explored in greater detail in other chapters. Once decisions have been made, they are recorded in schemes of work and session plans. Example formats and how to complete them are also included in this chapter.

When you have completed this chapter you will be able to:

- recognise the reasons for planning teaching and learning sessions
- describe the different aspects of planning that teachers need to consider
- identify the sequence in which decisions are made in a systematic approach to planning
- write learning objectives in a 'SMART' manner
- identify the different types or 'domains' of learning objectives
- differentiate between 'aims', 'general objectives' and 'specific objectives' and the context in which each is used
- recognise the factors to be taken into account when choosing which teaching and learning strategies, resources and assessment methods to use in a teaching and learning session

(Continued)

- employ a structured approach to the delivery of a teaching and learning session
- engage in a process of self-evaluation
- translate a syllabus into a scheme of work
- design session plans for use in both whole-class and workshop environments.

WHY PLAN?

Within teaching, attitudes towards planning are mixed but broadly fall into two camps – those for and those against. Whilst it is generally accepted that any activity in which we engage will proceed more smoothly and efficiently if we plan it, the process of planning can involve the investment of some time and effort. The view expressed by some experienced teachers is that it is unnecessary to write session plans. They argue that life as a teacher is busy enough as it is, so why spend valuable time, which could be spent on other pressing matters, writing session plans, particularly if you know your subject? If you are reasonably well organised, you can just go and teach it. Isn't this a valid argument? It is true that there are few, if any, idle moments in the life of a teacher and it can be a stressful occupation. One of the main strategies for relieving stress, however, is that of planning ahead, and avoiding the need for making snap decisions in pressurised situations. Moreover, the reality is that actually very few, if any, teachers just teach their subject; they will invariably have thought about what they can fit into a session, the best order in which to teach it and what resources they will need; in other words, they will engage in planning at some level. The argument centres more around the time and depth of thought that should be put into the process and whether or not there is a need to record these thoughts in a teaching plan.

Planning is a natural response to most activities we engage in, the detail involved largely depending on the complexity of the task in hand. If I go shopping, I write a shopping list to make sure I buy everything I need. If I go on a car journey, I plot the route in advance, to make sure I go the shortest or quickest way. If I build an extension to my house, I have detailed plans drawn up to ensure that everything is completed in the most effective order and I make best use of the time available for the build. I can, of course, do any of these things without planning first, but if I do it is likely that the process will be less effective and the result less satisfactory. In short, I would fall foul of the old adage: *fail to plan, plan to fail.*

The other argument raised against writing session plans is that they are too rigid, stifle spontaneity and creativity and things rarely go to plan anyway. These observations are largely based around the view of a plan as being 'set in stone'. If we return to the earlier examples of planning, can I not buy that special offer I come across in the supermarket because it was not on my original shopping list? If I run into a traffic jam on my car journey, do I have to sit in it rather than find a way around it because a detour doesn't fit with my original route? What happens if, when building my extension, I want to change to a new cheaper roofing material that has just come on to the market? Most people, being reasonably sensible, would adapt their planning to take account of these unexpected circumstances and this is exactly what we would do with a session plan. If we have considered carefully all that we need to, the plan we end up with should be fairly robust, but it is important to recognise that all plans are plans of *intention* – they reflect the decisions we make at the time based on the information at our disposal at that time. Sometimes, the realities of the situation fall outside of the plan; at other times the mood, interest and contributions of the group may prevail. Teaching is a responsive activity and often we have to adapt what we intended to do in order to respond to the moment. Rogers and Horrocks (2010: 249) remind us of this in suggesting that 'pursuing the teachable moment may mean deviating from the "session plan" so as to take advantage of that "spark" to explore something not planned for that session or indeed at all'. This means that 'the teacher needs to develop confidence to follow such matters through, even if it means at times abandoning the tidy and cherished structure of the teaching session'.

All plans have to be implemented in a flexible manner and it is much easier to adapt an existing plan to the situation as we find it, than it is to start out with no plan at all. This notion of flexibility in application of all aspects of the planning process should be kept at the front of your mind as you work your way through the rest of this chapter.

WHERE DOES PLANNING START FROM?

Getting started is often the most difficult part of any project in which we engage. We may have lots of ideas floating around in our heads but which comes first? What is the most logical order in which to proceed? Looking back at the planning activities already discussed, in writing my shopping list I started by looking round my kitchen to see what I already had and didn't have. I could then work out what I would need in order to eat for the rest of the week. My journey planning started from a consideration of the different possible routes available to reach my destination and then working out which of these was the most suitable. Planning an extension started by identifying what I wanted to end up with and then working out the best way to achieve this. So, depending on the nature of the task, the planning of each of these activities started from a number of different positions. Teachers also often start planning from different points. Having decided on their topic, some may start from a specific activity which they know will go down well with the group they are to teach, others from a particularly effective resource they have used before, whereas others again may start from a course textbook. A number of options exist. Which of these is the best starting point? Is there a logical sequence in which planning decisions can be made?

To answer these questions, it is useful to think of the analogy of a journey. When planning a journey, a number of decisions have to be made – decisions on how you will get to your destination and what you will take with you, for instance.

You first have to decide on the destination itself – all other decisions then flow naturally from this. In teaching terms, the destination is the learning that is to take place and this is normally expressed in the form of *learning objectives*. In arriving at the learning objectives for a teaching and learning session, you would normally start with a consideration of what you, the teacher, wish to achieve in this particular session, what you see as its purpose. You are deciding on your *aims*. You can now identify what it is that your learners will have to learn if these aims are to be realised. It is this learning that is spelled out in the learning objectives.

Once the learning objectives have been decided on, the remaining planning decisions can be made in a logical, systematic manner as outlined below:

1. Set aims and learning objectives.
2. Decide on what needs to be learned to achieve the objectives (content) and how this might best be achieved (teaching methods/learning activities).
3. Select the resources needed to support the teaching methods/learning activities you have chosen.
4. Decide how you will check that learning is taking place (assessment).

As we go about the daily activities of our lives, we are often reminded of the wonders of hindsight and how, with its benefit, we might have done things differently. Would we have bought that expensive television yesterday if we had known then that it was to be reduced for a quick sale today? Teaching is another activity which benefits from hindsight. When you have delivered the session you have planned, you might like to review your decisions in light of your experience with a view to possibly changing

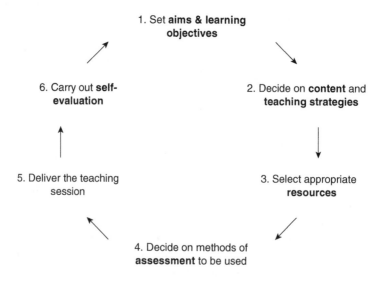

Figure 2.1   The planning cycle

some things to improve the session overall. This process of *self-evaluation* will influence the planning decisions you make when next you deliver this session, and so when added to the sequence of events outlined above, leads to a recurring process known as 'The Planning Cycle' (Figure 2.1), in which the decisions made at each stage inform those to be made at subsequent stages.

We will next explore each of these stages in a little more detail before looking at how they can be applied in producing schemes of work and session plans.

STAGES OF THE PLANNING CYCLE

1. SET AIMS AND LEARNING OBJECTIVES

Some examples of aims are to:

- introduce the skills required in order to engage in critical thinking
- explore the stages of child development and their application in the nursery setting
- develop skills in using spreadsheets to present data in graphical form
- review New Labour's strategies in widening participation in education.

Aims give an initial sense of direction. Avis et al. (2010: 122) consider an aim to be 'a general statement of aspiration, usually associated with a course or subject as a whole'. As previously mentioned, however, aims also indicate what the teacher sees as the purpose of the session or what they hope to achieve by teaching it. As Fairclough (2008: 53) suggests, 'an "AIM" is to do with the teacher's intention'. Aims, then, operate at both course and session level but, in both instances, although rather general in nature, give an initial sense of direction and structure. From a planning perspective, it is important to establish your aims clearly in your mind from the beginning because the next stage of the planning process is to identify the learning that must take place in order for these 'intentions' or aims to be achieved. As an illustration of this, the aims of this chapter are to:

- introduce a systematic approach to the planning
- show how this approach is used in writing schemes of work and session plans.

Learning objectives

Deciding on these aims was the first stage in the writing of this chapter. Although rather broad, they gave some initial purpose and structure, setting out what we wanted to achieve by writing it. We could now think about what you, the reader, would have to learn in order for these aims to be successfully achieved. To cover the first aim, we decided that you would have to be able to:

- recognise the reasons for planning teaching sessions
- describe the different aspects of planning that teachers need to consider
- identify the sequence in which decisions are made in a systematic approach to planning.

We have now begun to pinpoint the learning that is required to achieve the initial aim – we are arriving at the learning objectives. It is evident that the point of focus has now moved – whereas aims apply to teachers (or courses or even chapters of books!), learning objectives apply to learners (or readers in this instance – see the introductory box at the beginning of this chapter).

You might think that the way we have phrased these learning objectives is a little unusual. Why not just say that we think you will have to 'learn about the reasons for planning', rather than you will be able to 'recognise the reasons for planning teaching sessions', or you will have to 'learn about the different aspects of planning', rather than you will be able to 'describe the different aspects of planning that teachers need to consider'? The reason for this is that when we write a learning objective, we do so in a manner that allows us to decide fairly quickly and easily if it is being achieved by learners. Although we may consider learning as a process that goes on inside people's heads, we cannot actually see this happening and so it can be argued that we are not really in a position to say whether or not learning is taking place. If we phrase our learning objective as 'learn about the different aspects of planning', how do we know if this is actually occurring? If we phrase our learning objective as 'describe the different aspects of planning that teachers need to consider', however, it becomes much easier to make a judgement as to how successful learners are in achieving this. Broadly speaking, they can or cannot 'describe the different aspects of planning that teachers need to consider' what we have taught them about, and we can put this to the test by asking for a spoken or written description. As Fairclough (2008: 53) suggests, a learning objective is a statement of 'what the learners will be able to do by the end of the session'. For this reason, when we write learning objectives, we avoid using words like 'learn', 'understand' and 'know' that concern internal 'in the head' processes and instead use words like 'describe', 'list' and 'state', as these allow us to actually 'see' if learning is taking place. This makes assessment much more straightforward and effective. We call these types of words 'action verbs', and, by using them, ensure that the learning objectives we write are both specific and measurable, two of the characteristics of a well-written learning objective. The remaining three characteristics are contained in the mnemonic 'SMART' and we shall now examine these in more detail:

Specific

Measurable

Achievable

Relevant

Time-based

Specific and measurable   Before we look at the other characteristics, let us check that you have grasped this idea of specific and measurable. We have said that a learning objective should describe the desired learning exactly, stating clearly what the learner will be able to do as a result of your teaching. This should be observable, resulting in some form of learner activity that allows you to satisfy yourself that learning has indeed taken place. To achieve this, care should be taken in choosing the appropriate action verb when writing learning objectives.

ACTIVITY 2.1

In the table below, pick out the examples of good action verbs for writing learning objectives.

Table 2.1

define	select	understand	list
realise the significance of	measure	have a good grasp of	justify
really know	construct	select	be aware of
solve	be familiar with	demonstrate	distinguish between
describe	recall	explain	know
think	perform	appreciate	state
prepare	give reasons	report	be acquainted with

Source: Francis and Gould, 2013: 57

You can check your answers at the end of the chapter, but a 'good' learning objective has to be more than just written in a specific and measurable manner. Thought also has to be given to the learners who are to achieve the learning that the objectives spell out. That is what the next two characteristics are concerned with.

Achievable   Learning can be an extremely frustrating experience when what you have been set to learn is, for one reason or another, just too difficult. Similarly, it can be rather boring if the learning is too easy. Ideally then, learning objectives are written to fall within the capabilities of the intended learners but, at the same time, sufficiently stretching to give a sense of achievement on attainment. Learning objectives need to be written with learners in mind and so it is important to find out as much as you can about your learners prior to planning – after all, it is they who are to do the learning. This is the first step in the process of differentiation which was introduced in Chapter 1.

Relevant   What is the point of this learning described by your learning objective? If learners cannot see why it is important or how it will help them, then they may ask themselves why they should bother. Our options in deciding on appropriate objectives are somewhat limited as these are dictated to a large extent by the syllabus we are teaching to, but, as far as is possible, learner interests and capabilities should be taken into account when formulating learning objectives.

Time-based   How long will it take to achieve this learning objective? Learning objectives can be short term or long term so it may take one session, a week or even a lifetime of trying. Learners need to be aware of the length of time within which the learning objective is expected to be achieved. This is normally indicated at the outset of the objective by a phrase such as 'by the end of this session/module/course…'.

REFLECTIVE TASK 2.1

Review some session plans you have recently used by looking at the objectives. Are they SMART? Is it easy to see how you might assess each of them?

Types of learning objective

Benjamin Bloom (1956) separated learning objectives into three different types or *domains*. Consider the three examples below:

1.   State the characteristics of a learning objective.
2.   Write learning objectives which are both specific and measurable.
3.   Value the use of learning objectives as the basis for planning.

The first of these is asking for a statement of the knowledge that has been learned. Learning objectives which relate to knowledge are said by Bloom to fall within the *cognitive* domain. Sometimes, however, the learning that is to be achieved involves not just knowing about the subject, but being able to put that knowledge to use, applying it as part of a skill, as in the second learning objective above. A learning objective which is skill-related is said to fall within the *psycho-motor* domain. The third example addresses neither of these domains. At times, the learning that is sought is to do with bringing about an attitude change. Knowing the characteristics of learning objectives and being able to write them in an appropriate manner is of limited use – for example, if the process of using them is not seen as a worthwhile activity. Lots of the teaching that we engage in includes an attitudinal component – not just what we do, but also how we do it. Skills, for instance, have to be performed in a manner that is in line with health and safety requirements, and have to arrive at an end product which is of a good standard – a proper job completed in a safe manner. Learning objectives which look to bring about attitude change fall within the *affective* domain. By their very nature, although they have a behavioural component, attitudes tend to reflect a state of mind, and, consequently, affective objectives can present problems when trying to express them in a specific and measurable manner. This in turn makes assessment difficult. Generally, attitude change is achieved over a lengthy period of time, which will vary from learner to learner, and assessment strategies would have to take this into account.

REFLECTIVE TASK 2.2

Using the same session plans as in Reflective task 2.1, look this time at the TYPES of objectives they contain. How important do you think it is to address attitudes within your teaching? Do you include attitude objectives in your planning? Do you give attention to the teaching of attitudes without writing related objectives?

Levels of learning

As well as placing objectives into types or domains, Bloom also classified them in order of complexity – Bloom's hierarchy of objectives. His most comprehensive work occurred in the cognitive domain which he divided into the following categories:

1. Knowledge – being able to recall or recognise basic facts, ideas or information
2. Comprehension – understanding the meaning of knowledge; being able to explain in own words
3. Application – using the knowledge acquired; applying it in practical, real-life situations
4. Analysis – recognising the relationship between different components of an idea, patterns in information; seeing internal structures
5. Synthesis – reorganising knowledge to form new ideas; drawing conclusions
6. Evaluation – making judgements on the basis of the information given; assessing the value of ideas or theories based on reasoned argument.

Each level of the hierarchy increases in difficulty, knowledge being the least complex and evaluation the most complex of the categories. Each level in the hierarchy must be mastered before progressing on to the next. This means, for example, that we cannot put anything into practice (application) unless we first have all the information required (knowledge) and can make sense of it (comprehension). Bloom's taxonomy has been subject to revision by other writers who have renamed some of the levels and debated the order in which they occur. When reflecting on a teaching session, for instance, it could be argued that we do not come up with new ideas for future sessions (synthesis) until after we have reviewed and made judgements on the current session (evaluation). This is the view taken by Anderson and colleagues (2001) who, in the most well-known revision of Bloom, made the adaptations set out in Figure 2.2.

Level	Bloom	Anderson and Krathwohl
1	Knowledge	Remembering
2	Comprehension	Understanding
3	Application	Applying
4	Analysis	Analysing
5	Synthesis	Evaluating
6	Evaluation	Creating

Figure 2.2   Comparison of Bloom's categories with those of Anderson and Krathwohl

Despite the various revisions, however, Bloom's is still the most frequently used model. Try Activity 2.2 which demonstrates the use of Bloom's taxonomy.

ACTIVITY 2.2

In the days when David Beckham still played for Manchester United, Michael Parkinson conducted an interview with him. Some of Parkinson's questions are listed in the table below. Categorise each question using Bloom's categories of knowledge, comprehension, application, analysis, synthesis and evaluation.

Table 2.2

Parkinson's Questions	Level of Bloom's Taxonomy
How old were you when you signed for Manchester United?	
Could you explain the off-side rule?	
Give reasons why you are such a good midfielder.	
How do you cross a ball so accurately?	
How do you rate Manchester United's chances of winning the league this year?	
If you were managing United, how would you run the team?	
What would cause you to leave Manchester United?	
What do the lyrics of your wife's last single mean?	
George Best is your favourite footballer – what were his strengths and weaknesses as a footballer?	
What do you have written on the front of your boots?	
How would you improve the quality of England's game?	
How do you go about taking a corner?	

Getting the 'right' answers to the above exercise is not crucial, but you can compare your thoughts to ours if you wish, by reference to the table at the end of this chapter.

This exercise reminds us that any topic we teach contains a variety of possible levels of learning. This is an important consideration in both assessment and differentiation, and we will be referring back to Bloom's taxonomy in Chapters 3 and 4. In the meantime, let us return to planning.

This has been a fairly in-depth discussion of learning objectives as a starting point to planning but if a systematic approach to planning is to be used, it is important to get these learning objectives right. Perhaps, however, a cautionary note is appropriate at this point. Although an objectives-based approach provides clarity and logic to the planning process, Avis et al. (2010: 123) ask whether 'they (objectives) actually diminish our view of learning by reducing it to observable behaviour'. There are other starting points for planning and the objectives-based approach may not always be the most appropriate to achieve the learning that is sought, as we shall see in Chapter 8. The current educational climate, however, is very results-oriented and so evidencing that learning is taking place has become an increasingly important consideration. Expressing learning in a measurable manner is central to this process and this is evident in other approaches to planning and structuring learning such as outcomes and competencies. A more thorough discussion of these and other approaches to planning can be found in Chapter 8.

In summary, well-written learning objectives:

- identify clearly the learning that is to take place
- help in making appropriate choices of teaching strategies, resources and assessment strategies.

2. DECIDE ON CONTENT AND TEACHING METHODS/ LEARNING ACTIVITIES

We can view teaching strategies in much the same way as a carpenter, a plumber or an electrician considers the tools in their toolbox. There will be a variety of tools to allow all sorts of tasks to be undertaken. The choice of which tool to use will depend on the demands and nature of the specific job to be tackled. Similarly, as teachers, when deciding on the most appropriate method or activity to use out of all of those at our disposal, choice will be influenced by the demands and nature of the anticipated learning. If you are teaching a knowledge- or 'theory'-based session with learning objectives that fall mainly in the cognitive domain, the type of approach you adopt will probably include:

- lecture/verbal explanations
- question and answer
- brainstorming

- seminar
- projects
- problem solving.

A skills-based session with learning objectives, mainly in the psycho-motor domain, would doubtless include:

- demonstration
- practical exercises
- giving feedback
- simulations.

Attitude change is more likely to be achieved if it comes from 'within'. Learners need to think through and debate the issues and arrive at their own conclusions rather than 'being told'. A session concerned with bringing about attitude change, with learning objectives mainly in the affective domain, would be more likely to include:

- discussion
- debate
- role play
- tutorials.

Whilst the above lists are far from being definitive or even mutually exclusive, they do illustrate the natural relationship between choice of teaching approach and the learning objectives which are to be achieved. Other factors have an influence, however. The nature of the students who are to achieve the learning objectives and the realities of the situation in which we shall be teaching also need to be taken into account.

(a) Student characteristics

As we have seen in Chapter 1, learners in the Further Education and Skills sector come with a range of previous experiences and a wide range of different backgrounds, so we can be sure that each group of learners we come across will possess different characteristics from the others. A particular teaching strategy which matches well with a learning objective may not suit the learner or learners who are to achieve it. Games, for instance, might be seen as patronising by adult students who might prefer to be talked through the subject, but this may not be the preference of a younger audience with much shorter attention spans. Some learners may like to work on a project in a group whereas others may prefer to work alone. The reason for attending the course may also influence learner preferences – learners on an 'intensive' course, wishing to achieve a qualification in a shorter than normal time span will prefer a more focused approach which gives them the essential information they require, rather than engaging in discussion which considers the issues in more depth. As well as matching learning objectives, teaching strategies must also be compatible with learner characteristics and preferences.

(b) 'Reality' factors

Planning is more than a paper exercise and rarely takes place against the backdrop of an 'ideal world' and so decisions made need to take account of practical considerations. These may relate to:

- the time available – some strategies are more time-consuming than others; giving information is quicker than drawing it out by questioning, for instance. Generally, strategies which are more learner-led or involve high levels of participation require longer periods of time
- the time of day or year – learners attending an evening class after a day's work would respond differently, in all likelihood, if the class was held during the day without other distractions. Similarly, the same learners on a Monday morning may display different levels of motivation and attention to a Friday afternoon. Attitudes also tend to change towards the end of a long first term or towards the end of the year when the pressures of exams or coursework deadlines tend to intensify
- the size and composition of the group – groups may be too small, too large or have insufficient experience or mix of experience to accommodate some strategies
- the space in which the teaching session is to take place – rooms may be small, large, wide, narrow or furnished in a manner which allows for or inhibits flexible use; workshops may have insufficient individual working space
- the available resources – are the required resources available to support the chosen strategy? This is often a particular issue in practical subjects but can have an effect in other areas as well. A research-based approach to a particular topic with a large group may not be possible without sufficient and reliable internet access
- the confidence we have in the use of a particular teaching strategy or resource – our own personal feelings and confidence also form part of the 'decision mix'. It may be, for instance, that an affective objective, seeking to shape attitudes, would be best achieved by role play and we have a group which is quite willing to participate in such activities. If, however, we felt unsure of our ability to manage this activity effectively, we may well opt for a discussion-based approach around a case study, feeling much more in control and comfortable with this approach.

Decisions on specific teaching strategies are influenced by a number of factors, as illustrated in Figure 2.3. Detail on a range of strategies can be found in Chapter 5.

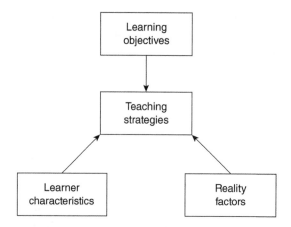

Figure 2.3   Influences on choice of teaching strategy

REFLECTIVE TASK 2.3

Review the teaching strategies you have used in your last few teaching sessions. Did your choice of strategies account for the factors listed above? Would you now go back and make any changes?

3. SELECT APPROPRIATE RESOURCES

There are many words in the English language that we use routinely but we rarely stop to consider exactly what they mean. 'Resources' is probably one of those words. The dictionary tells us that a resource is 'something that can be used for support or help', so we could consider an educational resource as 'something that can be used to support or help learning' (www.thefreedictionary.com/resource).

This definition is important in that it spells out two important factors concerning resources:

1. It is 'something' emphasises the fact that almost anything can be used as a resource – although there are some 'old favourites' that we are all familiar with and tend to use most frequently, the possibilities are fairly endless.
2. 'Used to support or help learning' suggests that when we choose from the range of possible resources, this is not our first consideration in the decision-making process. We first have to identify the learning that is to be supported or helped and then decide which resource can best achieve this and how.

Although teaching strategies can stand on their own, they are greatly enhanced in their effectiveness if supported by appropriate resources. Resources can be used to arouse motivation, focus attention, make understanding easier and help with memory, all important factors in the learning process. Resources and their use will be examined in greater detail in Chapter 3, but what is evident at this point is that we do not want to use resources as '"decoration", with no clear purpose in mind apart from some vague belief that they ought to be used' (Armitage et al., 1999: 97).

The more common resources listed in Figure 2.4 should help your thinking about the options that are available to you. The resources itemised in the list have been put into broad categories of potential usage but these are offered as suggestions rather than clear-cut guidelines.

Recording learner contributions	Presenting content
• Whiteboard	• Overhead projector
• Interactive whiteboard	• PowerPoint slides
• Flip chart	• Video clips
	• DVDs
	• Photographs
Reference materials	**Simplifying/Helping memory**
• Textbooks	• Handouts
• Internet/websites	• Worksheets
• Journals	• Models
	• The 'real thing'
	• Charts and posters
	• Case studies

Figure 2.4   Examples of resources

REFLECTIVE TASK 2.4

Use the categories above to reflect on your own practice. Do you favour one category more than another or do you have a more balanced approach? Can you see possibilities for increasing the range of resources you currently use?

4. DECIDE ON THE APPROPRIATE METHODS OF ASSESSMENT TO BE USED

Much of the learning that we undertake is sequential in nature, i.e. we have to fully grasp the current bit of learning before we can carry on to the next, and so methods of checking that learning is taking place need to be built in to our planning. Some of the activities we use as part of our overall teaching strategy will, by their very nature, accomplish this for us. Learners completing practical or written exercises, taking part in short quizzes, reporting back from discussions, engaging in problem-solving activities, giving short presentations or demonstrations, all fall into this category. As teachers, we are alert to the non-verbal signs that learners exhibit – frowning, smiling, making/not making eye contact, alert posture – as these also provide a good impression of whether or not learning is taking place. If we are unsure, we can ask questions, either of individual learners or generally of the group as a whole. We will often begin a session by asking questions relating to what has been learned in previous sessions, in order to check that the learning on which we wish to build is firmly in place. Detail on these and other ways of checking learning can be found in Chapter 4.

REFLECTIVE TASK 2.5

Do your session plans include a method of checking each objective? After teaching each session, how confident are you that learners had achieved all of the objectives? On what do you base the answer to this question?

5. DELIVER THE TEACHING SESSION

Every teaching session is unique and the way in which it is delivered will reflect this. Delivery will be influenced by a number of factors, such as the dynamic of the group and the nature and purpose of the session, but the following sequence provides a useful general format for most teaching and learning sessions:

- an introduction which sets the scene for what is to follow
- development of the main body of the session
- a conclusion which summarises the session and looks forward to subsequent sessions.

ACTIVITY 2.3

Before you read the next section, cast your mind back to the last time you watched a news programme on the television. How was the programme introduced? What was the overall format adopted?

Introduction

It is likely that you noticed the newscasters introduce themselves and then read through the headlines for the news items that were to follow, giving you an overall picture of the programme so you knew what to expect. Before specific items, you may be warned of 'distressing scenes' or 'strobe lighting', so you can decide whether or not to watch that particular part of the programme. In introducing a teaching session, we follow a similar pattern. If this session is the first time that you and the group have met each other – perhaps it is the beginning of the academic year or the session is a 'one-off' – it is important to establish an initial relationship and give learners some idea of what to expect. The introductory phase of the session would therefore include:

- **an initial welcome** – introduce yourself and give a little relevant background to establish credibility; and give the learners an opportunity to introduce each other
- **addressing practical matters** – give the location of any appropriate facilities; run through any health and safety requirements and point out fire exits; and complete any necessary paperwork
- **setting the scene** – introduce the session, setting out the objectives and briefly how these are to be achieved; establish links to what learners already know (some initial question and answer at this stage helps in getting a 'feel' for the group); explain the relevance and anticipated benefits of the session; and, finally, agree some appropriate ground rules.

Once you and the group know each other and have established both a relationship and a way of working together, a possible procedure would be to involve learners straight away with an active start to the session – a short, sharp exercise that can be given to learners as they enter the room, sufficiently flexible in nature to allow you to stop it at a convenient moment; perhaps a 'gap-fill' exercise, word search, paired question and answer activity or brief case study which involves the use of material covered in the previous session. This approach allows you to integrate any latecomers into the session with minimum fuss and disruption and affords an opportunity for some initial individual contact. You can bring the exercise to a halt at the appropriate moment and acknowledge the work that has been completed before formally recapping previous learning, perhaps using a question and answer format. The next stage would involve an outline of the proposed objectives of the session, their relevance and usefulness and the types of activities that are to be used.

As well as the content of the introduction, the manner in which it is conducted is also of paramount importance. Part of the function of the introduction is to arouse interest and encourage learners to adopt a receptive frame of mind. Interest can be aroused by strategies such as posing a problem initially which will gradually be solved as the session unfolds. Sometimes, however, no matter how enthralling we find our subject to be, we recognise that, to others, certain aspects of it may appear quite 'dry'. On other occasions, the subject matter may be fine but, for whatever reason, we ourselves do not feel particularly excited by the prospect of teaching it. Regardless of circumstance, we need to present an enthusiastic role model as this can have the greatest impact in setting the tone for the remainder of the session.

REFLECTIVE TASK 2.6

How did you normally introduce the sessions you teach? Having read the above, do you have any fresh thoughts about how to introduce the next session you teach?

Development

This is the main body of the session and so will occupy the majority of the total time. It is here that the intended knowledge or skills are developed using the different teaching strategies that have been decided on. These should be varied to maintain attention and engagement from learners and be well supported by appropriate resources. Skills sessions normally involve a lot of practical work and encourage 'active' learning. This is a trend that should be encouraged in theory-based sessions as well, in order to maintain attention levels and concentration, as these tend to diminish fairly quickly when learners are put into a more 'passive' role. Francis and Gould (2013: 176) suggest the following sequence:

1. Initial explanation and introduction of new material with some questions and answers.
2. Some form of exercise/group work/pair work using the new material.
3. Learning check, summary and link to the next stage of the session.
4. Repeat of a similar pattern until the session objectives are achieved.

This is similar to Petty's (2009: 443) 'PAR' or present–apply–review approach, in which he suggests that each of the three phases will be repeated several times in a given session.

Conclusion

A teaching session benefits from a distinct ending in much the same way as it does from a well-defined and structured beginning. It needs to be 'rounded off' rather than reaching an abrupt ending and learners need to leave with an overall picture of their learning fresh in their minds. Hillier (2005: 95), drawing on her own experience as a learner, suggests that 'it is unsatisfying for people to drift away without a formal end'. The conclusion of the session is the point at which all of the threads are drawn together and the important points highlighted.

In a skills session, this may involve allowing packing away and clearing up time before collecting the group together to share experiences. This can be achieved through taking contributions from individual learners on progress, points of difficulty or techniques they have discovered or found particularly useful. This could then be followed by the teacher commenting on what they had observed – common mistakes, points of technique – as the session had progressed, before looking forward to the next session and how it will relate to the current one.

In a more theoretical session, the conclusion may initially invite questions on matters arising from the session before going on to ask questions on the main points covered, finally leading into a review of the session as a whole. A formal summary is also of great value as it allows learners to take away a mental structure of the session. Research on memory suggests that this is most effectively achieved by including around seven main points in the summary. Homework or follow-up exercises can also be mentioned at this point. Last, but not least, links between the current session and future sessions are made.

REFLECTIVE TASK 2.7

Are the endings of your teaching sessions orderly or sometimes rushed? If the latter, why is this and what can you do to achieve a more effective ending? Any thoughts on how you might most better conclude future sessions?

6. CARRY OUT SELF-EVALUATION

An unfortunate incident in the life of the Scottish poet Robert Burns prompted him, in 1785, to write the poem *To a Mouse on Turning her up in her Nest with the Plough*, in which he stated:

The best-laid plans o' mice an' men

Gang aft a-gley,

An' lea'e us nought but grief an' pain

For promised joy.

Whilst hopefully the outcome is not grief and pain, it is inevitable that some sessions will share a similar fate to that of the mouse. This is where self-evaluation becomes particularly important. In reality, every session we teach involves a constant process of evaluation. Most, if not all, teachers share Jenny Rogers's (2007: 262) desire 'to know the answer to the question: Is it working?' Learners are conscious of whether they find teaching sessions to be interesting, boring, easy to understand, difficult, relevant or meaningful, and convey these opinions to us through their behaviours and body language. We are constantly on the lookout for such signs and are making our own judgements on whether or not 'it is working' as the session proceeds. We may change our plan as we go, based on the feedback we receive. This process of remaining alert to and interpreting the signals that learners give, followed by the making of instant judgements on how to react or respond appropriately, is one of the many factors that makes teaching the interesting and challenging job that it is. A more considered opinion, however, can be arrived at by evaluation after the event. Post-session evaluation allows for a more objective and measured approach, although, of course, it can only influence future rather than present practice.

The process of self-evaluation outlined above can be considered as a form of experiential learning and as such is most effective if it follows a structure based loosely on Kolb's (1984; Kolb and Fry, 1975) model in Figure 2.5.

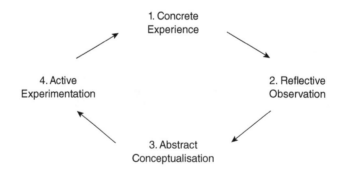

Figure 2.5   Kolb's Model of Experiential Learning (Kolb and Fry, 1975)

1.   Although the language is somewhat dense, the message conveyed by the model is simple. Kolb maintains that we learn through experience but only if we process that experience and make sense of it. Experience alone is insufficient to lead to

improvement, as is suggested by the point of view that 'thirty years' experience can be one year's experience repeated twenty-nine more times'. Experience is what Usher (1985: 60) describes as 'raw material' and as such requires 'processing' before it can lead to real learning. Applying Kolb's model to the self-evaluation of a teaching and learning session would lead to a sequence similar to the following:

1. Teach the session. This is Kolb's Concrete Experience.
2. Afterwards, re-run the session in your mind: what were the significant features, what went particularly well, what didn't go as well as you had hoped, did anything surprising happen? You are now engaging in what Kolb describes as Reflective Observation.
3. Then ask the question 'why did that happen?' You would engage in some analysis of the events you had identified in stage 2, looking for reasons as to why some things went well and others didn't. This is what Kolb calls Abstract Conceptualisation.
4. The results of this analysis would lead you to some conclusions about how you might do things differently and hopefully more effectively next time. Kolb's term for this is Active Experimentation.

This process can follow any experience – that first date, a job interview, taking part in some kind of sporting event … the list is endless … but in each case finding the answer to that 'why?' question is crucial and often the most difficult part of the process; it is only by searching for the answer to this question that we can really understand our practice and develop it in a meaningful way.

As well as our own thoughts, evaluative comment can come from a number of sources and can temper a natural inclination to be overly self-critical. We will explore these other options in Chapter 8. What is important at this point is that we recognise the value of making sense of and learning from our experience and the role that this plays in the overall planning cycle.

ACTIVITY 2.4

Most self-evaluations consider the following issues:

- What went well?
- What didn't go so well?
- What will I change?

How does this compare with Kolb's cycle? Can you use Kolb's cycle to make your own approach to self-evaluation more effective?

APPLYING THE PLANNING CYCLE TO WRITING SCHEMES OF WORK AND TEACHING PLANS

We have identified the factors that influence the decisions made during planning and established a systematic approach to the process as a whole. Now we will turn to applying this process to the two main planning documents used in teaching:

(a) Scheme of work.
(b) Session plan.

(A) SCHEME OF WORK

If you teach on a course which does not lead to a formally recognised award of some kind, you have considerable freedom in deciding how you will run your course and the kind of content which it will include. Most teachers, however, deliver courses which lead to an award, and so follow a set syllabus detailing what is required of learners in order for them to qualify for the award. Syllabi from different awarding bodies vary in what they include – they may or may not contain information on assessment requirements and guidance on how the course is delivered, for instance, but all syllabi, whether written in the form of topics, learning outcomes or competences, will tell you the content that must be covered in the delivery of the course.

What the syllabus does not tell us about, however, is:

* the best sequence in which to deliver course content
* how much time to spend on each different area
* how, in detail, it is to be delivered
* what resources will be needed
* the number and characteristics of the learners who will be on the course
* how progress will be measured throughout the course.

These are the kinds of planning decisions we need to make in order to deliver the course in the most effective manner, regardless of where the content comes from. The syllabus tells us WHAT we have to teach. The function of the scheme of work is to translate the syllabus into a working plan which tells us HOW we will teach it.

The format of a scheme of work varies from institution to institution. The steps outlined below, which take you through the process of designing and writing a scheme of work, can be adapted to your own particular circumstances.

1. Work out the time available to you to deliver the course

For award-bearing courses which span the academic year, check to see if there is a final examination. If so, you need to count backwards from its date to see how many sessions this leaves. You then need to check the dates of bank holidays and possible college closures to see if these affect your scheme of work. You now know the number of sessions at your disposal. You may, however, want to use some of these for purposes such as tutorials or revision sessions. Again, you need to identify how many sessions this will involve before you can finally arrive at the number of teaching sessions available to you for delivering the content of the course. For shorter or non-award-bearing courses, the procedure tends to be considerably simpler but still needs to be completed as the first stage in writing your scheme of work.

2. Decide on the best order in which to teach the different topics you will be covering in the course

Reece and Walker (2007: 244) suggest factors that may influence the ordering of topics, including:

- Is there a logical sequence dictated by the structure of the subject?
- Should the more interesting topics come at the beginning of the course in order to arouse motivation and interest or should they be kept till later when 'course fatigue' sets in?
- Do you cover topics you are most familiar and confident with first, allowing more preparation time for that with which you are less familiar and confident?
- Will the availability of resources be a determining factor?

If you have previously taught this course, you may be happy with the order you used at that time. Alternatively, you may wish to make some changes based on that experience or subsequent student evaluations.

To organise your thinking, Rowntree (1981) suggests writing down all the topics for consideration on a sheet of paper which is then cut up into smaller pieces, each with a topic written on it. These can then be laid out on a convenient surface in an order which reflects your initial thoughts. You now have a visual overview of the course as a whole and can examine different sequencing possibilities by moving the pieces of paper around until you arrive at an order that you are happy with. Having established an appropriate sequence, you can now consider how many sessions out of those available can be allocated to each topic before progressing to the next stage.

3. Devise learning objectives

The syllabus from which you are working may have expressed content in the form of learning objectives for you. If not, the next stage in devising your scheme of work is to relate its content to the learning that it requires. The learning objectives we discussed earlier in this chapter were quite specific and are the kind of objective we would expect to see on a session plan. The scheme of work is intended to give an overview of the course as a whole and provide the basis for the design of the individual session plans. The type of learning objectives we write on a scheme of work are consequently much more general in nature and are broken down into a more specific form when the session plans are written. This sequence is illustrated in Figure 2.6.

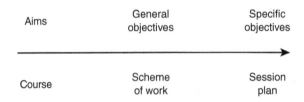

Figure 2.6   General and specific objectives

Avis et al. (2010: 122) consider a general objective to be a 'broad statement of what the learner is expected to achieve as a result of the learning session' as opposed to a specific objective which is a 'precise and verifiable statement of expected learner behaviour or potential'. Moreover, 'for an individual learning session, there would normally be a single general objective', which is taken from the scheme of work and then broken down into 'a smaller number of specific objectives (typically four or five)', which are recorded on the session plan.

Here are some examples of how this might work in practice.

Course: Paediatric First Aid

Aim (course)

- To provide the knowledge and confidence to give first aid in emergency situations involving children

General objective (scheme of work)

- To identify the reasons and causes for unconsciousness and how to respond to these in a first aid situation

Specific objectives (teaching plan)

- Identify the causes, signs and symptoms of anaphylactic shock
- Describe the use of the epi-pen in treating anaphylactic shock
- Recognise the causes, signs and symptoms of the following: drowning, poisoning, hyperventilation, croup, breath-holding, fainting and febrile convulsions

---

Course: Level 2 Motor Vehicle

Aim (course)

- To develop knowledge of light vehicle mechanical and electrical systems

General objective (scheme of work)

- To describe the operation of light vehicle lubrication systems

Specific objectives (teaching plan)

- Recognise the component parts of an engine lubrication system
- Classify the different types of lubricants
- Differentiate between full flow and bypass systems
- Describe the difference between a wet sump and a dry sump

Course: Level 2 Diploma in Sport

Aim (course)

- To develop a working knowledge of the anatomy of the body

General objective (scheme of work)

- To describe the different types of muscle and muscle movement

Specific objectives (teaching plan)

- Name the three different types of muscle
- Describe the particular structure of each
- Distinguish between concentric, eccentric and isometric muscle contractions
- Describe the use of each in a specified sporting example

ACTIVITY 2.5

Pick out a course that you currently teach. Complete the blank table below in a similar manner to those above.

Table 2.3

Course:

Aim (course):

General objective (scheme of work):

Specific objectives (teaching plan):

---

4. Consider teaching strategies

You can now consider the type of teaching strategies that you wish to employ. We are not looking to be specific at this stage, but you will have decided on the overall approach you want to take to the teaching of the course, and entries at this point will reflect this.

5. Identify resources that will be required

There are few things more annoying than finding that a particular resource you need for a teaching session is unavailable, already booked by someone else or out of stock because it hasn't been ordered in time. These circumstances are avoidable, however, if you plan in advance. Having decided generally on objective and teaching strategy, you are now in a position to identify the more important resources you will require for teaching the sessions planned into your scheme of work. This will allow you to make sure that the ICT room, DVD held by the library or consumables necessary for your practical task are available on the day. At this stage, you may identify that you need a worksheet, slide presentation or handout, without having produced it yet or thought about exactly what will go into it, although if you have taught this course before you may be in a position to be more specific.

6. Identify opportunities for embedding functional skills

Chapter 1 identified the responsibility we have towards our learners in meeting their functional skills needs. Although planning is of a rather general nature at the scheme of work stage, this is nonetheless a good point at which to begin thinking about this issue. Petty (2009: 407) goes so far as to suggest that it is a 'common mistake' to put content only into a scheme of work at the expense of functional and other skills. Aspects of functional skills that might need to be addressed at each stage of the scheme of work can be identified and thoughts further developed and refined when a more detailed session plan has been devised.

(B) SESSION PLAN

Session plan formats

Although there is no one standard way of setting out session plans – the institution in which you work will probably have its own particular approach that they require you to use – there are many similarities between the different suggested formats. The format will also reflect the nature of the session, and we will see in this section how the plan used for teaching a group will differ from that used in a workshop or one-to-one type of session. A general discussion of planning formats and their contents follows but as well as the blank formats that follow, completed examples can be found in Appendix 2 (whole-group teaching) and Appendices 3 and 4 (one-to-one/workshop environment) and you may like to have a look at these before reading further. (Figure 2.8, later, gives a general template around which the following discussion is based.)

1. Whole-group teaching   Most teaching plans used for whole-group teaching consist of two parts. The first outlines the context within which the session is to take place

Group:	Topic:	
Date:	Room:	Time:

Aims:

Specific Learning Objectives:	Assessment:

Differentiation Strategies:

Functional Skills Opportunities:

Time	Content	Teacher Activity	Learner Activity	Assessment	Resources

Figure 2.7   Teaching plan format for whole-group teaching

and records the 'process' elements. The second is directly related to the delivery of the session. We shall look at each in turn, but first have a look at the layout of the session plan in Figure 2.7.

Context

The top set of boxes gives the context of the session; the bottom set records how the session is to be taught. The first items to be recorded describe the 'who, what, when and where' of the session, which is useful information if the plan is to be used again. The aims of the session come next, followed by the specific learning objectives, written of course in 'SMART' style! Assessment methods (see Chapter 4) are recorded alongside the learning objectives so that the relationship between the two is clear. It is evident which assessment method is being employed to check the achievement of each objective. The next box down records the way in which the diversity within the group is acknowledged and is to be managed through the use of appropriate differentiation strategies (see Chapter 5). The final box describes how any functional skills (see Chapter 1) are to be embedded in this particular session.

Delivery

The first column in the 'delivery' section of the plan contains the timings of the session. These can be written as clock times or as the number of minutes a particular phase of the session will take. Clock times make management of time a little easier as they can be directly compared with the actual time during the delivery of the session. They have to be changed, however, if the plan is to be reused. The use of minutes allows for universal usage but has to be mentally converted to actual times to check progress during the session. Management of time in a session is an essential teaching skill. The session needs to be paced so as to cover everything that needs to be covered in the time available – you don't want to run out of time. Whilst in theory you can catch up next session, this puts more pressure on managing the time on that occasion and if this becomes a regular occurrence, you will fairly quickly find yourself out of step with your scheme of work. Equally, you don't want to have used up all of your prepared material and find you still have another 20 minutes or so before the session ends. Both of these situations can arise if you are not aware of them until either the end of the session or the point at which you run out of material, and in both cases it is too late to do anything about it. The question, then, is how to avoid it.

It is best not to regard the timings on a session plan as a timetable which should be rigidly adhered to. The need to implement the session plan in a flexible manner has already been stressed and this is particularly true in the case of managing time. There are a number of ways in which anticipated timings can prove to be less than accurate. Many activities, particularly those such as group work which are more student-led, can take a longer or shorter period of time than expected. Sometimes learners respond well to activities such as discussion and this takes longer than the time allowed. On other occasions, participation may be less enthusiastic and the time taken is less than you had thought. You may take some time to pursue a particularly interesting point. In short, there are a variety of factors which can throw your timing out. The only two times that you can rely on are the start time and the finish time, so these are the only two you regard as fixed. The times in between should be regarded as markers or reference points against which you gauge progress. Suppose you set off on a car journey for which you have allocated two hours. After 20 minutes of driving, you find you have covered a quarter of the distance. At this point, you know that you can slow down, spend a little longer at your coffee stop or even make a short detour from your planned route to see more of the sights along the way. If, on the other hand, you find that road conditions have been bad and it has taken you 45 minutes to cover a quarter of the distance, you now know that in order to still arrive at your destination at the planned time, you will have to make time up by not stopping for that coffee after all or by driving more quickly than you had planned for the remainder of the trip. The point is that you need to know if you are ahead of or behind time *during* your journey in order to take the appropriate actions to ensure that you arrive at your destination at the intended time. The times on a session plan fulfil a similar function. If you find that you have either taken a longer or shorter time than planned to complete the first section of your teaching plan, this is not the issue. What is important is that you know *at that stage* that you have either more or less time than you had planned for the remainder of the session. You are now in a position to make appropriate adjustments before it is too late. Times on a teaching plan are intended to help you manage time in a flexible manner rather than provide a timetable which is to be strictly adhered to.

So, having discovered a mismatch in our timing, how do we deal with it? In the car journey, driving faster or slower provides a straightforward answer but unfortunately the parallel of speaking more quickly or slowly isn't an option. We need a more creative solution. One option is to use a different activity to that which we had planned. If we are short of time, instead of having that discussion, we might just tell the group the conclusions we would expect to arise from it. If we now have more time than we anticipated, we might do the reverse or use a questioning approach instead of a telling approach. Another option is to split what we intend to cover during the session into three different categories:

1. Must cover: This is the material essential to the achievement of the session objectives.
2. Should cover: For a well-rounded session, this should be covered, but if the worst comes to the worst…
3. Could cover: This would be interesting, but isn't essential to the success of the session.

Obviously, 1 has to be covered but 3 can be included or not, depending on the available time. Thus, it is available to you if the session has proceeded at a quicker pace than you had anticipated, or you can choose not to include it if you find that time is in short supply.

The next column outlines the delivery of the content of the session and, as previously discussed, is structured to provide an introduction, the development of content in a logical manner and a conclusion. Links to the learning objectives can be made, as illustrated in the completed plan in Appendix 1.

The teaching strategies to be employed are recorded next. It is common practice to separate these out into activities such as lecture, demonstration and questioning in which the teacher leads and is the focus of attention (teacher activity) and those in which the learner is more in control and the more active party (learner activity) such as small group work, discussion and seminar. This allows us to see, at a glance, the overall balance in the session between the more passive, teacher-led approaches and the learner-led activities which encourage a more active approach to learning. See Chapter 5 for a more in-depth discussion of these categories.

The last column identifies the resources that will be required to support learning. We would try and be as specific as possible here. A quick glance down this column prior to teaching ensures we remember to take all the resources we need into the session with us.

2. Teaching in a workshop or one-to-one environment Teaching does not always involve taking a group as a whole through a session with everyone covering the same material at the same time. In many skills subjects, for example, when the basics have been mastered, learners engage in individual projects where they apply what they have learned. Although they may meet as a group, learners on competence-based programmes, which are delivered on a 'roll-on, roll-off' basis, are also likely to be engaged in different tasks. Basic education classes usually offer an individual approach as different learners have different needs and starting points. Situations such as these require a more individual approach to planning which incorporates:

- a record of progress to date
- what is to be covered in the current session
- a look forward to the next session.

The formats in Figure 2.8 achieve this in a fairly straightforward and easy-to-use fashion.

The format shown in version 1 allows an overview of planning on a session-by-session basis. The initial entry regarding the target for the session and associated resources is made by the teacher prior to the session. When the session starts, the teacher knows what each learner is to do and has the necessary resources to hand. During the session, progress can be discussed and recorded and a target or outcome for the following session agreed with the learner. The resources are also identified at this stage. Each learner now knows their starting point for the next session and can, in theory, make a start on entering the room as the resources they require have also been identified and can be made available. If kept up to date, this system of planning provides a comprehensive record of progress made by individual learners during the course, as well as allowing for advance planning and preparation. It also provides learners with an opportunity to have an input into their learning as they discuss progress and negotiate

Course:	Group:		Topic:	
Date:		Room:	Time:	
Name:	Outcome/target:		Resources needed:	Progress:
Learner 1				
Learner 2				
Learner 3				

Version 1

Course:		Room:		Time:
	Date:	Date:	Date:	Date:
Learner 1	Target:	Target:	Target:	Target:
	Resources:	Resources:	Resources:	Resources:
	Progress:	Progress:	Progress:	Progress:

Figure 2.8   Teaching plan formats for one-to-one/workshop teaching

(Adapted from Francis and Gould, 2013: 178)

targets which can have a positive effect on motivation. Ultimately, it could be the responsibility of the learners themselves to complete the entries, after discussion, thus giving them a degree of independence and control over their own learning. In this case, the format may have to be altered to make it more individual in nature, giving learners sight of only their own plan. This can be achieved by adopting a format similar to version 2. Each individual sheet could be given out at the beginning of the session as learners enter the room and collected, completed, for the following session, as they leave.

SUMMARY OF KEY POINTS

In this chapter, we have looked at effective planning for teaching and learning. We argued for the need to plan to ensure a higher likelihood of a smoother running, more effective teaching session. Planning formats for both whole-group teaching and a more individualised or workshop situation were identified, and completed examples of each are included as appendices for guidance.

The key points in this chapter are:

- Plans indicate intentions. They are responsive to the moment and should be implemented in a flexible manner.
- Planning is a systematic process in which decisions are made in the order of aims and objectives, content and teaching strategies, choice of resources, and assessment methods. After delivering a session, self-evaluation takes place to identify improvements that can be made.
- Learning objectives can be classified as falling within the cognitive, psycho-motor or affected domains and should be written using a SMART format.
- The choice of teaching strategies is influenced by the learning objectives, learners and the realities of the situation.
- Resources can take a number of forms but in all instances are intended to support the process of learning that is to take place.
- A teaching session should be structured to include an introduction, the development of material and finally a summary or conclusion.
- Self-evaluation identifies improvements through a process of reflecting on the main points of the session and exploring why they occurred as they did.
- Schemes of work are course plans which are devised from a syllabus and identify the sequence and timing of the various topics to be covered.
- Schemes of work are broken down into more detailed session plans. The format for a session plan depends on the nature of the session to be delivered.
- Rather than a timetable of events, timings on a session plan serve as a reference point, allowing more effective management of time.

ANSWER TO ACTIVITY 2.1

The verbs which are italicised are those which we would not use to write a SMART learning objective.

Table 2.4

define	select	*understand*	List
realise the significance of	measure	*have a good grasp of*	justify
really know	construct	select	*be aware of*
solve	*be familiar with*	demonstrate	distinguish between
describe	recall	explain	*know*
think	perform	*appreciate*	state
prepare	give reasons	report	*be acquainted with*

ANSWER TO ACTIVITY 2.2

Compare your answers with this completed table.

Table 2.5

Parkinson's Questions	Level of Bloom's Taxonomy
How old were you when you signed for Manchester United?	Knowledge
Could you explain the off-side rule?	Comprehension
Give reasons why you are such a good midfielder.	Analysis
How do you cross a ball so accurately?	Application
How do you rate Manchester United's chances of winning the league this year?	Evaluation
If you were managing United, how would you run the team?	Synthesis
What would cause you to leave Manchester United?	Analysis
What do the lyrics of your wife's last single mean?	Comprehension
George Best is your favourite footballer – what were his strengths and weaknesses as a footballer?	Evaluation
What do you have written on the front of your boots?	Knowledge
How would you improve the quality of England's game?	Synthesis
How do you go about taking a corner?	Application

REFERENCES

Anderson, L., Krathwohl, D., Airasian, P., Cruikshank, K., Mayer, R., Pintrich, P., et al. (2001) *A Taxonomy for Learning, Teaching, and Assessing: A Revision of Bloom's Taxonomy of Educational Objectives*. Oxford: Pearson Education.

Armitage, A., Bryant, R., Dunnill, R. and Flanagan, K. (1999) *Teaching and Training in Post-Compulsory Education*. Buckingham: Open University Press.

Avis, J., Fisher, R. and Thompson, R. (eds) (2010) *Teaching in Lifelong Learning: A Guide to Theory and Practice*. Maidenhead: Open University Press/McGraw-Hill Education.

Bloom, B. (1956) *Taxonomy of Educational Objectives*. London: Longman.

Fairclough, M. (2008) *Supporting Learners in the Lifelong Learning Sector*. Maidenhead: Open University Press/McGraw-Hill Education.

Francis, M. and Gould, J. (2013) Achieving Your PTLLS Award: A Practical Guide to Teaching in the Lifelong Learning Sector (2nd edn). London: Sage.

Hillier, Y. (2005) Reflective Teaching in Further and Adult Education (2nd edn). London: Continuum.

Kolb, D. (1984) Experiential Learning: Experience as the Source of Learning and Development. Englewood Cliffs, NJ: Prentice-Hall.

Kolb, D.A. and Fry, R. (1975) Toward an applied theory of experiential learning. In C. Cooper (ed.) *Theories of Group Processes*. London: Wiley.

Petty, G. (2009) *Teaching Today* (4th edn). Cheltenham: Nelson Thornes.

Reece, I. and Walker, S. (2007) *Teaching Training and Learning: A Practical Guide* (6th edn). Sunderland: Business Education Publishers.

Rogers, A. and Horrocks, N. (2010) *Teaching Adults* (4th edn). Maidenhead: Open University Press/McGraw-Hill Education.

Rogers, J. (2007) *Adults Learning* (5th edn). Maidenhead: Open University Press/McGraw-Hill Education.

Rowntree, D. (1981) *Developing Courses for Students*. New York: Harper & Row.

Usher, R. (1985) Beyond the anecdotal: adult learning and the use of experience. *Studies in the Education of Adults* 17(1): 59–75.

 # FURTHER READING

Harper, H. (2013) *Outstanding Teaching in Lifelong Learning*. Maidenhead: Open University Press.

The content of this book is based around 20 lessons judged to be outstanding by inspectors. As well as looking at inclusive practice and the use of questioning, it discusses approaches to planning and the various factors and areas (objectives, strategies, resources, assessment) that should be taken into account in the planning process. The points made are illustrated by reference to four outstanding lessons which were based on solid planning foundations.

Marzano, R.J. and Kendall, J.S. (2007) *The New Taxonomy of Educational Objectives* (2nd edn). California: Corwin Press.

If you would like to extend your thinking around the concept of objectives and Bloom's taxonomy, this book sets out some of the perceived limitations of Bloom's Taxonomy and looks at other approaches to classification before suggesting an alternative approach. The authors have also produced an accompanying text on application of their taxonomy – *Designing & Assessing Educational Objectives: Applying the New Taxonomy* (2008).

3
CHOOSING AND USING RESOURCES

Without the use of resources, learning can become a fairly sterile and less engaging process than it might otherwise be. Resources can be used by teachers to give added impact and interest to the sessions they deliver, and by learners to increase their understanding and ability to study independently. An extensive range of different resources is available to both groups, and to make an informed choice as to which resource should be used and then to obtain the greatest benefit from it, requires an understanding of the function, operation, strengths and limitations of these different resources. That is what this chapter provides.

When you have completed this chapter you will be able to:

- identify the different ways in which resources can be used to support both teaching and learning
- classify the different types of handout and recognise when best to distribute them to groups of learners
- demonstrate the different ways in which PowerPoint can be used
- describe how to make best use of a traditional whiteboard
- recognise the potential applications of the electronic whiteboard
- indicate the different uses to which a flip chart might be put
- list the different technologies that can be used in teaching and in learning
- differentiate between ICT and e-learning
- compare face-to-face, online and blended learning approaches

(Continued)

- recognise the different ways in which technology can assist in the creation of a variety of different types of resources
- describe the ways in which emerging technologies are increasing the communication channels between teachers and learners
- recognise the increasing use of technology in researching subject material
- access a range of adaptive technologies.

WHY USE RESOURCES?

ACTIVITY 3.1

Given a choice, in each of the following instances which approach would you prefer to use in learning about the subject?

1   A talk about the parts of a camera and how the camera works

or

2   A talk using an actual camera to demonstrate what was being said?

1   A description of the tools used in plumbing

or

2   An exhibition of plumbing tools accompanied by a description?

1   An explanation of different types of car tyres and their uses

or

2   An explanation using different types of car tyres to illustrate what is being said?

Give the reasons for your particular choices.

In responding to the first part of the above activity, you undoubtedly opted for the second choice in each case and it is highly unlikely that anyone who had to teach these subjects would choose any differently. You will recognise the camera, plumbing tools and car tyres as examples of resources and these obviously give some kind of 'added value' to the process of teaching. To find out what this is, we need to focus on your responses to the second part of the activity where the question asked is less straightforward, asking 'WHY do we prefer to be taught in this way?' The reasons you gave may well have included: the resource makes it more interesting, it's less complicated to understand, it's less boring or perhaps less difficult to remember afterwards. These and similar responses suggest that resources make the act of learning easier in some way, supporting Hillier's view (2005: 101) that resources 'are usually artefacts that can support learning'. Wallace (2001: 79) takes a slightly different but complementary view, stating that resources are 'a means to enliven, facilitate or inform the learning method you have chosen to use'.

These definitions suggest that resources take on a role in the teaching process of either supporting the learning that is to take place, or supporting the strategies that will be used in the achievement of that learning. This is why decisions involving resources come third in the planning sequence discussed in Chapter 2, after identifying the learning objectives and the teaching strategies to be used. It is only when these first two decisions have been made that a judgement can be made concerning the most appropriate resources to use – we need to know first what learning and teaching strategies the resources will be supporting. A distinction is often made between 'teaching resources' and 'learning resources', but this is not particularly helpful as many resources can fall equally well into either category, depending on the way in which they are used. For the purposes of this chapter, we will use the generic category of 'resources'.

RESOURCES AND PROMOTING LEARNING

The examples in Activity 3.1 all used actual real-life examples of what was being learned about and are commonly known as 'the real thing'. Whilst this is the best resource we can use, it is not always a realistic option. If we teach First Aid, we don't often have access to a real body with a broken arm; physics – a Hadron Collider; art – the *Mona Lisa*; floristry – spring blooms in winter; and in PSE classes we would not be allowed to bring knives, other offensive weapons or drugs into the classroom. Sometimes, for reasons of cost, availability, size or safety, we are unable to use the 'real thing' and so have to turn to other types of resource such as a picture or a model as a substitute. Chapter 2 identified a range of different types of resources; a selection has been taken from that list for the next activity.

ACTIVITY 3.2

Complete the table below by suggesting how each resource might support learning.

Table 3.1

Resource	Supports learning by...
Whiteboard	
Handout	
The 'real thing'	
DVD clip	
PowerPoint slides	
Flip chart	
Model	

In your response to the above activity, you may have considered some of the following resources.

Whiteboards highlight and organise the main points to be learned. Teachers can use them to clarify more complex points by drawing diagrams, making lists or producing mind maps. Handouts allow us to focus on the content of the session rather than on note taking and form a useful memory aid. The 'real thing' brings the real world into our learning, making it more interesting and easier to understand. Models perform a similar function when the 'real thing' is not available. Videos can also help in providing a representation of reality, and along with PowerPoint slides help to maintain our attention. Flip charts can help us keep track of discussions or a brainstorming session by recording contributions as they are made.

Generally, we learn best when:

- we want to learn about something because it interests us, excites us or arouses our curiosity
- what we are learning catches and holds our attention
- our learning makes sense; we can understand what is going on and it has some meaning for us
- we can commit what we are learning to memory reasonably easily.

As your answers to the last activity no doubt demonstrate, resources can help with all of these factors.

VISUAL RESOURCES

We communicate with the world through the five senses of sight, hearing, smell, touch and taste. Particular activities may rely on one sense more than the others – smell and taste are heavily used in cooking, touch is an essential sense in pottery or massage, hearing in music – but, in general, the degree to which we rely on each sense in the performance of everyday activities is approximately:

Sight – 83%

Hearing – 11%

Smell – 3.5%

Touch – 1.5%

Taste – 1%

If you were driving your car or going shopping, for instance, a bad head cold, which deprived you of a sense of smell, although irritating, would not provide a major obstacle to performing either of these activities. If the cold led to an ear infection, leaving you temporarily unable to hear, it would be more difficult, but still possible to engage in either activity. Suppose for some reason, however, you temporarily lost your sight. This would have a serious impact on your ability to perform any everyday task. In a learning situation, all of our senses are available to us but, often, the one that is expected to do the majority of the work is hearing. As hearing is not normally our main sensory input, listening intently is hard work on our part; we tire relatively quickly and maintaining concentration becomes difficult. If some visual stimulation is introduced, it comes as quite a relief and so attention is immediately turned towards it. By enabling us to appeal to more than one sense at the same time, visual aids add impact and interest to a session. They are extremely effective in attracting and maintaining attention and allow us, as teachers, to focus attention where we would like it to be. To be effective in this, however, visual aids need to be carefully managed as they can easily become an attention distractor. When not being used to complement the spoken word, whiteboards should be cleaned, flip charts turned to a blank page, projection systems switched off, models and realia placed out of sight, and handouts given out at relevant times. Used appropriately, the combination of explanation and visual aids can increase the amount of information retained by a considerable margin, as illustrated in Figure 3.1.

Studies suggest that three days after an event, people retain 10 per cent of what they heard from an oral presentation, 35 per cent from a visual presentation, and 65 per cent from a combined visual and oral presentation. Visual aids also help clarify and reinforce what is said. One of the ways in which we make sense of the spoken word is to form mental images of what has been said. Visual aids help in this process and increase comprehension and understanding, which, in turn, increase retention.

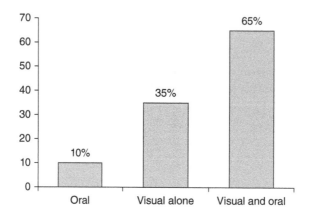

Figure 3.1   Amount of information retained after three days

The majority of the resources we use are visual in some way, but, when using slides, handouts, whiteboards and flip charts, we are in a position where we can determine the shape and form they take. Bearing in mind that their main function is to draw attention to the important points, and organise them in such a way that they can be most easily committed to memory, we need to consider how they might be designed to most effectively support learning in this way. Attention can be drawn to specific points by using larger writing, UPPER CASE, **bold**, *italics*, <u>underlining</u>, frames or different colours. Information can be organised by use of bullet points, numbers or sub-headings. Generally, visual aids should be uncluttered, with no more than five points, and all words and illustrations contained in them should be large enough to be seen by everyone in the room.

FREQUENTLY USED RESOURCES

1. HANDOUTS

Handouts are a versatile resource and form part of the staple diet of any teaching session. Their prime purpose is to relieve learners of the burden of taking copious notes, allowing them to focus attention on the content and process of the teaching session, but they have other uses as well. The exact purpose of a handout will determine the type to be used, how it is used and when it is to be given out.

Types of handout

(a) Trigger   This type of handout contains some form of scenario, case study, a series of short statements or similar which are intended to promote discussion, perhaps by answering accompanying questions, and set the scene for what is to follow. It can give an active, structured beginning to a session and can also be used as an informal assessment method if based around work covered in the sessions previous to the one in which it is used.

(b) Skeletal/gapped/incomplete   As can be seen from the various names given to this type of handout, it can offer different levels of structure, which provide a form of 'scaffolding' for note taking, but requires an active approach as learners have to consider and record information onto it. This can be achieved by:

- labelling diagrams provided on the handout
- completing the plotting of graphs, tables of data or calculations
- filling in gaps in written text or making brief notes under the sub-headings that have been supplied.

This type of handout can be completed in sections following short presentations of information. The pause for note making gives a change of activity and the use of a different set of skills and senses, and can be helpful in maintaining energy and attention levels. Alternatively, the handout can become part of the activity itself if filled in as part of a discussion or question and answer session. However used, it balances the need for accurate notes with an active approach to learning whilst maintaining and directing attention.

(c) Worksheets   The effectiveness of a teaching session lies not in how much material we can cover, but rather in how much of that material learners take away with them. The best way of achieving the latter option is to provide opportunities within the session for learners to engage with and use the material to be learned. We may therefore choose to consolidate what has been learned by setting a problem-solving type of activity in the form of a worksheet, in which learners, either individually or in groups, apply what has been learned. A differentiated approach, using either a series of short graded exercises or different level worksheets, can be used to extend learning as well as consolidate. In effect, this approach uses handouts as learning activities or informal assessment methods and has the advantage of providing opportunities for one-to-one time within the session.

(d) Summary   Summary handouts provide a review or record of the main points and information that are to be taken away from the session. They allow learners to focus attention solely on the session itself rather than divide their attention between the session and the need to take notes. When using this type of handout, it is customary to let learners know this is the case at the beginning of the session so they are aware of the choices they have in taking notes. Learners may still wish to make some notes of their own if they feel it helps them in their learning, but they can now make notes that will complement those they will be given rather than having to record every detail. If PowerPoint is used, the summary handout can be based around the slides, either in copy form or with the space to make notes alongside. If the handout is included as part of the session, perhaps by basing the conclusion to the session around reading through or referring to it, learners are more likely to file it away with other materials from the session and refer back to it at a later stage. Handouts given as 'add-ons' are the ones that are generally found left lying around at the end of a session. The importance we place on the handouts we give out needs to be reflected in the way in which we use them.

(e) Follow-up   At the end of a teaching session, we may want to set learners up or orientate them for the following session. A follow-up handout can be given relating to what will be covered next, setting short preparatory tasks for learners to complete. These can be as simple as noting down, in the space provided on the handout, two examples of what has been discussed that they notice in real life, perhaps with a short description. The purpose is to encourage learners to think through what they have learned (even if only fleetingly) and recognise its relevance and potential use. The responses can contribute to an active start to the next session. There is, of course, an element of risk in using this approach, and you may have to have a 'plan B' ready for the start of the next session if you feel that learners cannot be relied on 100 per cent to complete the tasks set. Ideally, plan B would acknowledge the work done by those who did complete the tasks, as we would like to reward the effort they have made. You may have to think carefully about ways in which you manage this approach (which will encourage compliance), or about its suitability for your particular learners, but it is well worth it if you can make it work!

Timing of distribution

Distributing handouts to a large class is not necessarily a straightforward activity and can cause considerable disruption – you might like to consider how this is best achieved with your own groups. The most appropriate time to issue handouts also requires some thought. Broadly speaking, the options are:

- at the beginning of the session
- during the session
- at the end of the session.

Which of these you decide on will depend on the purpose you intend the handout to fulfil. Figure 3.2 gives a 'rule of thumb' approach for guidance.

Type of handout	Best time?
Trigger	At the beginning of the session
Skeletal/gapped/incomplete	At the beginning of the session/During the session
Worksheet	During the session
Summary	At the end of the session
Follow-up	At the end of the session

Figure 3.2   Timing and distribution of handouts

Design of handouts

REFLECTIVE TASK 3.1

Ask colleagues and mentors to contribute to a collection of handouts used in the teaching of your subject. First, identify what type they are, using the categories introduced in the previous section. Now divide them into three piles:

1.   Those that you like the look of.
2.   Those that you don't like the look of.
3.   Those which you feel fairly neutral about.

What do the contents of the different piles tell you about handout design? How do your own handouts compare? Can you make them a more effective resource by thinking about the form they take, the visual impression they make and the amount and type of information they contain?

The Reflective Task above should give you some ideas on what constitutes good and bad design of handouts. Thinking back to your own experiences of receiving handouts, how do you feel when presented with a handout which is a page from a book which has been copied so often it is barely legible and contains dated information? Television programmes on selling houses emphasise 'kerb appeal'. Many people won't even set foot in a house if they don't like the outside, and, similarly, if we wish our handouts to be taken seriously and provide genuine support for learning we need to think about their visual impact on learners. With the technology that is now available, it should be possible to produce a professional-looking handout with good visual impact. As well as first impressions, visual impact also involves the way in which information on the handout is organised. Font size, style and white space can be used to good effect to highlight and arrange the information contained in the handout. Rather than using dense text, distinct titles, margins, spacing and clearly indicated sub-sections make information easier to find and sort out. Pictures can be used to brighten up your handout and emphasise structure but need to be chosen carefully so they do not reinforce undesirable stereotypical images. They also need to be used sparingly as they can distract from the points being made if over used. Use of subject jargon and language in general should be appropriate to the level and experience of the intended audience.

Your learners may include those with some form of dyslexia and you will need to consider their needs both in the design and management of your handouts. Although there is still some debate over the most suitable fonts to use, there is a website (www.bdadyslexia.org.uk/about-dyslexia/further-information/dyslexia-style-guide.html) which gives advice in this respect.

Dyslexic readers may have a preference for a particular colour of handout but you will need to ask what that preference is as it can vary from individual to individual. A supply of different coloured acetate overlays can be useful in overcoming this particular issue.

2. POWERPOINT

PowerPoint is a computer program forming part of the Microsoft Office suite that allows us to create and show slides to support our teaching. It is a versatile resource which can combine text, graphics and multi-media content. Collections of slides can be stored electronically and easily updated or modified for use in other sessions on related topics. It can be used to:

- contribute to the organisation and structure of your session
- create a consistent format with excellent visual impact
- link directly to the internet
- generate complementary handouts.

PowerPoint has become enormously popular as a teaching aid and its use seems to be a 'given' in most classroom-based teaching.

Not all teaching and learning require support from PowerPoint, however, and so the first consideration is whether it will serve a useful function in the session you are planning. PowerPoint has its origins in industry, where presentations were made in the boardroom. Its purpose was to present the greatest amount of information in the shortest time to a specific and knowledgeable audience, and so it was often used to *lead* and structure a presentation, displacing the presenter as the main focal point. In a teaching session, it has to be used in a different manner as its purpose is to *support* learning and teaching. We have already seen that the purpose of a visual aid is to attract and maintain attention, help understanding and make it easier to commit material to memory, and this purpose needs to be borne in mind when using PowerPoint and designing slides to use.

ACTIVITY 3.3

You will have been on the 'receiving end' of PowerPoint presentations on a number of occasions such as conferences or staff development activities, as part of the experience of your diploma course, etc. Focus on the times you found it useful. What does this tell you about the effective use and design of slides?

There are a number of features to consider when designing effective PowerPoint slides. How do your responses to the activity above compare to the list below?

(a) Text

- Avoid cluttering slides with too much text and resist the temptation to read from them.
- Use headings for structure. Make these **bold** for emphasis rather than using upper case, *italics* or underlining.
- Text needs to be around a minimum of 24pt to be readable in all parts of the room.
- Be consistent in the use of fonts. Too many variations in font size and type can be visually confusing.
- Bullet points provide a clear summary of key points, and do not need to be complete sentences.
- As a 'rule of thumb', slides should have no more than six bullet points and each bullet point should be no more than six words long.

(b) Colour and graphics

- Be consistent in the use of colour. All slides should have the same or similar background images and colour schemes.
- Use a bold colour contrast between background and text.
- Information can be easier to understand and remember if images are used in addition to text, and may even be used to replace text where an image might be easier to understand.
- All graphics should be relevant to the text rather than decorative.
- Images taken from the internet may pixelate (lose their smoothness) when you project them onto a large screen and may be subject to copyright.

(c) Animations and transitions

- Animations can be used to build up a process step-by-step to help understanding.
- Animations can be used to focus attention by revealing selected bits of information or bullet points one at a time.
- Animations and transitions should be used sparingly and in a consistent manner to avoid distraction from the content of the slides.

PowerPoint can be operated directly from the computer keyboard by using the 'Enter' key, from a distance using a wireless remote control or, if used in conjunction with an interactive Smart Board, by tapping on the board surface. There are also a number of keyboard shortcuts which can be useful and introduce additional functions.

Pressing the F1 key whilst running a slideshow will reveal these but the more useful shortcuts are included in Figure 3.3.

Effect	Shortcut key
Start slideshow	F5
Advance to the next slide	'N' key, spacebar, right or down arrow, page down
Return to the previous slide	'P' key, backspace, left or up arrow, page up
Go to a specific slide	Slide number followed by 'Enter'
Return to the first slide of the presentation	Home
Display pointer	Ctrl plus 'A' key
Hide pointer	Ctrl plus 'H' key
Change pointer to a pen	Ctrl plus 'P' key
Make the screen black	'B' key (press again to return to slideshow)
Make the screen white	'W' key (press again to return to slideshow)
End slideshow	Esc

Figure 3.3   Useful shortcut keys in PowerPoint

PowerPoint is constantly evolving and each new version brings its own added refinements. You need to check that the machine you will be using has a version of PowerPoint compatible with the one on which you devised your slideshow. If you have used a newer version of the program in constructing your slideshow, it may not work on a machine with an earlier version of the software.

Apple has a similar application called 'Keynotes'. The user chooses a pre-designed background or 'theme' for their slides which can then be built up by substituting the desired text and images. Elements such as tables, charts, shapes and various forms of media such as music, video clips or photographs can be added to slides by use of the appropriate tools, and animation and transition effects can also be accessed. Compatibility with other systems is achieved by uploading the completed slideshow to iWork.com where others can download it in Keynote, PowerPoint or PDF format.

An alternative presentation medium which claims to recreate the 'wow' factor which PowerPoint has now lost through familiarity, is Prezi. Prezis are created on a single 'canvas' rather than on a series of slides. Movement between the different items on the canvas is achieved by 'zooming' in and out from one to the other. This effect allows contrasts with the linear approach to presentation used by slide-based systems, although 'zooming' needs to be used carefully as it can induce dizziness or possibly even nausea in the audience. This YouTube clip (www.youtube.com/watch?v=1gCm L0P5RNA) will give you an idea of what a Prezi looks like. Although it takes a little time to get used to, it is a relatively easy system to use, as can be seen in this YouTube clip (www.youtube.com/watch?v=wmMGX0_HBwQ).

Although the overall canvas contains all of the information in the presentation in varying sizes and orientations, you can print a version to distribute as a handout by conversion to a series of PDF files. The system is 'cloud-based' which means that the software, and subsequently anything that is produced by its use, is hosted centrally on the internet rather than on your own computer in the way that PowerPoint is. Users can therefore access and share each other's work. Prezi allows free use for anyone in education, but upgrades can be purchased which allow a privacy option (for more information, go to http://prezi.com).

REFLECTIVE TASK 3.2

Think about your own use of PowerPoint. Do you use it to 'support' or 'lead' the learning that is taking place. How can you use it in such a way as to make it more of the former and less of the latter?

3. WHITEBOARDS (TRADITIONAL AND INTERACTIVE)

The whiteboard is a modern, cleaner, easier to use version of the old school chalkboard and fulfils much the same purpose. It can be used in a planned manner, such as recording the main points or headings of the material being covered, but it is normally more responsive in nature. We may use it to illustrate a complex or technical point that is proving difficult to explain or to record learner contributions to questions, the results of brainstorming exercises or feedback from group work. We would normally have some idea as to how we would arrange this information on the whiteboard, however, despite this more spontaneous use. This might involve mentally dividing it into sections and using these in turn, using colour, bullet points, headings or any of the other strategies previously discussed to help learners make sense of and organise what we record. Writing on a whiteboard is something of an art. The writing needs to be large enough to be seen in all parts of the room and this alone can take some practice to master. More difficult, however, is using the board whilst both maintaining some eye contact with learners and not obscuring their view. A sideways-on stance to the board can help in this respect, whilst moving across it as we write. As with all visual aids, the whiteboard can become an attention distractor after it has served its immediate purpose, and so cleaning after use also needs to become part of the ritual of working with it.

REFLECTIVE TASK 3.3

Next time you use a whiteboard in your teaching, stand back and take a look at it before you clean it, or take a picture of it with your mobile phone.

How well organised is it? What can you do to improve your use of it?

The modern-day counterpart of the whiteboard is its electronic or interactive version which connects to a computer and a projector, opening up further possibilities for its use. It can function as an ordinary whiteboard, an electronic copy board, a projector screen or a computer screen. This last application means that not only can the internet, PowerPoint or any other application that can be accessed by computer, be displayed on the whiteboard, but anything which is recorded onto it can be saved to the computer and retrieved for future use. If a printer is attached, instant handouts can be created. The computer can be controlled by touching or writing on the surface of the board instead of using a mouse or keyboard, and so users, whether teacher or learner, can input both at the computer and at the board. Software which allows materials to be prepared in advance and stored electronically, allowing for use on multiple occasions, can be loaded onto work or home computers. These prepared materials can be further annotated during a teaching session and the changes saved for future reference or discarded to preserve the materials in their original form, ready for further use.

There are a number of different manufacturers of interactive whiteboards and each supplies supplementary software providing additional functions and resource banks which contain different activities such as quizzes and templates. Some of the additional functions provided include:

- Reveal blind – this acts like a roller blind, shutting out parts of the screen; it can be made to go up/down/left/right and so can be used with columns as well as with lists
- Spotlight – acts in the manner in which its name suggests, exposing only a section of the content on the board; its shape and size can be varied and it can be moved around the board, which allows attention to be focused on specific items
- Timer – this is a digital or analogue clock which can either count down or up and sits in the corner of the board; it can be used to allow groups to self-regulate the timing of group work
- Camera capture – this allows parts of text or images from any displayable source to be captured, re-sized and placed on a clean page for further discussion and annotation.

Examples of teacher-led use include:

- showing PowerPoint slides to supplement information given
- viewing and surfing the internet from the whiteboard to illustrate topical issues
- showing video clips to initiate discussion, explain or show applications of new concepts
- writing over the top of slides, diagrams or text to highlight and annotate points.

The above uses exploit only part of the potential of this resource and it is important to remember the whiteboard's interactive function. It can be used by teachers or learners or collaboratively between the two. Examples of learner-led use include:

- adding their contributions to the discussion by writing them directly onto the whiteboard
- working in groups on Word documents or spreadsheets which can be displayed and discussed
- contributing individually to, or working in small groups on, labelling diagrams, creating drawings or producing mind maps.

To make the whiteboards even more interactive, they can be linked to classroom response systems. Each learner has a handheld device like a remote control or small mobile phone. In its simplest mode, this offers an A to F choice so, as simple multiple-choice questions come up on the interactive whiteboard, the group can respond. If used for purposes such as initial assessment, the responses are recorded by the white-board and can be viewed (probably at a later date) either as a pie chart (anonymously) or by learner name. Results can also be exported to Excel for future analysis and fed into a college data management system for record keeping. As well as allowing responses to prepared material, the system can be used spontaneously as a classroom resource. At any point in the session, questions can be asked or written on the white-board and responses gained instantly using the handsets. Opinions can be sought through questions such as 'do you agree or disagree with…?' Those who strongly agree can input 'A' and those who strongly disagree input 'F'; the results of the poll can be seen by everyone. The exercise can be repeated at the end of the discussion/debate to see if options have shifted. If respondents are identified, the initial responses can also be used to sit people of opposing views within smaller discussion groups. If not, the responses can be presented anonymously and collectively in a number of ways such as bar charts, graphs or pie charts. Response systems allow for comprehensive, instant feedback from learners, lending themselves easily to short, sharp formative assessments. It is relatively simple, for instance, after giving a short explanation, to test understanding by posing a few questions to respond to, providing an indication as to whether learners have absorbed the key points.

Other advances such as wireless keyboards and tablets allow use and involvement of learners anywhere within the room but as always these come at a price. The basic set-up is sufficient for most needs, however, and can be mastered in a relatively short period of time. Under the Labour Government's 'Harnessing Technology' policy (DfES, 2005), most schools in the country have interactive whiteboards in place and their use is now fairly commonplace. The implication here is that the next generation of learners may well consider the normal whiteboard to be outdated, as we now consider the old chalkboard to be, and consequently have higher expectations of both resources and their uses.

REFLECTIVE TASK 3.4

If you have access to an electronic whiteboard, think about the ways in which you currently use it. Come up with one idea on how to use it in a more interactive way which involves learners and put this into practice at the next available opportunity.

4. THE FLIP CHART

Flip charts are easy to use, don't need to be plugged in and are simple and small enough to be readily portable, so although they can be used alongside other resources they are particularly useful in circumstances where these are unavailable. They can be used much in the same way as a whiteboard for recording contributions and illustrating explanations but also fulfil other functions such as encouraging participation and organising group work. The results of group activities such as problem solving, brainstorming, decision making or devising lists can be recorded by the group on a blank page for presentation to and sharing with fellow learners. The simple act of recording group thoughts on a blank flip chart page provides a focus to the activity and provokes discussion and debate amongst group members. It is also a way of acknowledging contribution and effort, as well as ensuring a tangible end product to the activity. The completed pages can be hung around the room for all to see and to be referred back to if necessary. Although unashamedly low-tech, the flip chart is probably the most user-friendly and flexible resource available to us as teachers.

RESOURCES BASED ON EMERGING TECHNOLOGIES

Technology is transforming the nature and scope of resources that are available to us. Word-processing and graphics packages allow us to build up, fairly quickly, a comprehensive bank of professionally produced resources which can be modified and updated with relative ease. These resources can be organised and stored in a straightforward and efficient manner and used in a variety of locations, provided the appropriate hardware is available. In some instances, technology is put to use in updating current resources, as we have seen in the case of the whiteboard. In others, completely new avenues are opened up.

ACTIVITY 3.4

List as many different technologies as you can which are put to use, either directly or indirectly, in a teaching or learning capacity. How are these used by either teachers or learners?

Compare your list with that in Figure 3.4.

Virtual Learning Environment (VLE)	Flickr	Online videos (YouTube)	Google Books/Scholar
Skype	Speech recognition software	Text messaging	Podcasts
Wikis	PowerPoint	Search engines such as Google	Discussion boards
Visualiser	Wikipedia	Blogs	Animations
Social networking sites	E-books	Mobile phones	Turnitin

Figure 3.4   Technology in education

In the present day, the use of information and communications technology (ICT) has become a fact of teaching life. In this chapter, ICT is used to refer to the equipment (hardware and software) whereas e-learning refers to the use of ICT for the purpose of education. Whilst acknowledging that it is far from comprehensive, Clarke (2011: 28) provides the following list of ways in which the use of ICT can assist in both teaching and learning:

• researching your subject
• locating e-learning and other sources to integrate into your session
• creating learning materials from a straightforward handout summarising the key points to producing interactive multimedia resources

- extending your face-to-face sessions through communication technologies (e.g. email discussion forums)
- adding interest and flexibility through technology (e.g. electronic whiteboard)
- improving formative and summative assessment (e.g. annotating assignments with feedback)
- improving reflective skills (e.g. blogs)
- assisting peer support (e.g. wikis).

The potential use of technology in education is acknowledged at a strategic as well as a practical level. Clarke (2011: 3) informs us that better use of e-learning and other 21st-century IT solutions are required to 'drive up quality whilst reducing unnecessary costs in FE'. Despite the apparent strong measure of support for technology, however, take-up is variable, and Buckingham (2007: 30) reminds us of the 'significant gap between the imagination of policy-makers … and the realities of teaching and learning', as demonstrated by the sight, during a recent Ofsted inspection, of an FE lecturer pushing a traditional whiteboard on wheels along several corridors to a classroom which possessed only an electronic whiteboard and placing its more traditional predecessor firmly in front of it. Whalley et al. (2006) suggest that teacher resistance to the use of technology stems from the numerous other pressures placed on time and energy, and it is certainly the case that using new technologies involves a fairly steep learning curve and requires a greater effort than carrying on as normal. A lack of equipment and appropriate training in its use is a further factor and some concern has been expressed regarding technology taking over from teachers. Perhaps the biggest barrier, however, arises from the feeling many teachers have that the use of technology in the classroom is being imposed on them.

This is not a universal picture, however, and others in the profession embrace technology as an important part of their toolkit which can bring variety into the delivery of teaching sessions and support the process of learning in ways which have not been possible in the past. The best practice tends to be observed in instances where it is self-initiated and generally falls into the following categories:

- to create teaching and learning resources
- to open up new avenues of communication
- to research information
- to supplement or replace taught sessions.

CREATING TEACHING AND LEARNING RESOURCES

One of the most significant applications of ICT is the use of word-processing packages such as Microsoft Word to produce legible, visually attractive and professional-looking handouts and other classroom material with relative ease. Good typing skills are useful in this respect but even these are becoming less essential as speech recognition software is becoming more reliable and accurate. Dragon produce a series of reasonably priced packages (at the time of writing, the latest version is Dragon 13), which not only type as you talk but allow the use of voice commands to perform a variety of functions ranging from using the internet to answering and managing your email account. A short period of training is necessary to familiarise the package with the particular idiosyncrasies of the user's voice but it takes little time to have the system functioning.

Graphics can be easily imported into a document by using shapes, the clip art facility, SmartArt or charts (Microsoft Office 2016). Pictures can be taken from 'My pictures', the internet or sites such as Flickr, which has an archive of over 5 billion photographs from sources as wide as individual contributors to organisations such as NASA. Storage and modification are also made easy. Headers and footers can be used to customise, with page numbers, dates, mathematical equations and symbols inserted, and a little experimentation reveals other applications as each new version of the programme increases the options at our disposal.

Word has other possible uses, however, particularly if projected onto a screen. Text boxes can be used for matching or labelling exercises as they can be moved around the document with the mouse. The 'Drop boxes' and 'Comments' facilities within Word can also be put to good use in creating an interactive resource.

It is not always necessary to produce your own resources as the internet houses many ready-made materials which can be downloaded and used in their original form or modified to better suit the purpose you have in mind. Resources for use at different levels within a wide range of subjects can be found at http://xtlearn.net/nln; www.excellencegateway.org.uk/node/18239; www.bbc.co.uk/learning/ (now archived material only); www.heacademy.ac.uk/disciplines; and www.slideshare.net/featured/category/education

Templates for a variety of interactive quiz-based activities can be found at the 'Hot Potatoes' site (http://hotpot.uvic.ca/). Here, you will find six applications which will allow you to create multiple-choice, short-answer, jumbled-sentence, crossword, matching/ordering and gap-fill exercises, which can be used as part of a teaching session or accessed by learners for self-assessment purposes. If we add the different types of presentation packages, such as those discussed earlier, and the ability to link these directly to any site on the internet, it is evident that the whole process of producing resources and the variety that can be achieved have moved on to a different level.

OPENING UP NEW AVENUES OF COMMUNICATION

The days when communication was conducted only in a face-to-face manner are now long gone. Perhaps the biggest impact is that of email. The first email pre-dates the internet and was sent in 1971 by a computer engineer by the name of Ray Tomlinson.

The message contained in this first email also contained instructions on the use of @ in setting up email addresses. Now, some 40 years later, checking emails is an integral part of the daily routine at work, and, in an educational setting, emails are now used for a number of different purposes. Hill (2008: 59) provides a list which ranges from administrative tasks such as responding to course enquiries to direct learner contact relating to absence, assignment submission and sending work to those who miss a class. Emails are just one of the ways in which communication between teachers and learners has been revolutionised. Others are:

Blogs which, as their original name of weblog suggests, consist of a diary or collection of thoughts and ideas. They are generally created and written by a particular individual. The contents can remain personal or can be made available to others who can then comment on the entries if they wish. A useful single contributor blog that you may well have come across during your studies is that of Jim Crawley (which can be found at www.itslifejimbutnotasweknowit.org.uk/). A blog can provide an excellent medium for keeping a learning or reflective diary. If used as an open forum (preferably with some teacher control), it can provide a useful discussion forum on which opinions and ideas on a specific topic can be shared, entries being recorded in date order. Free sites such as www.blogger.com allow you to create a blog quickly and efficiently. A microblog such as Twitter differs from a normal blog in that it only accepts short posts (of up to 140 words) which can be replied to but only if the respondent has permission to view the site.

Wikis produce an entry on a website that is created collaboratively. It is either started by one person and others can correct or add to their contribution, or it can be organised so that different contributors cover different aspects of the topic under consideration. Wikipedia is the most well-known example, but the idea of a wiki can be used on a smaller scale as part of a group project when the members of the group have limited face-to-face contact.

Most younger (and, increasingly, older) learners use *social networking sites* to keep in contact with each other, share information and photographs, and meet new people. Users create their own profile and can apply privacy settings to make different parts of their profile more or less accessible to others. The popularity of such sites is demonstrated by the number of people on Facebook, which was launched in 2004 and now has over 800 million users worldwide. Such popularity and familiarity have now been tapped into by educational users to provide an alternative method of presenting information and to set up study or support groups.

Most teachers would like to see *mobile phones* banned within the classroom environment as they provide a distraction and are associated with, or can lead to, inappropriate behaviours. Outside of the classroom, however, they can provide a useful tool for communication and learning. The late Steve Jobs commented that mobile phones are gradually evolving into a 'remote control for your life'. Although talking to others is still their main function, mobile phones can be used for a variety of other purposes such as texting, receiving and sending emails, taking and sending pictures or videos, surfing the web, and can be connected to a computer to download information from it or vice versa. Each new generation of mobile phones brings further applications, increasing the possibilities for use. Informally, we use mobile phones as a source of information and learning on a regular basis when we are out and about and do not have access to other technology. We might consult the internet for a weather forecast, use the GPS application to find our destination, take a photograph or video of something of interest, listen to music, send an email or even pay directly for our ticket if we have no change at the car park. Many of these applications can be adapted for use in an educational setting. Text messages concerning absence or class announcements are now fairly commonplace, and mobile phones are often used to produce photographic evidence of work to be included in a portfolio. The huge range of possible uses has given rise to the concept of M-learning (learning through use of the mobile phone), and, as few learners do not possess a mobile phone, this is an approach to learning which is rapidly expanding and becoming more and more common.

Skype is a software application with text, voice and video capability which allows you to speak to and see others over the internet. Both you and the person you wish to communicate with need to open a Skype account and have access to a headset for listening and speaking and a webcam to establish visual contact. Skype differs from the other applications discussed so far (unless a mobile phone is used for talking to others), in that it is synchronous in its use: communication takes place in real time as the participants are in simultaneous contact. Asynchronous communication involves a delay in transmission, reception and response to a message. Skype can be put to good use in conducting tutorials, although time limits must be strictly adhered to – perhaps not a bad thing! This can relieve part-time learners of the inconvenience of travelling considerable distances in some cases, probably in the evening, for a one-to-one tutorial which will probably be of a short duration, allowing them to use their time more profitably.

ACTIVITY 3.5

Consider your own teaching. Do you wish to make communication with your learners easier? If so, which of the above technologies could you use to achieve this most simply?

RESEARCHING INFORMATION

When researching material for a teaching session or an assignment, we are no longer limited to books and other printed materials. The computer provides access to up-to-date information and expertise from a variety of different sources. Information is found by using a search engine. The most common general search engines are

Google, Yahoo, Bing, Ask, Altavista and AOL, but many specialist search engines exist which are dedicated to specific areas of expertise. Search engines open up a world of possibilities, but this can be a double-edged sword as the number of 'hits' produced on an individual search can be overwhelming. In 2003, the comedian Dave Gorman coined the term 'googlewhack' to describe the phenomenon of entering two words into Google to find it comes back with one and only one hit. Instances of this are so rare, he travelled around the world identifying any he came across in his great 'Googlewhack Adventure'. A more likely scenario is that achieved when entering the two words 'learning theories' and getting 6,090,000 results in the space of 0.08 seconds. The first rule of using a search engine is to filter out responses, reducing them to a more manageable number. It is suggested that we use key words only but these still produce a vast number of hits. Other strategies for refining a search are shown in Figure 3.5.

What to do	What it does
e.g. reflective practice – nursing	Typing a minus sign immediately before a key word indicates that you do not want web pages that contain this word to appear in your search results
e.g. Teaching ~ methods	If you want to search not only for your search criteria but also for its synonyms, type a tilde (~) immediately in front of your search term
e.g. Teaching methods OR theory	To search for web pages that include either of two search terms, add an uppercase OR between the terms
e.g. Obtaining "qualified teacher status"	By adding double quotes around a phrase, you are asking the search engine to look for the exact words in that exact order

Figure 3.5   Some simple internet search strategies

You may well have access to a 'teacher librarian' who can help you not only search for the sources you want but give you a short tutorial in searching the web more effectively. Failing that, there is also the web itself. Sites such as https://searchengine watch.com/static/tips provide short tutorials which will sharpen your surfing skills quickly and easily. An alternative approach is to find a site which has been put together specifically for a particular subject or topic and contains ready-made collections of material. The NLN and Excellence Gateway sites, previously mentioned, fall into this category. Alternatively, try this site – www.neilstoolbox.com/lazy-researcher/.

As well as general information, specific texts can be located through Google Scholar and Google Books. The latter provides free access only to parts of books, but this can still prove extremely useful. Many books are now provided in an online format and most libraries will hold a stock of these. If linked into an institutional library catalogue or VLE, they can normally be accessed off-site.

When consulting books or journals, we can be reasonably sure that the content is accurate and trustworthy, as it will have been written by someone with acknowledged expertise in that particular field and subjected to a process of critical evaluation by a combination of editor and reviewers prior to publication. The same does not apply to the World Wide Web. Anyone, regardless of expertise or lack of it, can contribute to internet sites which are not subjected to any systematic form of monitoring. Sites like Wikipedia, for example, although useful as a starting point in researching a topic, cannot be regarded as authoritative, as although peer-monitored, contributions to an entry can be made by the public at large. Information can be potentially inaccurate or biased. Many other sites are even less credible. Care has to be taken therefore in selecting information from the web. One set of guidelines for evaluating websites is provided by Schrock (cited in Herring, 2011: 38) and consists of being satisfied with the answers to the following five groups of questions asked of the proposed source:

WHO

Who wrote the pages and are they an expert?

Is a biography of the author included?

How can I find out more about the author?

WHAT

What does the author say is the purpose of the site?

What else might the author have in mind for the site?

What makes the site easy to use?

What information is included and does this information differ from that on other sites?

WHEN

When was the site created?

When was the site last updated?

WHERE

Where does the information come from?

Where can I look to find out more about the sponsor of the site?

WHY

Why is this information useful for my purpose?

Why should I use this information?

Why is this page better than another?

(Schrock, 2001: 9)

The other major issue with using the web as a research tool is the temptation to plagiarise. In the same way that it is easy to copy information from the internet, however, it is just as easy to identify where this occurs through the use of plagiarism checkers such as Turnitin. A number of these, such as: https://www.grammarly.com/plagiarism and www.quetext.com/ can be found on the internet for free.

ACTIVITY 3.6

If your institution does not already run a plagiarism checker such as Turnitin, go to the web and find a free checker and run your next assignment through it. What does it tell you? Does it help you with your citing and referencing skills?

SUPPLEMENTING OR REPLACING TAUGHT SESSIONS

It is now possible to take a course of study completely online (often for free) with the advent of Massive Open Online Courses (MOOCs). These are Web-based distance learning programmes that can be accessed by anyone who logs on to the appropriate website and signs up. Providers such as eDX host a whole catalogue of courses – an indication of the range on offer can be found at https://www.edx.org/. Here, however, we are concerned with ways in which we can use technology on an everyday basis to complement our current practice.

Although less common in other areas of the sector, the 2010 Becta review of the use of technology in education reported that 92 per cent of colleges of further education possessed a Virtual Learning Environment (VLE). This is an application which allows learners to access, by computer, a variety of course-related learning materials and interactive systems contained within a dedicated website. Learners are issued with a username and password. When they log on, they are greeted by name and arrive at a site which gives them access to a variety of course-related materials. Typically, these would include:

- learning materials such as handouts, PowerPoint presentations, video clips, useful web links
- course information (handbooks, module specifications, schemes of work, templates for course documents, tutor contact details)
- an announcement board for messages and course updates

- access to library catalogues and other online resources such as e-books and e-journals, RSS feeds
- discussion forums, blogs, wikis
- email connection with other learners or groups of learners
- self-assessment tests
- assignment drop boxes and grade books.

As we want to encourage use, such an abundance of material needs to be carefully organised so learners can easily find what they want and can navigate their way around the site with relative ease. Methods of organising VLE content vary from system to system. Blackboard uses a folder system, for example, whilst Moodle organises materials in a linear fashion. Using release dates to control the flow of information onto the VLE also helps to reduce the initial 'clutter' on the site when learners are still familiarising themselves with its contents and finding their way around it. Not all learners take to the VLE to start off with and they may well have to be encouraged to log on and use the site. Clarke (2011: 20) suggests that 'the key is to integrate the approach into the course so that learners can easily see the relevance and benefits of participation'. The VLE needs to be regarded as part of the course delivery rather than an 'add-on'. This can be achieved by requiring learners to engage in activities such as contributing to a discussion or taking part in creating a group wiki as part of an assessment early on in a course, or encouraging them to take some ownership of the site by consulting them as to what they would and wouldn't find useful to have on it. They need to see value in it and recognise that it presents advantages such as the provision of 24-hour access to course materials if illness or family or work commitments affect attendance. This last point raises the question of whether a device such as a VLE could be used as an alternative way of delivering a course.

For some time now, the government has encouraged increasing use of new education technologies, in a bid to expand provision, widen participation and generally stimulate a greater acceptance of lifelong learning. The Higginson report of 1996 suggested that all FE colleges should be linked to a national information highway. This would enable colleges to share electronic teaching materials and to widen access for students who need to study off campus. It was thought that learning delivered at a distance by electronic means would remove many of the barriers to learning faced by non-traditional learners, as:

- e-learning could be accessed at any time and in any appropriately equipped location, allowing self-paced learning
- the variety of different activities and media used cater for different learning styles
- the different approach may help relieve negative attitudes relating to a previous lack of success in traditional classroom settings.

This approach was also thought to present benefits for tutors and institutions. E-learning has never quite taken off, however, in the intended manner. It has not turned out to be as cost-effective as first thought, and, arguably, there are areas of the curriculum, such as those dealing with soft or hard skills, that do not lend themselves to this type of delivery. The main barrier to acceptance, however, seems to be more to do with human nature as 'While student success and high levels of student and instructor satisfaction can be produced consistently in fully online environments, many faculty and students lament the loss of face-to-face contact' (Dziuban et al., 2004: 3). Although technology is increasingly becoming an integral part of life in general and we all use it to a greater or lesser degree on a daily basis, when we learn we still place a high value on the social interaction that comes from contact with and learning from others. Education is rarely black and white, however, and Figure 3.6 indicates another possibility.

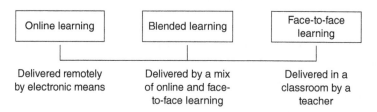

Figure 3.6   Possible delivery modes

Blended learning is an approach to learning and teaching which combines and integrates learning undertaken in face-to-face sessions with learning opportunities created online. It combines the flexibility offered by e-learning with the interaction and support which the company of a teacher and fellow learners provides. The influential *Harnessing Technology: Transforming Learning and Children's Services* report of 2005 suggests that blended learning can take learners 'beyond the confines of the traditional classroom, extending collaboration and enabling teachers to bring new resources into their teaching, culled from a world of digital libraries' (DfES, 2005).

When e-learning is used to supplement course delivery, it provides learners with an additional learning resource over and above the normal time allocated for face-to-face contact with a teacher. In a blended learning approach, e-learning acts as an alternative method of delivering portions of the course with an accompanying reduction in the course hours allocated to face-to-face contact with a teacher. This has implications for both course design and recruitment and selection procedures. A number of questions need to be asked before embarking on a blended learning journey:

- Why use this approach – what is the need it will satisfy?
- What will blended learning achieve that face-to-face delivery will not?
- What benefits will this approach bring to both learners and yourself?

- Which parts of the course readily lend themselves to delivery via e-learning?
- How much of the course should be delivered by face-to-face contact and how much by alternative means?
- Will it provide a cost-effective solution (both in terms of money and effort) to the identified need?

These questions need to be considered carefully as setting up and subsequently maintaining a blended learning approach involves a considerable investment of time and effort. The nature and characteristics of potential learners also need to be taken into account. You may design an excellent course but do the learners for whom it is intended possess the required skills and attitudes to successfully take advantage of it? Any form of e-learning involves a degree of learner autonomy. Autonomy is accompanied by responsibility, and decisions need to be made on the degree of autonomy to be built in to the course. As well as possessing the technical skills, do learners possess the time management skills, commitment, self-discipline and levels of independence required to succeed in using this approach?

A blended learning approach assumes that learners have reasonable access to a home computer. According to recently published figures from the Office for National Statistics, this is currently the case in only 75 per cent of UK households. Although free access to computers is available at public and college libraries for the remaining 25 per cent, the convenience factor has disappeared as usage is limited to opening hours which rather undermines the rationale behind an e-learning approach. Computer and internet access are related to economic circumstances, and of the previously quoted 75 per cent of households, the figures rise to 99 per cent for professionals, compared to 65 per cent for the long-term unemployed. It would appear that those whom the government would most like to target have the least chance of benefiting from e-learning. Some institutions operate schemes whereby learners can borrow a laptop, but this provides only a temporary solution to the problem. Set against this, the 2007 Becta report, *Survey of FE Learners and E-learning*, found that over eight in ten learners surveyed had access to a computer in the home, with the majority also benefiting from broadband connection to the internet (Becta was closed down in 2011).

For determined learners, access may be less of a problem than the statistics indicate, and certainly blended learning is an approach which is part of the wider movement to increase the use of technology in teaching and learning promoted by organisations such as the Joint Information Systems Committee (JISC, 2009: 8), which declares that in a digital age effective planning must include the ability to 'design, plan and orchestrate learning activities which involve the use of technology as part of a learning session or programme'. Blended learning approaches are becoming more common, especially within higher education, and are popular with private education and training providers as they allow them to appeal to a wider market.

FLIPPED LEARNING

The flipped classroom is a form of blended learning in which the traditional approach to teaching is reversed or 'flipped'. Instead of using classroom time to introduce and explain new material which is then consolidated and processed through activities outside of the classroom (homework), the new material is introduced to students prior to the lesson and classroom time is spent in exploring it through discussion, practical application, problem solving activities etc. Time spent with the teacher can be devoted to fostering a deeper understanding. Often this involves students in watching pre-prepared videos before the lesson but other ways of accessing content prior to the lesson such as loading articles, PowerPoint presentations or links to appropriate web pages onto the VLE for example, are also possible. See http://flippedinstitute.org/ for further information.

REFLECTIVE TASK 3.5

Consider your own teaching. Can you identify any opportunities to make use of technology such as a VLE to either supplement your current provision or per-haps deliver some aspects of it, especially in circumstances where you find yourself under severe time constraints? Can you identify instances where an approach based around the idea of 'flipping' your session might provide a more effective strategy? Do you think your learners could benefit from this type of approach?

ICT AND INCLUSION

Chapter 1 identified the responsibility we have as teachers to deliver courses and ses-sions in an inclusive manner. This responsibility also extends to ICT and 'reasonable adjustment' has to be made where barriers to its use are encountered. The issue of availability discussed above is not the only consideration relating to inclusion. Some learners, particularly those who are older, may lack the knowledge or skills required to make use of some technologies. This may necessitate building in some additional support during the course – perhaps some kind of 'buddy' or 'help desk' system to ensure learners can acquire the necessary skills and confidence to be able to meet any ICT requirements. Some learners may have an impairment which creates a difficulty, but here the technology itself can help as 'adaptive' or 'assistive' technologies (AT), which are designed to enable full access to users with any form of physical impair-ment, are built into many operating systems.

- Text-to-speech devices can help those with a visual impairment and also anyone with dyslexia or a similar impairment which makes reading on-screen text difficult.
- Screen magnification can help those with low vision.
- Display characteristics such as text size, font, colour and background can be changed to accommodate difficulties with reading from a screen.
- Alternative input devices exist for those with a physical impairment which makes use of a mouse or keyboard difficult.

The following features can be accessed in Windows 10 for example, by going to 'Control Panel', clicking on 'Ease of Access' and then 'Ease of Access Centre'. You will arrive at the menu shown in Figure 3.7.

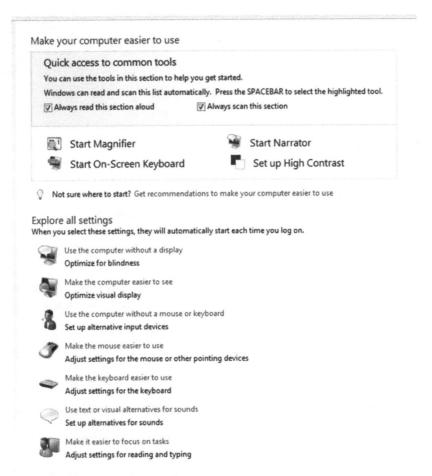

Make your computer easier to use

Quick access to common tools

You can use the tools in this section to help you get started.

Windows can read and scan this list automatically. Press the SPACEBAR to select the highlighted tool.

☑ Always read this section aloud   ☑ Always scan this section

Start Magnifier   Start Narrator

Start On-Screen Keyboard   Set up High Contrast

Not sure where to start? Get recommendations to make your computer easier to use

Explore all settings

When you select these settings, they will automatically start each time you log on.

Use the computer without a display
Optimize for blindness

Make the computer easier to see
Optimize visual display

Use the computer without a mouse or keyboard
Set up alternative input devices

Make the mouse easier to use
Adjust settings for the mouse or other pointing devices

Make the keyboard easier to use
Adjust settings for the keyboard

Use text or visual alternatives for sounds
Set up alternatives for sounds

Make it easier to focus on tasks
Adjust settings for reading and typing

Figure 3.7   Accessibility menu in Windows 10

Magnifier assists those with low vision, and can either magnify the entire desktop or zoom in on particular areas whilst still allowing normal computer operation. You can click buttons and input text in the normal manner inside the Magnifier window. Narrator can read on-screen text aloud and Audio Description can provide commentary on certain videos.

Alternatively, turning on text captions for spoken dialogue means text captions can be displayed instead of sounds to indicate what is happening on the computer (for example, when a document starts or finishes printing). On-Screen Keyboard allows for alternative input methods and can be combined with a touchscreen PC, allowing control by tapping on or moving your finger(s) across the screen. Windows also possesses a speech recognition system, allowing operations like sending emails or surfing the web to be activated by voice commands.

REFLECTIVE TASK 3.6

Locate the adaptive devices in Windows. Activate each in turn and note what the effect is so that you can point your learners towards an appropriate application if they have need of it.

More sophisticated and specialised applications, such as Braille display devices that can be attached to the keyboard to display screen content in Braille form, can also be obtained. Your institution may well have a disability adviser who can assist in accessing devices such as these and help with funding; if not, the following websites may prove helpful: www.abilitynet.org.uk/ and www.jisctechdis.ac.uk/

A CAUTIONARY NOTE

As with most innovations and technological advances, the advantages and benefits are to some extent offset by their potential abuse or misuse. We have already referred to the potential for plagiarism, and alongside this lie possible copyright issues. For teachers who make extensive use of technology during their working day, there are also issues of health and safety to consider. Workstations need to be set up correctly, to avoid a variety of strains, and augmented with footrests, wrist rests, document holders and anti-glare filters where necessary. Issues of what can be downloaded and sites which can be accessed have to be addressed, and most institutions will have policies relating to the acceptable use of technology. There are many reported instances of abuse of technology such as grooming, cyber bullying and identity theft, and this raises issues of safeguarding. Whilst most issues such as these will be dealt with through institutional monitoring and filtering of IT use, areas such as discussion boards need to be monitored and most will contain settings which allow the vetting of contributions before they are accepted.

SUMMARY OF KEY POINTS

In this chapter, we have looked at resources which can be used to support learning and enhance teaching. We explored the ways in which this might be achieved before going on to examine the use of a number of different resources and the benefits that can be derived from their use. The latter part of the chapter focused on resources arising out of recent advances in technology and demonstrated how these might be most appropriately employed in both a teaching and learning context.

The key points in this chapter are:

- Resources offer a practical alternative to the 'real thing'.
- Motivation, attention, understanding and memory are all aspects of the learning process that can be directly supported through the use of resources.
- The visual aspects of a resource have the greatest impact in attracting attention.
- Handouts fall into the categories of trigger, incomplete, worksheet, summary and follow-up, and their use is determined by their function.
- PowerPoint is a popular resource but has limited effect when used to present rather than support learning.
- Alternative systems to PowerPoint, such as Prezi, are gaining in popularity.
- The traditional whiteboard can be used in a spontaneous manner to highlight and record contributions as well as to prepare material in advance.
- The electronic whiteboard possesses the same capabilities as the computer and opens up a number of possibilities for interactive use.
- The flip chart is a versatile, easily managed resource which can be used spontaneously or with prepared materials in a wide variety of settings.
- Technology has greatly increased the possibilities for creating resources, improving communication, researching information and supplementing or even partially replacing taught sessions.
- Blended learning offers a combination of face-to-face and electronic modes of course delivery.
- The type of course and the characteristics of its likely learners have to be taken into consideration when making decisions around adopting a blended approach to learning.
- ICT offers a range of adaptive technologies which can be used to make learning more inclusive.

REFERENCES

Becta (2007) *Survey of FE Learners and E-learning*. Available online at: http://dera.ioe.ac. uk/8298/1/fe_learners_report.pdf (accessed 25/04/17).

Buckingham, D. (2007) Beyond Technology: Children's Learning in the Age of Digital Culture. Cambridge: Polity Press.

Clarke, A. (2011) How to Use Technology Effectively in Post-Compulsory Education. London: Routledge.

Department for Education and Skills (DfES) (2005) *Harnessing Technology: Transforming Learning and Children's Services*. Available online at: http://webarchive.nationalarchives.gov. uk/20130401151715/; www.education.gov.uk/publications/eOrderingDownload/1296-2005 PDF-EN-01.pdf (accessed 25/04/17).

Dziuban, C.D., Hartman, J.L. and Moskal, P.D. (2004) Blended learning: Educause Centre for Applied Research, *Research Bulletin*, Issue 7, 30 March, p. 3.

Herring, J. (2011) Improving Students' Web Use and Information Literacy. London: Facet Publishing.

Higginson, G. (1996) *Report of the Learning and Technology Committee*. Coventry: Further Education Funding Council.

Hill, C. (2008) Teaching with E-learning in the Lifelong Learning Sector (2nd edn). Exeter: Learning Matters.

Hillier, Y. (2005) Reflective Teaching in Further and Adult Education (2nd edn). London: Continuum.

Joint Information Systems Committee (JISC) (2009) *Effective Practice in a Digital Age: A Guide to Technology-enhanced Learning and Teaching*. Available online at: www.webarchive.org. uk/wayback/archive/20140615094835/; www.jisc.ac.uk/media/documents/publications/ effectivepracticedigitalage.pdf (accessed 25/04/17).

Schrock, K. (2001–9) *The Five W's of Website Evaluation*. Available online at: www.schrockguide. net/uploads/3/9/2/2/392267/5ws.pdf (accessed 25/04/17).

Wallace, S. (2001) Teaching and Supporting Learning in Further Education. Exeter: Learning Matters.

Whalley, J., Welch, T. and Williamson, L. (2006) *E-Learning in FE*. London: Continuum.

 # FURTHER READING

Clarke, A. (2011) How to Use Technology Effectively in Post-Compulsory Education. London: Routledge.

A sector specific book, the chapter on e-assessment is particularly interesting and provides ideas for using technology not only for summative assessment purposes but also as a means of fostering assessment for learning.

Smith Nash, S. and Moore, M. (2014) *Moodle Course Design Best Practices* Birmingham: Packt Publishing.

Most of us acquire knowledge about setting up and operating a Moodle site in a piecemeal 'need to know' basis. If, however you want to take a more systematic approach to learning about the benefits and management of Moodle this book will help you achieve that. A range of topics from setting up to archiving, managing resources, setting assessments and generally organising your site in the most effective manner are covered with easy to follow step-by-step instructions.

White, J. (2015) Digital Literacy Skills for FE Teachers. London: Sage.
If you would like to increase the presence of the digital world in your teaching but currently possess limited skills to achieve this, this is the book for you. As well as giving the background to the digital revolution within education, it identifies the different 'tools' that can be used to enhance learning. Issues such as appropriate use of devices and sources, management of resources, safety, security and legal concerns are all covered in an informed manner with accompanying case studies which provide a practical context.

4

ASSESSING FOR TEACHING AND LEARNING

Assessment is an integral part of the planning and delivery of teaching, being used to both consolidate and check learning. It serves a number of purposes, supplying feedback to a variety of interested parties and the assessment decisions made can have important consequences. The identification, selection and use of appropriate assessment methods and conducting assessments which are fair, valid and reliable are all key areas for staff in the Further Education and Skills sector, whether they teach on vocational or non-vocational programmes. Having carried out an assessment, the final stages of recording the results of that assessment and providing feedback to learners are carried out. This chapter explores both the conceptual and practical concerns of the assessment process, as well as the skills involved in its implementation.

When you have completed this chapter you will be able to:

- identify the functions of assessment
- list a range of assessment methods and make appropriate choices as to which to use
- define the following terms used in assessment: diagnostic, formative, summative, formal, informal, validity, reliability, fairness, equity, authenticity and sufficiency

- differentiate between criterion-referenced, norm-referenced and ipsative-referenced approaches to assessment
- distinguish between 'assessment of learning' and 'assessment for learning'
- describe how assessment for learning can be achieved in practice
- describe the characteristics of effective feedback
- recognise the benefits that arise from self and peer assessment activities
- explain the characteristics of assessment within vocational qualifications
- identify the different aspects of the role taken on by an assessor of vocational competence
- recognise the different levels within the quality assurance chain
- explain the role of Internal and External Verifiers with regard to Quality Assurance
- discuss the contribution that technology can make to the assessment process.

WHAT IS ASSESSMENT?

Assessment forms an integral part of the teaching process and can be defined as 'all those activities and processes involved in judging performance or measuring learner achievement' (Francis and Gould, 2013: 129). The key words in this definition are 'judging' and 'measuring'. But why do we bother?

ACTIVITY 4.1

Well, why do we bother? Come up with as many reasons as you can as to why we assess our learners before reading on and comparing your response to what comes next.

Your first thought may well have been that the purpose or reason for assessment is to find out how learners are doing, testing their progress. Although this is an important reason, there are others. For instance, it's not only the teacher who wants to find out about progress made – learners need to know too! Assessment can increase and enhance learners' motivation, especially when they know they are doing well, but also, as we shall see later, when progress is limited. Assessment can also be used as a tool for selection as it gives an indication of whether learners possess the background knowledge and skills required to be successful on a course they apply for; it can identify learner strengths and areas that require further development; the results of assessment acknowledge the learning that has taken place in a formal manner and can be used to contribute to an accreditation system; stakeholders, such as employers, may be interested in the results of assessments, especially if they have invested in a learner by contributing to course fees or by allowing time for study. Finally, assessment contributes to the process of self-evaluation which informs us, as teachers, of the effectiveness of our own practice. If, after the teaching of a session, module, unit, programme or course, we find that learners produce low scores in the associated assessment, then something needs to be improved on. Close examination of the results of the assessment can help to pinpoint the particular areas that have caused the greatest difficulty. Further probing and evaluation may reveal that a reason for the disappointing results was that the teaching methods employed or use of resources were not the best choice in this instance, or perhaps the learning objectives themselves were not realistic. The outcomes of assessment inform and are part of the process of evaluation which, as the planning cycle in Chapter 2 demonstrates, will lead to a better informed planning process on the next occasion that particular topic is taught. Assessment, then, fulfils a number of functions and is a crucial aspect of the overall process of teaching and learning.

WHAT DO WE ASSESS?

In order to fulfil the above functions, what exactly is to be assessed? Whilst this may seem a straightforward task at first sight, it is not necessarily that easy. As an example, take a simple maths calculation. Would you just look to see if the answer was correct or would you take into consideration how the learner got to that answer as well? Is it the 'product' or is it the 'process' that you are assessing? Would you give marks for parts of the method that had been correctly applied, despite the fact that the answer arrived at was incorrect? Is it the knowledge or the application of that knowledge that you wish to assess? The starting point to assessing that learning has taken place is to return to the learning objectives that were set and identify exactly what is to be achieved. Effective assessment is tied in closely with well written SMART learning objectives, and this is an issue we will return to later in the chapter.

WHEN DO WE ASSESS?

Arguably, assessment of learners takes place from the moment they apply for a course, or sometimes even before then, as, for instance, when they attend an open evening or just make a general enquiry by telephone or email. We inevitably begin to make some sort of judgement as to their suitability for the course. This is hardly a scientific process, however, as it is based only on impressions which, particularly if first impressions, can be misleading in many instances. A more reliable approach is needed and this is where the process of initial assessment described in Chapter 1 comes into play. You will remember that the purpose of initial assessment is to establish whether the particular course applied for is the most appropriate choice and if any additional support might be required. Once a learner has enrolled, and is attending the course, assessment takes a different direction. When meeting learners for the first time, we may well spend some time asking them questions in order to get a better feel for the levels of knowledge, skill and experience they bring with them. We are trying to establish the particular strengths and limitations of this specific group of learners. As part of this process, we will undoubtedly find out more about some individuals within the group as well. When assessment is used for this type of purpose, it is termed *diagnostic*. In the same way that a doctor makes a diagnosis before deciding on the most appropriate treatment for their patient, we are using the results of our diagnostic assessment to decide on the most appropriate approach to teaching and learning to take with regard to this particular group. At an individual level, diagnostic assessment informs both us and our learners where they can best focus their attention and their energies.

The subsequent assessment that takes place on a regular basis throughout the course is referred to as ongoing or *formative* assessment. The main purpose of formative assessment is to provide feedback to the teacher and the learner on the progress (or lack of progress) being made. More recently, formative assessment has begun to be known as 'assessment for learning', and this approach to assessment will be discussed in more detail later in this chapter. As we are all aware, there is normally some form of final assessment at the end of a course as well. This is known as a *summative* assessment. Its purpose is to provide evidence of achievement and usually results in some form of certification. When summative assessment is referred to, you may come across the use of the term 'assessment *of* learning' rather 'than assessment *for* learning'. In the case of a single teaching session, you might find out what the learners already know (or can do) about the topic at the beginning of the session (diagnostic); you then assess them during the session, making sure everybody is following what is taking place (formative); and, finally, at the end of the session check the learning objectives have been achieved (summative).

HOW DO WE ASSESS?

We now turn to the different ways in which we carry out assessment – the methods we use. You will be familiar with a variety of different methods of assessment that can be used both from your own experience of being assessed throughout your time as a learner and from the experience you may have had of teaching your own particular specialism.

REFLECTIVE TASK 4.1

Reflecting on your own experiences of assessment, both as teacher and 'taught', make a list of as many different assessment methods as you can think of. After comparing your list with Figure 4.1 on page 105, can you see other possible assessment methods you could use?

In completing Reflective task 4.1, you may have gravitated naturally towards assessment methods that seem most appropriate to your own teaching. Whatever your subject, it will involve learning across *all* of the domains identified in Chapter 2 to some extent, and viewing your teaching in this way opens up the possibilities to extend the range of assessment methods you currently use. With so many different assessment methods available, however, it can be difficult to choose which ones to use. See how you get on with Activity 4.2, which asks you to find the best match between a series of learning objectives and the list of assessment methods you now have at your disposal.

ACTIVITY 4.2

Complete the following table by suggesting an appropriate assessment method that could be used with each learning objective listed.

Table 4.1

	Learning objective	Method of assessment
1	List the ingredients of a white sauce	
2	Discuss the use of the 'outdoor classroom' in an early years setting	
3	Analyse the role of Mrs Bennet in Jane Austen's *Pride and Prejudice*	
4	Prepare your CV	
5	Replace a window	
6	Identify the correct tyre pressure for a Multi Purpose Vehicle, carrying 4 adults and 5 dogs	
7	Perform a half-head colouring using foils	
8	Explain how teaching assistants can support pupils with emotional and behavioural difficulties	
9	Define assessment	

For most of the above learning objectives, there isn't only one 'correct' method of assessment, as each can be assessed in a number of ways. For instance, number 1 (list the ingredients of a white sauce) can be assessed by questioning the learner or by asking them to write the ingredients down in a 'short-answer' test. Number 2 (discuss the use of the 'outdoor classroom' in an early years setting) can be assessed by listening to the discussions taking place or by asking learners to write an essay. Number 6, about tyre pressure, can be assessed by direct questioning or by a multiple-choice test/quiz or by a practical task. Which method you decide on depends largely on the purpose of the assessment, the time available, and even on the characteristics of your learners – some learners may find it hard to write down the ingredients of a white sauce but can quite easily tell you what the ingredients are. Some methods of assessment are better suited to some types of learning objective than others, however. For instance, if your learning objective is from the cognitive domain, your methods of assessment are likely to be oral questioning, written questions, essays or assignments. Psycho-motor learning objectives are best assessed by observation of the learner whilst they are carrying out a practical task or by examining the end product. There seems to be little point in writing an essay on applying a hair colour using foils, for instance. In order to be employed as a stylist in a salon, the learner needs to be able to perform such a task competently and is not able to prove this is the case by writing an essay. Chapter 2 suggested that learning objectives from the affective domain can take some time to be achieved, as a change in attitude is unlikely to come about within a single teaching session. As it is difficult to write SMART objectives relating to attitude change, it is equally difficult to be precise in their assessment. Methods such as the keeping of a diary/personal journal or a reflective piece of writing can, however, be used to support a change in attitude.

- Responding to verbal questions
- Being observed in some kind of performance in a real or simulated environment
- Completing an essay or written assignment
- Taking a multiple-choice test
- Responding to written short answer questions
- Taking part in an oral or aural test
- Undertaking a project
- Giving a presentation
- Responding to questions on a case study
- Keeping a journal or diary
- Completing a gap-fill exercise
- Participating in a quiz
- Completing a word search
- Demonstrating a skill to others
- Taking part in a debate

Figure 4.1   Some assessment methods

FORMAL AND INFORMAL APPROACHES TO ASSESSMENT

Some of the assessment methods we have looked at seem to have quite an 'official' tone to them, whilst others suggest use in a more casual and relaxed manner. It is this difference that we turn to next. Complete Reflective task 4.2 before reading on.

REFLECTIVE TASK 4.2

Think about times in your life when other people have assessed you. It may well be to do with education but does not necessarily have to be (e.g. driving test, job interview). For each example you think of, answer the following questions:

Who did the assessing?

What was the purpose of the assessment?

What form did the assessment take?

How did you feel during the assessment?

Did being assessed affect your performance?

What conclusions can you draw from Reflective task 4.2? Think back for a moment to the diagnostic questioning used with a new group of learners. How would this particular assessment activity be conducted? Hopefully, not in the style of the Spanish Inquisition! If an assessment procedure puts us 'on the spot' or in a stressful position, we tend not to perform at our best. Sportspeople, for instance, can 'freeze' on the big occasion, conscious of all the watching eyes, and, as a result, perform a skill poorly that under different circumstances would be second nature. In using diagnostic questioning, we do not wish to put learners under pressure. Questions could be asked in such a manner that learners may not be aware that they were being assessed. In this case, we would be adopting an *informal* approach to assessment. Summative methods of assessment are usually conducted in a *formal* manner; they tend to be pre-arranged, with some recording of results. Think back to your GCSE exams, your driving test or the essays and assignments you have to submit to pass this course. Other methods of assessment lend themselves more easily to an informal approach. They include: asking questions, observation of a practical task, listening to discussions, student presentations, micro-teaching sessions, quizzes, seminars, gap-fill exercises, group activities based around multiple-choice questions … the list is fairly endless, and you can probably add to it by referring back to the responses you gave in Reflective task 4.1. Some of these methods, however, can also be used formally. Presentations are often used as part of the interview process for a job – very formal. A Viva Voce is a formal part of the process of gaining a PhD but consists largely of being asked questions, and gap-fill exercises are often included in exams set by awarding bodies. It is the manner of carrying out the assessment rather than the method itself that decides whether it is deemed formal or informal.

VALIDITY AND RELIABILITY OF ASSESSMENT

In a previous section, it was suggested that it would not be appropriate to use an essay to assess a practical skill. An essay would assess whether a learner understood what had to be done and why, rather than whether they were able to perform the skill in a competent manner. It was also suggested that whilst some learners may be able to tell us the ingredients of a white sauce, they may face some difficulty in supplying that answer in a written form. If we were to insist on a written answer, it may be that although the learner knew what the correct ingredients were, they would not receive any credit for that knowledge due to their inability to communicate it to the assessor in the required written form. We would actually be putting their writing ability to the test rather than their knowledge of white sauces.

Both of the above examples illustrate an important quality that all assessment methods should possess. They should test the exact performance that the learning objective specifies. The term given to this particular quality is *validity*, which is defined by Reece and Walker (2007: 329) as 'how well a test measures what it is supposed to measure'. Validity is not an absolute term and assessments can exhibit different degrees of validity. A test (or, more accurately, the results obtained from it) can be considered to be high in validity or low in validity. Validity also comes in different types. The approaches to assessment in the examples above demonstrate low *construct validity*, as they do not provide a good measure of the specific ability (or construct) we wish to assess. If we wished to assess your ability to control a noisy class, we could ask you to answer a series of questions based around a case study on noisy learners, or alternatively we could conduct one of your teaching observations when you were teaching your noisiest group. Whilst the second method is not foolproof, it would possess higher construct validity than the first.

The course that you are following has been carefully mapped against the professional standards for teachers within the sector. The assessment procedures it uses should address all of these standards. Suppose, however, insufficient time had been allocated to allow for this. Assessment has been selected with care and precision to provide an overall assessment strategy high in construct validity. However, can it be claimed that the assessment procedure matches Reece and Walker's criteria for validity in that it 'measures what it is supposed to measure'? Unfortunately not! The overall assessment strategy, whilst high in construct validity, is low in *content validity*, as it measures only a limited range of the learning objectives (or standards in this case) of the course as a whole. Validity concerns such as these apply to assessment at all levels: within courses, as explained in the examples above, but also within planning a teaching session. Figure 4.2 shows a portion of a plan for a teaching session on 'Reports & Returns – VAT'.

Learning Objectives:	Assessment:
To:	Question and answer (LO1)
1. Define VAT.	Matching exercise (LO2)
2. Differentiate between VAT-free items and those on which VAT is charged.	Results of group work (LO4)
3. Calculate the VAT charged on given items.	Peer marking exercise (LO3, LO5)
4. Recognise the layout of a VAT return form.	
5. Correctly fill in a VAT return.	

Figure 4.2   Learning objectives and assessment strategies

The assessment methods used are largely informal in nature but have been carefully chosen to match the learning objectives, so ensuring high construct validity. Each learning objective has been linked to a particular assessment method, so all of the learning that is to take place in the session will be assessed. Some assessment methods may be used to check more than one learning objective simultaneously but overall high content validity has been ensured.

REFLECTIVE TASK 4.3

Review the session plans you have submitted so far on your diploma course. Can you improve the validity of the assessment procedures you have used in them? Look at the specification of the diploma unit you are currently studying. How effectively do you think the assessment procedures used match and cover the learning objectives/outcomes of the module?

We now turn to the other essential quality of all forms of assessment – *reliability*. First, complete Activity 4.3 below. You will find the two pieces of work it refers to in Appendix 5.

ACTIVITY 4.3

Mark the extracts taken from two essays, giving each a mark out of 100.

Activity 4.3 may have proved more difficult than it initially seemed. When you marked the extracts, what did you base your judgement on? How did you decide to award the marks? If the criteria had been pass/fail, would you have passed both? If you were to ask a colleague to mark the same two extracts, do you think their marks would be the same as yours? It is unlikely that you and your colleague would be in total agreement, as you would each place different importance or interpretations on the various points raised. In short, your judgements would be very subjective and therefore likely to differ. Each of you may approach the task of marking in a different manner. Some markers are very strict on accurate citing and referencing, for instance, whereas others may be more lenient in this respect but feel strongly about spelling. As you can imagine, this causes some issues for learners. It seems unfair that the same piece of work receives different marks from different teachers. It is an important principle of assessment that learners who achieve learning outcomes equally well should receive equal marks for that achievement.

Child (2004: 369) cites research on the disparity in examiners' marks in an essay question which shows differences in the marks awarded for the same question of between 25 and 36 per cent. There is an apocryphal story of one examiner in a similar experiment who left his model answer in with the sample scripts by mistake, only to have another examiner grade it as a fail. By their very nature, essays are difficult to mark with any degree of consistency but the situation can be improved by use of a mark scheme which sets criteria against which a piece of work should be judged.

ACTIVITY 4.4

Look at some mark schemes provided by awarding bodies. A sample of AQA mark schemes can be found at: www.aqa.org.uk/exams-administration/exams-guidance/find-past-papers-and-mark-schemes

Compare the mark schemes for two contrasting subjects, such as chemistry (http://filestore.aqa.org.uk/sample-papers-and-mark-schemes/2016/june/AQA-74041-QP-JUN16.PDF) and English literature (http://filestore.aqa.org.uk/sample-papers-and-mark-schemes/2016/june/AQA-77111-QP-JUN16.PDF – look at both Section A and Section B).

How do they differ?

Mark schemes differ in their levels of specificity and this is to some extent a function of the subject, as you will have seen in the above activity, and the degree of flexibility built into the assessment process. If all markers work with the same criteria as outlined in the mark scheme, however, they should be able to make a similar judgement, and therefore the outcomes of the assessment should be similar, regardless of teachers' personal preferences. In other words, the assessment should be more objective. This achievement of some kind of uniformity between different markers is one example of 'reliability'. Reece and Walker (2007: 331) define the reliability of an assessment method as 'the extent to which it consistently measures what it is supposed to measure', and state that an assessment is considered reliable when:

- different examiners assessing the same work award the same scores
- examiners award the same score to the same script if they score it again on a subsequent occasion
- students get the same score on a test when it is administered at different times.

Like validity, reliability is not an absolute term but can vary between high and low. A high level of reliability can be found in multiple-choice questions, as they are an example of objective testing; items in an objective test have only one predetermined correct answer – their reliability therefore should be 100 per cent. The same marks will be given regardless of who does the marking. Examples of objective items include:

- multiple choice
- true/false
- matching lists
- multiple response
- assertion/reason
- short answer
- odd one out
- rearrangement.

Objective testing is not without its critics, who point out a number of limitations in its use. These include the difficulties of constructing test items which are truly objective, the possibility of gaining marks purely through guesswork and concerns about the relatively low levels of knowledge that can be tested. Its supporters, however, contend that depending on the manner in which an item is phrased, higher levels of knowledge can be assessed by this approach, particularly when using items such as assertion/reason where there is an element of having to justify the answer selected. It is also possible to apply 'guessing correction' formulae to results to counteract the gaining of marks through guesswork. Whatever the relative merits of objective testing, it provides a highly reliable form of assessment which also lends itself well to achieving results with high content validity, as large areas of the syllabus can be covered relatively easily.

The less objective an assessment is, the greater the requirement is for a mark scheme. As well as bringing some level of consistency into the marking process when different markers are involved, a mark scheme helps in ensuring consistency in the marks awarded by the same marker over a number of pieces of work.

ACTIVITY 4.5

You have just sat down for the evening with a pile of marking (again!). You have a good specific mark scheme as a guide, so in theory your marking should be consistent over all of the pieces of work in front of you. It is highly unlikely, however, that this will be the case. What factors can you identify that will affect the marks you award?

A number of possible responses spring to mind. One of these concerns the state of *your* mind whilst engaged in the task of marking. Did you have a stressful day or did it run fairly smoothly? Are you feeling 'on top' of your workload or are you beginning to feel somewhat overwhelmed by it? Were you also up all last night marking or are you coming fresh to the task? How about the actual pieces of work – are some well-presented and easy to read whilst others are somewhat disjointed and require reading through several times before you can make sense of them? If handwritten, are they legible or an indecipherable scrawl? Does the last piece of work in the pile receive the same level of consideration as the first? Will the identity of the person who submitted the work have any bearing on your decision? Are you likely to give the same benefit of the doubt to that pleasant, conscientious student who sits near the front of the class as you would to that surly, lazy learner who always sits at the back? There appear to be a number of factors that influence our judgement and affect the overall consistency of the marks we award. These are not confined to the scenario described in Activity 4.5. Suppose you were to conduct a practical test in an outdoor environment. Would you feel the same about the performances you assessed if some took place in the warmth of the sun whilst others took place during a hailstorm?

Factors such as those described above cannot be overcome through a convenient straightforward solution like a mark scheme. 'Blind marking', in which we are unaware of the identity of the person who has submitted the work, can be used to counteract our previous knowledge and experience of particular learners which might lead to positive bias (halo effect) or negative bias (horns effect), but we are all human and with the best will in the world, our marking will be subject to the influences discussed above.

One way of addressing this issue is for teachers to check each other's work. This process is carried out formally as part of the overall quality assurance procedures of an institution. It is generally known as internal moderation when applied to HE programmes which are validated by a university, or internal verification when applied to FE programmes which come under the control of awarding bodies such as City and Guilds, Edexcel and AQA. The OCR website describes the process of internal verification as 'the process by which a centre regularly samples and evaluates its assessment practices and decisions, and acts on the findings to ensure consistency and fairness'.

It is time-consuming to check every piece of work, so a sample of work is selected for each marker and checked. The size of each sample is normally determined by the level of experience of the marker, but must be sufficiently large to be representative of the marking experienced by the group as a whole. After this internal process is completed, external checking takes place by either an External Examiner (HE) or External Verifier or Standards Verifier (FE) to ensure there is consistency in the marks awarded by different centres that offer the same award or qualification.

FAIRNESS AND EQUITY

So far, we have looked at how assessment decisions are arrived at and the factors which might influence this process. We now turn to learners and issues relating to their performance during an assessment.

REFLECTIVE TASK 4.4

On the occasions in the past when you have had to make an assessment of some kind, are you confident you have always performed to the best of your abilities? If not, can you identify the factors which have had an effect on your performance? What does this tell you about ways in which you can better prepare your own learners for the assessments they take?

You have probably come up with a number of instances in which your performance in an assessment was adversely affected to some degree. As an example, consider someone who suffers from hay fever. Will their performance and subsequently the mark they receive be affected by the time of year at which they take their test? Alternatively, consider an assessment that requires everyone to have access to a particular piece of equipment. Most have the latest model but some are given an older version of the equipment. These and other factors you have probably identified in Activity 4.5 illustrate the concept of fairness in assessment. Lam (1995) tells us that in a fair assessment students are given equitable opportunities to demonstrate what they know. Ideally then, an assessment should not discriminate between learners, other than on grounds of the ability that is being assessed. It is clear, however, that there are some factors relating to fairness which we can attend to and others that are outside of our control. We cannot provide any relief from hay fever, for instance, but it is within our power to make sure that everyone taking an assessment has access to appropriate equipment of the same quality. Race et al. (2005: 3) tell us that 'assessment should be fair', with all learners having the opportunity to succeed and 'all assessment instruments and processes ... seen to be fair by all students'. What then, might contribute to *unfairness?* If a particular learner does not do themselves justice because of nerves, we can help by giving them experience of 'mock exams'; the simple act of briefing learners about an assessment so that they know what is expected of them, the criteria against which they will be judged and the relative weightings of different parts of the assessment, will make a significant contribution to the assessment process being a fair one. Making the assessment criteria explicit to learners contributes to making assessment a more transparent process.

It may be that learners will not be able to perform to their full potential for reasons of language or culture. This is a particular aspect of fairness known as 'equity'. In order to be equitable, an assessment should not disadvantage any group or individual. Procedures such as giving learners with dyslexia extra time to complete an assessment or access to scribes or signers for other impairments fall into this category. To ensure equity for all, however, we have to consider introducing differentiation into our assessment practices. This would involve the use of a range of assessment strategies and methods to meet the different needs of learners. If equity was taken to its logical conclusion, assessments would be designed on an individual basis. This does not sit well with a desire for standardisation in assessment, but, as Armitage et al. (2011: 180) point out, 'Allowing learners to demonstrate their knowledge and skills in different ways, to best suit them, does not mean that standards are lowered, as ultimately, the end-product or outcome has not been changed'.

This debate takes us back to the issue of equality and diversity discussed in general terms in Chapter 1, but in the specific context of assessment. The same general principles still apply, however. In order to provide all learners with an equal opportunity of demonstrating the full extent to which they possess the knowledge or skills that are being assessed, different individual arrangements for the assessment process may have to be made. Consider the following example:

Jim used to teach science in a secondary school in London which had an intake of students covering a range of cultures and first languages. This was a completely new subject for all pupils and for the first real 'exam' that they took at the end of the first term, each class was divided into two groups – native English speakers and pupils for whom English was an additional language. The native speakers took the exam in the conventional manner but the other group had the exam paper read out to them. Although not a complete solution, it was an attempt to achieve fairness. There were some in the school who disagreed with this approach as they believed it 'made the exam easier' for some, gaining them higher marks than they should have received.

Were they right or had they missed the point? The Armitage quote above would suggest that although the method of measurement was different for some, what was measured (science knowledge) remained the same. A variety of methods can increase both fairness and the construct validity of the assessment as a whole.

AUTHENTICITY AND SUFFICIENCY

A Premier League footballer was arrested on suspicion of committing fraud by false representation, as he allegedly had someone else sit the theory part of his driving test. This highlights an issue of authenticity for this particular assessment. All assessments should be authentic, meaning that the work assessed should be the learner's own. When the assessment takes the form of an exam or observation of the learner carrying out a task, authenticity is easily established. This is not the case for all assessment methods, however.

In the case of written work, how does your tutor know that what you have produced is all your own work and hasn't relied heavily on chunks taken from the internet or other people's work, without declaring this? It is even possible you have bought a complete assignment off the internet or, like our footballer, got someone else to write it for you. To safeguard against this, you may have been asked to submit your assignment electronically so it can be run through a plagiarism checker, and have had to sign a declaration on your assignment front sheet verifying that your submission is your own work. Authenticity with respect to written work is becoming a major problem in this electronic age, but fortunately the same means that facilitate plagiarism can also be successfully used to detect it.

REFLECTIVE TASK 4.5

Reflect on your own teaching. Are there aspects of your assessment process that might raise problems as far as authenticity is concerned? What steps can you take to minimise this possibility?

An alternative use of the term 'authentic' in the language of assessment refers to any activity which assesses a learner's knowledge, skills or attitudes being used as they would in a real-world situation. Authentic assessment mirrors real life, although reasons of practicality or expense often lead to assessment in a simulated rather than a 'real' environment. This approach is extensively used on vocational and technical courses (Tummons, 2007: 56), and here authenticity is related to construct validity.

Another issue which is particularly significant in vocational and technical courses is that of 'sufficiency'. In academic subjects, writing an assignment or essay is usually regarded as being sufficient to demonstrate knowledge and understanding of the topic. In a vocational setting, if a learner demonstrates a skill to an assessor on a single occasion, is that sufficient to demonstrate mastery of the skill or is it just an indication of good luck on the day? Ollin and Tucker (2008: 45) deem that sufficiency is satisfied when 'the evidence is enough to prove competence'. Therefore, before the assessor signs the learner off as being competent, they may want to see the learner perform this skill on more than one occasion. Although seemingly tiresome, this does have a benefit for the learner. Whilst sufficiency ensures that the teacher or assessor can be certain a learner is competent, it also means that learners are not dependent on one occasion only to demonstrate their competency. If they have a 'bad day', they have the opportunity to do better the next time. Sufficiency, therefore, is related to the reliability of assessment. Sometimes the number of times the task needs to be performed is stated by the awarding body for the course; in other situations, it is up to the professional judgement of the teacher or assessor to make this decision. When a portfolio is used as a method of assessment, it may be that the learner will have to use a range of supporting evidence, such as personal statements, witness accounts or professional discussions, to demonstrate their competency. These need to be chosen carefully so that they directly address the ability to be assessed, as in Ollin and Tucker's experience 'insufficient evidence does not usually mean too little evidence but too little evidence of a relevant kind' as learners adopt 'a "shopping trolley" approach to the assessment, where all sorts of documentary items are collected in the vague hope that they will provide something of substance' (2008: 45).

MARKS AND REFERENCING SYSTEMS

ACTIVITY 4.6

If you had a child who came home from school and told you they had a score of 15 in a test that day, how would you respond?

Your initial reaction would probably be that of bemusement as, on its own, a mark of 15 has little meaning. It needs to be put into some kind of context to make sense. You need a point of reference against which to compare it, so you may ask questions like:

1. What did everyone else get?
2. What was the pass mark?
3. What did you get in your last test?

If you asked question 1, you are using the performance of others to make sense of the mark. If most of the other children scored less than 15, then you consider it to be a good mark. If, on the other hand, most children gained a score higher than 15, you are less impressed. Comparing performance to that of others is known as *norm referencing* or 'grading on the curve'. It is based on the assumption that any type of individual difference that exists in the population as a whole, from shoe size to intelligence scores, will be 'normally distributed amongst its members'. If we were to represent this distribution as a graph, most people would be clustered in the middle with fewest people at the ends, as shown in Figure 4.3.

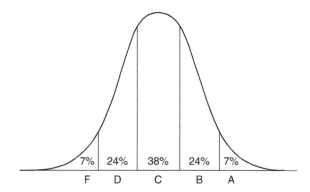

Figure 4.3   Normal distribution curve

The curve is then divided into sections and the grade you receive depends on which section of the curve you fall into. Norm referencing was originally introduced to overcome the varying difficulty of national exams from year to year. If you were unlucky enough to hit a year when the exam was difficult, your score would suffer accordingly. Alternatively, if the exam was easy in the year that you took it, your score would reflect that. If, however, instead of using a raw score, your final mark is decided on the basis of how well it compares to everyone else, this anomaly would disappear. Norm referencing is a competitive system as it ranks learners by comparison with each other. This is of interest to employers and universities who wish to select the best candidates available to them each year, and norm referencing helps in identifying who these are.

If you asked question 2, you are using an externally set standard to make sense of the mark. If a score of 15 is higher than the pass mark, then you consider it to be a good mark. If, on the other hand, a score of 15 is lower than the pass mark, you are less impressed. Your performance has to meet a number of criteria. Broadly speaking, the pass mark is decided by the number and combination of criteria that have to be met. If you meet the required criteria, you pass; if not, you fail. The driving test is a good example of this. The examiner has a checklist of criteria arranged into categories that correspond to the different driving skills you are expected to exhibit. The examiner marks your performance against this checklist as you go round the test route.

If, at the end of the test, you have met a sufficient number of criteria from each category, you have passed the test. This approach is known as *criterion referencing* and it measures whether learners have, or have not yet, reached a specific level of achievement. Of course, there can still be some debate about how the criteria are interpreted. To minimise any ambiguity in the criteria, they need to be transparent. If learners have access to the criteria before the assessment, they know exactly what their work will be marked against, and teachers, when marking, should all come to the same result. Criteria describing different levels of performance can also be used to give different grades. Ofsted grades teaching performance by this method.

Although transparency of criteria can be seen as an advantage, it may lead to what is referred to as 'teaching to the test', making sure that your learners do well in the assessment. Nothing wrong with that, you may think, as we all want our learners to do well, especially when we, as teachers, are sometimes judged on the performance of our learners. If your learners achieve high marks, you must be a good teacher (unfortunately, the opposite logic also applies!). Arguably, this may encourage a surface approach to learning, and a narrowing of what is taught, as the sole focus is on achieving the assessment criteria rather than on the learning that is to take place.

If you asked question 3, you are using an internally set standard to make sense of the mark. If a score of 15 is higher than your child normally achieves, then you consider it to be a good mark. If, on the other hand, a score of 15 is lower than their normal score, you are less impressed. This type of referencing is known as *ipsative* and is also referred to as 'self-referenced' assessment, as the learner's performance is measured purely against their own previous performance. Think about when you learned to ride a bicycle or maybe play the piano or even speak a new language. At first, you probably weren't very good – you needed stabilisers on your bike, could find only middle C on the piano or your Italian did not exceed ordering a pasta dish. After practising, however, you improved: the stabilisers came off, you're good at cornering now; you play 'Claire de Lune' on your piano; you can hold a simple conversation in Italian (or even do all three at the same time!). You are not interested in how others are doing, whether they make quicker/slower progress than you; you just measure yourself against your previous performance. This can, of course, be considered as a form of criterion referencing, but the criteria are not externally set by someone else and are not common to everyone. They are your own individual criteria which are appropriate to your current stage of development. This type of assessment complements the setting of individual targets and goals.

This may seem like a fairer way of assessing your learners, and certainly provides the motivation to learn as it focuses on the progress made. It can be misleading, however, if learners are not made aware of the way in which judgements are made. A teacher could, for instance, whilst monitoring a group of learners at work, give positive feedback to one learner whose work was actually the worst in the room, whilst giving less positive feedback to another learner who was producing the best work in the room. In this instance, the comments would be made from an ipsative point of view. Learner 1 would be producing work which, although not of a good general standard, was better than that which they normally produced. Learner 2, although producing work of a generally high standard, would be capable of better.

Ipsative referencing does not sit happily within a culture of accountability and its accompanying results-based funding and inspection systems. One area where this type of assessment is used is in the teaching of learners with specific learning difficulties, where progress is measured and targets are set on an individual basis. Learners do need to recognise, however, if and how these targets relate to what is required to achieve a formal qualification.

ASSESSMENT FOR LEARNING (AfL)

> The nature and impact of assessment depends on the uses to which the results of that assessment are put. A system whose main priority is to generate information for internal use by teachers on the next steps in pupils' learning may have different characteristics and effects from one where the drive is to produce a qualification which will provide a grade on which an employer or a university admissions tutor might rely in order to judge the suitability of a candidate for employment or further study. (Mansell et al., 2009: 5)

If you skipped over the above quote, go back and read it now as it provides a context to the recent debate concerning the purpose and use of assessment which will be explored over the next few pages. Traditionally, assessment has been seen to be focused on the testing and measuring of achievement. Its purpose was to see whether or not learning had taken place – what has previously been referred to in this chapter as summative assessment or assessment of learning. A shift towards a more formative approach is now beginning to emerge in which assessment is regarded not solely as a testing procedure but also as another tool for learning.

The impetus for this movement was provided by the work of Black and Wiliam with their publications *Inside the Black Box* (1998) and *Assessment for Learning: Beyond the Black Box* (1999). The 'black box' they refer to represents the classroom. It was Black and Wiliam's contention that government initiatives focused heavily on the inputs and outputs relating to the black box, with far less concern with what happened inside it. Teaching and learning were apparently of less consequence than the summative assessment procedures that contributed to the collection and recording of data for the purposes of certification and evaluation (see Figure 4.4).

Black and Wiliam advocated a greater use of formative assessment or 'assessment for learning' to redress the balance. It is perhaps important to stress at this point that the suggestion is not for a 'one or the other' approach, a point reinforced by Spendlove (2009), who reports that AfL is not an attack on summative assessment; it is about getting an appropriate balance between the two. The debate is not really about methods of assessment, but more about their perceived purpose. Mansell et al. (2009: 9) remind us that 'formative' and 'summative' are not labels for different types or forms of assessment but describe how assessments are used.

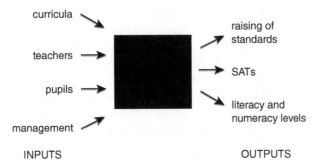

Figure 4.4   A 'Black Box' model

So, given the above, what does AfL mean? Black and Wiliam (1999) describe it as a process which is intended to promote students' learning rather than having account-ability ranking or the certifying of competence as its primary purpose. Learning is aided through the provision of information that both students and teachers can use in assessing one another and which encourages the modification of teaching and learn-ing activities.

The Quality Improvement Agency (QIA) also stresses the purpose of AfL as improv-ing learning through the provision of constructive feedback in order to:

- agree actions to help the learner improve
- adapt teaching methods to meet the learner's identified needs (QIA, 2008: 2).

Figure 4.5 illustrates how this works.

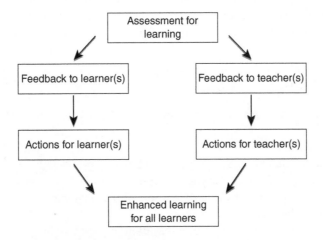

Figure 4.5   QIA assessment for learning cycle

The Assessment Reform Group (ARG), an informal network of academics who lay emphasis on the ways in which assessment can help to advance learning rather than merely measuring it, offers a similar viewpoint, defining AfL as 'the process of seeking and interpreting evidence for use by learners and their teachers to decide where the learners are in their learning, where they need to go and how best to get there' (ARG, 2002).

It is evident, then, that AfL prioritises the development of learners and can therefore be seen as situated at the core of the process of teaching and learning, with learners actively involved in their own learning. The ARG identified 10 principles that underpin AfL. Assessment for learning:

- is part of effective planning
- focuses on how students learn
- is central to classroom practice
- is a key professional skill
- is sensitive and constructive
- fosters motivation
- promotes understanding of goals and criteria
- helps learners know how to improve
- develops the capacity for self-assessment
- recognises all educational achievement (ARG, 2002).

Whereas assessment of learning creates a culture of competition and all that this implies, assessment for learning seeks to create a culture of success. By now, you will have a good 'feel' for AfL and what it seeks to achieve, so we turn next to putting it into practice. The main aim, as we have seen, is to use assessment as a tool to promote learning and as such to embed it within the teaching and learning strategies we use. According to LSIS (2009: 9), this is a natural consequence of most teaching activity as 'judgements on learners' performance happen quite naturally in the course of any teaching and learning session and require two-way dialogue, decision-making and communication of the assessment decision in the form of quality feedback to the learner on their performance'.

REFLECTIVE TASK 4.6

Check how well your current practice promotes AfL by answering the following questions:

- How well do you use questioning to stretch and include all of your learners?
- How detailed is the feedback you give your learners? Does it make them think?
- Do you share the objectives with learners at the beginning of a session? If so, what type of language do you use?
- Do you use much self and peer assessment in your teaching?

You will probably have guessed from the questions in Reflective task 4.6 that the four main strategies associated with AfL are:

- rich questioning
- effective marking and feedback
- sharing learning goals
- peer and self-assessment.

RICH QUESTIONING

Questioning learners is an integral part of teaching. We use it to check individual understanding, improve participation and help clarify any misconceptions. It enables learners to develop their analytical and critical thinking skills; they may gain a deeper understanding by listening to other people's responses and comments. It consolidates previous learning and, perhaps most importantly, promotes confidence and self-esteem when a correct answer is given. *Rich questions* are those which focus on exploring and enhancing understanding rather than testing knowledge of facts. The next chapter explores questioning techniques in more detail and discusses open and closed questions. Closed questions encourage recall rather than thinking about an answer. Asking open questions, on the other hand, can lead to more in-depth discussions with more learners taking part, giving a more informed idea about our learners' understanding, including any gaps in their knowledge. If you ask a learner a question which requires a yes/no answer, and they say 'hmmm, yes, I think so; hmmm, no, maybe not', that does not provide you with a clear picture of the depth of their knowledge. A more appropriate way of asking might be 'why is...' or 'how would you explain...'. *Rich questions* are *open* questions, focusing on the 'how will' and the 'why do' rather than a straightforward 'what is'. When using rich questioning, Black et al. (2003: 32) found that if more time was allowed to reply, more thoughtful answers were given. They cite the work of Rowe (1974) who found that longer 'wait time' meant that:

- answers were longer
- failure to respond decreased
- responses were more confident
- students challenged and/or improved the answers of other students
- more alternative explanations were offered (Black et al., 2003: 33).

All of these characteristics suggest a more active approach to learning and a deeper, more complex thought process. Research has indicated that the average time between teachers asking a question and intervening if the answer isn't immediately forthcoming, is 0.9 seconds! Learners may be able to answer a closed question in that time but find it difficult to consider an open question and formulate and articulate an answer without some 'wait time'.

REFLECTIVE TASK 4.7

Consider your own questioning techniques. What kind of questions do you ask? How do you feel about silences whilst learners formulate a response?

The kind of questions we might use in a 'rich' approach include:

- How do you...?
- How can you be sure...?
- Suppose you were to ... how would you then...?
- How can you explain that when...?
- What evidence do you have to be able to say that...?
- Why might this be/not be the case if...?
- What does that lead you on to think?

You have already encountered Bloom's Taxonomy of Objectives in Chapter 2 and so will have realised that closed questions (and therefore lower-order thinking skills) relate to the knowledge and possibly comprehension and application sections of the hierarchy. Answers to open or 'rich' questions generally require the application of the higher-order thinking skills of analysis, synthesis and evaluation.

ACTIVITY 4.7

Most of you will be familiar with the following nursery rhyme:

Jack and Jill went up the hill

To fetch a pail of water,

Jack fell down and broke his crown and

Jill came tumbling after.

What questions might you ask to prompt answers relating to (a) knowledge, (b) analysis and (c) evaluation? (Consult Figure 4.7 later for some suggestions.)

Finally, here are some tips for rich questioning:

- Plan your questions, remembering that open questions invite a deeper, more reflective response.
- Ask questions that are at an appropriate level for the learner, ensuring all learners are involved.
- Allow time for learners to formulate their answers.
- Value the responses.
- Redirect questions that do not receive an answer to other learners or the group as a whole.
- Resist the temptation to answer your own questions.

EFFECTIVE MARKING AND FEEDBACK

Whilst we recognise that the giving of feedback is an essential part of the process of teaching and learning, there is considerable debate over the form that feedback should take. Probably the most common type of feedback given on a piece of work is a mark (out of 10 or a percentage) or a grade. Both learners and teachers appear to be keen on giving or receiving a mark or grade, as it gives an indication of 'where the learner stands'. What does it actually tell you though? If you have gained a mark of 68 per cent and your friend has received a mark of 57 per cent for the same piece of work, you know that you have performed better than your friend. This information might make you feel good, although not so good for your friend perhaps. If the pass mark for the piece of work was 50 per cent, you know that you have passed with some room to spare. If you wish to take an ipsative view, you will compare your 68 per cent to your last mark for a similar piece of work to see if you have improved. What a mark or grade does not do, however, is tell you the strengths and limitations of the particular piece of work or what might be done to bring about improvement.

Research carried out by Butler (1988) suggested that giving learners a mark does not improve their learning. She found that the greatest increase in learner attainment occurred when comments only were given on the work. These comments needed to be more extensive than 'well done' or 'try harder'. Instead, they identified what had been done well and focused on what had to be done to improve. This is one of the central principles of AfL. This is not the same as giving learners the correct or complete answers, as a further principle of AfL decrees that learners should take responsibility for their own learning and learn to think things through for themselves. The teacher's role is to provide the scaffolding that allows this. Most teachers give both marks and comments. The marks tend to distract from the comments, however. Black et al. (2003) found that when given both, learners rarely read comments, preferring to compare marks with peers as their first reaction. Teachers rarely gave learners time in class to read comments and few, if any, learners read them at home. Butler's findings suggest that ideally comments only should be provided, although this can prove initially unsettling in practice as the awarding of a mark seems to create some sense of security in both teachers and learners. As a further refinement, Black et al. (2003) suggest a follow-up activity which learners could try to show the teacher that they can put the suggested improvements into practice.

Petty (2009: 482; see also Petty, n.d.) suggests the use of the 'medal and mission' model with respect to the giving of feedback. The medal is represented by what the learner has done well. Its function is not just to provide encouragement for the learner but, more importantly, to provide precise information on what was good about their response to the assessment. A mission explains exactly what was not so good about the response and indicates how improvements can be made. The emphasis is on improvement rather than focusing on what was wrong without giving any further feedback. Figure 4.6 illustrates this process.

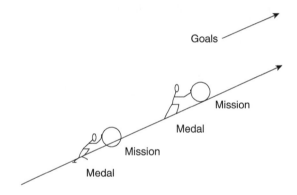

Figure 4.6   Medals, missions and goals

Source: http://geoffpetty.com

ACTIVITY 4.8

Looking at the following examples of feedback, identify the medals and missions.

1. This is a good piece of work; you have clearly identified the purpose of initial assessment.
2. Well done, however don't forget your citing and referencing.
3. A clear description of the purpose of initial assessment and how you use this in your own practice. To improve, be accurate in your citing and referencing. You need to include the date of publication, as explained in the handout on Harvard referencing.

Learners can also benefit from verbal feedback through group and plenary sessions. This is most effective when, rather than teachers telling learners what they have done wrong, learners themselves identify how they can improve, discussing this with the teacher. These types of discussions teach learners to be reflective about their work and responses.

SHARING LEARNING GOALS

It is now fairly standard practice to make a statement of objectives at the beginning of a teaching session, but it should be borne in mind that when we write objectives we do so in a specific manner for a specific reason. We do not normally talk in the same way. Learning objectives, assessment criteria and any other information that is shared with learners in order to involve them and give them an understanding of what is to come and what is expected of them, really needs to be communicated in language that makes sense to them. Objectives, for instance, can be presented as a number of short simple questions. Rather than enter into a lengthy explanation of a task, it may be more helpful to show a completed example.

A useful structure, borrowed from the school sector, for the sharing of learning goals, is the WALT, WILF and TIB technique:

Learning intention: We Are Learning To… (WALT)

Success criteria: What I'm Looking For… (WILF)

Purpose: This Is Because… (TIB)

Knowledge	Who went up the hill with Jack?
Analysis	Explain the series of events that may have led to Jack's fall.
Evaluation	Give a rationale for why Jack and Jill should, or should not, be given another chance to fetch water.

Figure 4.7   Some suggested answers for the Jack and Jill exercise

SELF AND PEER ASSESSMENT

Self-assessment involves learners taking responsibility for monitoring and making judgements about their own learning. This is a process that does not necessarily come easily to all learners, as they do not always value or trust their own judgements or necessarily possess the skills required to make a judgement. As a result, self-assessment often requires quite a strong structure in the initial stages until learners feel more comfortable with it as a process and have acquired the skills required to make it a productive activity. Teachers also may feel uncomfortable with the notion of self-assessment, feeling that they need to keep control of the assessment process and worrying that learners may not take it seriously or will be too generous in their judgements. A structured approach can help allay such fears.

To engage in self-assessment, learners need to possess a degree of self-awareness concerning their own levels of understanding and need. This requires an environment which allows them to have the confidence to share their insights without fear of loss of face or even ridicule. This can be encouraged by means of a simple prompted thumb-up or thumb-down to indicate understanding or a lack of it. Alternatively, a slightly more sophisticated approach makes use of a 'traffic light' system when learners are engaged in some form of task. This involves placing a red, amber or green block or card on their table. Red means they are finding difficulty with the task, amber, that they need a bit more help and green, that they are coping with the task without difficulty. The teacher can now see at a glance who is making progress and who needs varying degrees of assistance. A different way of indicating the same is 'HIT': the H stands for 'I need more Help', the I for 'I can do this Independently' and the T for 'I can Teach this to others'. At first, learners may over- or under-estimate their skills or knowledge, but will become more accurate in their judgements as they become familiar with the system.

As well as self-awareness, some reflective skills are required, and again some initial structure will assist in the development of these skills. To this end, you can ask learners to complete a 'PMI diagram', in which they identify what they consider to be a Plus of an activity, what they regard as a Minus and what they found Interesting. Figure 4.8 shows a PMI completed by a learner training to be a beautician, following her first hands-on experience in her college's training salon.

Plus	Minus	Interesting
Real salon experience;	Was really nervous;	To realise how much I depended on colleagues for clean bowls and towels, etc.;
All products were on the trolley;	Forgot to check for allergies;	
	Didn't mention purpose of the products;	Chatting to the client
Nice, friendly client	Overran	

Figure 4.8   A completed PMI diagram

A 'KWHL grid' provides a structure for learners to use when assessing their current position and what they need to do to progress further. The learner first identifies what they already *Know* about the topic. Next, they specify what they *Want* to know or find out. They then have to consider *How* they are going to do this. They finish by recording what they have *Learned* (see Figure 4.9).

Peer assessment occurs when learners check each other's learning. It allows learners to use their own language, phrases and figures of speech, leading sometimes to

What do I know	What do I want to know	How will I learn	What have I learned
Dyslexia affects 4–8% of the population. It is a learning difficulty which makes it more difficult to read and write.	How can I support dyslexic learners?	Contact the British Dyslexia Association; research the Internet.	Dyslexic learners benefit from having a clear overview of the lesson; use different colour pens on the whiteboard; use multi-sensory/kinaesthetic methods.

Figure 4.9   A completed KWHL grid

the kind of understanding that a teacher cannot communicate in quite the same way. Judging someone else's work can also lead to a more objective viewpoint, as there is less of a vested interest in the final mark awarded. This can result in a greater willingness to discuss and debate the relative merits of an answer in a more balanced and rational manner – this is when learning takes place! As well as enhancing learning, learners also achieve a greater insight into the assessment processes they will be subject to and the criteria against which they will be judged. Black et al. (2003: 51) are strong advocates of both self and peer assessment as 'learning can be enriched by marking their own or one another's work' and 'students learn by taking the roles of teachers and examiners of others'.

Black and Wiliam (1998) cite homework, test scripts and presentations, as their research was carried out mainly within a classroom setting, but we can add practical tasks and skills to the list as the workshop environment provides an excellent backdrop for peer assessment.

In learning a skill, particularly in the latter stages, learners can work in pairs. Whilst one carries out the skill, the other uses a laminated checklist to assess performance. The checklist can be used to give prompts if necessary but serves mainly to guide feedback which is given on completion of the routine. Roles are then reversed. As well as providing some variety within the repetitious nature of skill acquisition, this approach encourages learners to think more about the skill itself and analyse their own performance in a more critical manner. The teacher meanwhile can observe progress within the group as a whole, giving help where it is most required and also monitoring and giving advice on feedback skills. As well as process, learners can also peer-assess the end product resulting from application of a skill. They are asked to take on the role of a customer and are tasked with explaining to their fellow learner why they would or would not be satisfied with the job done and their thoughts on paying for it. This can be adapted easily into a self-assessment approach as well, with the teacher asking the learner, 'If you were a customer, would you...', and discussing their response.

Whilst the benefits of peer assessment are plain to see, the practice may not always be as straightforward as portrayed above. Dix (2010) alerts us to some possible difficulties. Friends working together may start chatting about other things; some learners may find it difficult to share their judgements with others or may find it difficult to accept feedback from their peers and so careful management of this activity is required. Learners need to be made aware of the purpose of the activity and what is expected of them in carrying it out. Peer assessment needs to be set up in a structured manner rather than initiated with a simple 'discuss in pairs' instruction. Groups need to be formed on the basis of the most productive combinations, despite pressure from learners wanting to work in friendship groups or not wanting to work together with certain other learners. In a classroom setting, strategies such as 'blind' marking can be used to overcome some of these objections but initial firmness and a belief in what you are doing are most often required in the practical environment. Once learners have experienced the approach on a few occasions and seen the benefits it can bring, objections should soon disappear.

The most important factor in introducing self and particularly peer assessment, however, is the establishment of an environment in which learners feel psychologically safe. A culture needs to be put in place in which 'mistakes' or 'not yet understanding a concept' are looked on as an opportunity for learning rather than signifying failure. Learners should feel free to discuss what they don't understand or have answered incorrectly without the fear of being ridiculed or laughed at. The focus has to be on the positive, accepting and striving for improvement with all learners responsible for the learning process, rather than on the negative or non-achievement. Modelling what is expected is essential in achieving an appropriate atmosphere, and the expectations we have of learners also figure prominently. The 'Pygmalion' effect (Rosenthal and Jacobson, 1992) relates to the self-fulfilling prophecy which is embedded in teachers' expectations. It tells us that if we have high expectations of our learners and they are aware of these, they will perform to a standard that matches that expectation. Equally, when learners are aware that we have low expectations of them, they will live up (or down?) to these expectations. It is only when an appropriate climate has been set that learners will enter into the spirit of self and peer assessment and gradually acquire the skills of self-evaluation and giving feedback that make for a really productive learning activity.

REFLECTIVE TASK 4.8

When you plan your next teaching session, take a look at the assessment methods you propose to use. Can you take one of these and turn it into either a self or peer assessment activity?

ASSESSING VOCATIONAL QUALIFICATIONS

Vocational qualifications (VQs) are work-related qualifications that relate directly to specific job roles, providing the skills that employers are looking for. They can be delivered as full-time courses in college using simulated work environments for those with little or no vocational experience (learner responsive) or in the workplace for those with the necessary experience and employment (employer responsive). It is this focus on application of skills and competency and the role taken on by the assessor in facilitating the accreditation process that make vocational qualifications different. As well as having sufficient occupational knowledge and experience at or above the level of the unit being assessed, assessors must also possess either the appropriate Training, Assessment and Quality Assurance (TAQA) qualifications, Al and A2 assessor awards, or (if of a certain age) the D32/33 assessor qualifications. Assessment takes place largely by observation of performance and testing for underpinning knowledge through questioning.

Until recently, the majority of vocational qualifications were delivered through the National Vocational Qualification (NVQ) route as part of the National Qualification Framework (NQF), a national system of comparing qualifications by level. The different qualification titles still caused some confusion, however, and the NQF was replaced in 2011 by a new qualification structure, the Qualifications and Credit Framework (QCF), in the interests of simplification and flexibility. The QCF works on the basis of packaging learning into units of varying size and level which can be combined to acquire a qualification. There are three types of qualification, each with a maximum credit value – see Figure 4.10.

Qualification	Credit range
Award	1–12
Certificate	13–36
Diploma	37 or over

Figure 4.10   QCA qualification structure and credit range

The type of qualification thus indicates its size. Each can be achieved at a level of difficulty between 1 and 8. The title of the qualification therefore specifies the subject, level and maximum credit rating. The Award, Certificate and Diploma in Further Education and Training were devised under this framework and all conform to this naming system.

In 2015, the QCF in turn was replaced by the Regulated Qualifications Framework (RQF). Under this framework, a qualification is defined by level and by the number of hours involved in its achievement – the total qualification time (TQT). The total is arrived at by adding together the number of hours of tutor contact, or guided learning hours (GLH), the number of required hours of independent study, or directed Learning hours and the hours taken up by assessments. 10 hours of course time can be considered as 1 credit. By 31st December 2017 all courses should have a TQT. Unlike previous qualifications, with RQFs there is no set deadline for completion – instead students can finish them at their own pace.

Despite changes in names and qualification structures, assessment procedures remain largely the same, as vocational qualifications are still competence-based in nature. The NVQ Criteria and Guidance from 1995 define competence as 'the ability to perform to the standards required in employment across a range of circumstances and to meet changing demands'.

Assessment is thus criterion-referenced, each area of competence being represented in the form of a number of 'performance criteria'. Performance criteria are arrived at by starting from a specified job role and breaking it down into a number of units. Each unit is further broken down into its constituent 'elements' from which the performance criteria are derived. This leads to a pass or fail judgement rather than a grade, as learners (or candidates, as we shall now refer to them) are found to be either competent, in which case they pass, or not, in which case they fail. As proof of competence, candidates are required to gather evidence showing how they have met the various performance criteria, and this evidence is normally stored and submitted in the form of a portfolio. The evidence gathered can be *direct*, meaning it is either produced wholly by the candidate or is evidenced through observation of their performance by the assessor. As assessment is conducted on an individual basis, however, possibly in a variety of settings and with each assessment activity only covering so many performance criteria, resource implications arise. Candidates can therefore also produce evidence derived from other sources and people. This is *indirect* evidence.

ORGANISING THE ASSESSMENT PROCESS

The assessment process comprises three main stages:

1. Planning for assessment.
2. Making judgements on performance and knowledge.
3. Providing feedback and recording results.

1. PLANNING FOR ASSESSMENT

The first encounter with a competence-based approach can prove to be a daunting experience for many. There are so many different competencies and performance criteria and so many ways of assessing these that it is often initially difficult to see 'the wood for the trees'. The assessor's first task, therefore, is to help the candidate make some sense of the process and see how it applies to them. The best way of initiating this is simply to talk to the candidate about their work and what they do, relating this to one of the units of the programme. During this conversation, it may transpire that the candidate has previously achieved a qualification that overlaps with a unit or part of a unit. Provided the original certificate can be produced and has appropriate currency (i.e. it is up to date with current practice), then Accreditation of Prior Learning (APL) can be awarded, avoiding repetition of learning. As a rule of thumb, qualifications normally have a 'shelf life' or currency of five years but this can vary depending on subject area; qualifications in subjects with a strong technological bias, for instance, can become out-dated very quickly. Awarding bodies normally provide guidance as to what they regard as acceptable or not for the purpose of APL. At the conclusion of the conversation, both candidate and assessor should have reached agreement as to the most appropriate types of evidence and methods of assessment to be used to demonstrate competence. Health and safety issues and the procedures to be adopted in the case of any disagreement concerning competency may also form part of the discussion. A plan can then be drawn up summarising what needs to be assessed and how this will be achieved and setting out an initial timetable. Ollin and Tucker (2008: 37) provide a useful checklist of questions that might be asked of the planning process, to ensure it has identified the key areas of agreement:

- *What* competencies or criteria will be assessed?
- *Who* will be involved in the assessment?
- *When* will they be assessed?
- *Where* will they be assessed?
- *How* will they be assessed?
- *How* will achievement be recorded and confirmed to the candidate?
- *When* will feedback be given?
- *How* will feedback be given?

2. MAKING JUDGEMENTS ON PERFORMANCE AND KNOWLEDGE

There are a number of different methods which can be used to judge competence and knowledge. In NVQ programmes, assessors are required to use at least four different methods, and, although not a requirement, other vocational qualifications also tend to use a variety of approaches. The main methods of assessment are:

(a) Assessing performance

1. Observation – this is the main method by which competence is judged. Observations need to be recorded in some detail on a form that makes it clear as to the evidence observed which proves competence. It is usual to use a checklist approach which itemises the competences to be observed.

2.   Witness statement, audio or video recordings – these provide an alternative to direct observation by the assessor. A witness statement needs to be supplied by someone who has the experience and/or qualifications to be able to make a judgement. All three approaches need to be accompanied by a clear rationale or explanation showing how the evidence presented matches the performance criteria being claimed.

(b) Assessing knowledge and understanding

1.   Questioning – this is the main method by which knowledge and understanding are assessed. Candidates need to demonstrate not only that they can perform the required skill, but that they understand what they are doing and how and why they are doing it. It is impossible to assess performance in all of the different situations and contexts in which the skill might be used, so candidates also need to show that they understand how they might have to adapt performance to fit the range of circumstances they might encounter. Questioning (see Chapter 5) is therefore an important skill in vocational assessment.
2.   Written tests, projects and professional discussions – these are alternative methods to questioning and their use is largely dependent on the level and complexity of the knowledge and understanding that need to be demonstrated. A professional discussion provides the candidate with an opportunity to talk through, in a fairly relaxed manner, aspects of evidence that require clarification or fill gaps left by the other forms of assessment used.

In certain situations, simulations can be used as an assessment method, but assessors need to check that this is an allowable alternative for the particular competence(s) they wish to assess in this way.

3. PROVIDING FEEDBACK AND RECORDING RESULTS

We have already looked at effective feedback, whether written or spoken, and how it should give guidance on how matters can be improved. Vocational qualifications make extensive use of spoken feedback, normally in the form of a discussion between assessor and candidate. Ollin and Tucker (2008: 49) stress that 'the skill of giving constructive and helpful feedback is at the heart of successful assessment', resulting in candidates being clear on what they have achieved and what they need to do to develop or maintain performance, leading to a positive motivational effect.

REFLECTIVE TASK 4.9

When you give feedback, do you have a set procedure you follow? How do you start and finish the feedback session, for instance? Why do you do it in this way?

There are a number of approaches that can be taken to the giving of feedback. The model of effective feedback, given below, proceeds through six stages. Although looking rather complicated, the approach is actually relatively easy to use in practice and provides a systematic and consistent approach to giving feedback.

The six stages are:

1. Listen
2. Confirm
3. Inform
4. Focus
5. Summarise
6. Agree.

Listen

This first stage consists of gathering impressions from the candidate on their performance. In all likelihood, a lot of effort and practice will have gone into preparing for this assessment and candidates will want to have done themselves justice. Sometimes, however, things will not have gone exactly as planned. Most candidates are quite self-critical and will recognise aspects of their performance that might have been better and the reasons why it was not. Until they have had an opportunity to express these thoughts, they will not really be focused on anything that you have to say at this stage. Their response also gives an indication of their level of self-awareness and helps to gauge the tone and level of feedback that will be given.

Confirm

Having asked for a response, there may be a need to reassure the candidate that you have really listened to what they have said and understood their position. This involves summarising what the candidate has said and checking for a common understanding.

Inform

The next thought in the candidate's mind is whether or not they have been deemed competent. Some assessors prefer to give the rationale for the decision first and give their verdict at a later stage, thus also avoiding the possibility of defensive responses from the candidate during the discussion. The suggestion here though is that the result of the assessment is made known at this stage, otherwise it becomes a distraction and can divert attention away from constructive discussion.

Focus

Specific points can now be picked up on. Remember at this stage to:

- start by reference to the positives
- discuss what you actually saw, rather than give your opinion
- prioritise your feedback and limit it to two or three areas for development
- be specific and limit your observations to matters which the candidate has the capability to change.

Summarise

The points that have been raised are reviewed and clarified before drawing them into a summary.

Agree

As the hallmark of good feedback, whatever form it takes, is that it leaves the recipient knowing what they can do to improve future performance, the final stage of the feedback process is to agree an action plan to address the development points identified. These may contribute to gaining a pass on a future assessment or build on competence already displayed.

THE QUALITY ASSURANCE CHAIN

In the bigger picture of assessment, quality assurance consists of putting a series of checks in place to maintain the integrity of a qualification. This can be considered in two ways:

- the quality of the assessment process and judgements
- the quality and fitness for purpose of the qualification itself.

The process of arriving at a vocational qualification starts when the relevant Sector Skills Council creates a set of Occupational Standards which define the competencies required to perform a job role within that particular occupational sector. Awarding bodies then devise and offer qualifications based around these occupational standards. These qualifications are then offered in approved centres which meet criteria laid down by the awarding body. The first stage in quality assurance involves the awarding body and is designed to preserve the credibility of the qualification. The awarding body appoints a lead verifier and a number of external verifiers (or standards verifiers) or moderators to monitor and audit the approved centres to ensure they operate within the awarding body guidelines. External verifiers also offer support and guidance to the centres they are responsible for and act as a channel of communication between the centres and the awarding body. Each centre in turn operates its own internal quality assurance policy which spells out its in-house quality procedures. Adherence to these procedures is monitored by a number of internal verifiers, one of whom is attached to each vocational qualification that the centre offers. Internal verifiers also monitor the judgements on competency made by the assessors on each qualification with respect to accuracy and consistency. The external verifier samples and checks the work of the internal verifier and the efficiency of the centre's quality assurance procedures. The first part of the chain of quality assurance measures for vocational qualifications is represented by the diagram in Figure 4.11.

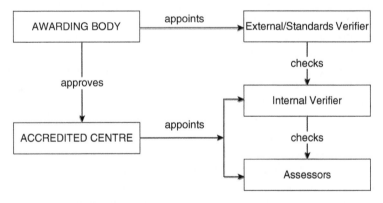

Figure 4.11   Chain of quality assurance checks

The remainder of the quality assurance chain involves monitoring the performance of the awarding body itself. This is carried out by the Office of Qualifications and Examinations Regulation (Ofqual), which ensures that all awarding bodies delivering vocational qualifications meet the regulatory requirements concerning quality, rigour, fairness and consistency.

E-ASSESSMENT

We have seen in the previous chapter how ICT is taking on an increasing and more active role in teaching and learning. Similar inroads are being made into the assessment process and the use of technology in checking and testing learning, under the heading of e-assessment, is becoming more common. The 2005 Education and Skills White Paper heralded the formal adoption of e-assessment as a strategy with its claim that 'in the medium term we expect e-assessment to make a significant contribution to cutting the assessment burden and to improving the quality and usage' (DfES, 2005: 70). One of the stated aims of the QCA's 2007 *Regulatory Principles for E-assessment* report was to 'ensure that sector qualification strategies encourage the development and take-up of innovative forms of e-assessment' (p. 4).

Here, however, we are more concerned with the use of e-assessment as a tool which teachers and learners can use in a more informal way. The advantages claimed for e-assessment over the traditional pencil-and-paper approach centre on:

- the amount of paperwork being reduced
- it providing a less stressful process for learners
- marking being more objective and therefore results possessing greater reliability
- marking being completed and feedback being given more quickly
- assessment being provided on demand and repeated to consolidate learning.

The last two of these apply particularly when e-assessment is used for formative purposes. We have already seen the importance of assessment for learning and e-assessment provides an excellent platform for this approach. Online assessments can be quickly and easily delivered through the VLE. Quizzes can be uploaded and simple exercises can be created in a matter of minutes using the Hot Potatoes site (http://hotpot.uvic.ca). Learners can now self-assess as immediate feedback is given to the responses they make. Although by its nature, such feedback is generic and brief, it is sufficient to allow learners to diagnose and respond more effectively to their own learning needs. Its greatest benefit is its immediacy and the way in which it encourages learners to become actively engaged in their own assessment. This presents a gain for teachers as well, as it relieves them of some of the responsibilities for marking and giving feedback, freeing up more time for other activities, although this has to be balanced against the time spent in creating the assessment in the first place. The approach can be extended beyond individual use: learners can pair up and peer-assess or it could be used as a focus for whole-class team games and discussion.

A more modest use of technology has had an impact on assessment by allowing learners to submit draft pieces of work for formative feedback via email. Feedback can be provided using either the 'track changes' or 'comments' facilities in Word.

Drop boxes on the VLE can also be used for assignment submission. They can be set up to allow submission only during a given time period and will record the exact date and time of submission. The grade book facility also allows a record of the marks obtained to be kept.

E-PORTFOLIOS

Clarke (2011: 105) describes e-portfolios as being 'collections of digital evidence that show the learners' skills, knowledge and understanding'. They are becoming more popular, partly because they are less cumbersome and more eco-friendly than their paper-based counterparts, but mainly because they allow evidence to be collected in a greater variety of formats. When used for assessment purposes, they can include videos and digital images, allowing skills to be demonstrated and end-products to be recorded, audio recordings of discussions, question and answer sessions or witness statements, links to blogs, reflective logs or other personal documents. E-portfolios can be used as developmental logs or function as a record of achievement, showcasing individual accomplishments perhaps in relation to specific work or personal goals.

Whatever purpose the e-portfolio is put to, it must be organised in a logical and systematic manner so that an assessor or other interested party can gain an initial overview of its contents (rather like an index in a paper-based portfolio) and subsequently locate individual items within the portfolio as required.

SUMMARY OF KEY POINTS

In this chapter, we have looked at the assessment process, its purpose and how it might be implemented in practice. The language of assessment was explained and the importance of assessment for learning highlighted. The particular requirements of vocational qualifications with their emphasis on competency-based assessment were explored, along with the approaches adopted for quality assurance. The chapter concluded with a brief look at the potential of e-assessment.

The key points in this chapter are:

- Assessment fulfils a variety of purposes and these are reflected in the form an assessment takes.
- Assessment can take place at the beginning (diagnostic), during (formative) or at the end (summative) of an episode of learning.
- All assessments need to be devised and carried out in a manner that maximises the reliability and validity of the results they produce.

(Continued)

- Increased consistency in marking can be achieved by using a mark scheme.
- Safeguards need to be put into place to ensure the authenticity of work submitted for assessment purposes.
- The marks obtained in an assessment can be referenced against the marks achieved by other learners (norm), set criteria (criterion) or individual progress (ipsative).
- Assessment for learning enhances learning through identifying areas for improvement and strategies to achieve this.
- Self and peer assessment allow learners to take responsibility for their own assessment and lead to a more thoughtful and considered approach.
- The assessment of vocational qualifications is based around judgements relating to competence.
- Observation and questioning are the two main methods employed to test competence and knowledge respectively.
- Assessors need to plan the assessment process carefully in conjunction with their candidates.
- Vocational qualifications employ a quality assurance system based around internal and external verification.
- E-assessment reduces paperwork and provides a route to instant feedback on demand.

REFERENCES

Armitage, A., Donovan, G., Flanagan, K. and Poma, S. (2011) *Developing Professional Practice 14–19*. Harlow: Pearson Education.

Assessment Reform Group (ARG) (2002) *Assessment for Learning: 10 Principles*. Available online at: www.aaia.org.uk/content/uploads/2010/06/Assessment-for-Learning-10-principles.pdf (accessed 25/04/17).

Black, P. and Wiliam, D. (1998) *Inside the Black Box*. London: NFER.

Black, P. and Wiliam, D. (1999) *Assessment for Learning: Beyond the Black Box*. London: Kings College London.

Black, P., Harrison, C., Lee, C., Marshall, B. and Wiliam, D. (2003) *Assessment for Learning: Putting it into Practice*. Maidenhead: Open University Press.

Butler, R. (1988) Enhancing and undermining intrinsic motivation: the effects of task-involving and ego-involving evaluation on interest and performance, *British Journal of Educational Psychology*, 58: 1–14.

Child, D. (2004) *Psychology and the Teacher* (7th edn). London: Continuum.

Clarke, A. (2011) How to Use Technology Effectively in Post-Compulsory Education. London: Routledge.

DfES (2005) *14–19 Education and Skills*. Available online at: http://webarchive.nationalarchives.gov.uk/20050301194752/http://dfes.gov.uk/publications/14-19educationandskills/pdfs/14-19WhitePaper.pdf (accessed 25/04/17).

Dix, P. (2010) The Essential Guide to Classroom Assessment. Harlow: Pearson.

Francis, M. and Gould, J. (2013) Achieving Your PTLLS Award: A Practical Guide to Teaching in the Lifelong Learning Sector (2nd edn). London: Sage.

Lam, T.C.M. (1995) Fairness in performance assessment. *ERIC Digest*. Available online at: http://ericae.net/db/edo/ED391982.htm (accessed 25/04/17).

LSIS (2009) *Assessment for Learning*. Available online at: http://archive.excellencegateway.org.uk/pdf/Assessment%20for%20Learning.pdf (accessed 21/10/13).

Mansell, W., James, M. and the Assessment Reform Group (2009) *Assessment in Schools: Fit for Purpose? A Commentary by the Teaching and Learning Research Programme.* London: Economic and Social Research Council, Teaching and Learning Research Programme.

OCR website: www.ocr.org.uk (accessed 25/04/17).

Ollin, R. and Tucker, J. (2008) *The NVQ Assessor, Verifier and Candidate Handbook* (4th edn). London: Kogan Page.

Petty, G. (2009) *Teaching Today* (4th edn). Cheltenham: Nelson Thornes.

Petty, G. (n.d.) *Medal and Mission*. Available online at: http://geoffpetty.com/for-teachers/feedback-and-questions/ (accessed 25/04/17).

QCA (2007) *Regulatory Principles for E-assessment*. Available online at: www.publications.parliament.uk/pa/cm200607/cmselect/cmeduski/memo/test&ass/ucm3102paper4.pdf (accessed 25/04/17).

Quality Improvement Agency (QIA) (2008) *Skills for Life Improvement Programme Booklet 5: Assessment for Learning*. Reading: CfBT Education Trust. Available online at: https://colleenyoung.files.wordpress.com/2016/06/10_assessment_for_learning_guide.pdf (accessed 25/04/17).

Race, P., Brown, S. and Smith, B. (2005) *500 Tips on Assessment* (2nd edn). Abingdon: Routledge Falmer.

Reece, I. and Walker, S. (2007) *Teaching, Training and Learning: A Practical Guide* (6th edn). Sunderland: Business Education Publishers.

Rosenthal, R. and Jacobson, L. (1992) Pygmalion in the Classroom: Teacher Expectation and Pupils' Intellectual Development. New York: Irvington Publishers.

Rowe, M.B. (1974) Wait time and rewards as instructional variables: their influence on language, logic and fate control. *Journal of Research in Science Teaching*, 11: 81–94.

Spendlove, D. (2009) Putting Assessment for Learning into Practice. London: Continuum.

Tummons, J. (2007) *Assessing Learning in the Lifelong Learning Sector* (2nd edn). Exeter: Learning Matters.

FURTHER READING

Bartlett, J. (2015) Outstanding Assessment for Learning in the Classroom. Abingdon: Routledge.

This book starts by establishing the rationale behind an assessment for learning approach before proceeding to look at implementation. Although written with a schools audience in mind, this book includes a wealth of practical strategies covering a range of subject areas which can be easily adapted for use in an Education and Training environment.

Coffield, F., Costa, C., Muller, W. and Webber, J. (2014) *Beyond Bulimic Learning*. London: IOE Press.

This is a book which covers a variety of themes. Chapter 2, for instance gives an interesting take on 'best practice' and is well worth a read. In terms of assessment, however, Chapter 8 gives a comprehensive review of approaches to the giving of feedback and provides an excellent framework against which to analyse your own practice in this area.

Wiliam, D. (2011) *Embedded Formative Assessment.* **Bloomington: Solution Tree Press.**
A very readable text which gives some theoretical background to formative assessment in the earlier chapters but later focuses on practice, explaining overall strategies with sections on 'practical techniques' at the end of each chapter.

5

COMMUNICATION AND TEACHING STRATEGIES

Teaching is based around communication with learners through the teaching strategies employed. We use a variety of communication skills in everyday life and transfer these into the teaching situation, but at an intuitive level. Recognising and understanding the skills we possess at a more conscious level allows them to be used in a more deliberate manner. One way of achieving this is by comparing what we do to theory. This chapter provides such a point of comparison, beginning with a brief look at theories, models and types of communication. This is followed by an overview of some of the different types of teaching strategies that we employ in communicating with our learners. Sometimes we communicate with learners in groups and sometimes on a more individual basis, and these two modes of communicating are explored initially before looking at two general strategies – question and answer and discussion – which can be employed within most teaching approaches. The teaching of practical skills is examined in more detail as an example of a specific strategy. The chapter concludes by placing two issues raised in Chapter 1 – differentiation and embedding functional skills – within the context of teaching strategies.

When you have completed this chapter you will be able to:

- analyse the communication process and identify different types of communication
- identify the characteristics of a learning group

(Continued)

- differentiate between the types of learning appropriate to small and large group activities
- manage large group and small group work effectively
- describe the purpose of one-to-one teaching and possible approaches to employ
- make effective use of questioning as a teaching strategy
- run productive discussion groups
- summarise the different stages in the acquisition of practical skills
- choose appropriate differentiation strategies for large group, small group and individual approaches.

MODELS OF COMMUNICATION

The American composer John Powell once said, 'communication works for those who work at it'. In order to work at it, we need some understanding of the process itself and so we turn here to some simple models of communication.

The most basic model of communication involves a sender passing some kind of information or message to a receiver.

This is one-way communication and is the kind of communication we engage in when, for example, listening to the radio. This is a useful form of communication for transmitting a one-way flow of uninterrupted information as when giving a lecture. When listening to the radio, however, if we don't quite understand, miss a bit of what has been said or need a moment or two to digest the information, we have a problem. We cannot ask the radio to explain what it meant or proceed more slowly to give us an opportunity for thought. One-way communication can thus lead to frustration on the part of the receiver and this is sometimes the case in a lecture situation, particularly if we have to cope with the added distraction of taking notes at the same time. If, instead of a radio, the sender was a person, that sense of frustration may well be shared, as without any form of feedback from the receiver the sender will not know if their message is being received and interpreted in the required manner. So, the person giving the lecture may also feel a certain amount of frustration as although they are imparting lots of information, they do not necessarily know if it is being understood by their audience. To overcome such problems, communication between two people normally proceeds in a two-way manner, with the roles of sender and receiver interchanging between the participants. If I ask you if you are enjoying that cake you are eating, I would be doing so for a purpose and would hope for a response. You may well reply along the lines of 'yes, thank you, I am particularly enjoying the marzipan on top' or 'not really, it's rather rich for my taste'. Our roles have switched – you are now the sender and I am now the receiver and so we are engaging in two-way communication. This is a more time-consuming process, but generally proves a more satisfying experience for both parties and results in a shared understanding of what has been communicated. For this reason, most of our teaching uses two-way rather than one-way communication.

Our model now becomes a little more complex.

As senders, we need to be able to formulate a clear and unambiguous message, normally achieved in a teaching environment by thorough planning and preparation. But we now have to be able to act as a receiver as well and so another skill – listening – comes into play. Effective listening involves clearing the mind of other thoughts and focusing on the incoming message. We can let the sender know this is the case in a number of ways, such as making eye contact, nodding, leaning forward and using appropriate facial expressions. This introduces another type of communication. In the example above, suppose you had cake in your mouth when I asked my question. Having been well brought up, your response might now be in the form of a smile, a nod of the head or even a thumbs-up sign. As well as using words (verbal), communication can also be achieved through non-verbal means. We show we are listening by non-verbal signals or cues. Again, the model increases in complexity.

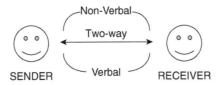

Non-verbal cues form an extremely important aspect of the communication process, prompting management consultant Peter Drucker to suggest that 'the most important thing in communication is hearing what isn't said' (Drucker, n.d.).

Non-verbal communication can serve a variety of purposes. As well as replacing verbal communication, it can also complement or emphasise the verbal communication, as in 'this cake is very nice', accompanied by eye contact, a smile and nodding of the head. It can also, however, contradict verbal communication, as in 'this cake is very nice' accompanied by a grimace and avoidance of eye contact.

This apparent contradiction occurs because non-verbal communication conveys information about feelings and attitudes, and sometimes what we say about something does not necessarily reflect how we actually feel about it. Research undertaken by Albert Mehrabian (1972) suggests that face-to-face communication has three components:

- words (what is actually said)
- tone of voice (how we say the words)
- body language.

Mehrabian claimed that 55 per cent of the meaning conveyed in a message is achieved through the use of body language, 38 per cent comes from the tone of voice used and only 7 per cent arises out of the meaning of the words used. This research was concerned specifically with the communication of emotions and feelings and so the relative importance of each component may well be different in normal conversation. Mehrabian's research does, however, give an indication of how important non-verbal communication can be. As teachers, an understanding of non-verbal cues as part of the communication process is an important skill to develop as it will allow us to become better receivers of the messages that learners (intentionally or unintentionally) send, and also better senders of signals to our learners.

ACTIVITY 5.1

What would you understand the following non-verbal signals to mean?

1. head nodding up and down
2. eyebrows raised
3. making eye contact
4. leaning forward
5. arms or legs crossed
6. avoiding eye contact
7. head shaking from side to side
8. frowning.

Generally, the signals in Activity 5.1 are considered to mean:

1. understanding or agreement
2. surprise or disbelief
3. interest and a wish to communicate
4. open-mindedness and interest

5. uncertainty and defensiveness
6. lack of interest or no desire to communicate
7. disagreement
8. lack of understanding or disagreement.

Interpreting non-verbal communication is not an exact science, however, particularly as it can be culture-specific. Western cultures see direct eye-to-eye contact as a sign of trustworthiness but become uncomfortable if it is maintained for too long. Arab cultures prefer to make prolonged eye contact as a sign of interest, whereas in some Asian countries such as Japan respect is shown by avoiding eye contact. Some would consider a belch whilst eating to be most impolite; in other cultures, it is a sign of satisfaction. A thumbs-up sign is usually taken as an indication that everything is fine, but it is considered an extremely offensive gesture in Nigeria and in Japan signifies 'five'.

Our own perceptions also influence our interpretation. Petty (2009) describes how a smile given by an intelligent cooperative learner may be seen as positive, but the same smile from an unmotivated and challenging learner means something is afoot! It is best therefore not to read too much into a single non-verbal cue but to look for other complementary cues before drawing a conclusion.

As well as interpreting the non-verbal cues our learners send, we also need to be aware of the non-verbal cues learners receive. Whilst we can, and do, use these in a deliberate manner, we may also respond to learners automatically, unaware of the non-verbal cues we give at the same time. We are prone to 'emotional leakage', as our body language may well give away what we are thinking but would rather learners did not know. We may, for instance, be teaching a rather 'dry' aspect of our subject. We know this is the case but have introduced the topic as interesting and relevant – does our body language match this statement as we teach it? What message does it send and how does it shape expectations?

REFLECTIVE TASK 5.1

Think about the non-verbal messages your learners receive as they enter the teaching room. What are they? How can you influence them? For instance:

Where do you position yourself in the room? Do you adopt an 'open' or 'closed' stance?

Is the room set up in an organised manner?

Do these 'say' anything to your learners?

How is your teaching room set out? Chairs/tables in straight lines, forming a horseshoe shape, a circle or maybe grouped in small clusters? All of these arrangements send a different signal as to the type of session and interactions that are to take place. Is the room tidy and organised? The way we set up a room gives an indication of the importance we give to the session, whilst the way we leave it probably gives a message to the next user. How are you dressed? Do you stand or sit when teaching? Where do you position yourself in the room? In the centre? To one side? How near are you to learners? From four to twelve feet away is considered to be 'social distance', and suggests informal interactions; further than this indicates a formal approach. A number of messages are being sent and received before a word has even been spoken.

ACTIVITY 5.2

Now think about the ways in which you use non-verbal cues both in your teaching and in your management of learners. Why do you use these instead of saying what you mean?

You will probably have thought of non-verbal cues which are intended to boost confidence and encourage participation, focus attention, emphasise important points, illustrate difficult points, discourage interruptions and disproportionate contribution, and discourage inappropriate behaviour. Quite often, a gesture or an expression can convey a message more quickly and less intrusively than a verbal comment; the momentum of the session is maintained. The way in which we say things, as opposed to what we say – differences in loudness, pitch, timbre, rate, inflection, rhythm, and enunciation – also conveys a message to the listener.

It would appear that the basic model of one-way communication that we started off with is a rare occurrence either in everyday contact or in teaching. A two-way approach involving both verbal and non-verbal interactions leads to more effective and satisfying communication.

POSSIBLE BARRIERS TO COMMUNICATION AND WAYS OF OVERCOMING THESE

The model of communication we have been building has hopefully encouraged you to think about ways in which you can make communication between you and your learners more effective. Despite our skills, however, the communication process sometimes breaks down as it encounters various obstacles or barriers – 'anything that interferes with the communication process and disrupts or distorts the message' (Appleyard and Appleyard, 2010: 7).

The above definition leaves us with a lengthy list of suspects. It may be that:

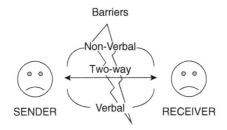

1. We use too much jargon without explaining it.
2. We give too much information to absorb in one go.
3. What we are teaching has no relevance to learners.
4. The room is too hot, cold, dark or light.
5. Distractions are caused by interruptions, external noise, inappropriate behaviour or teacher mannerisms.
6. Learners lack confidence in their ability.
7. Learners are preoccupied with other matters.
8. Learners don't like the teacher, the subject or the way it is being taught.
9. Learners have short attention spans and are easily bored.
10. Learners are tired or hungry.

Numbers 1–5 in the above list can be classified as 'external' and fall within our sphere of influence, provided we recognise them for what they are. Numbers 6–10 are more difficult to deal with as they are 'internal' to learners. We may not even be aware of them, although their effects may well be apparent. Internal barriers have to be identified before they can be addressed, and the first stage in doing this is creating a rapport with learners themselves.

COMMUNICATION AND THE TEACHING OF GROUPS

Much of the teaching we do involves groups of learners in differing situations – large groups when whole-class teaching, or managing smaller groups in a variety of activities. We will be looking at the skills required in each of these situations but first turn to a consideration of the nature and characteristics of groups as a whole. The term 'group' is used widely and fairly loosely in everyday conversation so, for the purpose of the discussion that follows in this chapter, we need to define more specifically what we mean when we use the term 'group', particularly when applied within a learning context.

ACTIVITY 5.3

To start thinking about the characteristics of a group, consider the two following situations:

1.   a number of passengers in a railway carriage
2.   a number of musicians in a band.

Do you consider both to be a group? What are the differences?
    It may also be helpful to think about a group that you are a member of:

*   Why did the group form in the first place?
*   Do you communicate with all or most (if it is a large group) of your fellow group members?
*   Do you feel a part of, and think of others as being part of, the group?
*   Do you know what actions and behaviours are approved and disapproved of within the group?

The term 'aggregate' is often used to describe a number of individuals who happen to be in the same space at the same time, as opposed to 'group' which implies something over and above this. Your thoughts on the above exercise may well have led you to the conclusion that a group differs from an aggregate in that:

1.   the members of a group have a common purpose, goal or task that they collectively wish to achieve
2.   there is some form of interaction between members of the group
3.   group members identify with others as belonging to the group
4.   some norms relating to procedures and conduct are recognised and adhered to by all members of the group.

In a learning situation, rather than an aggregate, we would want our learners to be part of a group as this brings a number of benefits:

*   A group can often achieve what cannot be achieved by its individual members.
*   The group acts as a forum for learning from others through the sharing and pooling of a wide range of knowledge and experience.
*   Individual group members provide each other with mutual support.
*   The group can provide a differentiated learning environment.
*   Being part of a group develops skills in areas such as working with others and communication.

A learning group (or indeed any other type of group) doesn't just happen, however – it forms or 'comes together' gradually, developing in a number of stages. There are numerous studies that identify the stages in group formation, some suggesting that there are as few as three stages, whilst others recognise as many as seven or eight. Tuckman (1965) arrived at what is probably the most well-known model of group development through a review of approximately 50 existing studies, identifying similarities and common features. His model identifies the four stages of forming, storming, norming and performing.

Forming occurs when the group first meets and is a time of uncertainty in which the potential group members try to identify their place in the group and how the group will operate. Storming occurs when members try to establish themselves within the group and a 'pecking order' begins to emerge. At the norming stage, the group begins to develop some cohesion as the unwritten rules which govern expectations and behaviour generally within the group begin to emerge. Finally, the group reaches the performing stage and members now work together to achieve their common goals and begin to derive the benefits of membership of the group. A group which has reached the performing stage is one in which learning is optimised and in which learners provide mutual support for each other. They can only remain as members of the group, however, as long as they abide by the norms established.

Tuckman's (1965) study reviewed groups which were passively led, with no attempts being made to influence the process of group development. As teachers, however, we would want the groups we teach to reach the performing stage as quickly as possible and so employ strategies to facilitate this. We wish to establish a group environment in which individuals feel valued, supported, confident and able to learn.

REFLECTIVE TASK 5.2

What strategies can you identify which might be used to encourage groups to proceed more quickly through Tuckman's (1965) stages of development? How can you manage your groups in such a way that they 'gel' more quickly and group members become mutually supportive?

STRATEGIES TO ENCOURAGE GROUP COHESION

The forming and storming stages of group development are most easily negotiated if learners communicate with each other and begin to feel more at ease in each other's company. This can be aided by the use of an icebreaking activity which 'encourages learners to talk to us, to each other and to the group as a whole' (Francis and Gould, 2013: 20). Icebreaking activities are designed to break down the barriers that invariably exist when a number of people meet for the first time.

In the early stages of a course, small group activities, in which the composition of the groups is constantly changed, encourages mixing within the group and talking to and getting to know other group members. Snowballing exercises are particularly useful in this respect. They start off individually, then form pairs which then join up to form a larger group, which subsequently joins up again with a similar sized group, thus gradually increasing the group size and the scope of learner contact.

Setting ground rules, as discussed in Chapter 1, assists in the establishing of group norms, particularly if a learner-led approach is adopted for this activity.

The initial management of groups, then, focuses on establishing a group identity and group cohesion, and helps to develop points 2, 3 and 4 of the group characteristics listed earlier in this chapter.

GROUP SIZE

The form taken by group teaching depends largely on the type of learning that is to take place. If the purpose is to deliver factual material in a structured manner, then whole-group teaching is the most appropriate approach to adopt. Small group activities are more appropriate when the material to be covered considers opinions rather than facts, involves making judgements, applies general principles to practical situations, benefits from some form of shared reflection or can be derived from a basis of learner experience.

LARGE GROUPS

A conversation between two boys about Spot the dog takes the following form:

Boy 1:   I taught Spot how to whistle.

Boy 2:   I can't hear him whistling.

Boy 1:   I said I taught him. I didn't say he learned it!

The teaching of large groups allows a relatively large amount of information to be conveyed to a large number of people in a structured manner in a short period of time. As such, it can lead to an efficient use of teaching time but also means that if we are not careful, we may end up 'teaching Spot to whistle'.

Large group teaching tends to involve passing on and explaining material of a factual nature, and, at the planning stage, thought needs to be given not only to the content of the session but also to how it might be delivered most effectively. Information processing theory (see Chapter 6) informs us that attention, perception and memory are the key processes in learning, and so the way in which we go about teaching large groups should take account of these if Spot is to have any chance of learning how to whistle.

MANAGING ATTENTION

With respect to attention, we need to consider the following:

- capturing attention initially
- maintaining it for the duration of the taught session.

ACTIVITY 5.4

Think about the tasks or activities you engage in in normal everyday life. Some will attract and hold your attention for longer than others – why is this? List the reasons you come up with.

Your responses to the above exercise will probably include the fact that some things interest you more than others, some activities arouse your curiosity and others you see as being useful and worthwhile. This has an obvious implication for our teaching in that if we wish learners to be attentive, they must be interested in or curious about what we have to offer and can see some point in it – we would establish the relevance and benefits of what we are going to teach at the beginning of the session. This will normally guarantee initial attention but our next task is to keep that attention at a good level for the rest of the session and one of the problems we face here is that attention spans can be fairly short. There are a number of reasons for this.

One of these is to do with the way in which we take in information through the senses. Sight is the sense on which we are most reliant under normal circumstances. When teaching large groups, however, we tend to communicate largely by talking and so learners are reliant on hearing as their main sensory input. Focusing exclusively on the spoken word involves a lot of hard work and this level of effort can only be maintained for a limited period of time. Typically, attention spans under these circumstances tend to be about 20 minutes in duration. To relieve the burden on hearing, we can use visual aids which also bring our major sense, sight, back into play. Showing as well as telling helps maintain attention levels and increases the amount of information we subsequently remember. Generally, visual aids create interest and prolong attention, as well as giving a focus to the important learning points.

So, introducing visual material brings more than one sense into play and introduces an element of variety into our teaching. Variety is an important factor in maintaining attention. If you watch a film, the camera shot changes frequently, rarely lasting for more than five seconds or so. Conversely, to avoid attention, an animal stalking its prey will remain very still. As well as varying sensory input, a variety of different activities and resources will help maintain attention.

The type of activity in which you were engaged may have featured in your response to the exercise on attention as attention spans also vary with the type of learning that is taking place. Listening to someone talk will not normally maintain attention levels for as long a period of time as, for example, a discussion. The difference between the two activities is that, in the first, learners only receive information, either verbally or visually – learning is passive – whereas in the second, learners also engage with and use the material to be learned – learning is active. Active learning involves 'doing' and thinking about the information presented and can include interaction with other learners.

Introducing short, sharp, active learning activities into sessions to break up the more passive 'listen and look' type of approach can increase attention spans considerably. A simple example would be the use of questioning but, with a little imagination, a number of resources such as case studies, problem-solving exercises, multiple-choice questions, diagrams or charts can be adapted to form the basis of short activities that learners can engage in singly, in pairs or in small groups as part of the overall session. The common characteristic of all such activities is that they require learners to think about, take further or consolidate the information they receive in an active manner, thus maintaining attention at a high level throughout the session and making learning more effective.

HELPING UNDERSTANDING

Many would argue that good teaching is about taking a potentially complex subject and putting it across in a manner in which it can be easily understood. Failure to do this can lead to frustration for learners, and the attention we have worked so hard to gain in the first place will inevitably begin to wander and eventually will probably be lost altogether.

We find things easier to understand if we can relate them to what we already know. For this reason, we often start a teaching session off with a review of previous related learning and possibly some question and answer to establish that the required previous learning is indeed in place. This is similar to what Ausubel (1960) calls an 'advance organiser', which, as the name suggests, organises the mind in advance of new learning, making it more receptive to what is to follow.

Advance organisers allow learners to connect new information to what they already know and prepare them for what they are to learn next. They can take different forms, ranging from a simple contextualised statement of objectives, an anecdote or an example to more complex visual representations such as a diagram, flow chart or mind map. The effect is similar to looking at a map before going on a journey or consulting a diagram before putting together some flat-pack furniture – we can see the bigger picture and how the different parts of it relate to each other.

When presenting the main bulk of the topic, content should be developed in a logical sequence at a pace which is appropriate to the rate of uptake in the group.

Summarising at the end of different sections and linking to the next helps learners organise their thoughts and make sense of the content as a whole. Activity 5.5 will help you think about how to make your explanations clearer.

ACTIVITY 5.5

Consider the following sentence:

'He caught the ball gracefully in his two hands.'

If you had to explain the meaning of the words in the sentence to someone who had not encountered them before, which of the following two words would you find the easiest/most difficult to explain?

(a) ball
(b) gracefully

How would you go about explaining the meaning of each word?

You will almost certainly have chosen 'ball' as an easier word to explain than 'gracefully'. This is because 'gracefully' is an abstract idea with no real form or substance, whereas 'ball' is what is described as concrete in nature – it is real and can be accessed through our senses.

Generally, as concrete concepts are easier to understand, we try to move in a concrete to abstract direction when introducing new material.

This can be achieved in a subject of a theoretical nature by starting our explanation not with the actual theory, but with examples of the theory at work. We have tried to do this above when asking you to think about groups with which you are familiar and how they work before going on to the 'theory' about the characteristics of a group. Another way of achieving this is to use analogies. We do this naturally in normal conversation to make ourselves more easily understood or to avoid more complicated explanations:

'You could cut the atmosphere with a knife.'

'My memory is getting more like a sieve every day.'

'Getting an answer from him was like drawing teeth.'

'She was singing like a bird.'

Perhaps in the previous section you would have found the concept of an advance organiser easier to understand if we had started our explanation by discussing looking at maps or diagrams.

HELPING MEMORY

Often, learners cannot remember everything they are taught because of the sheer volume of information that is presented to them. Due to the way in which memory is structured (see Chapter 6), it can only process relatively small amounts of information at a time. It is more effective, therefore, to give a manageable amount of information initially and then use it in a short exercise to consolidate it before moving on to give further information. Petty (1997: 123) quotes research which claims that only 5 per cent of the content of a lecture is remembered but this can be increased to 90 per cent if immediate use is made of what has been learned. This concurs with Dale's Cone of Learning, a modified version of which (Francis and Gould, 2013: 90) is shown in Figure 5.1.

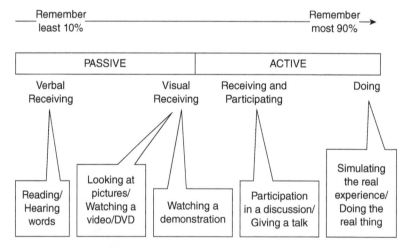

Figure 5.1   Adaptation of Dale's cone example

The visual organisation of information in groups or lists also helps the process of memory, as do mnemonics which try and impose order onto otherwise unrelated bits of information.

SMALLER GROUPS

Small group activities can take a variety of different forms. Some of the more common ones are:

BUZZ GROUPS

Small groups are set up and given a specific task to complete or an issue to consider in a fairly short time. The different groups may all work on the same task or issue, or different aspects of it, sharing their conclusions in a plenary session at the end of the activity. The name is taken from the buzz of conversation produced around the room when the activity is in full flow.

SNOWBALLS

Learners consider an issue individually and jot down their thoughts. They then form pairs and compare notes, looking for similarities and differences. The pairs then combine to form groups of four for further discussion, arriving at a conclusion which they can report back in a plenary session. The name snowball reflects the way the groups build in size, rather like a snowball rolling down a hill. As previously mentioned, this type of group activity is particularly useful when learners are still fairly new to each other, as it starts off with an individual learner talking just to one other person, having had time to think about what they say, before contributing to the larger group.

CROSSOVER GROUPS

This technique is also known as square root, as the starting point is to establish small groups containing a number of members equal to the square root of the group as a whole. A group of 16 forms four groups of four, for example, and similarly a group of 25 gives five groups of five. Each group is given a specific topic to discuss. After an allotted period of time, members of each of the original groups join together to form new groups, thus maximising the exchange of information. With a little imagination, this method can be adapted for use with different sized groups.

As has been seen earlier in this chapter, when working with large groups, planning and preparation centre around the content of the session and the best ways of putting it across. Small group activities, however, are generally set up with the intention of deriving the content of the session from learners' own thoughts and experiences. Planning therefore focuses on thinking through the process that learners will engage in to ensure that this is most effectively organised to achieve the aims and objectives of the session.

REFLECTIVE TASK 5.3

Think of an occasion when you worked successfully with others in a small group. What made this a satisfying and worthwhile activity for you?

You may have had experiences of working in a small group activity which you found to be unsatisfactory or frustrating. What were the reasons for this?

On the basis of the above experiences, what do you think teachers can do to make sure that working in small groups is an effective learning activity? How do you ensure that discussion is both lively and productive and all learners feel included in and contribute to the activity? Compare your thoughts with the strategies outlined below.

The main areas to consider in planning and managing small group activities are:

1. Setting up the activity.
2. Maintaining momentum.
3. Bringing the activity to a close.

1. SETTING UP THE ACTIVITY

(a) Choice of topic

The first thing to consider in choice of topic is its suitability for small group work. An area which is factual is more appropriate to large group work, as described above; there needs to be an element of discussion and sharing of experience or opinions for small group activities to work effectively. The chosen topic must also be sufficiently complex to sustain meaningful discussion amongst group members, but also capable of resolution within the available time. A wide-ranging topic can be split into different aspects, each of which can be allocated to different groups, contributions being shared in a plenary session at the end. This approach can also contribute towards an overall differentiation strategy, as the more challenging and less challenging aspects of the topic as a whole can be allocated to different groups depending on their experience or familiarity within the particular area.

(b) Introducing the activity

A good introduction ensures that learners have a clear idea of:

- the topic to be explored
- the purpose of the activity
- how it is to be carried out.

This can be achieved either simply by talking the issues through or giving some kind of written instructions. An example of what is expected often helps avoid potential misunderstandings and clarify exactly what is required.

Strategies which will assist in maintaining task focus during the group activity can also be introduced at this stage. Identifying a definite end product (report back, short presentation, flip chart notes, completion of handout) is helpful in this respect, as is the allocation of given roles (chair, scribe, reporter) to specific group members which helps encourage participation all round for the duration of the activity.

(c) The physical environment in which the group activity will take place

---

ACTIVITY 5.6

The following diagrams illustrate the different seating arrangements which groups might adopt during a small group activity.

Which do you think are the most and least effective and why?

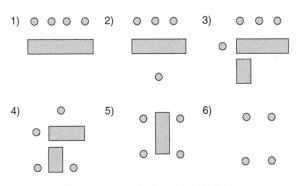

The arrangements shown in 1, 2, 3 and 4 have shortcomings for small group work as they either exclude or make it difficult for some learners to participate (1 and 3) or place one learner in a 'power or 'controlling' position (2 and 4). These, however, are the arrangements which learners often find easiest to adopt if left to organise themselves as they are most convenient, requiring the least amount of energy and movement to achieve. Arrangements 5 and 6 are much more effective, giving eye-to-eye contact with all members of the group and equal access all round. Sometimes it will require an assertive approach from the teacher to achieve these, but the ensuing group activity will be far more likely to lead to a successful outcome.

(d) The number of learners in the group

In general, larger groups provide a greater pool of knowledge and experience to draw on and consequently produce a more considered contribution. This does, however, mean that the group is likely to take longer to reach a decision and the opportunity for individual contribution to the discussion is more limited than in a smaller group. Conversely, a smaller group will arrive at a decision more quickly and is more likely to involve all of its members in some capacity, but may well arrive at a less well informed result. It is evident that any decision on group size will involve a compromise of some kind and a final decision is usually influenced by the intended purpose of the activity and more pragmatic concerns such as the length of time available for the activity. Petty (2009: 243) suggests that 'Up to six and many hands make light work; over eight and too many cooks spoil the broth'. Jacques and Salmon (2007: 25) concur, stating: 'Most theorists, researchers and practitioners agree that five to seven members is the optimum for leaderless groups.'

(e) Group composition

The kinds of factors that might be considered in arriving at a decision relating to the particular combination of learners that will work best together in a group include:

- the prime purpose of the activity – is it social or task oriented? If the former, learners can be randomly allocated to groups or numbered off, the purpose being to achieve social mixing within the group as a whole. If the latter, the nature of the task may well determine certain combinations of learners with particular experience or areas of expertise
- differentiation strategies to be employed – will learners be grouped in terms of aptitude for the task in hand or will more balanced groups be formed? If the former, more teacher time can be spent with the groups who will encounter the greater difficulty, if the latter, learners will provide support for each other
- compatibility of learners – are there some learners who are better kept apart? Some friendship groupings can be counterproductive, leading to a loss of task focus, but equally some combinations of learners will lead to personality clashes. Both instances are best avoided!

2. MAINTAINING MOMENTUM

Jacques and Salmon (2007) suggest that all groups fulfil a dual purpose which they divide into social and task dimensions. They argue that in a group situation, members derive an 'emotional satisfaction ... from being with people they like and enjoy'

(2007: 32), and that the success of a 'social' group is measured 'in terms of how enjoyable it is'. When learners form groups, they naturally tend to take the opportunity to engage in social 'chit chat'. A 'task group', however, measures its success 'in terms of how much work it achieves'. Learning groups, in common with all other groups, embody both of these characteristics, and the management of groups and group activities consists of achieving an appropriate balance between these two dimensions. Where that balance lies will depend on purpose. At the beginning of a course, small group activities may be used to encourage interaction between learners and contribute to the 'gelling' of the group as a whole. In such instances, the social dimension is the more important. Johnson and Johnson (1991: 393) remind us, however, that 'a learning group is a group whose purpose is to ensure that group members learn specific subject matter, information, knowledge, skills and procedures', and so, generally, once the group as a whole is reasonably established, management tends to focus on the task dimension. Monitoring progress is an essential part of maintaining task focus, ensuring the balance is maintained in this direction rather than towards the social dimension of the group. The purpose of monitoring initially is to ensure that all groups have understood the task to be undertaken and are making an initial start. Subsequent monitoring is more concerned with ensuring that task focus is maintained and should be carried out in an unobtrusive fashion – it is checking rather than interfering! Pre-prepared extension tasks can be allocated where necessary if groups progress through the activity at different rates.

3. BRINGING THE ACTIVITY TO A CLOSE

When to bring small group activity to a close is a matter of judgement and the monitoring process described above will help in arriving at a decision. If groups are working well and discussion is productive, we may well decide to prolong the activity beyond the time we had originally planned. If, on the other hand, discussion is flagging, we may end the task when we think it has run its course. It is now important to acknowledge the results of the work that has taken place. If this is not done, learners will begin to question the point of the activity and be less likely to want to participate in similar activities in the future.

Sharing the results of group activity can be achieved in a number of ways, as identified earlier (report back, short presentation, flip chart notes, completion of handout), but the role of the teacher at this stage is to clarify, summarise and record in some form the conclusions arrived at. When taking feedback, it is important to spread the activity around the various groups, as often if one group reports back first followed by the second and then the third, by the time the last group comes to make its contribution there is nothing left to say. The better strategy therefore is to get each group to report back on different aspects of the topic under discussion. A more student-centred alternative is offered by 'the round' (Brandes and Ginnis, 1986: 33), in which each person in the group makes a personal statement of what has been learned, although the individual freedom not to participate – 'pass' – is always an option.

INDIVIDUAL LEARNING AND DEVELOPMENT

The focus so far has been on working with learners in a variety of group situations but often, even in a group context, learning is largely an individual process. All will have sat through the same experience and so take away the same general picture and conclusions, but what each individual learner takes away from the session will not be identical to the others, as it will depend on who they are and their previous knowledge and experience. Some will find certain aspects of the topic more interesting than others, some will find parts more difficult or easier, and different levels of motivation and attention will also be on display. So, arguably, all learning is individual, even in a group context. Sometimes because of the diversity within the sector, the levels of individuality are such that teaching becomes more effective, and the learning and development of individual learners can be more easily facilitated if conducted on a one-to-one basis.

Examples of this would include:

- one-to-one contact in a workshop situation when practising or acquiring a skill
- tutorial sessions
- work-based learning visits
- the teaching of small groups with diverse needs such as might be found in a Skills for Life or Life Skills environment
- supporting individual projects or research-based learning
- supporting learners on distance learning programmes.

What is common to all of these circumstances is that:

- learners can work at their own pace
- individual issues or barriers to learning are addressed
- learners can influence the direction their learning will take.

REFLECTIVE TASK 5.4

Make a list of the instances where you have one-to-one contact with your tutor on your diploma course. What form did this contact take? Was it fruitful? If so, identify the reasons why this was the case. In what ways has this contact helped you to develop as a teacher.

You have probably found that informal one-to-one contact during large or small group sessions has helped clarify or extend your understanding of the topic under discussion.

Individual tutorials may have motivated you to keep on top of the workload and addressed barriers to you achieving this. Discussions of individual progress will have helped you identify your strengths and how to build on these. Your tutorials may also have helped you in identifying your own individual needs and ways of meeting these through the course. Observation feedback will have considered strengths and limitations in teaching performance, and identified areas for development and how to achieve this. Discussion of your practice may have helped to clarify aspects of theory about which you were unsure.

Sometimes an individual approach is used with a specific aim in mind, such as in coaching where the coach reviews existing skills and devises strategies to refine and improve them. Mentoring involves general development through sharing and learning from the experiences of a more experienced colleague as is the case with your 'subject mentor'.

In general, however, teaching on a one-to-one basis occurs in a variety of guises and settings, encouraging the learning process to be viewed from the perspective of the learner, addressing issues important to them and thus improving the effectiveness of their learning. The way in which this is achieved will depend largely on the opportunities afforded by the context in which learning is taking place but, within all of these approaches, some form of recording decisions arrived at and tracking progress made are essential to the process.

INDIVIDUAL LEARNING PLAN (ILP)

An Individual Learning Plan (ILP) is a document completed and maintained by learners with the intention of helping them to understand the bigger picture of their total learning experience whilst being on a course. It should help learners recognise their progress, identify what needs to be done to further develop their knowledge and skills, and identify any particular individual needs which may require additional support.

LSIS (2009: 3) sees the functions of the ILP as:

- providing a route for learners to become more involved in their learning experience
- helping learners take control of their learning
- keeping learners motivated in working towards their goals
- lying at the heart of assessment, learning, support and achievement.

The format used to record this process will vary from institution to institution, but Keeley-Browne (2007: 162) maintains that all should contain:

- a student record (full time/part time)
- key skills planning and tracking

- initial assessments and study support planning
- pro-formas for student self-assessment and one-to-one tutorial interviews
- a tutor log to record discussions and reviews against the set targets.

Some courses within the sector are classified as non-accredited provision, meaning that they do not lead to formal qualifications. Formal assessment is often regarded as inappropriate on such courses. There is, however, a need to evidence progress and development and this is an important component of the course quality assurance procedures. In 2002, the National Institute of Adult Continuing Education (NIACE) and the then Learning and Skills Development Agency (LSDA) developed a process known as the Recognition and Recording of Progress and Achievement (RARPA) in response to this need. The ILP is often used as a device to fulfil the requirements of the RARPA process.

The ILP, then, provides a record of the individual educational journey, identifying its beginning and end points. It shows how development has occurred between these points, along with the support provided in achieving this, whilst affording learners some say in the direction their learning takes. In order for an ILP to achieve its purpose, however, it needs to be regarded positively by both teachers and learners. This depends on whether each party fully understands the purpose and usefulness of the process of completing the ILP and whether sufficient time is made available to carry out this activity in a meaningful way, but, where the process is valued, the ILP can be a useful tool in promoting learner autonomy and individual development.

LEARNING CONTRACTS

Once the basic concepts or skills within a course have been mastered, individual project or research-based approaches, allowing for application of knowledge and skills in practical contexts, are often introduced. A learning contract is a useful device for planning and tracking such activities. A learning contract is an agreement drawn up between a teacher and a learner specifying an episode of learning that is to take place. Like any other contract, it is binding – in this case, on the learner to complete the course of learning. Learning contracts are frequently used in Adult and Community Education (ACE) and were popularised by Malcolm Knowles et al. (1998), who distinguished between learning for personal development and learning for improved competence which may have to meet the requirements of outside agencies, and argued that 'learning contracts provide a means for negotiating a reconciliation between these external needs and expectation and the learner's internal needs and interests' (1998: 211).

Learning contracts can increase motivation as they try to match the learning to be undertaken to individual needs, thereby increasing its relevance. The active role of the learner in devising the contract further enhances motivation and helps to

develop the skills of independent learning, particularly those relating to time management, planning and decision making. The devising of a learning contract can be
approached in a number of different ways but according to Boak (1998: 5) should
be characterised by 'a degree of choice for the learner, a learning plan and (usually)
an agreement between the learner and someone who will help them – a tutor,
trainer, coach or mentor'.

An example of a format is shown in Figure 5.2.

Learning Contract
Course: ....
Name: ....
1. What are you going to learn? (State learning objectives using SMART terminology)
2. How will you achieve this? (List the strategies you will employ)
3. What will you need? (Identify any resources you think you will need)
4. How will you know that you have been successful in your learning? (Describe how you will evidence that learning has taken place)
5. By what date will you have completed this contract? (Identify a realistic target date for completion)
Signed .... (Learner)   Date: ....
Signed .... (Tutor)   Date: ....

Figure 5.2   Example of a learning contract format

The format is reasonably self-explanatory but the success of a learning contract relies
on more than just completion of the document. It is the process behind and beyond
this that determines whether or not the learning contract will achieve its purpose.
Boak (1998) suggests this process consists of a number of distinct stages:

1. Preparation of learners

Ideally, it is the learner rather than the teacher who will make the bigger contribution
to setting up the contract and also bear the ultimate responsibility for doing the work

required to ensure successful completion. This will involve a considerable investment in terms of time and effort and so learners need to be confident that results will justify the investment. Other than practical matters such as organising a suitable time and environment in which to meet and preparing a suitable contract format, the teacher's initial contribution lies in preparing the learner for the task in hand. Boak refers to this as 'priming' which consists of:

- explaining the purpose of a learning contract and the form it takes
- establishing relevance and building confidence in using the approach and its ability to reach a useful and practical outcome
- clarifying exactly what the learner is expected to do.

2. Agreement on the content of the learning contract

A learning contract is intended to fulfil individual needs, and so the first task is to clarify exactly what these are and to express them in a clear and unambiguous (SMART) manner. The remaining decisions should flow naturally on from this stage and so it is worth spending some time on getting it right. Having established the desired outcomes, the criteria for successful completion need to be agreed. The exact nature and level of formality of these criteria will depend on the purpose of the contract – if it is being used in part fulfilment of the requirements of a qualification, the criteria will need to be more robust than if the concern is personal development. Most importantly, this stage should produce a contract which is not only relevant and useful but is also realistic and achievable within the constraints of the available time and resources.

3. Monitoring progress and providing support

Support can take a number of forms such as providing a sounding board for ideas, guidance on sources of information, reassurance on progress to date or the maintenance of motivation levels. It can be provided from a distance by telephone or email but an agreed time and place to meet for actual face-to-face contact is the approach that most learners generally welcome. Sometimes, particularly in the early stages, this can take place as a group meeting with other learners who are also engaged in contract learning. The feelings of mutual support and camaraderie that can be generated by such meetings can have a very positive effect on motivation and morale. Generally, however, as work on the contract progresses, a more individual approach will be preferred. An agreed target or action plan should be negotiated at the conclusion of each meeting, in preparation for the next.

4. Evaluation of results

Although formative mutual evaluation will be a natural part of the monitoring process, some form of summative evaluation is also required. If the learning contract is to be used to count towards a qualification, it needs to be checked against the requirements of the qualification, even though it may be a complete piece of work in its own right. A slightly different approach can be adopted if the learning contract serves a personal development function, but here also there are questions to be answered. Has the contract reached completion? Has it served its purpose? What has been learned both from the outcome and process of the contract? Where does it lead next?

COMBINING THE TWO APPROACHES

It can be seen that working in a one-to-one setting is a valuable activity as it allows individual needs to be addressed, resulting in increased motivation and more effective and relevant learning. It needs to be an organised process, however, with some element of formal recording which shows evidence of:

- identification of individual needs
- choice of appropriate strategies to address these
- an action plan with appropriate parameters
- periodic review of progress
- evidence of successful achievement
- directions for further development.

It is not just the mechanics which are important, however; the process itself and the way in which it is managed are crucial to the success of any one-to-one approach in ensuring individual progress and development. The relationship established between teachers and learners is significant in making this work, with teachers and learners operating in a fairly relaxed and informal atmosphere. The role that we play becomes much more one of facilitator, and the section on humanism in Chapter 6 provides detail on the nature of the qualities of a 'good' facilitator and the elements of the facilitative process. One-to-one teaching is not always conducted in such a deliberate fashion, however, and in most of the teaching we do, group and individual approaches complement each other. Most sessions have some kind of practical or small group elements built into them which provide opportunities for interacting with learners on a one-to-one basis on a more informal footing, and we need to make the most of these opportunities as they arise. Some strategies span both group and individual approaches to learning and we now turn to look at one such strategy, question and answer, in more depth.

SOME SPECIFIC STRATEGIES USED IN TEACHING

QUESTION AND ANSWER

ACTIVITY 5.7

Think of occasions when you have asked questions of friends, colleagues or parents in conversation. What was your purpose in asking those questions? What did you hope to achieve or find out?

We use questions a lot in normal everyday conversation for a variety of different purposes. Perhaps we wish to know if we have been understood, maybe we are looking for a particular piece of information, or possibly we wish to find out the reasons behind someone's actions. Similarly, questioning is used in teaching to fulfil a variety of purposes which include:

- checking that learners have understood what we have been saying to them
- finding out what learners already know in relation to the topic we are to teach
- promoting an inclusive approach by encouraging participation and contribution from all members of the group
- motivating learners by giving them the opportunity to demonstrate their knowledge in front of others
- maintaining attention
- building knowledge in a step-by-step manner.

Our reasons for using questioning will influence the type of questions we ask and the way in which we ask them, but generally questioning skills can be thought of as falling into two parts.

1. Asking questions.
2. Dealing with the responses.

Asking questions

The types of question we ask generally fall into two different categories – closed and open – each being used to achieve a different purpose. *Closed questions* are asked when we are seeking a specific answer. This would be the case if we were testing for recall, wishing to focus attention on a specific area, or using questioning to build up knowledge in a step-by-step fashion. Closed questions therefore have to be phrased in a sufficiently narrow fashion to give the learner some indication of the required response (see Figure 5.3). Lack of response may not be due to insufficient knowledge but uncertainty as to what is being looked for, if questions are phrased in an overly general or ambiguous manner. Generally, the best way to devise a closed question is to first consider the answer you are seeking and then formulate a question which will elicit it. There is, however, a fine line between making a question sufficiently specific to indicate the response required and so narrow that the answer is obvious and therefore lacking in challenge.

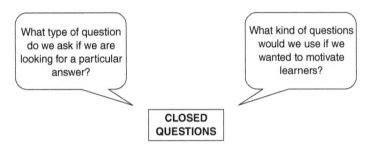

Figure 5.3   Closed questions

On other occasions, we may want to find out what the learner thinks, what their views and perceptions are, or we may wish them to come up with a variety of ideas around a specific topic or consider a specific issue. We may wish to initiate discussion, debate or divergent thinking. Rather than guide learners towards a predetermined answer or indeed influence their answer at all, we want them to think creatively and express themselves freely. In this case, *open questions* are much more appropriate and we are likely to be posing questions which encourage learners to think more broadly: How? Why? Where? When?

Whichever type of question we use, it should:

- be reasonably short; effort can be put into arriving at an answer rather than trying to remember the question
- contain only one idea; effort can be put into arriving at an answer rather than trying to work out which part needs answering
- use language with which the learner is familiar; effort can then be put into arriving at an answer rather than trying to decipher the question.

Another consideration is whether to direct questions towards the group as a whole or whether to nominate individual learners to answer. General questioning of the group is non-threatening and allows the momentum of the session to be maintained but it is often the same individuals who offer an answer whilst others are content to let them do the work. The biggest disadvantage of a general approach to questioning, however, is that we tend to make assumptions on behalf of the group as a whole, based on the answers of individual members. Although we can make some judgement on the ability of everyone to provide the answer to a question by scanning the room and looking for eye contact or other non-verbal indications, we can only be certain of the understanding displayed by the one (often the same) person who provides the answer. Directed or 'nominated' questioning is therefore often preferred as questions can be distributed evenly around the group as a whole, ensuring everyone in the group provides an answer at some point in the session, giving a better indication of the collective understanding of the group.

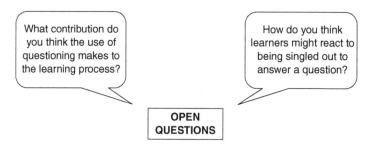

Figure 5.4   Open questions

The purpose of using questioning can often be more effectively realised by the use of a directed approach. In encouraging inclusion or motivation, for instance, learners are asked specific questions that are within their ability to respond to them but still constitute a challenge. More able and confident learners can be asked more difficult or abstract questions, whilst less able or less confident learners can be given less complex questions or questions that require them to recount an experience or are of a descriptive rather than analytical nature. One way of putting this into practice is to use the 'pose, pause, pounce and praise' approach in which the following sequence is followed:

1.   One of the limitations of directed questioning is that as soon as the name of the chosen recipient of the question is mentioned, the remaining members of the group relax and may 'switch off'. We therefore initially *pose* the question to the group as a whole.
2.   A *pause* then ensues to allow consideration of the question and thinking time relating to the answer. We would like questioning to be a helpful, positive experience for learners, as if they find it a relatively stress-free experience and see the

benefits, they are more likely to contribute and learn. During the pause, we scan the group, deciding who the question is best directed at.

3. We then name the person we wish to answer the question (*pounce*), acknowledging the answer and giving *praise* where appropriate. It is often helpful to repeat the answer to the others as they may not have heard it. Repeating the answer also gives an opportunity for 'tweaking' if it was not exactly what we were hoping for.

Dealing with the responses

In order to deal with the response to a question, we have to listen to it properly in the first place. This is an obvious statement but sometimes we are distracted and engage in what Brown and Wragg (1993) call 'skim listening'. We might be pre-occupied with what is happening in the group, thinking about our next question or even, in the interests of time management, wondering how long this answer is going to take, and so don't give full attention to what is actually being said. A more careful approach to listening needs to be adopted if we are to deal appropriately with the responses we receive. Responses fall broadly into four categories, each of which needs a slightly different treatment:

*   the correct answer
*   the partially correct answer
*   the wrong answer
*   no answer.

The correct answer

If we have phrased the question well and directed it towards an appropriate member of the group, this is the likeliest outcome. This is a situation we would like to encourage so we give positive acknowledgement of the answer, praising where appropriate and possibly repeating the answer for the benefit of the group as a whole.

> Well done X, that was a good answer. What X said was...

The partially correct answer

To maintain our positive approach to questioning, we would first acknowledge the part of the answer which is correct before attending to the incorrect part. It is important to correct any misconceptions, and, having identified the incorrect part of the response, it can be opened out to the rest of the group. Usually, this will resolve the issue but if no one else can supply the correct answer, we know that there is a problem that possibly needs to be dealt with before continuing with further questioning.

> Thank you, I liked the first part of your answer which was ... but I'm not sure about the second part. What do the rest of you think?

The wrong answer

The natural assumption following a wrong answer is that it is a lack of knowledge or understanding that is at the root of the problem. Brown and Wragg (1993: 18), however, point out that 'questions are only as good as the answers they get', and so we should not dismiss the possibility that it was poor questioning technique that led to a lack of understanding or misinterpretation of the question.

Our first response, therefore, might be to rethink the question and ask again or ask shorter closed questions to lead the learner towards the correct answer. Alternatively, the question could be redirected. We want to encourage learners to continue to respond positively to questioning, so the original answer needs to be treated in a non-critical manner which nonetheless makes it clear that it was incorrect. To maintain learner confidence, the original individual could be asked another question fairly soon afterwards that we are sure they can answer.

> I can see why you say that, but...
>
> That's a good answer but it doesn't really address the question.

No answer

The first step is to redirect the question to the group as a whole. It is possible that the first person you asked simply didn't know the answer and someone else can supply it. If this fails to produce a response, however, it may be that the question asked was too open so rephrasing the question or breaking it down into smaller, simpler components can be tried next. A continuing lack of response suggests that perhaps some re-teaching is called for!

> Okay, let's reconsider that question. What do you think is...?

DISCUSSION

Not everything that we teach is black and white in nature – sometimes there are shades of grey that need to be explored and discussion is an activity best suited to this purpose. Discussion involves the sharing of knowledge and the debating of ideas and opinions in order to arrive at some form of conclusion and can take place in either a large group or small group context. This does mean that learners need to have some background knowledge and experience of the discussion topic but it can be complemented by the use of 'trigger' materials such as a short video clip, case study or newspaper article to contextualise the discussion and provide an initial focus. Trigger materials can also minimise the dangers of 'pooling ignorance' – voicing assumptions as facts, making inappropriate comments or lines of argument or maybe reinforcing undesirable stereotypes. In such cases, we would tend to manage and guide discussion to some extent rather than allowing it to be free-ranging.

REFLECTIVE TASK 5.5

Think back to discussions in which you have participated. Some will have been productive, some not. Why was this the case? What strategies were, or could have been, used to make the discussion an effective learning activity? What does this tell you about the way in which you manage discussion activities involving your own learners?

In considering those less productive discussions in which you have participated, you may have identified reasons relating to the participants, such as:

- some learners do not find it easy to participate in discussion and 'opt out' whereas others tend to dominate
- some do not take the discussion seriously or miss the point altogether
- some deviate from the topic and introduce 'personal agendas'
- some don't like discussion as an activity and prefer more direct and focused approaches.

On the other hand, it may have been about more practical considerations such as the unsuitability of the physical environment (it is difficult to discuss if you cannot make eye contact with everyone else in the group) or that the discussion just seemed to end or peter out without reaching any kind of conclusion. The management of discussion tries to address these kinds of issues. The levels of intervention that are necessary will depend on the nature of the group and how well the activity is progressing, but the following general principles may help to ensure that the discussions you run fall into the 'productive' category.

Discussion is most effective when:

- it has a clear agreed purpose and a subject which lends itself to some form of debate:

    o   Choose a topic which is relevant, well defined and allows scope for discussion.
    o   Ensure everyone is aware of the purpose of the discussion.

- everyone feels involved and their contributions matter:

    o   Set ground rules for the discussion.
    o   Use verbal or non-verbal cues to encourage active listening and discourage over-talking, interruptions and competitiveness.
    o   Use questions to direct and redirect, encouraging involvement from all.
    o   Encourage continuing participation by acknowledging contributions.
    o   Avoid expressing your own views; try to act as a 'neutral chairperson'.

- it remains focused:

    o   Control the pace of discussion, allowing time for response and reflection.
    o   If necessary, break up the discussion into smaller segments.
    o   Keep discussion focused and limit digression.

- some definite conclusions are drawn:

    o   Summarise throughout the discussion at appropriate points.
    o   Help individuals or groups to identify what has been learned and how it might be used in the future.

STRATEGIES AND SUBJECT SPECIALISM

Different subject specialisms seem to lend themselves more readily than others to particular approaches and are traditionally taught in a certain way. This is largely dependent on the type of objective they are based around and there is some agreement at a basic level of fit between objectives and the strategies used to achieve them.

Arguably, however, all specialisms are similar in that each involves the achievement of a mix of all three types of objective, the nature of the specialism determining the degree of emphasis placed on each. All specialisms involve a concern with learners acquiring appropriate attitudes. These may be attitudes relating to safety, accuracy, standards, other learners, confidence in self, and so on. In an academic subject like maths, a knowledge of the underlying theory is of limited use if learners do not also possess the skills required to apply it. In specialisms which are more vocational or practical in nature, the required skills cannot be effectively mastered without an understanding of the appropriate underpinning knowledge. The strategies considered so far in this chapter are most applicable in addressing knowledge and attitude objectives, so the next section considers the teaching of practical skills.

Type of objective	Most appropriate strategies
Knowledge/cognitive	lecture, seminar, games, project, questioning
Skill/psycho-motor	demonstration, practical exercise, simulation
Attitude/affective	discussion, role play, tutorial

Figure 5.5   Objectives and teaching strategies

TEACHING PRACTICAL SKILLS

If you teach in a military environment, you will be familiar with the mnemonic EDIP. This spells out the stages in teaching a skill:

Explain

Demonstrate

Imitate

Practise

The explanation stage sets the scene, focusing on when and how the skill is used and any significant features such as safety issues. The next stage normally involves a demonstration of the complete skill, followed by a slow, step-by-step demonstration accompanied by commentary. During the imitation stage, learners repeat the actions of the skill, following further demonstration of each step. Practice builds confidence and gives the opportunity to develop speed and accuracy in performance. This is often followed by a consolidation stage, which involves a summary and possibly some form of testing of competence in performing the skill.

If you teach in a different environment, you will still recognise elements of the above approach as fairly customary in the teaching of skills. You will remember from Chapter 2 that the name given to objectives within the skills domain is 'psycho-motor'. This suggests that there are two parts to a skill:

1. A knowledge part – knowing what has to be done and in what order (psycho).
2. A performance part – being able to actually carry out the appropriate actions which make up the skill in an efficient manner (motor).

Demonstration

The knowledge part of the skill is imparted through demonstration. In order to conduct a demonstration, you must be skilled yourself and so will have reached a stage at which you perform the skill automatically. Whilst this is good for credibility, it can cause problems in demonstration as you may well be performing actions that you are not aware of and this can lead to the making of assumptions on behalf of learners. To overcome this, a skills analysis is conducted prior to conducting the demonstration. This involves breaking down the overall skill into a series of sub-skills. Each sub-skill is then broken down further until a degree of detail appropriate to the level of knowledge and experience of prospective learners is reached.

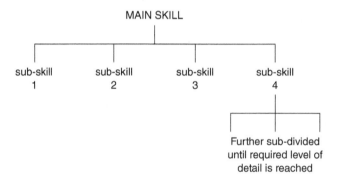

Figure 5.6   Skills analysis

This procedure heightens awareness of all the steps involved in the skill, ensuring they are highlighted in the demonstration and accompanying commentary. Petty (2009) describes demonstration as 'showing how' through example. This involves not only 'showing how' in the sense of 'what is done' but also in the manner of 'how it is done'. The attitudes we present during demonstration are as equally on display as the actions we perform. These might include attitudes toward safety, standard of work, care of equipment, hygiene, models/clients and assistants/technicians. We would want to present a professional image in all of these areas, particularly as it is difficult to encourage these traits in learners and point out their absence if we do not provide an appropriate role model of them ourselves.

In terms of technique, the secret of good demonstration is the same as for most activities – good preparation and planning. This will involve preparation of:

- learners – are they aware of the purpose of the demonstration and any specific points on which to focus?
- yourself – have you conducted a skills analysis, breaking the skill down into all of its component parts and actions? Are your own skills a little 'rusty' or out of date? If so, have you rehearsed and practised them sufficiently to provide an effective

role model? Have you thought about the commentary you will give to accompany the demonstration? Do learners possess similar skills and have you considered how these might help or hinder their learning of this skill? Will you need to take account of a mix of right-handed and left-handed learners? Have you decided what proportion of the skill is best demonstrated at one time and what your overall strategy will be?

- the environment – how can learners be best positioned so all will be able to see and hear? Is the demonstration best observed from behind or from the front? Is it best to demonstrate to the whole group or best to split them up into smaller groups and demonstrate to each group in turn? If the latter, how will you keep the non-demonstration group usefully occupied?

- materials and equipment – do you have sufficient quantities of the necessary materials? Is all of the equipment to be used in good working order? Do you need technician support and, if so, have you made sure a technician will be available when required?

The actual demonstration can be organised in a number of ways but the sequence of 'whole to parts to whole' is most frequently used:

1. The complete skill is first demonstrated at normal speed. As well as focusing attention, this gives learners a picture of the skill as a whole and reminds them, at a later stage, how the different parts of the skill fit together. This is not dissimilar in purpose to Ausubel's (1960) advance organiser which was referred to earlier. Some reassurance may be necessary at this stage, however, as the perfect demonstration can prove intimidating to inexperienced learners.

2. The skill is now broken down into a number of smaller parts or chunks (see skills analysis) and each is demonstrated, with commentary, at a pace which allows learners to absorb what is happening. Practice may take place between each of these shorter demonstrations or the practice element may be left until the completion of the whole demonstration procedure, depending on the complexity of the skill and the previous experience and knowledge of the learners.

3. Finally, the skill is demonstrated again in its entirety to consolidate the required learning, attention being drawn to the key learning points. At all stages, time for learner questions is provided.

Although demonstration is considered to be primarily visual, the accompanying commentary is just as important. The commentary will be informed by the skills analysis, which will have raised awareness of the detail involved in the performance of the skill. It is used to draw attention to these points and might also give the reasons behind them, thus addressing the 'why' as well as the 'how' of the skill. Receiving and responding to feedback through the senses is an important aspect of the performance of any skill and this is another area of the commentary we will seek to attend to.

Sight	'if you watch for...'; 'at this stage you will probably see...'
Hearing	'if you hear ... you will know that...'; 'you should listen carefully to...'
Touch	'it should be smooth to the touch at this stage...'; 'if it feels brittle, you will know that...'
Taste	'normally produces a taste like...'; 'if it tastes of ... you will know that'
Smell	'it should now smell like...'; 'note this particular smell. It means that...'

Although in some skills the role of a particular sense is greater or lesser (e.g. cooking: taste and smell; pottery: touch; music: hearing and touch), all skills have some kind of sensory input and drawing learners' attention to this gives a greater feel for and understanding of the skill in question.

REFLECTIVE TASK 5.6

So far, demonstration seems to be a fairly passive approach as far as learners are concerned. How can learning from demonstration be made a more active process? List as many ways as you can. Use this list as a checklist against which to analyse your own approach to demonstration.

The simplest approach to making demonstration a more participative and 'active learning' experience is through the use of questioning. Questions can ask learners to *explain* – 'how can this be done?'; *predict* – 'what do you think comes next?'; *analyse* – 'why do you think I did that at this point?'; or *summarise* – 'what were the first three things I did in this demonstration?' Other possibilities for a more active approach to demonstration include:

- Learners take it in turns to demonstrate part of the skill and receive feedback from their peers.
- An incorrect demonstration is carried out and learners are asked to identify the faults (this would only be used when we were sure learners were sufficiently sure of the procedure that an incorrect demonstration would not confuse them).
- A silent demonstration is performed and learners have to provide the commentary.
- Learners prepare a set of instructions for the skill. Other learners use these to demonstrate the skill, receiving feedback from the group as a whole.

The effectiveness of the demonstration can also be enhanced by the use of a number of resources. A working model or poster to highlight important points can support the demonstration, particularly if it is 'larger than life'. A good step-by-step handout, laminated to preserve it in a practical environment, can also prove an invaluable aid and can be used in conjunction with the demonstration, helping to establish the sequence of events firmly in learners' minds or to support peer-assessment activities such as those suggested above. In some subjects (e.g. dance, beauty therapy), mirrors can be used, both alongside the demonstration and in the feedback process, although care needs to be taken to avoid potential confusion between left and right sides.

Practice

After the demonstration, learners know what is involved in the skill and what has to be done. The performance element of the skill can now be acquired through practice, accompanied by appropriate feedback. If the skill is relatively straightforward and not overly complex, 'whole practice' is used where the skill is practised in its entirety. More complex skills can be broken down into parts or sub-routines which are then practised separately until mastered before putting them together again in the complete skill. The parts can be recombined either after each has been successfully mastered separately or in a more progressive manner where the first two parts of the skill are learned and then practised together. The third part is then practised and added to the first two before moving on to the fourth. This sequence continues until the whole skill is mastered. As with the demonstration, this part of the skills session will run more effectively if carefully planned and prepared. The questions to ask now are:

(a) of learners – are they equipped with and wearing any personal protective equipment (PPE) that is required for this particular skill? Are they fully aware of the various health and safety rules and requirements? Do they recognise that learning a skill may take time and progress may at times be slow? Are they aware of what is commercially viable?

(b) of yourself – have you thought through your differentiation strategies? Have you identified the learners who are more and less likely to learn the new skill quickly, the more and less enthusiastic learners, the more and less disciplined learners? Have you decided on the best combinations of learners if they have to share equipment – possible buddying strategies? Do you have extension tasks in mind for those who acquire the skill easily and quickly? Have you considered ways in which you might involve learners in the demonstration? Do you need to record progress and, if so, how will you do this?

(c) of the environment – does everyone have sufficient working space and light? How will you allocate learners to spaces? Are learners able to move safely about the room? If not, how will you deal with this? Does the staff/learner ratio fall within safety guidelines?

(d) of materials and equipment – does the equipment match exactly that used in the demonstration? Are there sufficient materials and equipment of a suitable quality to meet the needs of the session?

Chapter 2 and, later, Chapter 7 remind us of the need to start any teaching session in a calm, organised and orderly manner, as this sets the tone for what is to follow – this is particularly important in a practical session as over-excited learners or inappropriate behaviour can have serious consequences. Learners will be keen to 'get stuck in' but the start of the session should consist of gathering the group together in a convenient spot and addressing them as a whole. Clothing and equipment can be checked, and health and safety considerations reinforced, along with ground rules. More practical matters can then be covered before learners start work; matters such as time limits and procedures for the session – working singly or in pairs, expectations of progress, use of equipment and even a reminder to read the manufacturer's instructions and follow these for any products used in performing the skill. This collective beginning also reminds learners that although they may well spend the majority of the session working individually or possibly in pairs or small groups, they are still part of the larger group.

Once everyone understands what is required, is appropriately equipped and has made a start, the teaching role becomes one of monitoring progress and giving feedback.

ACTIVITY 5.8

What do you consider to be the particular issues that need to be addressed as part of the monitoring and feedback process?

Monitoring and feedback need to be responsive to individual needs and progress, and the emphasis shifts as learners gradually acquire the skill. Issues addressed will include:

Correct practice

Ralph Nader is attributed with the saying 'Your best teacher is your last mistake'. Mistakes only tell us what 'not to do', however, and can have severe consequences which might lead us to rephrase Nader's original statement as 'your best teacher is someone else's mistake'! Whilst mistakes in learning a skill rarely have such momentous consequences as those we might make in life, they are best avoided at this stage of the learning process. Mistakes can lead to incorrect technique which can easily become habitual and therefore difficult to eradicate if not caught early, making acquiring the correct technique even more difficult to master. Initially then, monitoring involves ensuring that everyone is using the correct technique to carry out the skill and intervening when learners are having difficulty or

are using incorrect methods. This may involve us in using 'on the spot' mini demonstrations, questioning or using the performance of other learners to guide
individuals back on to the correct track.

Standards

Once the basic skill has been mastered, feedback will relate more to the level of performance required. As well as adopting a professional rather than 'good enough'
attitude to their work, learners also need to know how their performance relates to
the real working environment and the standards expected within the industry they are
to enter. This need not involve reference to technical specifications at this stage
(although these need to be constantly reinforced where they are part of a legal
requirement) but can be addressed through a simple invitation to the learner to consider 'If you were the customer...'.

Motivation

Whilst learners are enthusiastic to start off with, progress can slow down as a 'skills
plateau' is reached where consolidation rather than progress takes place. Rates of
progress will vary from learner to learner. Some will acquire the skill relatively quickly
and easily so the session no longer holds much challenge for them, and some will
progress more slowly and may begin to lose heart. These situations need to be managed to maintain motivation levels. Often, learners need to be reminded of their
achievements as they tend to focus in the 'here and now' on any difficulties they are
encountering. A few motivational words can help here: 'Although you are finding this
difficult at the moment, yesterday you couldn't ... today you can...'; 'It may be taking
a little time, but look how much more accurate/fluent/quick you are becoming'.
Different rates of progress can be managed through differentiation strategies: extension tasks (different and more complex contexts within which to practise the skill,
introducing problem-solving activities, using advanced learners to explain or give
feedback to others) for those who are making good progress and short-term targets
and goals for those whose progress is more limited.

If a learner is really struggling, there is a temptation to offer assistance to a level
where it is debatable as to who is performing the skill. Whilst this may provide short-
term relief in terms of maintaining motivation and getting them over the immediate
problem, it is unhelpful in the long term. Whilst we wish to be supportive towards
our learners and see them succeed, how far should we go in this direction? Perhaps
this is an ideal moment to revisit the notion of boundaries raised in Chapter 1. Ideally,
we would find other ways around the problem, which allow the learner to overcome
the particular obstacle that is impeding progress by themselves and so still maintain
control over their own learning.

'Personalising' the skill

Once the skill has been mastered to a good standard, learners can begin to develop their own style. Performance is adapted to make the most of individual strengths and make the skill more economical in terms of demands put on energy levels and the body as a whole. We can use the feedback process to discuss and encourage such modifications.

Encouraging learner independence

The ultimate goal in giving feedback is to enable the learner to perform the skill on their own, independent of any assistance or supervision. The way in which we give feedback has an influence on learners developing this ability. When we give spoken feedback, we have two options – we can tell:

'That's good so far although you might have … Just try that and when you have finished, let me know and I'll come back and check it for you.'

Or we can ask:

'That's interesting – why did you do it that way? Do you think it's the best way? Can you think of a different approach? What do you think you need to do next?'

Telling tends to lead to reliance on the teacher, whereas asking makes learners think about what they have been doing and helps develop their skills of self-assessment and self-evaluation, enabling them, eventually, to provide their own feedback. If learners are lacking in confidence, however, they can find a questioning approach to be intimidating so a more direct approach to feedback may be appropriate at this stage in their learning. Which approach is adopted is therefore a matter of professional judgement and quite often a mixed approach – some telling, some asking – is adopted, with the balance between the two tipped in the direction appropriate to the particular learner.

Time is another influencing factor as telling is generally a more straightforward and quicker approach than questioning, but ultimately the underlying aim is to encourage learners to become more autonomous in their learning and more confident when transferring it to a work environment.

DIFFERENTIATION STRATEGIES

Chapter 1 established the diverse nature of learners within the sector and how this diversity is reflected in the makeup of the groups that we teach. We need to consider, therefore, how to use each of the teaching strategies discussed in this chapter in a differentiated manner in order to create an inclusive learning environment. Some of the differentiation strategies we might employ have already been mentioned in passing but what follows is a more comprehensive list.

WHOLE GROUP

- Use a variety of teaching strategies and resources to cater for the various preferred learning styles within the group.
- Come up with differentiated objectives to allow learners to work towards an appropriate level of learning within the same topic (an excellent account of how this can be achieved practically is given in Ginnis, 2002: 234).
- Provide graduated worksheets, from easy to hard, with learners working through these as far as they are able.
- Make additional resource packs available for those who wish to delve deeper into a subject.
- Ask learners to answer questions appropriate to their level of previous knowledge and experience by using a nominated questioning technique.
- Work with open rather than closed tasks, allowing learners to 'self-differentiate'; this should be accompanied by higher teacher expectations of stronger learners.
- Make best use of learning support assistants and plan how to make the most effective use of their time.

SMALL GROUPS

- Consider group composition – mixed groups allow for 'buddying' and peer support; ability groups can result in some self-sufficient groupings, giving more teacher time to those that need it.
- Prepare extension tasks for groups who finish the original task quickly and easily; an extension task can be as simple as a short question that should ensure learners are now being asked to operate one level higher on Bloom's Taxonomy.
- If using ability groupings, split the overall task into smaller tasks of differing complexity and allocate accordingly.
- Use peer assessment and peer tutoring strategies.

INDIVIDUAL

- Set individual targets; decide on these through a process of negotiation with the learner or, better still, encourage learners to set their own goals and targets.
- Encourage self-assessment and evaluation, providing a structure within which to do this.

FUNCTIONAL SKILLS AND TEACHING STRATEGIES

Chapter 1 alerted us to the functional skills needs of our learners and the responsibility of teachers within the sector to respond to these where they form a barrier to learning. Improvement in functional skills is best achieved through practice in their use, but there is reluctance on the part of learners to do this when they cannot see the point in it. Embedding functional skills within the subject provides a relevant context in which to use these skills, as well as stressing their importance within the particular subject. We need to bear in mind, however, the quote from a contributor to the NRDC report on embedding functional skills and vocational programmes (Casey et al., 2007): 'You wouldn't expect a maths teacher to teach plastering... so why on earth do you expect a plasterer to teach maths?'

We do not have the necessary expertise and skills to be teachers of functional skills – Chapter 1 also introduced the notion of professional boundaries; knowing the limits of our expertise and when to involve others with the required specialist knowledge – but we are expected to look for and make the most of any naturally occurring opportunities within our teaching strategies that allow learners to address their functional skills needs through practice.

SUMMARY OF KEY POINTS

In this chapter, we have looked at those teaching strategies which provide the main form of communication between ourselves and our learners. We have explored a number of different general and specific teaching strategies, relating these both to the communication process and to the different combinations of learners we encounter. The detail of implementing these strategies has been examined with the intention of encouraging reflection on and further development of practice.

The key points in this chapter are:

- Communication can take a number of forms: one-way, two-way, verbal and non-verbal. Factors which cause a breakdown in communication can be internal to the learner or stem from the external learning environment.

- Much of the teaching we do concerns learners working in groups. Strategies such as icebreakers assist the group in negotiating its stages of development, allowing learners to gain maximum benefit from membership.
- Large groups are normally worked with when delivering sizeable amounts of information. Information can be made more accessible to learners by careful management of the processes of motivation, attention, understanding and memory.
- Giving prior consideration to size, composition and the working environment increases the effectiveness of small group activities. Monitoring is required to achieve a suitable social and task balance.
- Successful one-to-one teaching relies on a good rapport between teacher and learner. Individual needs are catered for through the setting of personal goals and targets, recorded on ILPs and learning contracts.
- Question and answer can be used in a variety of teaching situations and requires skill in devising questions and dealing appropriately with the answers received.
- Discussion is used to share knowledge, ideas and experience amongst learners. It requires an appropriate topic or question and may need managing to keep the discussion on topic and ensure it remains an inclusive experience.
- All subjects involve the teaching of knowledge, skills and attitudes. The nature of the specialism determines the relative emphasis placed on each.
- Skills are taught through demonstration and practice. Preparation of learners, yourself, the environment and materials and equipment is crucial to both activities.
- All teaching strategies should be employed in a differentiated manner.
- Teaching strategies provide opportunities for the embedding of functional skills.

REFERENCES

Appleyard, N. and Appleyard, K. (2010) *Communicating with Learners in the Lifelong Learning Sector*. Exeter: Learning Matters.

Ausubel, D.P. (1960) The use of advance organizers in the learning and retention of meaningful verbal material. *Journal of Educational Psychology* 51(5): 267–72.

Boak, G. (1998) A Complete Guide to Learning Contracts. Aldershot: Gower.

Brandes, D. and Ginnis, P. (1986) *A Guide to Student-centred Learning*. Oxford: Blackwell.

Brown, G. and Wragg, E.C. (1993) *Questioning*. London: Routledge.

Casey, H., Cara, O., Eldred, J., Grie, S.F., Hodge, R., Ivanic, R., et al. (2007) You Wouldn't Expect a Maths Teacher to Teach Plastering... Embedding Literacy, Language and Numeracy in Post-16 Vocational Programmes: The Impact on Learning and Achievement. London: NRDC.

Drucker, P. (n.d.) Retrieved from BrainyQuote.com website: www.brainyquote.com/quotes/quotes/p/peterdruck142500.html (accessed 25/04/17).

Francis, M. and Gould, J. (2013) *Achieving Your PTLLS Award* (2nd edn). London: Sage.

Ginnis, P. (2002) *The Teacher's Toolkit*. Carmarthen: Crown House Publishing.

Jacques, D. and Salmon, G. (2007) Learning in Groups: A Handbook for Face-to-Face and Online Environments (4th edn). London: Routledge.

Johnson, D.W. and Johnson, F.P. (1991) *Joining Together: Group Theory and Group Skills* (4th edn). Needham Heights, MA: Allyn & Bacon.

Keeley-Browne, L. (2007) Training to Teach in the Learning and Skills Sector: From Threshold Award to QTLS. Harlow: Pearson Education.

Knowles, M., Elwood, F.H. and Swanson, R.A. (1998) *The Adult Learner* (5th edn). Woburn, MA: Butterworth-Heinemann.

Learning and Skills Improvement Service (LSIS) (2009) *Individual Learning Plans in Foundation Learning at Key Stage 4*. Coventry: LSIS.

Mehrabian, A. (1972) Silent Messages: Implicit Communication of Emotions and Attitudes. Belmont, CA: Wadsworth.

Petty, G. (1997) *Teaching Today: A Practical Guide* (1st edn). Cheltenham: Nelson Thornes.

Petty, G. (2009) *Teaching Today: A Practical Guide* (4th edn). Cheltenham: Nelson Thornes.

Tuckman, B. (1965) Developmental sequence in small groups. *Psychological Bulletin* 63: 384–99.

 # FURTHER READING

Harvey, B. and Harvey, J. (2013) Creative Teaching Approaches in the Lifelong Learning Sector. Maidenhead: OU Press.

Whilst drawing on the authors' wealth of experience to introduce a variety of activities and suggestions for use with learners, this book also supplies a framework within which creativity can flourish. It looks not only at practical activities but also at the processes engaged in by creative teachers along with potential barriers and how to overcome these, and organisational context. Catering for all levels of experience, this is a productive read for both new and experienced teachers.

Rossa, J. (2014) *The Perfect Further Education Lesson*. Bancyfelin: Independent Thinking Press.

This rather optimistically titled book provides an easy read for busy teachers and covers all aspects of a lesson from preparation through to marking. Examples and case studies are drawn from a variety of subject areas and practical ideas and 'tips' on successful teaching are offered in plenty. There is also helpful reference to ways of embedding, which considers employability skills, equality and diversity, numeracy and literacy.

6
LEARNING: THEORY AND PRACTICE

Learning means different things to different people, so a number of different theories as to the nature of learning and the learning process exist. A particular view of learning leads to a particular way of teaching; it is important therefore that, as teachers, we have a working knowledge of these different theories and their application. This chapter explores the main theories of learning that inform and underpin our everyday practice. In the spirit of James Cask Penney's (n.d.) assertion that 'Theory is splendid but until put into practice, it is valueless', the implications for practice will be examined as each theory is discussed.

When you have completed this chapter you will be able to:

*   describe the following theories of learning and recognise the ways in which they inform practice:

    o   behaviourism
    o   cognitivism
    o   information processing theory
    o   neuro-cognitive approaches
    o   social learning
    o   humanism
    o   andragogy.

THE NATURE OF THEORY

First, a cautionary note about theory. Popper (1959/1992: 51) suggests that theories are 'nets cast to catch what we call "the world", to rationalise, to explain and to master it'.

Achieving such mastery, however, initially involves simplification and generalisation and so it is important to bear in mind whilst reading this chapter that theory, by its very nature, rarely provides a complete match with reality. Teaching and learning invariably don't fit neatly into the boxes that theory provides for us. What those boxes do provide, however, are reference points against which we can compare and analyse practice. The third stage of Kolb's model of experiential learning, 'abstract conceptualisation', informs us that to learn and benefit from the experiences we have, we need to analyse and make sense of them. Theory provides the tool with which to do this. Theory can guide future practice or lead to a better understanding of current practice, enabling us to become more effective in what we do.

As teachers, we all have our own personal theories of learning, derived mainly from our own experience as learners – we have views on what learning is and how it can best be achieved, and these views shape the way in which we teach. This chapter encourages looking beyond immediate experience for guidance, however, supplementing it with knowledge of the established, recognised theories of learning which form the basis of our professional knowledge.

BEHAVIOURISM

When psychology was in its infancy in the late 1800s, the popular method of investigation was that of introspection. This involved subjects 'looking inwards' and describing their thought processes. It was believed that through the use of introspection, information could be gathered on how a person's mind worked. Many thought this approach to be unreliable and lacking in any scientific rigour. The American psychologist John B. Watson (1919) was a particularly vocal opponent of introspection and was of the opinion that for psychology to become accepted as a true science, it could not rely on an examination of individual internal mental processes that could not be observed and agreed on. What *could* be directly observed and directly and accurately measured, however, were the behaviours that people exhibited. These behaviours, according to Watson, indicated how people responded to their environment and the stimuli that it provided. If behaviour was made the focus of investigation, observations could be made which were free of bias and could be independently checked and verified. Behaviourism, then, came about as a response to the previous practice of introspection and introduced an approach in which the world is interpreted in terms of 'externally observable behaviour'. It does not concern itself with a person's internal processes on the basis that, as we cannot see what these are, how can we say what is happening? Learning therefore is viewed not as a process which goes on in a person's head, but as a change in behaviour brought about by some form of action or experience. Learning is said to have taken place when a new behaviour pattern is established and added to a person's existing behaviours. This argument may remind you of the discussion of SMART learning objectives (Chapter 2), and it should now be evident that the objectives-based approach to planning is derived from a behaviourist view of learning.

If learning is the establishment of a new behaviour pattern, how then do we achieve this? The work of Ivan Pavlov gives us some answers. He used dogs for his experiments, one of which involved collecting and measuring the amount of saliva produced when food was placed in a dog's mouth. In the language of behaviourism, the food is known as the *stimulus* as it produces or triggers the salivation. The salivation itself is termed the *response*. He conducted a series of experiments whereby he would ring a bell immediately before presenting the dog with food. He found that after he had repeated this procedure a number of times, the bell by itself was sufficient to cause the dog to salivate. According to Pavlov, the dog had now 'learned' to salivate to the sound of the bell. Learning had taken place because the dog was now exhibiting a form of behaviour it did not exhibit before. The new behaviour pattern involved salivating (response) to the sound of the bell (stimulus). Learning, then, is brought about through the association of a specific stimulus and response. This is often represented as *S–R*, the line joining the stimulus (S) and the response (R) representing what is variously termed the 'connection' or 'bond' between them. A specific stimulus will automatically bring about an identical response each time it is presented: *Learning is brought about by the association or pairing of a stimulus with a response.*

ACTIVITY 6.1

Pavlov has shown how a dog can be made to 'drool' at the sound of a bell, but how can this inform your practice? Can you identify any applications of Pavlov's work in your teaching?

It is important to recognise that the production of saliva under these circumstances is an *involuntary* or *reflex* action. It is not a conscious act. The dog does not think about salivating, it responds automatically. From a behaviourist perspective, this is true for all learning. Learning is an external rather than an internal process and takes the form of automatic response to environmental stimuli. The term 'conditioning' is used to describe this process. Pavlov's work is known as 'classical conditioning' and involves the pairing of an existing response with a new stimulus – dogs have always salivated but not normally in response to a bell. Classical conditioning is therefore of limited use to us as teachers as we are looking to establish completely new learning, i.e. a new or original response to a given stimulus rather than an existing reflex action. In this respect, 'operant conditioning', the work of Skinner, is far more helpful as in this approach an entirely new behaviour is established; the subject 'operates' on the immediate environment rather than passively responding to it as in classical conditioning.

Skinner's research involved rats; when they accidentally touched a particular lever within their cage, they received some food. The rats soon 'learned' which lever to touch in order to be rewarded.

Skinner was less concerned with the part played by the initial stimulus in bringing about learning, attaching greater importance to the consequence which follows a response. He used the term 'reinforcement' to describe 'any consequence which increases the frequency with which a response occurs'. Reinforcement encourages a particular behaviour, especially if the consequence is pleasant.

Reinforcement is an important concept for a number of reasons. Learning is only retained as long as there is a connection between stimulus and response. Under normal circumstances, when new learning or a 'change in behaviour' is established, the new S–R connection will gradually disappear unless it is strengthened intermittently. If you played a fruit machine, you would eventually stop if you never won anything. You would only continue playing if every now and again you won. The occasional win reinforces or encourages your 'fruit machine playing' behaviour. Reinforcement is necessary to maintain learning.

When we are learning something new, how do we know we are doing so in the correct manner? We cannot decide for ourselves as that would involve an internal process and, in a behaviourist view of the world, learning is an external activity. If we are told 'that is good' or 'you are doing well', not only are we motivated to learn, but we now know that what we are learning is correct. So, as well as maintaining established knowledge, reinforcement is instrumental in establishing new learning by giving feedback during the learning phase. Skinner's work also informs our approach to classroom management.

When it comes to the issue of classroom management, the point of focus for the behaviourist is not the individual who is displaying the behaviour but rather the behaviour itself. The strategies employed are therefore aimed at influencing and controlling the actual behaviours. As a starting point, rules are set, identifying those behaviours which are deemed acceptable and those which are not. Punishment and reinforcement are used to ensure compliance with the rules.

'Punishment' is the opposite of reinforcement, as it is an unpleasant consequence to a response which is intended to *weaken or eliminate* a given behaviour pattern by decreasing the frequency with which the response occurs. Unlike reinforcement, which encourages the desired behaviours, punishment is intended to discourage undesirable behaviours.

Reinforcement can be one of two types – positive or negative. Negative reinforcement is often confused with punishment but there is a critical difference between the two. Negative reinforcement, like positive reinforcement, is designed *to strengthen or increase the likelihood* of a given behaviour, whereas punishment is intended to *weaken or eliminate* a given behaviour. Unlike positive reinforcement, which encourages the desired behaviour through pleasurable consequences, negative reinforcement encourages the desired behaviour through the removal of an unpleasant consequence.

Consider the following example: a parent is fed up with their child leaving the bedroom in a mess so bans them from watching television. This is a punishment as it is intended to act as an unpleasant consequence to the undesirable 'leaving the bedroom in a mess' behaviour, thus discouraging it. If the child now begins to tidy the bedroom, they may be allowed to watch television again. This is negative reinforcement as the unpleasant consequence has been removed, thus encouraging the desired behaviour of keeping the bedroom in a tidy state. Maintaining this desired behaviour could then be further encouraged by positive reinforcement in the form of praise. A combination of these three consequences can be used to manage behaviour, as illustrated in Figure 6.1.

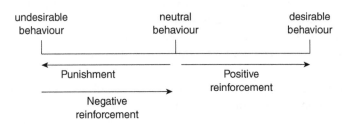

Figure 6.1   Managing behaviour through the use of reinforcement and punishment

REFLECTIVE TASK 6.1

Consider your own approach to managing learners and their behaviour. Do you use any behaviourist techniques? Reflect on a recent incident. Did you or could you have used a combination of punishment and positive and negative reinforcement to arrive at a satisfactory outcome?

A number of behaviour management techniques such as 'assertive discipline' and 'ABC' (antecedent–behaviour–consequence) are based on the work of Skinner, as, to a lesser extent, is the laying down of 'ground rules' at the beginning of a course.

Skinner's other major contribution to practice was to show how complex learning could be brought about by building it up in a step-by-step fashion. He called this process 'shaping', suggesting that 'operant conditioning shapes behaviour as a sculptor shapes a lump of clay' (1953: 91). Shaping is achieved by breaking down the desired behaviour into a number of smaller steps and reinforcing these sequentially until eventually the complete and more complex behaviour is achieved. As we saw in Chapter 5, many skills are typically taught in this way by initially conducting a skills analysis in which the overall skill is broken down into a number of sub-skills. This is then followed by a combination of demonstration and practice.

ACTIVITY 6.2

How do the actions of Skinner's rat differ from those of Pavlov's dog? Does Skinner's work open up any new avenues for you as a teacher?

Generally, the teaching strategies used in a behaviourist approach involve repetition and breaking learning down into smaller chunks. Consider the traditional method of learning the times-table. This is achieved through constant repetition, bit by bit, until eventually the complete table is learned, the teacher correcting mistakes and reinforcing correct answers throughout. The teacher would ask '3 times 2?' and the answer would come back as '6'. There are two things to note in this exchange:

- The answer is given automatically – it does not involve conscious thought.
- There is only one correct answer – '3 times 2?' is the stimulus and '6' is the correct response.

As learning in a behaviourist approach involves giving the correct response to the appropriate stimulus, this is what assessment methods seek to measure. Checking knowledge involves looking for the correct answer and so the methods used fall into the category of closed questions or objective testing. Skills are more usually assessed through observation where the observer uses a checklist which itemises the various stages that the skill has been broken down into.

A behaviourist approach to teaching and learning, therefore, offers a number of positive features:

- It is straightforward and unambiguous.
- It provides a systematic approach to teaching and learning.
- It allows learning to be measured easily.
- It focuses on the learning that is to take place.

ACTIVITY 6.3

Can you see the potential limitations of a behaviourist approach? List the reasons you can think of before you read on. Can you identify any areas of your teaching in which you make use of this approach and others in which it would be unsuitable?

COGNITIVISM

Behaviourism provided the first real thoughts on defining learning, how it takes place and how it is planned, delivered and assessed. It was not without its critics, however, who were of the opinion that it took an overly simplistic view and could not fully account for a number of different aspects of learning. Behaviourism was also regarded by many as being too prescriptive and over-reliant on teacher-led methods.

It was against this backdrop that a new perspective on learning arose – cognitivism.

The cognitive perspective on learning is concerned with internal mental processes which seek understanding and meaning in the material to be learned. Meaning is derived from relating new learning to existing learning. Piaget was one of the first cognitivists. He believed that instead of merely responding to stimuli in the environment, as behaviourists suggest, we interact with the environment to actively construct our own knowledge and understanding of the world. He considered children to be 'little scientists', actively constructing and testing out their own theories and ideas about the world, rather than 'blank slates' to be subsequently filled.

Piaget suggests that knowledge is stored in the form of *schemas*. A schema is a mental model of everything we know about a given subject at a given time and allows the storing of information in categories that clarify relationships. A network of such schema forms our 'world view'. If we now have a new experience, we try to make sense of it – in other words, fit it into or relate it to what we already know (our existing schema). If we can do this, we are said to have *assimilated* the new knowledge. If, however, it does not make sense (we cannot make it fit with what we already know), we either have to alter our existing schema so that the new experience or knowledge does fit, or we have to form a new schema, in which case we are said to *accommodate* the new knowledge or experience. From a cognitive perspective, learning takes place not through a change in behaviour but through a change in our internal cognitive structures. Rather than adding to the store, new knowledge 'transforms' or redefines existing knowledge.

In a behaviourist approach, learning was built up in a step-by-step manner, taking 'bits' of information and adding them to others in a linear process. The nature of knowledge from a cognitive viewpoint, however, is one in which the 'bits' of information are all interrelated and collectively have a specific meaning. When new information is taken in, it becomes part of that 'larger picture' but, as a consequence, the picture changes. The following analogy will help make this clearer.

Consider making a cup of coffee. A spoonful of coffee is placed in the cup. How many items are in the cup? You will probably agree that the answer is 'one'. Water is now added and the mix stirred. How many items are in the cup? Is it one or is it two? Similarly, milk and sugar are added with stirring. Are there four items in the cup now or one? The answer is that there is always one item in the cup but it changes each time something else is added. This is analogous to learning when considered from a cognitive perspective. We have a particular view, picture or cognitive structure relating to a given subject. We now learn something new about this subject, but it is not merely another fact that is added to an existing store of knowledge; it becomes part of what we know but in doing so alters our overall view of the subject. Rather than adding to the store, new knowledge 'transforms' existing knowledge. We describe this as our understanding becoming deeper or our awareness being raised.

The behaviourist perspective now had a rival which was becoming more popular. The tension between the two approaches and the challenge that behaviourism now faced was summed up by Amsel (1989: 1) who stated: 'I like to point out that the S–R psychologists, who at one time formed the government, are now in loyal opposition, the cognitivists being the new government.'

There are a number of different strands to the cognitive perspective. Gestalt psychologists, for instance, have as their motto, 'the whole is greater than the sum of its parts', by which they mean viewing the whole picture rather than its constituent parts leads to the establishment of meaning, as illustrated in Figure 6.2.

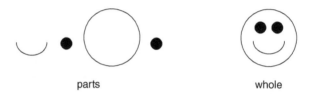

parts   whole

Figure 6.2 The whole is greater than the sum of its parts

They suggest that learning occurs through 'insight' which takes place on realising the relationship that exists between all of the different parts of the situation. Instead of seeing the 'parts', we see the 'whole' and how the different 'parts' make this up. This moment of insight is popularly known as 'the penny dropping' or the 'aha' moment.

All cognitivists, however, agree on the following general principles:

- Current learning builds on previous learning.
- Learning involves deriving understanding and meaning.
- Meaning is dependent on establishing relationships.
- Relationships are stored internally as cognitive structures (Gould, 2012: 44).

ACTIVITY 6.4

Previously, you were asked to identify aspects of your current teaching in which a behaviourist approach would be unsuitable. Is a cognitive approach likely to be more appropriate in those instances?

Use the four characteristics of a cognitive approach listed above to help you arrive at your decision.

As a cognitive view of learning takes such a different form from that of a behaviourist approach, the methods and activities used to achieve it will also be different. Questions will be open, of a 'how' and 'why' nature, rather than the more closed 'what' type of questions used in behaviourism. Their purpose is not to identify the correct answer but to encourage thinking, debating and theorising. The purpose of methods and activities from a cognitive approach, generally, is to promote understanding and reasoned thinking. Commonly used strategies include problem solving, projects, mind mapping and discovery-based activities. Learning tends to be more learner-led than teacher-led as it involves the individual reorganising and restructuring of knowledge. As Reece and Walker (2007: 85) point out, this does mean that 'if you have a class of sixteen students, they probably have sixteen slightly different understandings'. Discussion, in which all learners participate in the same activity but arrive at their own individual conclusions, is an example of this.

Understanding can be reached in different ways, as illustrated by two other cognitivists, Ausubel and Bruner. Both subscribe to the same basic underpinning principles of the cognitive approach, agreeing that new learning builds on existing learning, that understanding and meaning are paramount in learning and that meaning is dependent on establishing relationships. They also agree that to achieve this, knowledge must be structured and organised. What they differ on is where that structure should come from – teachers or learners.

Ausubel (1963) suggests a model where information is presented to learners in an organised manner. His argument is that if the organisation of learned material is required in order for meaningful learning to take place, then this is the form in which it should initially be presented to learners. The 'tell them what you are going to tell them, tell them, tell them what you have told them' approach is based around Ausubel's ideas. The sequence of presentation is:

1. The topic of the session is first stated and then explained fully and clearly. The relationships it contains are identified and emphasised.
2. Examples are considered and in each case an explanation of how they fit and illustrate the topic is given.
3. Some non-examples are also introduced with a clear explanation as to why they do not qualify.
4. Learners are given some further examples to work through.
5. The session ends with a summary which revisits the overall structure of the topic.

Ausubel suggests that the most effective sequence in teaching is to start from a clear explanation of the topic and then use examples as illustrations to deepen understanding. This is known as the deductive approach.

Bruner (1963) takes a different viewpoint, believing that when learners are presented with information in a highly structured manner, they become over-dependent on the teacher. Bruner maintained that learners should be encouraged to discover pieces of information and their interrelationships for themselves, as this would allow them to remember the information for a longer period of time and also increase their ability to apply new knowledge to real-life situations. This is a form of constructivism which centres on the belief that learning is individually derived or 'constructed' by building on and linking to existing learning. Instead of using examples to illustrate what has been explained, as suggested by Ausubel, Bruner advocates that learners are presented with carefully chosen examples first, and then encouraged to arrive at the learning related to the session topic for themselves. There are a number of ways in which examples can be presented to learners in order to achieve this result, but Joyce et al. (2011: 117) suggest using positive and negative examples in pairs in the following sequence:

1. Teacher presents labelled examples.
2. Students compare attributes in positive and negative examples.
3. Students generate and test hypotheses.
4. Students state a definition according to the essential attributes.

This method of proceeding, in which learners arrive at the answers themselves through a process of discovery, is known as the inductive approach.

REFLECTIVE TASK 6.2

Identify instances from your own experience of learning that have taken a discovery approach.

Identify one area from your own teaching that might benefit from a discovery-based approach to learning. How might you implement this approach?

Assessment methods need to match the type of learning that is taking place. From a cognitive viewpoint, the priority is not to arrive at 'the correct answer'. Assessment is concerned with testing the ability to interpret and structure information and to engage in reasoned thought, and this purpose is reflected in the methods used. Typically, the essay is used in the cognitive approach, as it asks learners to explain, justify and reason, and generally demonstrates their understanding of a subject. Projects, presentations, poster presentations and discussion/debate types of exercises can also be used.

By now, you should be familiar with the idea that cognitivists are interested in the 'whole picture' and how the different parts contained within it relate to each other. They do not view anything in isolation. This principle also holds true for classroom management. Unlike behaviourism, where the behaviour itself is the sole concern, behaviour is viewed as merely one part of a more complex picture in a cognitive approach, and in order to arrive at an understanding of behaviour the person as a whole has to be taken into consideration. A cognitive approach does not see behaviour as the main issue but rather as a symptom of a deeper underlying problem.

McPhillimy (1996: 57) reminds us that 'another central aspect of the cognitive approach is the importance it attaches to the influence on a pupil's behaviour of his self-concept'. Self-concept is an indication of how learners see themselves as a whole and can be either positive or negative. In a learning situation, a positive self-concept arises out of consistent previous success in learning. New learning situations are therefore approached with an expectation of success and such a positive attitude to learning means inappropriate behaviour is unlikely to occur.

The Further Education and Skills sector is often seen as a 'second chance' and a proportion of learners will bring a negative self-concept to the learning situation arising out of previous unsuccessful learning experiences. Expectations may now be of difficulty and failure. If in any new learning, success is also difficult to come by, avoidance of failure rather than the achievement of success becomes the goal. Tactics employed by learners in the evasion of failure include avoidance strategies such as not bringing equipment with them, self-deprecation ('I've never been any good at...'), putting the blame elsewhere (on the teacher or the boring nature of the subject) and, as a last resort, a refusal to do the work.

Rather than dealing with the actual behaviour, a cognitive approach to classroom management is based around trying to turn a negative self-concept into a positive one. Establishing some kind of rapport or relationship with learners generally has a positive effect on self-concept, but learners need to experience success in their learning to turn a negative self-concept around. The general strategy is to help learners to recognise and accept their own successes. This means setting short-term achievable targets, accompanied by work which is carefully structured to allow these to be successfully met but which still contains an element of challenge for the learner. In short: using effective differentiation strategies.

ACTIVITY 6.5

Which of the two approaches to behaviour management – behaviourist and cognitive – do you think is more appropriate to the sector, or do you consider each has a place?

INFORMATION PROCESSING THEORY

As well as theorising about the nature of learning and the structures within the mind, cognitive theory also attempts to explain how information is processed. Information processing theory compares the workings of the mind to that of a computer, in its attempts to account for the ways in which people receive, store, integrate, retrieve and use information through the processes of attention, perception and memory.

Attention

Like the computer, the mind has a limited capacity in terms of the amount and nature of the information it can process. In the same way that a computer will 'crash' if asked to perform too many tasks simultaneously, the brain suffers from overload if asked to process too many stimuli at the same time. The purpose of the attention phase of information processing is to prevent such overload by filtering out the majority of presented stimuli, allowing only those which are selected to proceed to the next phase of the process. This begs the question as to what determines which stimuli are selected and which are not.

Broadbent's filter theory (1958) suggests that it is the physical characteristics of the stimulus that are responsible for attracting attention:

- Some colours are more likely to attract attention than others. Generally, red is a good attracter of attention which is why we use it to denote danger. The greater the intensity of the stimulus – the brighter the colour, the louder the sound, the stronger the smell or taste, the greater the pressure of touch – the more likely it is to attract attention.
- Variety in stimulus attracts attention. A police siren, as well as being high pitched and loud (intense), is also irregular. Variety in learning activity, switching the focus from teacher to learner and resources from written to graphical, will help in maintaining attention throughout a session of learning.
- Anything which is different and so stands out from its surroundings will attract attention. Underlining, colour and different styles of print such as capital letters, bold or italic type are often used to achieve this effect.

If we engage in conversation in a crowded room, the immediate conversation is loudest and therefore holds our attention, as suggested by Broadbent. If, however, someone mentions our name as part of a different conversation over on the other side of the room, this becomes our new focus of attention. This 'cocktail effect', as it is known, suggests that another mechanism is at work whereby stimuli which have some personal meaning or interest are also selected for attention. These stimuli include anything that relates directly to us or our current areas of interest.

It would seem therefore that two factors influence attention – some stimuli are selected on account of their physical properties whilst others are selected because they have some personal significance.

REFLECTIVE TASK 6.3

What strategies do you use within your own teaching to influence the attention of your learners?

In a learning situation, there are three important aspects of attention management:

- Attract attention.
- Focus attention.
- Maintain attention.

We can identify strategies for attracting and focusing attention from the discussion above, but maintaining attention is dependent on attention span. Learning is directly affected by our attention span, which varies with each individual but is generally determined by the type of activity in which we engage and the length of time it takes. Attention spans are shorter in passive approaches to learning and longer when learning is active, so varying the type and length of activities helps keep attention levels high. A summary of strategies used to manage attention is given below in Table 6.1.

Table 6.1

Purpose	Strategy
Attract	• Pose problems or questions to start the session off
	• Use colours and images to good advantage in projection systems
Focus	• Use questions and monitor group activities
	• Use the whiteboard to highlight main points; avoid clutter
	• Reveal only one item of information at a time
Maintain	• Use a variety of activities and resources
	• Give clear short directions before, not during, an activity
	• Use movement, gestures and voice inflection to good effect
	• Clean whiteboards and close down projection systems when not directly using them

Having focused on the appropriate messages, the information we encounter now has to be interpreted and made sense of.

Perception

Perception can be defined as 'the acquisition and processing of sensory information in order to see, hear, taste or feel objects in the world; it also guides an organism's actions with respect to those objects' (Sekuler and Blake, 2002: 621). In essence, it is concerned with interpretation and making sense of incoming information, and as such has already been touched on in the general view of cognitive approaches which noted that rather than merely acting as passive receptors of external stimuli we need to extract personal meaning from them. Here, we will briefly consider the factors which influence perception and the ways in which they affect learning.

Previous experience   According to Solso et al. (2005: 75), 'If past learning did not influence our perception, the curious lines on this page you are now reading, which we call letters, would not be perceived as parts of words and the words would be devoid of meaning'. Previous experience plays an important role in perception as new learning builds on existing experience and ultimately becomes part of it. If you are approached by a stranger asking for directions, invariably you will start by asking them if they know where such and such a particular landmark is. You will try and find out what their existing knowledge is and use this as the basis for your explanation of how to arrive at the required destination. You are acknowledging the fact that previous experience provides a frame of reference against which incoming information can be interpreted.

One practical approach to facilitating perception through the linking of new information to previous knowledge is the use of analogies. As previously noted, this section is based around the analogy of the brain as a computer. Other commonly used analogies include the flow of electricity along a wire and the flow of water along a pipe, memory as a filing cabinet, light as water ripples or waves, the heart as a pump, fractions as slices of a cake and the earth as acting like a greenhouse in causing global warming.

REFLECTIVE TASK 6.4

Think of any topic that you teach which is either difficult to explain or is abstract in nature. Devise an analogy to make this particular topic easier to understand. Try it out and evaluate its success.

Context   Context also provides a clue as to interpretation. The word 'chip', for instance, can be interpreted in a number of different but equally valid ways. Previous experience will suggest a 'chip' could be something eaten with fish, a small piece of wood, a token used in gambling, a flaw in an otherwise perfect piece of china or a working component in a computer. If I was in a computer shop and overheard a conversation about 'chips', I could be fairly certain as to which was the appropriate interpretation. 'Advance organisers' (discussed in Chapter 5) and the way a session is introduced can be used to establish an initial context in a teaching situation, preparing the mind to interpret what is to be learned in an appropriate manner.

Hypothesising   Have you ever sat in a railway carriage and looked out of the window to see another railway carriage on the track next to yours? Your carriage moves off in a forward direction, or is it the other carriage moving off in a backwards direction? The more you look, the more difficult it is to tell which is the case. According to Gregory (1990), when we are presented by the senses with new information, we form hypotheses as to its possible meaning. More often than not, a single hypothesis stands out as the most likely interpretation and we consequently accept it. In the case above, however, two equally plausible hypotheses can be formulated. Hypothesis 1 is 'my carriage is moving forwards', whilst hypothesis 2 states that 'the other carriage is moving backwards', hence the confusion. To resolve this confusion, Gregory suggests that we seek 'confirmatory cues' to verify one of the competing hypotheses. In the case of the railway carriage, this is easily done by either looking out of the opposite window or turning to information from the other senses – can we feel vibrations caused by movement? Can we hear the wheels of our carriage moving over the railway track? Once one of the hypotheses is confirmed through these means, we are no longer confused when looking at the other carriage. Similarly in teaching, more perspectives confirm our understanding – demonstrating or giving examples as well as describing, using different resources to accompany explanations or contributions from learners describing their own experiences.

Language   The earlier quote on 'the role of previous experience' refers to making sense of the written word, but the same argument applies to the spoken word, the most widely used form of communication in teaching and learning. Language, or the way in which the spoken word is used, is an important factor in perception. Interpretation of the spoken word is influenced by a number of factors such as accent, dialect, register or whether the language used by the teacher is the first language of the learner. In the teaching of any subject, however, you will be introducing new terminology and using the specialised language, concepts or 'jargon' of your specialist subject. A sound knowledge of the terminology or jargon is an essential component of the learning that takes place within any specialist area and at some stage it has to be learned so that everyone 'speaks the same language'. The introduction of too much specialist language on the same occasion, however, can be overwhelming, leading to learners 'switching off' or a general lack of understanding, and so a gradual introduction is normally most effective. Arriving at an understanding of the particular concept before naming it, in a manner similar to that suggested by Bruner in Chapter 5, can also be very effective. Once learned, engaging learners in activities which give them an opportunity to use the new language helps in establishing it as the norm and, at the same time, provides feedback on how well it is understood. A summary of strategies used to facilitate perception is shown in Table 6.2.

Table 6.2

Strategy	Effect on perception
Use a variety of approaches	Captures and covers all learning/perceptual styles
Encourage contributions, ideas and examples from learners	Makes use of previous knowledge and experience
Use resources and hands-on approaches to full advantage	Provides plentiful auditory, visual and tactile stimuli and 'confirmatory cues'
Give total picture first; use advance organisers and signposts	Presents structure so learners can identify relationships from the start
Use plenty of analogies and examples	Builds on what is already known
Ask learners to explain new concepts	Assesses understanding; introduces different language register
Try starting from examples to introduce new terminology	Moves from the concrete to the abstract
Use 'jargon' only when appropriate – introduce the concept before naming it	Uses accessible language
Use problem-solving approaches	Ensures engagement with material to be learned leads to understanding
Point out patterns in new material to be learned	Establishes structure
Review learning and assist learners to identify how new learning relates to what they already know	Integrates new learning with existing knowledge and experience
Start learning sessions by reference to what has been previously learned and how it relates to what is to be learned	Provides context and establishes relationships in learned material
End learning sessions by looking forward to the next session, establishing links with current learning	Provides context and establishes relationships with current and future learning

Memory

Information which has passed through the previous stages now needs to be retained in such a way that it can be later accessed at will. This is the function of memory.

Memory is an information storage system and the way in which it works can be compared to another information storage system – the filing cabinet. The first stage in putting a document into the filing cabinet would be to decide what to file it under – where you will store it – and this would depend on how you had organised your filing cabinet. When information is first received for storage in memory, a decision must be made as to how and where it will be stored. This process, analogous to deciding what to file the information under, is known as 'encoding'. Encoding normally involves changing the information into a form in which it is able to be stored. To find and retrieve the document from the filing cabinet at a later date, you would need to remember what you had originally filed it under. Similarly, the retrieval of stored information from memory depends on how it was stored in the first place and retrieval 'cues' are dependent on the original encoding mechanisms used.

To work effectively, memory must be capable of carrying out three processes:

1. Encoding information – information must be registered and converted to a form in which it can be stored.
2. Storing information – information is stored and is available for future use.
3. Retrieving information – information is recovered from storage when required.

REFLECTIVE TASK 6.5

What strategies do you use to make it easier for your learners to commit what they learn to memory? Can you relate these strategies to any of the processes above? Can you identify any further strategies that you might be able to use?

A number of models of memory have been devised to explain how these processes take place – the most common is the multi-store model which suggests that information is passed between three types of memory store, as illustrated in Figure 6.3.

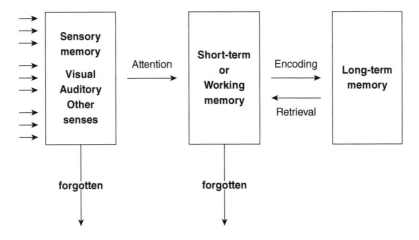

Figure 6.3   The multi-store model of memory

Sensory memory has a large capacity but holds only a fleeting trace of incoming sensory information of between 0.5 and 3 seconds duration. This allows a decision to be made as to whether the information should be retained for further processing by passing on to short-term memory.

Short-term memory has a limited capacity and is only capable of holding approximately seven items of information at one time. The trace formed by incoming information fades or decays quickly, only lasting for between 5 and 15 seconds. It is renewed by repetition or 'rote' rehearsal and if this process is repeated a sufficient number of times the information becomes encoded. So, if you repeat a piece of information such as a telephone number a sufficient number of times, it will transfer to long-term memory. The concept of short-term memory, however, has been largely replaced by that of 'working memory'. This is considered a more active system than short-term memory as it processes information as well as storing it. Working memory contains a 'central executive' module which controls the operation of a number of 'slave systems' which deal directly with incoming sensory information, making sense of it and linking related pieces of information.

Long-term memory is considered to be limitless in capacity and stores memories on a permanent basis. It encodes information largely through 'elaborative' rehearsal which establishes a relationship between new and existing information. Information in long-term memory is organised in terms of hierarchy, meaning and understanding. This allows stored information to be more easily located and retrieved. Forgetting occurs when information is lost at some stage of the memory process or, in the case of long-term memory, by the inability to retrieve information due to the lack of an appropriate cue.

Knowing how memory works allows us to devise strategies to make the process of committing learning to memory a more efficient process, and some of these strategies are illustrated below in Table 6.3.

Table 6.3

Strategy	Effect on memory
Present information in a structured manner	Helps learners to encode
Summarise the key points (approximately seven) at the end of a learning session	Provides structure and avoids forgetting through interference effects
Do not overload learners with information	Gives opportunity for transfer from short-term to long-term memory
Use question and answer frequently and informal quizzes and short tests during learning sessions	With practice, makes the retrieval of information easier
Use mnemonics and encourage learners to devise their own mnemonics	Gives meaning to otherwise random information, thus assisting encoding of information
Present information in small meaningful 'chunks'	Helps encoding and eases the burden on short-term memory
Use visual approaches, particularly those which organise information in some way	Helps encoding through chunking and understanding
Use activities which encourage learners to actively use new information	Helps with processing of information and subsequent encoding

NEURO-COGNITIVE APPROACHES

In arriving at their conclusions regarding the internal organisation and workings of the brain, cognitive researchers relied on observing the behaviours that occurred as a result of their experiments. This was due to the fact, so forcefully pointed out by behaviourists, that we cannot see inside the brain and examine its workings at first hand. Or can we?

Cognitive neuroscience involves an examination of the biological and neurological aspects of the brain in order to better understand how it functions. It attempts to identify the biological underpinning of the various mental processes that take place. It achieves this through the use of various brain imaging techniques such as Functional Magnetic Resonance Imaging (fMRI) and Positron Emission Tomography (PET), which can identify the specific areas in the brain in which activity is taking place when particular tasks are being performed. Electroencephalography (EEG) scans can measure the duration and sequence of brain activity. Functional Magnetic Resonance Spectroscopy (fMRS) records various chemical levels within the brain whilst activity is in progress. This technology has been used to examine the rhythms of the brain and the effects on the brain of exercise, nutrition, stress, mood and emotion, as well as further exploring processes such as attention and memory. So, in the same way that the eyes are said to be the window to the soul, brain imaging techniques can be considered as providing a 'window into the brain'.

For obvious reasons, studies in this area are also referred to as 'brain-based' learning, which Jensen (2008: 4) defines as 'learning in accordance with the way the brain is naturally designed to learn. It is a multidisciplinary approach that is built on this fundamental question: What is good for the brain?'

Interest in the structure of the brain is not a recent phenomenon. Roger Sperry's 'split brain experiments' in the early 1970s (*Lancet*, 1999) led to the brain being regarded as consisting of two distinct halves or hemispheres – the right hemisphere, which is concerned with creativity, and the left, which is characterised by logic. This theory has a number of implications for learning and provides a possible explanation as to why we favour a particular learning style. Both hemispheres of the brain are involved in any activity in which we engage, but one side or the other can be more dominant. If the right hemisphere is the more dominant, we adopt a 'holistic' approach to learning – we like to 'see the whole picture'. If, however, it is the left hemisphere which is the more dominant, our approach to learning is sequential or linear – we prefer a systematic approach to learning which is built up in a step-by-step manner.

A later model of the brain, known as the 'triune brain theory', was developed by Paul MacLean (1985) and is based on evolutionary development. McLean considered the human brain to contain three layers or types. These are:

- the *reptilian complex*, which is regarded as the earliest evolutionary phase and is therefore concerned largely with physical survival. It is situated in the brain stem and cerebellum and controls the main body functions such as breathing, digestion and circulation and is also responsible for the 'fight or flight' response to stress.

- the *limbic system*, which is concerned with emotion and affects motivation, feeding, reproductive behaviour and parental behaviour. It helps determine whether we feel positive or negative towards something, and is the source of the value judgements that we make. It is situated in the hippocampus.
- the *neo-cortex*, which represents the most recent step in the evolution of the human brain, giving abilities relating to language, abstract thought, imagination, planning and perception – the higher cognitive functions which distinguish humans from animals. It is also known as the cerebral cortex or more colloquially as 'the grey matter' and is the outer, wrinkled portion of our brain. In humans, it accounts for just over 80 per cent of the brain as a whole and is regarded as the part of the brain in which learning takes place. (See Figure 6.4)

Each of the three brains interacts with and is connected to the other two by an extensive two-way network of nerves. To some extent, each also seems to operate independently as a separate brain system with its own distinct characteristics. In terms of learning, this has an important implication. One might reasonably assume that as the highest order functioning brain, the neo-cortex would control the other two. If, however, we are faced with a life-threatening situation, the reptilian brain becomes dominant. Because it is at the 'fight or flight' level of the brain, its response is automatic. When the reptilian brain is in a dominant position, learning cannot take place. Similarly, if we are in a situation which results in an emotionally unstable state, the limbic brain comes to the fore preventing effective learning. Learning is most effective when the neo-cortex is the dominant brain system and so the message here is that the learning environment should not contain any perceived threats or emotional upset if learning is to take place, as it is only then that the neo-cortex is the dominant system.

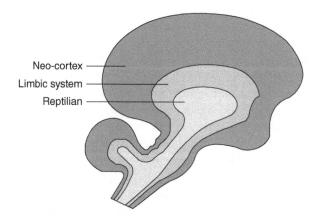

Figure 6.4   The parts of the triune brain

REFLECTIVE TASK 6.6

Learners will sometimes come out of an exam complaining their 'mind just went blank' or they would have done better if they 'had not been as nervous'. What can you do to make situations in the learning environment, such as assessment, less stressful so learners can perform at their optimum level? What can you do to prepare learners for formal exams that will help them approach these in a more relaxed frame of mind?

The above views are now considered rather dated and have given way to 'whole-brain theory' which is based on the premise that every part of the brain is involved in most activities. Activity occurs in the brain cells, one type of which is the neuron.

Neurons form the basic components of the brain and are constructed in such a way that they can connect to each other to form *neural pathways* in which information from one neuron flows to another neuron across a *synapse*. (See Figure 6.5) This is achieved through both electrical and chemical means. It is these neural pathways that constitute learning and so it is the number of possible connections and interconnections occurring between them that is important, rather than the actual number of neurons themselves (about 100 billion in the adult brain). This process of forming neural pathways is known as *plasticity* and is particularly active in the early years of our lives. The number of connections that can be made is not endless, and hand in hand with plasticity – the making of new connections – is the process of *synaptic pruning* in which old or weak connections are destroyed, making room for new ones. It is through these complementary processes of plasticity and synaptic pruning that the brain develops and adapts to new circumstances.

Learning then is the result of the formation of neural pathways, and imaging techniques provide some insight into how and where these are formed within the brain.

Cognitive neuroscience or brain-based learning is a relatively new area of research and so currently lacks any kind of definitive overall statement of direction and application. McNeil (2009: Introduction) describes the current situation thus: 'at present, the evidence from neuroscience that informs learning is like a huge and only partly-formed Roman mosaic; incomplete yet fascinating'.

Neuroscience does, however, seem to be largely agreeing with the conclusions of information processing theory, whilst also opening up some new areas relating to the physiology of the brain, such as those relating to rhythms of the brain and the effects of nutrition, exercise, stress, mood and emotion. Taking care of the brain and ensuring that it is in the best condition for effective learning has become an important strand of this approach. Simple measures include ensuring adequate supplies of

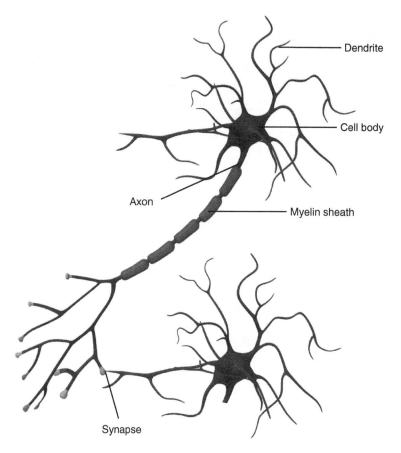

Figure 6.5   Neuron and synapse

Source: © Shutterstock.com/3drenderings

water, oxygen and nutrition. Challenge, active approaches to learning and operating within a safe, stimulating environment also contribute to the achievement of optimum brain efficiency. The ways in which the brain develops at different life stages – in the early years, adolescence and adulthood – also give some insights into various educational issues.

Neuroscience is still a relatively new area and further development is needed for it to have a more direct impact on practice. The 2006 Teaching and Learning Research Programme publication on 'Neuroscience and Education' informs us that 'Of course brain scans cannot give rise directly to lesson plans. There is a need for bridging studies that interpret scientific results in terms of possible interventions, and evaluation of these interventions in suitable learning contexts' (Nash et al., 2008: 22).

SOCIAL LEARNING

Ronald Regan is credited with suggesting that 'Each generation goes further than the generation preceding it because it stands on the shoulders of that generation'. This is the basis of social learning theory – rather than continually rediscovering our knowledge, each generation builds on and further develops the achievements of the previous generation. In contrast to Piaget's view of children as 'little scientists' discovering their own world, social learning theory suggests that knowledge can be derived from the child's social and cultural surroundings, as well as by individual discovery.

Bandura (1977: 22), one of the earliest social learning theorists, points out the laborious, and even hazardous, nature of learning everything through individual action: 'Fortunately, most human behaviour is learned observationally through modelling: from observing others, one forms an idea of how new behaviours are performed, and on later occasions this coded information serves as a guide for action.' Social learning theory, then, claims that we learn from each other through the processes of observation, imitation and modelling.

Generally, we tend to adopt behaviours that we observe as receiving a positive response when displayed by others, whilst not adopting behaviours which we observe as being received negatively. Bandura tells us that as teachers we should model the behaviours we would like our learners to display and respond positively to individual learner behaviours we would wish to encourage in others.

Modelling on its own, however, is insufficient to bring about a change in others. Bandura identified four necessary conditions that need to be fulfilled before others can adopt the desired behaviour:

1. Attention – the person must first pay attention to what is being modelled.
2. Retention – they must be able to remember what it consists of.
3. Reproduction – the behaviour must be within the person's physical and cognitive reach.
4. Motivation and opportunity – they must actually want to replicate what has been modelled. This is normally influenced by the observed consequences of modelling and is known as 'vicarious reinforcement'. We are more likely to imitate behaviour that we observe being rewarded and refrain from behaviour we observe being punished. The more opportunities we give to practise the new behaviour in a 'safe' environment, the more likely it is to be repeated.

We do not 'mindlessly' adopt the behaviours of others; we make decisions as to whether or not to follow the example set. Bandura renamed his social learning theory as social cognitive theory to better reflect how we learn from our social experiences.

We can also learn from each other in a more deliberate and planned manner, as suggested by Vygotsky and his Zone of Proximal Development (ZPD), which he defined as 'the distance between the actual developmental level as determined by independent problem solving and the level of potential development as determined through problem solving under adult guidance, or in collaboration with more capable peers' (1978: 86).

The ZPD suggests that a gap exists between what a child already knows, or is capable of learning independently, and what can be learned with the assistance of an adult or someone who has greater capability in the particular area. Vygotsky used the term of 'more knowledgeable other' (MKO) to identify the individual who assists in addressing tasks, skills or problems within the ZPD. Although the MKO is normally the teacher, others, such as peers, can take on the role as long as they have the necessary knowledge or expertise. The MKO gives support in the form of 'scaffolding'. This term arises out of the work of Bruner and is analogous to the use of scaffolding in the building trade, which supports the initial construction of a building but is gradually removed as the building nears completion. Similarly, support is given in the learning of new material and is gradually removed as understanding increases, until finally it is removed altogether when learning has taken place. Scaffolding can take a number of forms:

- explaining: providing guidance and practice
- giving cues: giving clues, constructive questioning and feedback
- sorting information into an appropriate sequence
- modifying tasks: limiting the amount of information
- modelling: thinking aloud (i.e. think-speak) (Pritchard and Woollard, 2010: 42).

REFLECTIVE TASK 6.7

Identify aspects of your teaching that might be described as scaffolding. You will probably find you use this approach quite often. How can you modify what you do to minimise the level of support you offer to learners whilst still helping them to a successful outcome. How might you use Bandura and Vygotsky's ideas on modelling?

Whilst the works of Bandura and Vygotsky focus largely on learning in the early years, they also have relevance for the Further Education and Skills sector. The role of a subject mentor is to 'scaffold' development, and indeed all forms of mentoring, coaching, apprenticeship, on-the-job training and internships provide examples of social learning.

Advertising makes full use of social learning theory. Television commercials show us 'perfect' people experiencing desirable outcomes whilst modelling the purchasing behaviour we are meant to adopt. In real life, as opposed to the world of television, our contact with other people means that instances of social learning can be found in most of our day-to-day activities. This is also true for the learning environment and social learning is incidental to most forms of group work or collaborative learning where learners discuss and learn from each other. Learners themselves are keenly aware of the benefits of social learning and frequently ask each other for advice and information, similar to the 'phone a friend' spot on a popular television show.

Social learning theory impacts on practice in a number of ways – as part of the skills demonstration in Chapter 5, we have seen how as teachers we model desirable professional behaviours and attitudes, but we also use learners' actions and work as examples to model what is looked for, pointing out their positive consequences to other learners. We create opportunities for scaffolding at a formal level through 'buddying' and peer-tutoring and assessment, and at a more informal level by inviting learners to look at and discuss each other's work at the end of a session, particularly in a workshop situation.

HUMANISM

In the different perspectives covered so far, the focus has been on deciding what learning actually is and the processes through which it takes place. When turning to a humanistic perspective, the emphasis shifts towards a consideration of learners themselves, their characteristics and how these influence the learning that takes place. At the heart of the humanistic perspective on learning is 'the person'. Humanism came to the fore in the 1960s when the prevailing views were those of the behaviourist and psychoanalytical perspectives. Both of these suggested that people's actions and behaviours are controlled by factors other than their own free will; behaviourism implied that we are controlled by our environment and psycho-analytical approaches suggested that the subconscious is the determining factor in deciding on our actions. In response to this viewpoint, a group of psychologists which included Abraham Maslow and Carl Rogers asked what it is that makes humans 'human'. The conclusions they arrived at formed the basis of an alternative to the two prevalent theories and so they called their approach 'third force', or 'humanistic' psychology.

The major aim of the humanistic approach is to help people to maximise their potential for personal growth, which Maslow (1968: 29–31) regards as '*in itself*, a rewarding and exciting process … like playing the violin or being a good carpenter'. We all try to 'be the best that we can be' or, as humanists would describe it, strive for self-actualisation. This represents a very positive, optimistic view of people as learners, but we only have to look around at our learners to recognise that unfortunately this is not the case for all. It would appear that barriers exist which prevent the achievement of the desired state of self-actualisation.

REFLECTIVE TASK 6.8

What do you consider the main barriers to learning that are faced by your learners? What strategies do or can you use to overcome these?

Maslow termed these barriers 'deficiency needs' in his well-known Hierarchy of Needs, represented in Figure 6.6.

The process of achieving self-actualisation cannot begin until the deficiency needs are satisfied and strategies such as organising rooms, taking breaks at an appropriate

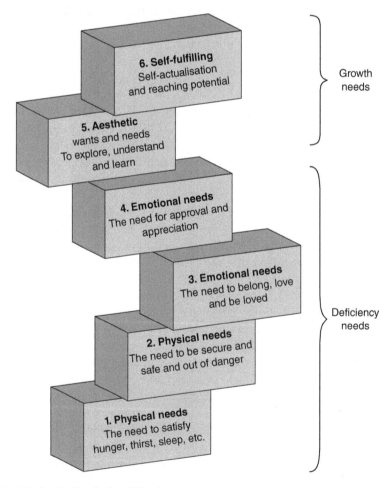

Figure 6.6   Maslow's Hierarchy of Needs

time, induction procedures, setting ground rules and icebreaking exercises are all intended to address this issue.

Carl Rogers started as a counsellor at a time when this was generally a directive process, with the counsellor offering advice and suggesting solutions to the client's problems. Rogers (1989: 12), however, came to the conclusion that:

> it is the client who knows what hurts, what directions to go, what problems are crucial, what experiences have been deeply buried. It began to occur to me that unless I had a need to demonstrate my own cleverness and learning, I would do better to rely on the client for the direction of movement in the process.

Clients, however, were not arriving at their own solutions. What was preventing them from doing this? Rogers argued that the job of the therapist was not to give advice but to help the client identify and overcome the 'barriers' that precluded them from arriving at a solution or, in the language of humanism, achieving self-actualisation.

Maslow and Rogers are like-minded in that they agree that humans strive towards self-actualisation, but barriers can exist which impede their progress towards this goal. Maslow's focus is on the nature of the barriers themselves, whilst Rogers is more concerned with the ways in which these can be overcome.

Rogers is mainly responsible for introducing the term 'facilitation' into common usage within education, and one of the more significant features of a humanistic approach is the role of the teacher as facilitator. This is a term which is rather difficult to pin down and define, although its purpose is fairly clear as the roots of the word come from the Latin 'facilis' which means 'to make something easy'. As Hunter et al. (1993: 5) explain:

> facilitation is about process – how you do something – rather than the content – what you do. A facilitator is a process guide, someone who makes a process easier or more convenient to use. Facilitation is about movement – moving from A to B. The facilitator helps to guide group members towards their chosen destination. Facilitation makes it easier to get to an agreed destination.

In terms of education, it would seem that the facilitator makes learning easy for others and is concerned with the process rather than the content of learning. This is associated with a movement towards empowerment, whereby learners begin to take control of and responsibility for their own learning.

Rogers saw the relationship between teacher and learner as the most significant factor in facilitation. He identified three characteristics that the facilitator needs to possess:

1. *Congruence* – genuineness, honesty with the learner and self.
2. *Empathy* – the ability to feel what the learner feels; to view the world through the eyes of the learner.
3. *Respect* – acceptance of and unconditional positive regard for the learner.

The facilitator creates a supportive environment and communicates this to the learner, thus creating the conditions that correspond with Rogers's famous quote: 'I know I cannot teach anyone anything; I can only provide an environment in which he can learn.' Rogers (1965) likened the process of facilitation to that of teaching a child to ride a bike, suggesting that you can't just tell them how. They have to try it for themselves. And you can't hold them up the whole time either. There comes a point when you have to let them go. If they fall, they fall, but if you hang on, they never learn.

The humanistic perspective lies behind the 'student-centred approach' to learning.

ACTIVITY 6.6

What does the term 'student-centred' mean to you? What aspects of your practice do you see as falling into this category?

This approach is difficult to define exactly but there is general agreement that what is important is not the activities engaged in but rather the climate and relationships which are formed. Brandes and Ginnis (1986: 6) echo Rogers in stating that 'In essence, student centred learning is not a bag of tricks; it is about attitudes and relationships'. They subsequently define student-centredness as 'a system of providing learning which has the student at its heart' (1986: 1). The determining factor in establishing a student-centred approach is the relationship between learner and teacher, and this determines the role of the teacher or facilitator.

Whilst the importance of relationship in underpinning the facilitative process is acknowledged, it doesn't actually tell us what to do. One of the major criticisms of the humanistic approach is that it is philosophical rather than scientific and less definitive in its practice. So how does a humanistic or student-centred approach work? Heron (1999) identifies the 'dimensions' of facilitation and also the different 'modes' in which the facilitator can operate. Interestingly, Heron (1999: 8) suggests that facilitation can take a directive or *hierarchical* form in which 'you [the facilitator] take full responsibility, in charge of all major decisions on all dimensions of the learning process', if that is appropriate to the needs of the group at that particular moment in time. A newly formed group with little knowledge or experience of the subject to hand, for instance, would require such an approach. As groups become more cohesive and gain knowledge and experience, facilitation becomes more a matter of *cooperation* and eventually will reach a stage of *autonomy* where control is largely handed over to the group itself. A parallel reasoning can also apply to the facilitation of learning at an individual level.

Brandes and Ginnis (1986) suggest a number of strategies appropriate to a student-centred approach:

- the circle
- the round
- brainstorming
- games
- open discussion
- problem solving
- contracts.

Rogers (2007: 107) adds discussion, role play and simulation to the list, however from the discussion above regarding facilitation it is apparent that it is not so much the activities themselves that are important but the manner in which they are conducted.

When it comes to assessment, we would not look to an externally set standard (criterion referencing) or the performance of others (norm referencing) to measure performance, as a humanistic approach concerns itself with the uniqueness of the individual. The type of referencing that is appropriate within a humanistic approach to learning is known as ipsative referencing. Ipsative referencing reflects individual achievement and so the point of comparison is the previous or usual performance of that individual. Self-actualisation is a measure of individual potential and ipsative referencing explores whether or not personal progress is being made; it is therefore developmental rather than judgemental. This can prove difficult to implement in practice, however, as in an educational system which is driven by results and accountability it is the reaching of a set standard (criterion referencing), the achievement of a higher grade than others (norm referencing) or a referencing system involving a combination of these two elements which is normally applied.

ANDRAGOGY

Andragogy is the name given to an approach to teaching adults popularised by Malcolm Knowles in the 1970s. He based his theory around 'what we know from experience and research of the unique characteristics of adult learners' after observing adults being taught in the same fashion as children, an approach he considered as inappropriate. Although the practice of teaching children (pedagogy) provided the initial impetus to Knowles's work, the comparison was later considered to be unhelpful and andragogy was subsequently presented as a general model of good practice.

ACTIVITY 6.7

Knowles considered adult learners to possess distinct characteristics. Reflect on your own experiences of learning. Do you learn differently to the way you did when a child? Consider also the characteristics of your own

(Continued)

learners. Do you consider them to be adults? If so, what are the character-istics they display? If not, what characteristics prevent them from coming into this category? See how your thoughts compare with those of Knowles outlined below.

In considering the nature of adult learners, Knowles initially identified four basic assumptions:

1. Self-concept

Self-concept relates to the way we view ourselves and has a strong bearing on the way in which we behave. Knowles defined adulthood as arriving at 'a self-concept of being responsible for our own lives, of being self-directing' (1990: 57). He considered that, with maturity, an individual's self-concept moves from one of dependency towards that of self-direction. Adults therefore need to be perceived as being respon-sible for themselves, otherwise resentment and resistance can result. On returning to an educational environment, however, the conditioning of their school experience can cause them to revert back to a dependent mode, a state which is at odds with their adult status. This raises the question as to whether adult learners see themselves as adults (independent, capable of making their own decisions) or learners (dependent, needing instruction and direction). Knowles (1990) advocates the use of learning activities that help adult learners make this transition from the dependency of the learner to the self-directedness of the adult.

2. Experience

Age brings with it an accumulation of rich and varied experience which provides both a resource for learning and a base on which to relate new learning. Many of the activi-ties commonly used in adult and community education, such as discussion, case studies and problem-solving activities, tap into this pool of experience. Knowles (1990) claimed that adults identify very strongly with their experiences; these form part of their identity and to acknowledge experience is to also acknowledge the person. Conversely, to ignore experience is equivalent to ignoring or rejecting the person. Knowles advances a strong case for the use of experiential approaches to learning but acknowledges that experience can also have a negative side as it can lead to habit and a closed mind.

3. Readiness to learn

Knowles (1990) believed that adults do not learn 'what they ought' but are ready to learn what is important to them at the time. This is influenced by the different social roles taken on as we grow older. Knowles cites the example of a girl who would not be ready to learn about infant nutrition or marital relationships whilst at school but would be very ready to learn about these things when she became engaged to be married.

4. Orientation to learning

Adults do not learn 'subjects' but learn in order to complete tasks or solve problems which are part of their daily life. As these tasks and problems need to be tackled now rather than on some distant future occasion, adults need to see immediate results in their learning.

These four original assumptions were first published in 1975 but a further two assumptions, relating to motivation and the need to know, were added in 1984 and 1989 respectively, as follows.

5. Motivation

Whilst acknowledging that adults can be motivated by rewards such as better jobs or higher salaries, Knowles maintained that as a person matures the motivation to learn becomes internalised. Self-esteem and quality of life or just the need to keep growing and developing become more important in giving adults a reason to learn.

6. The need to know

Knowles (1990) was influenced by the work of Alan Tough who regarded the major-ity of adult learning (80 per cent) as occurring through individual learning projects. Tough found that considerable energy was invested in weighing up the benefits of the proposed learning and the negative consequences of not engaging in it. Knowles surmised from this that adult learners need to be made aware of the 'need to know' in order to commit fully to learning.

You will doubtless have recognised strong elements of the humanistic approach in Knowles's work which may not be unexpected as he bases it around the characteris-tics and subsequent needs of the learner, albeit from a generalised rather than individualised viewpoint.

Knowles devised a number of 'design elements' in the learning process which should be applied in a manner appropriate to the adult status of learners. These were climate, planning, diagnosis of needs, formulation of objectives, design and activities, and finally, evaluation. All of the above should be approached as joint enterprises between teacher and learner, emphasising the role of the teacher as facilitator. Knowles cites activities such as planning, negotiation, needs diagnosis and re-diagnosis as 'mutual' pursuits.

Generally, an andragogical approach to learning is experiential in nature, with an emphasis on negotiation to ensure individual needs are being met. Knowles (1990) recognised the need for a structure of some kind, however, to convert his 'design elements' from statements of intent into actual practice. Learning contracts, as encountered in Chapter 5, are extensively used to achieve this.

The concept of andragogy is not without its critics, although none appear to have offered a practical alternative. A summary of their views, by Merriam, Caffarella and Baumgartner (2007: 85–90), include:

- It is unclear whether andragogy constitutes a theory of teaching, a theory of learning or a series of principles of good practice.
- Several of its assumptions are problematical.
- It ignores the social context within which learning takes place.
- It is culturally and politically specific.

Andragogy has nonetheless had a big impact on adult education and 'practitioners who work with adult learners continue to find Knowles's Andragogy, with its characteristics of adult learners, to be a helpful rubric for better understanding adults as learners' (Merriam et al., 2007: 92).

SUMMARY OF KEY POINTS

In this chapter, we have looked at the different theories of learning and how they inform our everyday practice. No one theory accounts for all aspects of learning and we draw on all of them in arriving at our own personal theory of learning on which we base our approach to teaching.

The key points in this chapter are:

- *Behaviourist* theory requires that learning is measurable and therefore evidenced in an observable form. Teaching is planned and assessed in a systematic manner, based around learning objectives. Teaching strategies tend to be teacher-led and classroom management techniques are based on rules, rewards and sanctions.
- *Cognitive* theory regards learning as a search for meaning and understanding. It favours active forms of learning such as problem-solving and discovery-based approaches. Classroom management techniques revolve around a view of the whole person rather than just the behaviours they exhibit.

- *Information processing* theory compares the brain to a computer and identifies attention, perception and memory as the main procedures involved in processing information. Teaching is carried out in a manner designed to increase the efficiency of these processes.
- *Neuro-cognitive* approaches use brain imaging techniques to examine how various mental processes are implemented in the brain. In common with information processing theory, processes such as attention, perception and memory are explored but the physiology of the brain and how it can best be looked after, increasing its efficiency, is also a point of focus.
- *Social learning* theory speculates that we learn from one another through the processes of observation, imitation and modelling. Learning from those more knowledgeable than ourselves through the technique of scaffolding allows us to achieve what we could not through our own efforts alone.
- *Humanism* places high importance on the uniqueness of the individual and their drive to reach their full potential. Learning is a response to individual needs and is planned and carried out through a process of facilitation.
- *Andragogy* is based around the characteristics of adults as learners. Adult learners are self-directing and capable of making their own educational decisions. This is facilitated through the use of devices such as learning contracts.

REFERENCES

Amsel, A. (1989) Behaviourism, Neobehaviourism and Cognitivism in Learning Theory: Historical and Contemporary Perspectives. Hillsdale, NJ: Lawrence Erlbaum.

Ausubel, D. (1963) *The Psychology of Meaningful Verbal Learning*. New York: Grune & Stratton.

Bandura, A. (1977) *Social Learning Theory*. New York: General Learning Press.

Brandes, D. and Ginnis, P. (1986) *A Guide to Student-centred Learning*. Oxford: Blackwell.

Bruner, J. (1963) *The Process of Education*. Cambridge, Mass: Harvard University Press.

Broadbent, D. (1958) *Perception and Communication*. Oxford: Pergamon.

Gould, J. (2012) Learning Theory and Classroom Practice in the Lifelong Learning Sector (2nd edn). Exeter: Learning Matters.

Gregory, R.L. (1990) *Eye and Brain: The Psychology of Seeing* (4th edn). London: Weidenfeld & Nicolson.

Heron, J. (1999) *The Complete Facilitator's Handbook*. London: Kogan Page.

Hunter, D., Bailey, A. and Taylor, B. (1993) *The Art of Facilitation*. Auckland: Tandem Press.

Jensen, E. (2008) Brain-based Learning: The New Paradigm of Teaching (2nd edn). London: Sage.

Joyce, B., Weil, M. and Calhoun, E. (2011) *Models of Teaching* (8th edn). Boston, MA: Pearson Education.

Knowles, M. (1990) *The Adult Learner: A Neglected Species* (4th edn). Houston, TX: Gulf Publishing.

Lancet (1999) 20 Nov.; 354(9192):1828. The Nobel chronicles. 1981: Roger Wolcott Sperry (1913–94); David Hunter Hubel (b. 1926); Torsten N. Wiesel (b. 1924).

MacLean, P.D. (1985) Evolutionary psychiatry and the triune brain. *Psychological Medicine*, 15(2): 219–221.

Maslow, A. (1968) *Towards a Psychology of Being* (2nd edn). New York: Van Nostrand-Reinhold.

McNeil, F. (2009) *Learning with the Brain in Mind*. London: Sage.

McPhillimy, B. (1996) *Controlling Your Class*. Chichester: Wiley.

Merriam, S., Caffarella, R. and Baumgartner, L. (2007) *Learning in Adulthood: A Comprehensive Guide* (3rd edn). San Francisco: Jossey-Bass.

Nash, I., Jones, S., Ecclestone, K. and Brown, A. (eds) (2008) *Students Reap Benefits but Lecturers are Under Stress: Challenge and Change in Further Education*. London: TLRP. Available online at: http://learning.gov.wales/docs/learningwales/publications/140721-challenge-change-in-fe-en.pdf (accessed 25/04/17).

Penney, J.C. (n.d.) 101 Kickass startup quotes via onboard. Available online at: http://onboardly.com/content-marketing/101-kickass-startup-quotes/ (accessed 25/04/17).

Popper, K. (1959/1992) *The Logic of Scientific Discovery*. London & New York: Routledge.

Pritchard, A. and Woollard, J. (2010) *Constuctivism and Social Learning*. Abingdon: Routledge.

Reece, I. and Walker, S. (2007) *Teaching, Training and Learning* (6th edn). Sunderland: Business Education Publishers.

Rogers, C. (1965) *Client-centred Therapy*. Boston and New York: Houghton-Mifflin.

Rogers, C. (1989) *On Becoming a Person*. Boston and New York: Houghton Mifflin.

Rogers, J. (2007) *Adults Learning* (5th edn). Maidenhead: Open University Press/McGraw-Hill.

Sekuler, R. and Blake, R. (2002) *Perception*. New York: McGraw-Hill.

Skinner, B.F. (1953) *Science and Human Behaviour*. New York: The Free Press.

Solso, R., Maclin, M. and Maclin, O. (2005) *Cognitive Psychology* (7th edn). Boston, MA: Allyn & Bacon.

Vygotsky, L.S. (1978) *Mind in Society: Development of Higher Psychological Processes*. Cambridge, MA: Harvard University Press.

Watson, J.B. (1919) *Psychology from the Standpoint of a Behaviorist*. Philadelphia: Lippincott.

FURTHER READING

Aubrey, K. and Riley, A. (2015) *Understanding and Using Educational Theories*. London: Sage.

Rather than using theory as a starting point, the initial focus of this book is the theorists themselves, exploring their background and the context of the time before reviewing their specific contributions within the field of learning theory. As well as the 'usual suspects' such as Piaget, Skinner, Bruner and Vygotsky, others such as Kolb, Schon and Montessori are also covered. A follow-up book – *Understanding and Using Challenging Educational Theories* (2017) – uses a similar format and will have a particular appeal if you are interested in Humanistic approaches as its first three chapters look at the lives and work of Maslow, Rogers and A.S. Neill, founder of Summerhill school.

Ormrod, J.E. (2012) *Human Learning* **(6th edn). London: Pearson.**
An excellent book to explore some of the theories explored in this chapter in greater depth. Part two of the book focuses on Behaviourism, Part three on Social learning and part four on Cognitive perspectives.

Rogers, C. and Freiberg, H.J. (1994) *Freedom To Learn.* **New York: Macmillan.**
Humanistic approaches to education are based around a number of beliefs and assumptions rather than conclusions drawn from objective scientific experiment. It is more of a philosophical approach and so it is best to go back to the original writers to gain a full understanding of what is entailed. *Freedom To Learn* is a seminal text in this respect and discusses concepts such as 'responsible freedom', facilitation and relationships in an accessible manner with plenty of examples to both help understanding of the rather abstract concepts involved but also to bring the text to life.

7

MANAGING LEARNERS

Successful teaching involves not only the management of learning, but also the management of those who are to undertake this learning – the learners themselves. This chapter explores different aspects of this process with the initial focus on the creation of the kind of inclusive environment which promotes learning as part of a well-formed and supportive group. As well as supportive surroundings, learners need to want to learn, and strategies for encouraging and maintaining motivation are discussed next. Instances of challenging behaviour on the part of learners can still be encountered, notwithstanding the above, and cause of, prevention of and response to such incidents completes the chapter.

When you have completed this chapter you will be able to:

- review the various factors which contribute to an inclusive learning experience
- discuss the factors which play a significant part in determining the kind of impression that is made at a first meeting with a group of learners
- evaluate the effectiveness of an induction programme
- describe the characteristics of the learning environment, teachers, teaching sessions and learners which influence the motivation to learn
- describe the type of relationship between teachers and learners that is appropriate to the Further Education and Skills sector
- identify instances of challenging behaviour
- review examples of good practice in managing learners and their learning

- explain the role of effective classroom management in preventing incidents of challenging behaviour
- differentiate between aggressive, passive and assertive responses to challenging behaviour and evaluate the effectiveness of each
- evaluate the use of rules-based approaches to managing challenging behaviour
- classify different approaches to the setting of ground rules
- describe the approach used in 'assertive discipline'.

CREATING A POSITIVE CLIMATE

Learners who feel secure and free from anxiety, and experience a positive, inclusive learning environment are more likely to turn their attention and energies towards their learning. Managing the learning environment therefore plays a significant part in managing learners. To start thinking about what this involves, complete Activity 7.1.

ACTIVITY 7.1

Reflect on your own experiences as a learner. If in the past you have felt anxious or insecure in your learning, try to identify the reasons for this. They may be personal factors or factors relating to teacher attitudes or the climate within the learning environment.

It is likely that your response to Activity 7.1 will include reference to teacher actions such as:

- poor planning and organisation
- lack of enthusiasm
- patronising learners or putting them 'on the spot'

or a learning environment in which you felt:

- the atmosphere was overly competitive
- unsure of others in the group
- you were not listened to or your opinions were not respected.

As part of a supportive group and with a teacher who recognises and responds to individual needs, the natural anxieties and insecurities felt by some learners can be reduced, with a resulting positive effect on learning. The importance of initial assessment in providing reassurance to learners, that their choice of course is appropriate and that their support needs are recognised, has already been discussed, but it is the first meeting between the teacher and learner(s) that can prove to be a significant time in establishing the sort of climate in which learning will flourish. One of the major aims of that first session is to reduce anxiety levels and to begin to establish some form of relationship or rapport between teacher and learners and between learners themselves.

FIRST IMPRESSIONS

First impressions are lasting and set the initial tone, so the initial impressions created both at individual and institutional level need to be positive.

Most institutions run induction programmes which are designed to ensure that all learners have as smooth a transition as possible into their new course and the culture and expectations of the institution. Their purpose is to welcome learners, to help them understand what their course is about and to settle in quickly. In a large institution, a typical induction programme will include:

- an introduction to staff who will be teaching on the course
- how to find your way about the site
- an introduction to any services such as the learning resource centre, information, advice and guidance (IAG), counselling and welfare
- health and safety information
- Learning Agreements
- developing Individual Learning Plans (ILPs)
- policies such as Complaints, Equality and Diversity.

The form that induction takes will depend on context, the nature of the course and the learners. For a group of younger learners embarking on a full-time programme, the process can be spread over a week. For an adult group on a short, part-time course, it may take no more than the first 10 minutes of the first session, but regardless of the form induction takes, at its conclusion learners should feel more secure and committed to the course they are to take.

At a personal level, some of the things learners notice about teachers on first meeting them are how well prepared and organised they are, the kind of body language they display, how confident they appear and how they are dressed. The impressions formed from these observations influence the level of confidence they have in their teachers and how they react to them.

The issue of dress is tricky. Sometimes the context of the teaching determines this – laboratories and workshop environments require white/brown coats or similar and appropriate protective footwear, goggles, etc.; sports subjects are normally taught in tracksuits – but generally a choice is made. Learners on professional courses may expect dress appropriate to that kind of environment; younger learners may be 'put off' by formal dress, whereas older learners may take offence at a more casual dress code. Whilst dress may be a matter of personal preference, the impression it gives to learners does need to be considered.

As part of the first meeting, steps can be taken to encourage the group to 'gel'. Chapter 5 described how theories of group development suggest that groups form in a series of stages. The first stage involves the coming together of the members of the potential group. This is followed by a 'jostling for position' before 'norms', or expectations of behaviour, from those in the group, begin to emerge. It is only after this last stage that the group begins to function as a working unit. These stages were summarised as forming, storming, norming and performing by Tuckman (1965).

The first steps towards creating a supportive and interactive group can be taken with the setting of ground rules as a guide to expected behaviours, helping to establish group 'norms', and the use of an icebreaking exercise to allow learners to get to know each other better. Icebreaking exercises help ease groups through the 'forming' stage. These can be quick activities amounting to no more than brief introductions around the group if time is at a premium or can take a longer, more involved form if time is available. Figure 7.1 illustrates Francis and Gould's (2013: 20) categorisation of icebreaking activities.

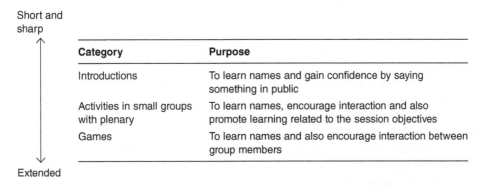

Short and
sharp

Category	Purpose
Introductions	To learn names and gain confidence by saying something in public
Activities in small groups with plenary	To learn names, encourage interaction and also promote learning related to the session objectives
Games	To learn names and also encourage interaction between group members

Extended

Figure 7.1 Types of icebreakers

Each category of icebreaker has a slightly different function but all go some way towards dispelling that initial nervousness and anxiety that exist when a group comes together for the first time. The type of exercise used will depend on the time available and what the teacher feels comfortable with and considers appropriate, given the age and nature of the group. Whatever the decision, some form of icebreaking exercise, no matter how brief, will invariably help in encouraging an otherwise disparate bunch of people take their first steps towards becoming a learning group.

REFLECTIVE TASK 7.1

Think carefully about the kind of first impression you wish to create with the groups you teach - formal, informal, approachable, serious, light-hearted, business-like, structured, interactive. What can you do and how would you organise that first meeting to ensure this is the case?

MANAGING MOTIVATION

We now turn from a consideration of the learning environment to a consideration of learners themselves. Further Education and Skills falls outside of the compulsory sector of education and so, by definition, learners who participate do so by choice. From an external perspective, it would therefore be reasonable to assume that learners are eager to learn and behave accordingly. This is probably true for the vast majority of learners but there will be others for whom this is not the case. Sometimes the choice to engage in learning may be made 'for' learners rather than 'by' them, either through circumstance or the influence of others. 'Other' reasons for engaging in further learning may well include:

- parental pressure
- the lack of employment opportunities
- a wish to avoid taking on personal responsibility.

With such learners, the motivational challenge for teachers is to show them that there is some personal advantage to be gained from the course they are to take. They need to see that what they will be studying has some relevance both to themselves and any future aspirations they may have; they need to be convinced that their studies will provide a worthwhile experience which will result in a productive outcome. Other learners may arrive with a clear aim in mind. The task here is to maintain their motivation at its initial level throughout the rest of the course.

There are many different theories regarding motivation and some of these have been touched on in Chapter 6. Some, particularly those with a behaviourist bias, take the view that motivation is dependent on factors in the environment – motivation is extrinsic. Others, such as Maslow, regard the internal needs of the individual to be what motivates them – motivation is intrinsic. Intrinsic motivation is considered to be the more effective of the two, but is difficult to influence directly. We can aim to arouse curiosity in the way in which we introduce a topic, using questions or a problem-solving approach, or perhaps encourage interest by starting from a consideration of practical application. Largely, however, we rely on strategies which influence extrinsic motivation with the intention that, over time, these will bring about a shift towards intrinsic motivation. The areas in which we can exert an influence are:

- If learners experience a *learning environment* equipped with appropriate facilities and within which they feel part of a supportive group, they are much more likely to be positively motivated in their learning.
- *Teachers* who are enthusiastic about their subject and are professional but approachable in their manner are more likely to produce motivated learners.
- *Teaching sessions* which encourage active participation, setting challenging but achievable tasks, complemented by constructive feedback and appropriate use of praise, are also likely to result in well-motivated learners.
- Perhaps most importantly, *learners* who are successful in their learning and feel they have some say in it, are the most likely to be highly motivated.

The above provides a guide to general approaches which will have a positive effect on learner motivation as a whole. When considering individual cases of learners with poor motivation to learning, however, we need to follow the example of a doctor who, in order to decide on the most appropriate treatment for a particular ailment, needs to know what is causing it in the first place. Is it a lack of success in learning, a lack of interest, a need for more or less structure, or simply a lack of urgency or drive? Does it stem from previous or current experiences of learning? Without the answers to such questions, it is difficult to decide on the most appropriate response to the lack of motivation being shown.

ACTIVITY 7.2

Identify three learners you have come into contact with who display poor motivation in their learning. For each, identify the cause.

In the same way that the causes of a lack of motivation vary from one person to another, what motivates a particular learner can also be quite personal. Generally, the use of rewards, for example, is considered to be a strategy for managing motivation, but what one person sees as a reward, another might view differently. The reward may have to be tailored to the individual. Managing motivation effectively, in common with most aspects of successful teaching, involves an awareness of the characteristics and individual needs of learners.

ACTIVITY 7.3

Refer back to Activity 7.2. You identified the cause of poor motivation in three specific learners. For each, now devise a strategy which would work for each individual learner.

Whilst motivation can be managed 'on the hoof', it can also be managed pro-actively as part of the planning process. The answers to the following five questions will serve as a general motivation checklist in planning:

1. How can I ensure that learners experience a supportive physical and social environment?
2. What can I do to help learners recognise the learning as relevant to them?
3. Have I planned for sufficient variety and opportunity for learners to participate in and contribute to this session?
4. How can I make sure that learners recognise they have been successful in their learning?
5. Can I include any opportunities within this session whereby learners take on some responsibility for their own learning?

It is important to consider learner motivation in planning as not only does poor motivation result in less effective learning but it can also be a contributory factor to any challenging behaviour which learners might display, and it is to this that we turn next.

CHALLENGING BEHAVIOUR

The second theme of this chapter focuses on 'classroom management', but may more accurately be considered as 'management of learners' given the wide range of possible teaching and learning environments, and the diversity of learners that exist within the sector. Although the majority of learners genuinely want to learn and will display appropriate attitudes and behaviours, it cannot be assumed that this is the case for *all* learners and some will present challenges that have to be met. The level of that challenge will vary, depending on who, what and where you teach, and the remainder of this chapter needs to be viewed from the perspective of your own working context and the nature of your own particular learners. Some parts will bear more direct relevance to your practice than others but the general principles can be interpreted and adapted to suit your own circumstances.

WHAT LEARNING THEORY TELLS US

We have already seen how learning theory can inform us of some of the issues related to challenging behaviour and suggest some general approaches to its management.

In behaviourism, the actual behaviour is the focus of attention and is managed through a system of rules and consequences. Desirable behaviour is encouraged through reinforcement and undesirable behaviour is discouraged through a lack of reinforcement or some form of punishment such as the withdrawal of privileges.

From a cognitive angle, the behaviour is only one part of the overall picture and a more holistic view of the person must be taken. Strategies focus on establishing a working relationship with learners, leading to identification of the cause of the inappropriate behaviour and strategies to remedy this. Previous negative experiences in learning are often a cause. A cognitive approach involves trying to see the situation from the point of view of the learner and showing them that it is in their interests to adopt the required behaviour.

For the humanist, inappropriate behaviour is seen largely as a response to a lack of control by learners over their own learning. Learners are given increasing responsibility for their own learning and behaviour, supported by teachers who can empathise with their view of the world.

In social learning theory, behaviour is learned through the example of and contact with others. Teachers should model appropriate behaviours and show how appropriate behaviour by others in the group leads to positive outcomes and how inappropriate behaviour leads to negative outcomes.

From a neuro-cognitive point of view, during adolescence the area of the brain situated in the prefrontal cortex is in an ongoing state of development which continues into early adulthood. At this stage, the potential for learning is high but so is the propensity for risk-taking and impulsive behaviour. The as yet underdeveloped processes include the ability to 'inhibit inappropriate behaviours'.

WHAT IS CHALLENGING BEHAVIOUR?

The types of behavioural issues we wish to discuss are variously known as 'challenging', 'inappropriate', 'undesirable' and 'difficult'. For the purposes of this chapter, we use the term 'challenging behaviour' as defined by LSDA (2007) which identifies the following areas:

- behaviours that disrupt routine teaching and interfere with the concentration of other learners
- violent or offensive behaviour that interferes with 'routine activity'
- behaviours which offend, ridicule or intimidate other learners
- non-engagement in learning (LSDA, 2007: 2).

The LSDA report also includes intermittent attendance, but we will focus on the four issues above.

First, we consider incidents which may be accompanied by or threaten to involve some form of violence. Research by various FE organisations suggests that an all-college approach is required to manage behaviour effectively, and so most organisations within the sector will have some form of policy and procedures in place to deal with more serious incidents. You should make sure you are thoroughly familiar with all procedures within your institution relating to behaviour management and disciplinary procedures and make full use of them. Such procedures are backed by the authority of the institution as a whole and using them will take some of the pressure off you. Mitchell et al. (1998) conducted a major research project into managing behaviour in FE and found that consistency was key in implementing an all-college approach. This applied at:

- the strategic level where policy is devised
- the systems level where procedures to enact policy are developed

but perhaps most importantly at:

- the delivery level where all staff need to be consistent and fair in their application of procedures.

Policies and procedures are there to be used and, moreover, rely on staff using them in a consistent manner to maintain their effectiveness. All forms of institutional support that are available should be called on when necessary, and certainly more serious instances of challenging behaviour should be reported and dealt with through the appropriate channels.

REFLECTIVE TASK 7.2

Are you aware of the behaviour management policies that operate within your institution? Find and consult them. Do you use them to support you in managing your students' behaviours? How might you make better use of them?

Dix (2010) suggests that, unlike schools, confrontation in the Further Education and Skills sector is more likely to occur between students rather than between students and staff. Even in schools, violent behaviour towards teachers is still relatively rare. Although serious incidents tend to be the exception, it is likely that you will be aware of the groups in which any potentially serious behaviour problems are likely to occur, and, as Dix (2010: 98) recommends, 'if you are working with particularly volatile groups, make sure you have a rehearsed procedure for calling on support/security'. As Rogers points out in the foreword to Gribble's (2006) book, its title is 'in a class *of* your own', not 'in a class *on* your own'.

The most common instances of challenging behaviour likely to be encountered, however, are normally classified as being 'low-level' in nature. In a similar fashion to Chinese Water Torture, although the individual 'drips' are fairly insignificant, their cumulative effect can be significant. Low-level disruption can be persistent in nature and constantly having to deal with it can be a draining experience. More importantly perhaps, if left unchecked it can escalate into more serious situations.

ACTIVITY 7.4

What kinds of low-level disruption occur within your teaching? You might like to keep these in mind as you work through the rest of the chapter.

Teachers in the sector normally identify the following as falling into this category:

- talking to others at the same time as the teacher is speaking
- ignoring instructions
- 'playing the fool', particularly during small group activities
- asking personal questions
- trying to 'catch the teacher out'
- texting on mobile phones
- throwing objects across the room
- using offensive language.

Reasons for such low-level disruption are numerous, and, in Chapter 6, we identified diverting attention from failure as one possible cause. *Behaviour and Motivation: Disruption in Further Education*, a discussion document created by the Further Education Unit in 1987, cites mismatch as a major cause. Some of the examples of mismatch identified in the report include those between:

- learning and teaching styles
- expectations and ability
- teacher authority and learner autonomy
- course content and learner aspirations
- constraints of provision and needs of learners.

Other more straightforward causes might be personal issues, the lesson learners have just come from, the weather or simply 'having a bad day'. Particular reasons can be more prevalent within certain groups of learners. Vizard (2007: 4–7), for instance, provides a comprehensive list of influences and possible reasons for challenging behaviours presented by learners aged 14–16.

RELATIONSHIPS

In exploring the issue of challenging behaviour, the type of teacher/learner relationship appropriate to the sector is worth exploring. Although we have identified instances in which this may not always be the case, attendance, within the sector, is generally voluntary. An authoritarian approach is therefore deemed to be inappropriate and many learners come in with the expectation that 'it will be different from school'. They expect a more informal environment in which they will be treated in a more adult fashion. It was noted in Chapter 6 that for Carl Rogers (1989) a relationship between teacher/facilitator and learner of mutual respect and trust is the most important factor in bringing about learning. Others also emphasise the importance of relationships. Vizard (2007: 36) includes relationships in his '10 Rs of positive behaviour management' (two others are the related areas of rapport and respect); Bill Rogers (2006) emphasises the importance of cooling off and re-establishing working relationships ('repair and build') as part of the overall process of behaviour management; and Smith and Laslett (1993) refer to 'getting on with them' as one of their four areas to address in classroom management. Relationships, then, are an important aspect of creating a positive learning environment.

REFLECTIVE TASK 7.3

Think back to your own experience of learning and consider the types of relationship you had with your own teachers that you found the most helpful to you in your learning. How would you describe these? How were you addressed? What kind of body language was used? How does your own practice compare? What can you learn from a consideration of these examples that might influence the relationship you have with your own learners?

A productive relationship is often confused with being friendly towards or being liked by learners. Whilst in real life we all like to be liked and to get on with those we come into contact with, this is not necessarily the most appropriate starting point in establishing a relationship within the learning environment. As Dix (2010: 100) suggests,

'It's not about trying to get down with the kids', a view supported by Fairclough (2008: 48) who suggests that 'learners do not want the teacher to be one of them', but adds that 'at the other end of the scale, learners are not comfortable if the teacher is psychologically too far removed from them, and therefore not easily approachable'.

A balance needs to be found in which a professional distance is maintained whilst establishing a good working relationship, which leads to effective communication and promotes cooperation in all classroom activities. A useful checklist of the characteristics of a good working relationship is supplied by Glasser (2005) who believed that the relationship between teacher and learner is the crux to meeting learner needs. He lists the following 'seven caring habits' that teachers should exhibit in the classroom:

- supporting
- encouraging
- listening
- accepting
- trusting
- respecting
- negotiating differences

contrasting these with 'the seven deadly habits' listed below:

- criticising
- blaming
- complaining
- nagging
- threatening
- punishing
- bribing/rewarding to control.

How do these compare with your response to the last activity?

PREVENTION

McManus (1995: 82) suggests that 'it often appears that experienced teachers have trouble-free lessons not through knowing how to cope with troublesome behaviour but simply because it does not seem to arise in their classrooms'. Within your own experience, you may well have noticed that the same group of learners often behave and react differently to different teachers. This difference can be attributed not only to the relationship that exists between the two but also to the way in which different practitioners teach and manage their groups. Well-delivered teaching, coupled with the use of appropriate management techniques, can prevent challenging behaviour. If learners feel part of the group, are presented with work that is interesting, relevant and within their grasp but still provides a challenge, and involved in active rather than passive learning which leaves them with a feeling of achievement, then their energies are likely to be channelled into their learning rather than challenging behaviour. This is the approach taken in a well-known study conducted by Kounin (1970). Kounin identified a group of teachers who were regarded by their peers as excellent 'classroom managers' and observed them at work, looking for common approaches in their practice.

His research indicated that effective teachers are those who prevent problems from occurring in the first place. His focus wasn't on how teachers dealt with misbehaviour, but on the reasons it did not occur in the first place.

In general, he observed that behaviour problems were kept to a minimum when students were actively engaged in their learning, and went on to identify specific teacher actions that influenced this. The key points fall into three areas:

1. Reacting to learners – the general management of learners.
2. Movement management – ways of keeping a session flowing.
3. Group focus – keeping groups busy and on task.

Reacting to learners

Kounin (1970) identified some significant features in the way teachers reacted to and gave signals to their learners:

*   ripple effect

Kounin observed that the effects of any interaction between a teacher and an individual learner were not confined to the two direct participants, but also influenced those directly around them, rather in the way that a stone dropped into still water sets up a ripple that spreads outwards for some distance. Praising one learner had a positive effect on other learners around; reprimanding a specific learner made those around more attentive to their work. When directly confronting a learner, the resulting ripple can either be 'positive' or 'negative' from the teacher's perspective, depending on the light it shows them in. This could influence decisions on whether to deal with particular issues within a whole-class setting or on an individual basis at the conclusion of the session.

*   withitness

Withitness, or what Rogers (2006) terms 'relaxed vigilance', refers to the need for the teacher to be aware of what is going on in all parts of the learning environment at all times and for learners to be aware that this is the case. Withitness makes a significant contribution to 'nipping in the bud' any potential problems before they occur. Learners soon pick up on whether teachers are 'with it' or not; they need to know that teachers 'have eyes in the back of their head'. Signs of 'withitness' include maintaining eye contact, the use of non-verbal signals, asking questions, moving around all areas of the learning environment and, in particular, standing near to learners who show signs of impending misbehaviour. Careful consideration of room layout, the composition of groups and positioning in the room are also signs of 'withitness'. Vizard (2007: 59) stresses the importance of adopting a position from 'where you can scan or "light-house" the whole group'.

- overlapping

Overlapping bears some similarities to 'withitness' and refers to situations where effective teachers tend to two or more events simultaneously, rather than focusing on one at the expense of the other(s). Examples include giving feedback to one learner whilst still monitoring the progress of others, introducing a topic whilst 'patrolling', dealing with latecomers whilst maintaining a watchful eye on the rest of the group or giving feedback to one group whilst addressing another group in another part of the room who are not focused on the task.

It appears that learners are more likely to focus on their work and less likely to misbehave if they think that the teacher is aware of what they are doing, and so the teacher lets them know this is the case by using a variety of verbal and non-verbal signals.

Movement management

This refers not to the movement of learners, but to the movement within a teaching session, which Kounin (1970) defines as the extent to which it proceeds smoothly without digressions, diversions or interruptions. Teaching sessions which flow well and maintain attention are less likely to offer opportunities for misbehaviour. Kounin identified two characteristics of such lessons:

- smoothness

There needs to be a smooth transition between activities, keeping lessons moving and avoiding abrupt changes. Each activity or topic area in a lesson is summarised and linked to the next, which is introduced in an appropriate manner, avoiding gaps or pauses in proceedings. Kounin identified a number of activities in which teachers engage that lead to a lack of 'smoothness'. These include leaving a topic or activity 'dangling' to be dealt with at another time, 'flip-flopping' between one activity and another, 'thrusting' irrelevant information or advice at learners when they are engaged in a task and over-exposing learners to a topic or activity, giving too much information at one time and leading to 'satiation' – where they have had enough.

- momentum

Momentum refers to appropriate pace and progression through a lesson, keeping learners busy and engaged throughout.

Group focus

This involves keeping the whole class involved and interested and makes use of two techniques:

- group alerting

The entire group is kept actively engaged through the creation of interest or suspense, by asking questions of both the group and individuals, but in a random rather than predictable manner.

- group accountability

The teacher makes the group aware that their contributions are being monitored and there is an expectation that their efforts will lead to an end-product of some description.

Prior to Kounin, the management of behaviour and teaching had been considered to be separate issues – in Victorian times, the qualifications required of a teacher were subject knowledge and the ability to administer a good thrashing! Kounin (1970) was one of the first to identify the connection between the two, arguing that challenging behaviour can be prevented by the effective management of learners and learning, and is more easily dealt with before rather than after it occurs. Rogers (2006: 108) echoes this sentiment, suggesting: 'The key question we need to ask is "How can I prevent, or minimise, unnecessary hassles or problems?"' Both suggest that approaches to classroom discipline should be built around keeping learners fully engaged. The message is fairly clear – when learners are stimulated by and involved in their learning, challenging behaviour of the type identified earlier is far less likely to occur.

Smith and Laslett (1993) consider prevention from the standpoint of different phases of a teaching session. Their four rules of classroom management are:

1. Get them in.
2. Get them out.
3. Get on with it.
4. Get on with them.

They consider that most behaviour problems arise from a poor start to the session and stress the importance of the way in which learners are greeted, where they sit and ensuring a brisk, business-like start with a 'warm-up' activity ready to occupy learners straight away. 'Getting them out' is considered the next most vulnerable time offering opportunities for misbehaviour and so, rather than bags being packed and an anticipatory shuffle towards the door taking place when learners decide the session has ended, an orderly conclusion is also of paramount importance as it sets the tone for subsequent sessions. Like Kounin, Smith and Laslett stress the importance of 'momentum' in a session in the 'get on with it' phase, ensuring that learners are kept busy and fully engaged in work that is of an appropriate level. The final phase of 'getting on with them' addresses appropriate teacher/learner relationships.

REFLECTIVE TASK 7.4

Review your own procedures for beginning and ending teaching sessions. Do they differ depending on the group you are taking? Do Smith and Laslett offer any suggestions you might find useful at these phases of a teaching session?

Another useful perspective is provided by the 'ABC' approach to managing behaviour. This is based on the premise that any incidence of challenging behaviour will contain three elements (ABC) which occur in the following sequence:

Antecedent (A) – the event that takes place before the behaviour. It is this event that prompts or triggers the behaviour itself.

Behaviour (B) – what the learner does. In this context of this chapter, the focus is on challenging behaviour that results from the antecedent, although this model can also be used to explore and analyse desirable behaviours.

Consequence (C) – what happens as a result of the behaviour displayed. Generally, positive consequences lead to repetition of the behaviour, whilst negative consequences make it less likely to recur (refer back to behaviourist theory, earlier in this chapter).

The antecedent or 'trigger' for the behaviour could be a number of things. It could be related to interactions with the teacher, other learners, the work set, the activity engaged in, personal factors, existing rules … the list is fairly endless, but if the event that triggers the behaviour in question can be identified, strategies can be formulated which will help to avoid or reduce further incidences of this behaviour.

REFLECTIVE TASK 7.5

If you have recently experienced any form of incident with learners, analyse it using the ABC framework. What 'triggered' the event? Does this suggest alternative ways of dealing with the incident or perhaps confirm that the actions taken were the most appropriate? What can be done to avoid such incidents in the future?

Prevention, then, is better than cure and the different areas we have looked at so far – creating a positive learning environment, relationships and effective management of learners and learning – all contribute to this. Sometimes, however, despite our best efforts, incidences of challenging behaviour can still occur and the next sections consider ways of managing these.

AGGRESSIVE, PASSIVE AND ASSERTIVE RESPONSES TO CHALLENGING BEHAVIOUR

Early on in human evolution, when the need to survive in a variety of dangerous or threatening situations was an almost daily occurrence, the body developed a physiological response to such situations which resulted in the release of adrenalin into the body, readying it to respond by fighting or running away. This is known as the 'fight or flight' response. Although physically we now live in an altogether safer world, the same response is triggered by any stressful experiences we encounter in our daily lives, such as incidences of challenging behaviour (see the triune brain in the neurocognitive section in Chapter 6). A number of such occurrences can lead to tiredness due to the energy levels involved and in extreme cases the body's natural defence mechanisms can eventually become worn down.

A fight response is accompanied by feelings of anger; a flight response by feelings of apprehension. The release of adrenalin causes an immediate emotional effect or 'gut feeling' and it is this that determines how we subsequently act. In 'fight' mode, the subsequent feelings of anger mean it is likely that teachers will react to challenging behaviour in an aggressive manner. This would be evident in their body language – posture, gestures and tone of voice – and also in the language used. Characteristically, this would involve criticism, sarcasm, direct commands and praise given in a reluctant manner.

In 'flight' mode, however, the emotion is that of fear or apprehension and body language would be passive, as would the language used. The aim would be to avoid any form of confrontation and so the language used would be characterised by a reluctance to give direct instruction or criticism and deny direct responsibility.

In their own ways, each of the above will serve to make the situation worse rather than resolve it. An aggressive demeanour will usually provoke a similarly aggressive response from the learner and invariably the situation will become more confrontational and may eventually spiral out of control altogether. On the other hand, a passive reaction can give the impression that the teacher is not sufficiently concerned to make a commitment and may well leave learners confused, lacking in direction and ultimately more frustrated than they were to start with.

These two approaches relate well to certain teacher stereotypes. Gribble (2006: 48) identifies 'the authoritarian or demanding teacher' and the 'indecisive teacher'. The former asserts their power over learners using condescending language, and sarcasm, similar to the aggressive approach outlined above. Mitchell et al. (1998: 7) use the term 'authoritarian professional' and suggest such a person 'demands social behaviour'. Gribble (2006: 49) argues that such a teaching style 'results in increasing levels of confrontation, poor working relationships and disaffection in pupils'. The passive approach is embodied in the style adopted by the 'indecisive teacher', which Gribble (2006: 50) describes as 'the antithesis of the demanding teacher' but which 'can be equally damaging when attempting to maximise pupils' learning potential'. Mitchell uses the term 'the abdicating professional', who is someone who 'hopes for social behaviour'.

Fortunately, there is a third category – 'the decisive or positive teacher' (Gribble, 2006: 51) or 'confident professional', who 'expects social behaviour (and usually gets it!)' (Mitchell et al., 1998: 7). The approach employed by this third category of teacher is neither aggressive nor passive, but assertive.

ACTIVITY 7.5

Think back to your own experiences as a learner. Can you identify teachers you have encountered who fall into the categories above? How do you place teachers into these categories? What particular characteristics do they display? How did your experience of each make you feel?

To understand the difference between aggressive, passive and assertive approaches, it is useful to look at the work of Watkins (2001: 17), who indicates that the following sequence of events occurs when we are faced with any incident.

1.   FEEL   Initial emotive reaction

    ↓

2.   THINK   Refer back to previous experience and knowledge

    ↓

3.   DO   Now decide on and carry through a course of action

He suggests that often when we react under pressure, the 'think' stage is left out of the sequence 'so that what we do is driven by what we feel'. Aggressive and passive approaches result from a sequence of 'feel' followed by 'do' and Watkins refers to this combination as *reacting*. The inclusion of the 'think' stage, completing the whole sequence, is termed *responding* rather than reacting. If we respond, our actions are determined by a rational rather than an emotional state of mind. We are calm rather than angry or apprehensive and so our response is assertive.

An aggressive reaction on the part of a teacher may involve a loud, threatening tone of voice, closed body language with tensed muscles and a finger pointing or banging on furniture. The type of language employed includes:

- direct instructions – 'do that in the way that I have shown you'
- refusals – 'you can't do that in here'
- reference to feelings of anger or annoyance – 'I'm getting really fed up with the poor standard of work you keep producing'
- criticism – 'is this really the best you can do after all that I've told you?'
- sarcasm – 'even my grandmother knows that'
- reluctant use of praise – 'well, I suppose it's not the worst piece of work you have produced'.

This leads either to compliant but resentful learners or an equally aggressive reply which can lead to further escalation.

The passive teacher, on the other hand, talks in a quiet voice which may be punctuated by sighs and accompanied by non-verbal communication such as a shrugging of the shoulders and avoidance of direct eye contact. The language employed is characterised by:

- the avoidance of direct responsibility – 'I know it's not very interesting but it's on the syllabus so we will just have to make the best of it'
- a reluctance to offer direct criticism – 'I think it's quite good, but I'm not sure it's the answer the examiners are looking for'
- the avoidance of direct instruction – 'I wonder if we could now/it might be an idea if you turned to page 63'
- a reluctance to say 'no' – 'perhaps it's best if you don't do that just now'
- allocation of blame elsewhere – 'I know it's quite soon to hand in work but the course leader set that date, not me'.

As nothing is definitive, this can lead to confusion or frustration on the part of learners, particularly those that need reasonably firm boundaries or structures to work within.

An assertive response exhibits open body language and language which is characterised by:

- clear instructions with reasons – 'I want you to sit down now as you are distracting others from their work'
- saying no but with reasons – 'you can't do that now as there isn't enough time left today'
- encouraging learners to express themselves – 'I can see that you don't agree with that. Can you tell me why?'
- the inclusion of praise when offering criticism – 'although you haven't made a lot of progress, you started off really well'
- acknowledging the learner's point of view – 'I can see why you think this is unnecessary, but there is actually a very good reason for it'
- suggestions as to alternative, acceptable behaviours – 'asking others in your group politely is far more effective than shouting'.

An assertive approach treats learners in a reasoned and adult fashion whilst letting them know in a clear but firm manner exactly what is expected of them. It finds a balance between achieving the teacher's purpose and maintaining the teacher/learner relationship. It provides firm guidelines without being confrontational and is normally used in conjunction with the spelling out of consequences of actions, as in Canter and Canter's 'assertive discipline' approach which is covered in the next section.

Assertiveness can involve specific techniques such as:

- broken record (repeating your requests when meeting resistance)
- fogging (acknowledging the other person's point of view, whilst restating your case)
- negative enquiry (asking for constructive criticism when being verbally attacked)
- negative assertion (agreeing with accurate parts of criticism whilst still stating your own case).

In terms of teaching, however, the main points to remember are:

1. Respond in a calm, logical manner. Count to 10 or use whatever device works for you, to pause, overcome the initial emotive reaction and get yourself into the appropriate frame of mind.
2. Have a clear idea in your mind as to exactly what it is that you want to achieve and how this might best be accomplished.
3. Adopt appropriate body language, particularly the making of eye contact.
4. Explain clearly, in a calm tone of voice, exactly what you require.
5. Be prepared to be flexible but only if the response you receive is reasonable and well explained.
6. Be prepared to be critical but only if your criticism is justified and you can offer a more acceptable (to you) alternative.

RULES AND PROCEDURES

If everyone drove on whatever side of the road they felt like, travel by car would soon become a chaotic and frustrating experience. Fortunately, we have rules governing this situation and we all know to drive on the left-hand side of the road when driving in the UK. As long as everyone continues to obey this rule, we can proceed on our journey in a safe manner and reach our destination with a minimum of fuss. A failure to comply with this rule attracts the attention of the police and the subsequent consequences. This simple example illustrates some general points about rules:

- Rules are introduced for our benefit.
- Rules govern our behaviour – what we do – by letting us know what is expected of us.
- The simpler the rule, the better.
- Everyone needs to obey the rule for it to have best effect.
- Rules have to be 'policed' to ensure compliance.

Generally, all social situations are subject to some kind of rules which let us know how to behave in that particular context – what is acceptable and what is not. A number of different types of rules operate within teaching, as outlined in Figure 7.2.

Type of rule	Comes from	Example	'Policed' by	Personal or impersonal
Institutional	Formulated by the institution	No smoking on premises	Institution	Impersonal
Situational	The requirements of the situation, e.g. Health and Safety	Wearing of appropriate PSE in workshops	Legislation	Impersonal
Learning environment	Teacher	No interrupting when teacher talking	Teacher	Personal

Figure 7.2   Types of rules

We have already noted the importance of institutional rules and the need for them to be acted on in a consistent manner by all members of staff in order to remain effective; the same is true of 'situational' rules. Both of these types of rules can be regarded as 'impersonal' as they are not devised by the teacher and are not reliant on the authority of the teacher to ensure compliance – they are supported by the weight of the institution itself or the legislation covering that particular situation. The third type of rule is less clear cut. This is the type of rule that we as teachers introduce to ensure the smooth running of our teaching sessions. Interactionist sociology takes an interesting view of the rules that operate within a learning environment. The suggestion is that when teachers meet their learners for the first time, there are two sets of rules that might emerge from the situation – one that the learners would like to operate by and one which is favoured by the teacher. If both sets of rules are in agreement, a harmonious learning environment is soon established but, if not, tensions arise. These tensions are resolved through a process whereby each party 'pushes' for their rules to be the ones that are accepted. This process is known as 'negotiating the boundaries' and eventually some form of compromise situation emerges. Reaching this compromise can, however, be a lengthy and uncomfortable process and will generally involve winners and losers to some extent, leading to possible resentments. Referring back to the previous section on passive and aggressive approaches, the situation may well resemble the position shown below.

| Aggressive | When you invade/attack someone else's boundaries | I win – you lose |
| Passive | When you allow your boundaries to be invaded | I lose – you win |

A better situation to arrive at would be to avoid unnecessary conflict by using an assertive approach to establish a set of rules at the outset.

| Assertive | Standing up for your rights without violating the rights of others | I win – you win |

Consequences are an important consideration in any rules-based approach. They directly affect and influence the behaviours engaged in and so need to be thought through carefully before being implemented. The rationale behind a rules-based approach comes from behaviourist psychology, and, according to this theory, consequences fall into the two categories of reinforcement and punishment (see the earlier section in this chapter on behaviourism), and positive and negative consequences. It has previously been argued that positive consequences are generally more effective than negative ones. Points to bear in mind when considering consequences include:

- Select consequences you feel comfortable in enforcing.
- Use consequences which have some significance for learners. Whilst ideally there should be consistency in application, some tailoring may be necessary for individual learners to achieve best effect.
- Keep them simple.
- Choose consequences which can be applied as soon as possible after the event.
- Have a sliding scale of consequences to accommodate different levels of behaviour.
- Apply consequences in a neutral manner using a firm tone of voice.

The structure provided by 'assertive discipline', first introduced in America by Lee Canter (Canter and Canter, 2001), can be used to introduce a rules-based approach. In common with most rules-based approaches, assertive discipline is a system of behaviour management which relies on the consistent reinforcement of a limited number of clear, concise rules. Positive reinforcement encourages behaviour within the rules and negative consequences discourage breaking them. There is, however, an emphasis on the positive, assertive discipline being focused on 'catching learners being good' and encouraging learners to make appropriate behaviour choices. The three main features of the approach are:

- a set of rules which are to be followed at all times
- positive reinforcement when rules are followed
- negative consequences that result from not following the rules.

Learners are made aware of what is expected of them through the establishment of rules and procedures. Consequences exist in a hierarchy dependent on the nature, frequency and severity of the offence but importantly are deemed to result from a choice that the learner makes. Learners can make the choice of engaging in the expected, desirable behaviours leading to positive reinforcement. Alternatively, they can choose not to behave in this manner, but the result of this choice is the acceptance of the resulting consequence, normally some form of sanction or punishment. If, however, the sanction or punishment leads to the desirable behaviour, it can be lifted, thus employing negative reinforcement to strengthen the desired behaviour. Learners, therefore, to a large extent, self-regulate their own behaviour. Consider, for example, a learner who chooses not to follow a rule concerning talking whilst the teacher is talking, leading to a sanction of staying on at the end of the session – the agreed consequence. If the learner is now quiet for the remainder of the session, thus showing the desired behaviour, the sanction may be lifted. The lifting of the sanction is an example of negative reinforcement and serves to strengthen the behaviour of not talking at the same time as the teacher.

Rules are best kept to few in number (about five) and are positively phrased, identifying what 'to do' rather than what 'not to do' and are confined to behaviour – they do not address academic matters. They are phrased in 'observable' terms to avoid ambiguity and uncertainty, and one way of arriving at a common understanding is to involve learners in devising the rules.

REFLECTIVE TASK 7.6

A rules-based approach will be appropriate to some aspects of your particular teaching context. How did you establish those rules? Do you think the rewards and sanctions you use are both realistic and appropriate to the groups you teach? Do you think the ways in which you apply these rewards and sanctions is proportionate to the behaviours you observe?

LEARNERS AGED 14–16

Although traditionally the 14–16 age range has been taught in secondary schools, provision within the FE sector has been expanded to include this group, largely through the increased flexibility programme (IFP). The IFP for 14–16-year-olds was introduced in 2002, with the intention of increasing vocational and work-related learning opportunities for 14–16-year-olds of all abilities, who it was thought would benefit more from this type of provision, rather than the more academic-based school curriculum. Eight new vocational GCSEs with a focus on work-related learning were introduced in 2002 to complement this initiative. The Key Stage 4 curriculum consists of core elements, entitlement elements and vocational elements. It is the vocational elements that are delivered as part of the IFP and learners for whom it is thought to be appropriate can thus take up to two vocational qualifications which will be delivered in a college environment. The remaining requirements of Key Stage 4 are fulfilled within the school environment.

Issues with challenging behaviour seem to be more prevalent when teaching groups in the 14–16 age range. Most teachers who work in a college environment are used to dealing with older and more mature learners and see teaching the 14–16 age group as different, but what form does this difference take?

One difference for the learners involved is that they will be dividing their time between attendance at (the more familiar) school and college, each of which will make different demands on them. They will also have different expectations of college and will mix with a different type of student body, within which they will hold a different status. This is not a straightforward situation; some of the quotes from learners interviewed in a report commissioned by the National Foundation for Educational Research (NFER) on implementing the IFP testify that 'it was a big scary place … you come to school, and you knew where everything was, and you come to college and everything was "wow"' (Golden et al., 2004: 47), 'around school I really know everybody, so it is a big change' (p. 44) and 'they call us schoolies' (p. 45).

So 14–16 learners are faced with different demands placed on them by the two environments within which their learning takes place. Similar issues surface in a list produced by Vizard (2007: 3) of a number of difficulties 14–16 learners face and which can lead to challenging behaviour:

- a lack of maturity
- an inability to handle the increased freedom of unsupervised time
- an inability to cope with the large size of college
- a difficulty in managing their time
- a fear of being split up from their peer group
- a fear of challenge and being taken out of their comfort zone
- a difficulty in adapting to health and safety requirements.

So, whilst coming to college may in some respects provide a preferable option to learning in school, the difference in the two environments and the demands and expectations they place on learners can, for some, prove difficult to cope with. Vizard suggests that challenging behaviour is a potential consequence of this.

Part of the rationale behind the IFP programme was to provide a vehicle through which to re-engage learners whose experience in the school system had proved unsatisfactory. It will come as little surprise therefore to find that one of the main reasons given to Golden and colleagues for participating in the IFP was a desire to 'learn away from school in a new environment where some felt they would be treated differently and it would be a different experience' (Golden et al., 2004: 43). Typically, such learners find difficulty in following courses which are content-led, rather abstract and heavily reliant on reading, writing and listening skills. It was thought that, for some, the IFP would better suit their preference for a practical style of learning and provide a more relevant path for a career aim (Golden et al., 2004: 47). Learners aged 14–16 therefore have expectations not only of how they will be treated, but also of how they will be taught. Generally, if these expectations are met, challenging behaviour will be minimal. If, however, learners experience 'more of the same', their response will be less positive.

Being treated differently is a recurrent theme in the literature relating to IFP and, as has already been mentioned, getting to know your learners is one of the fundamentals of teaching. Armitage et al. (2011: 164) lay particular emphasis on the importance of building positive relationships with younger learners, suggesting 'many students who are disengaged from education perceive their teachers to be too controlling or domineering'. Peart and Atkins (2011: 61) support this view but stress that this must be a genuine rather than a forced process.

Many teachers in the Further Education and Skills sector are used to contact with more mature and motivated learners and some consequently possess a negative image of 14–16 learners, being wary of this age group and the perceived problems they may bring. Such perceptions were recognised in an NFER report on the impact of 14–16 in colleges which reported: 'The main thing is you have to have lecturers who want to teach them. Young people are very astute and they can see if staff don't want to be there' (McCrone et al., 2007: 14).

So, in teaching the 14–16 age group, perhaps it is not so much a matter of finding appropriate behaviour management techniques – those mentioned in this chapter can be successfully adapted and applied – but more a case of recognising and responding to the particular circumstances and characteristics of the group and approaching the task with a positive attitude.

SUMMARY OF KEY POINTS

This chapter has looked at how learners might be managed in a way that increases the effectiveness of their learning process. Factors such as first impressions, induction procedures and the management of groups were discussed in relation to creating an inclusive learning environment.

The importance of the motivation to learn was highlighted, along with ways of both stimulating and maintaining this within learners. Finally, strategies which could be used to prevent or respond to incidents of challenging behaviour were examined in some depth.

The key points in this chapter are:

- A positive, supportive learning environment contributes to an inclusive learning experience.
- First impressions at both an individual and institutional level are important as they set the tone for what is to follow.
- Induction programmes should leave learners feeling both welcome and informed and able to settle in quickly to their new course and environment.
- Learners enter the sector on a voluntary basis but this in itself does not always guarantee high levels of motivation.
- The motivation displayed by learners is affected by a number of factors such as the learning environment, teacher characteristics and, most importantly, the degree of success experienced in their learning.
- Challenging behaviour is regarded as any actions which interfere with teaching or the learning of self or others.
- The relationship established between teacher and learner needs to be supportive without being overly familiar.
- Kounin suggests that potentially challenging behaviour can be pre-empted by effective classroom management.
- Smith and Laslett stress the importance of orderly beginnings and endings to teaching sessions in preventing challenging behaviour.
- The 'ABC' framework suggests that the management of behaviour should be informed by a consideration of the *antecedents* to the behaviour, the *behaviour* itself and its subsequent *consequences*.
- An aggressive reaction to challenging behaviour invites escalation; a passive reaction leads to uncertainty and frustration; an assertive response is most likely to lead to a successful resolution.
- Assertive discipline involves public recognition of a small number of rules, along with recognition of the consequences of following or breaking these.

REFERENCES

Armitage, A., Flanagan, K., Poms, S. and Donovan, G. (2011) *Developing Professional Practice 14–19*. London: Longman.
Canter, L. and Canter, M. (2001) Assertive Discipline: Positive Behavior Management for Today's Classroom. Canter & Associates.

Dix, P. (2010) *Taking Care of Behaviour* (2nd edn). Harlow: Pearson.

Fairclough, M. (2008) *Supporting Learners in the Lifelong Learning Sector*. Maidenhead: Open University Press.

Francis, M. and Gould, J. (2013) *Achieving Your PTLLS Award*. London: Sage.

Further Education Unit (1987) Behaviour and Motivation: Disruption in Further Education. London: Longman.

Glasser, W. (2005) *Choice Theory*. William Glasser Institute. Available online at: www.wglasser.com/the-glasser-approach (accessed 25/04/17).

Golden, S., Nelson, J., O'Donnell, L. and Rudd, P. (2004) *Implementing the Increased Flexibility for 14 to 16 Year Olds Programme: The Experience of Partnerships and Students*. Slough: NFER. Available online at: www.education.gov.uk/publications/eOrderingDownload/RR562.pdf (accessed 25/04/17).

Gribble, B. (2006) In a Class of Your Own: Managing Pupil Behaviour. London: Continuum.

Kounin, J. (1970) *Discipline and Group Management in Classrooms*. New York: Holt, Reinhart & Winston.

Learning and Skills Development Agency (LSDA) (2007) What's Your Problem? Working with Learners with Challenging Behaviour. London: LSDA.

McCrone, T., Wade, P. and Golden, S. (2007) *The Impact of 14–16 Year Olds on Further Education Colleges*. Slough: NFER. Available online at: www.nfer.ac.uk/nfer/publications/ICL01/ICL01.pdf (accessed 25/04/17).

McManus, M. (1995) *Troublesome Behaviour in the Classroom* (2nd edn). London: Routledge.

Mitchell, C., Pride, D., Haward, L. and Pride, B. (1998) *Ain't Misbehavin'*. London: FEDA.

Peart, S. and Atkins, L. (2011) *Teaching 14–19 Learners in the Lifelong Learning Sector*. Exeter: Learning Matters.

Rogers, B. (2006) Classroom Behaviour: A Practical Guide to Effective Teaching, Behaviour Management and Colleague Support (2nd edn). London: Sage.

Rogers, C. (1989) *On Becoming a Person*. Boston & New York: Houghton Mifflin.

Smith, C. and Laslett, R. (1993) *Effective Classroom Management: A Teacher's Guide* (2nd edn). London: Routledge.

Tuckman, B. (1965) Developmental sequence in small groups. *Psychological Bulletin*, 63: 384–99.

Vizard, D. (2007) How to Manage Behaviour in Further Education. London: Paul Chapman.

Watkins, C. (2001) *Managing Classroom Behaviour*. London: Association of Teachers and Lecturers.

 # FURTHER READING

Rogers, B. (2015) Classroom Behaviour: A Practical Guide to Effective Teaching, Behaviour Management and Colleague Support (4th edn). London: Sage.

Something of a 'guru' on behaviour management, this is Bill Roger's latest publication. As usual it offers clear guidance on many aspects of behaviour management illustrated by everyday examples and case studies with which most will be familiar. Written in an anecdotal, engaging style, every chapter constitutes a worthwhile read but we would particularly recommend chapter 3 on the use of language.

Vizard, D. (2012) How to Manage Behaviour in Further Education (2nd edn). London: Sage.
Written specifically for the sector, this book gives comprehensive coverage of a whole range of issues relating to the creation of a positive learning environment and dealing with difficult behaviour. It covers behaviour management at both the individual and group level and contains advice and strategies to employ in managing areas as diverse as cyber bullying and supporting additional needs. Written in a user-friendly style with short reflective exercises to help think through the issues raised.

Wallace, S. (2013) *Managing Behaviour in Further and Adult Education* (3rd edn). Exeter: Learning Matters.
A good general text full of case studies with accompanying tasks designed to make you think about the issues involved. The whole range of learners within the sector is covered from 14–19 through to adult students and the conversational style of the writing makes for an engaging read. A more recent book (*Motivating Unwilling Learners in Education*, 2017, Bloomsbury Education) looks at the allied topic of motivation and considers particular issues such as 'selling' English and Maths and the particular challenges of motivation within the 14–16 age group.

8

PROFESSIONALISM AND CONTINUING PROFESSIONAL DEVELOPMENT

The sector in which we work, and the role that we fulfil within it, are constantly and rapidly evolving and changing. As part of a professional approach, it is incumbent on us to broaden and update our knowledge and skills through active engagement in continuing personal and professional development. This chapter examines the process of reflective practice which provides the rationale behind such thinking and introduces a number of reflective activities designed to assist in identifying and addressing developmental needs in a systematic manner.

When you have completed this chapter you will be able to:

- describe the characteristics of 'profession' and 'professionalism'
- identify some of the barriers to a professional approach that might exist within the working environment
- recognise the tensions that can be generated by the different demands placed on those fulfilling the roles of manager and teacher
- define reflective practice
- describe Schön's model of reflective practice and distinguish between the three levels of reflective practice it identifies
- recognise the role played by experiential learning within the process of reflective practice

- differentiate between the models of learning through experience and reflection proposed by Kolb, Dennison and Kirk, Gibbs and Brookfield
- describe the purpose and benefits that can be derived from keeping a professional development journal
- relate the process of self-evaluation to Kolb's model of experiential learning
- explain the purpose and describe the format of an Individual Learning Plan
- differentiate between different categories of 'critical incident'
- distinguish between 'subject' observations and 'process' observations
- recognise the characteristics of reflective writing.

DOES TEACHING IN EDUCATION AND TRAINING QUALIFY AS A PROFESSION?

In this chapter, we will be exploring the concepts of profession and professionalism as they apply within the sector; to begin the process, we will first attempt to decide what is meant by the term 'profession'.

ACTIVITY 8.1

Identify three jobs that you would consider carry the label of profession. Now think of three jobs that would not be described as being a profession. What is the difference between the two groups of jobs? Pick out the characteristics that you consider define profession.

The above approach comes from the social sciences and tries to define profession by identifying its functions – a 'trait' approach. It gives rise to a number of definitions which nonetheless agree on a number of common characteristics of a profession.

(a) is based on a body of expert knowledge
(b) involves a lengthy period of training
(c) has a controlling body comprised of others in the same profession
(d) is governed by a code of ethics or set of principles of behaviour
(e) possesses a certain status in the community.

How do we compare to these characteristics?

(A) IS BASED ON A BODY OF EXPERT KNOWLEDGE

ACTIVITY 8.2

Do you regard your subject knowledge and your knowledge of teaching as having equal standing in terms of your teaching? What is your view on the perception of teaching reported by Robson (2005: 15) as 'more common sense than expertise'?

If you wish to become a doctor, you have to study medicine. If you wish to become a lawyer, you have to study the law. Is there an equivalent body of knowledge that we as teachers have to study? Many of you will have had a previous occupation before coming into teaching in this sector. You may well have been an accountant, a mechanic, a hairdresser, an engineer, a musician, a photographer, and so on. Whichever you were, you will have had to study and acquire qualifications to demonstrate your occupational knowledge and expertise. Does this constitute the body of expert knowledge required to be a teacher? Certainly, to teach you have to know your subject, but this form of study qualifies you to be an accountant, a mechanic, a hairdresser, etc. In order to be a teacher, as well as knowing your subject you have to be able to communicate it to others, and there is an expert body of knowledge associated with this particular skill. This 'dual professionalism', as it is known, is peculiar to the sector. It raises interesting questions, such as whether you consider yourself to be an accountant or a teacher, i.e. whether you are an accountant who teaches or a teacher of accountancy.

However you answer this question, it is arguable that teaching as an activity has its own body of expert knowledge involving the nature of teaching and learning. This body of knowledge may, as yet, be rather ill-defined but, for the moment at least, can be regarded as enshrined in the overarching professional standards for teachers, tutors and trainers, introduced in 2007 by LLUK and subsequently updated by the ETF in 2014. These latter standards underpin the Diploma course you are attending as they are intended to set out clear expectations of effective practice in Education and Training.

The areas they cover are:

- Professional values and attributes.
- Professional knowledge and understanding.
- Professional skills.

The twenty standards included in these categories can be found at http://www.et-foundation.co.uk/wp-content/uploads/2014/05/ETF_Professional_Standards_Digital_FINAL.pdf

(B) INVOLVES A LENGTHY PERIOD OF TRAINING

September 2013 saw the revocation of the Further Education and Skills Workforce Regulations, which means that the requirement of a teaching qualification is now decided by employers rather than being mandatory by government decree. Training for your diploma generally takes one year if completed through a full-time course and two years if the in-service route is taken. However, can we claim that it is lengthy? Medical and legal training both take about five years of full-time study, so we do not compare very favourably there. One could argue, however, that the time taken to gain subject qualifications should also be included within this category which takes us into a similar time frame.

(C) HAS A CONTROLLING BODY COMPRISED OF OTHERS IN THE SAME PROFESSION

Generally, a professional or controlling body fulfils the following functions:

- sets standards through codes of ethics and codes of practice
- maintains professional disciplinary procedures
- encourages and regulates CPD
- operates a complaints mechanism
- maintains a register of members
- safeguards entry into the profession.

Up until April 2013, the Institute for Learning (IfL) acted in this capacity within the sector. Originally conceived as the FE Guild, the Education and Training Foundation, a new FE employer-led partnership, was launched in August 2013 to support the improvement of teaching, learning, leadership and management. Part of its brief is to define and promote professionalism.

(D) IS GOVERNED BY A CODE OF ETHICS OR SET OF PRINCIPLES OF BEHAVIOUR

Although ceasing to operate in 2014, the IfL introduced a code of professional practice in 2008 outlining 'the behaviours expected of members – for the benefit of learners, employers, the profession and the wider community' (IfL website). The areas it covered were:

- integrity
- respect
- care
- practice
- disclosure
- responsibility.

(E) POSSESSES A CERTAIN STATUS IN THE COMMUNITY

How do people react at a social gathering when you tell them what you do for a living? We leave you to make your own decision on this particular characteristic, content in the knowledge that however others react to our status we can still sign passport photographs.

There is more to the claim of being part of a profession, however, than a set of externally measured characteristics. There is an internal process which must also be considered. Robson (2005) is dismissive of the trait approach outlined above, preferring to define profession from the perspective of 'a set of ideas, or a way of thinking about occupations' (2005: 10). She suggests that the three concepts of professional knowledge, autonomy and responsibility more usefully capture the essence of 'profession', not least because they are capable of change with time and context, as is the concept of profession. We have already explored the notion of responsibility in Chapter 1 and have referred to professional knowledge earlier in this section, but what about autonomy?

Professional identity is often related to the degree of autonomy and self-determination members possess, on the basis that 'professional practitioners require a high degree of individual autonomy – independence of judgement – for effective practice' (Carr, 1999: 23). Historically, teachers have been 'in charge' of the curriculum and have demonstrated 'independence of judgement' in curricular decision making. The 1944 Education Act made virtually no reference to the curriculum within this sector; ministers were happy to leave that to teachers, a situation which prevailed into the 1970s. James Callaghan's famous 1976 Ruskin speech, however, which triggered the Great Debate in education, attacked what was becoming known as the 'secret garden of curriculum', making a case instead for a centrally devised 'core curriculum'. Since then, government control over the curriculum has gradually increased and although, unlike the schools sector, the Further Education and Skills sector is not subject to the imposition of a 'national curriculum', teachers are falling behind employers and others in the pecking order of curricular decision making.

REFLECTIVE TASK 8.1

How much autonomy do you feel you have in your professional role – at institutional level, departmental level, individual level – is your classroom your castle? Do you agree with Robson's (2005: 13) assertion that 'Conventionally, teachers' autonomy still allows them freedom to resolve the uncertainties they are presented with, at least at the level of the classroom, workshop or lecture hall'?

CURRENT DEVELOPMENTS

In October 2012, Lord Lingfield published his review on professionalism in FE which changed the nature of the debate. In light of the 'government's intention to increase the autonomy of providers' (BIS, 2012: 6), the report suggested the sector be given greater independence and autonomy with respect to professionalism 'supporting and enhancing the professionalism which we consider already exists' (p. 6). In terms of definition, however, Lingfield seems not to be breaking new ground, listing the criteria said to underpin professionalism as:

- mastery of a complex discipline
- continuous enhancement of expertise
- acceptance that the field of expertise is a vocation to be pursued selflessly for the benefit of others
- public accountability for high standards of capability and conduct
- membership of a group earning and deserving the respect of the community
- membership of a defined group with similar skills, transcending local loyalties to achieve national and international recognition
- acceptance of responsibility for the competence and good conduct of other members of the professional group
- membership of a group which accepts responsibility for planning succession by future generations
- membership of a group which seeks continuously to extend and improve its field of knowledge
- membership of a group deserving an above-average standard of living (BIS, 2012: 22).

A 2013 discussion paper (Guild Development Project Team, 2013) for the then proposed FE Guild listed specialised knowledge (acknowledging that 'In our sector practitioners will often need dual professionalism, covering the vocational or subject knowledge skill set and teaching/training/assessment skills', p. 7), personal qualities, competency, public accountability and image as the key elements in definitions of the profession.

PROFESSIONAL AND PROFESSIONALISM

This takes us on to the terms 'professional' and 'professionalism'. If we ignore the distraction of the meaning of professional, which indicates that payment is made for services rendered, we would normally consider 'professional' as meaning doing a good job. Those who are not members of a profession can of course still go about their work in a professional manner. The plumber (regarded as being a member of a trade rather than a profession) who turns up at the appointed hour, completes the job in a proficient manner in a reasonable amount of time, charges in line with the original estimate and cleans up afterwards will be considered to have done a 'professional' job. This corresponds well with Keeley-Browne's suggestion (2007: 16) that 'the term "professional" in the modern world refers to the desire to strive for excellence in the service of others'.

Definitions of professionalism appear to be somewhat context-bound but Avis et al. (2010: 43) are of the opinion that professionalism 'indicates attitudes and responsibilities demonstrated within a specific social context'. For the purpose of the following discussion, professionalism will be considered as doing a professional job – providing a service you would be pleased to receive. This would appear to be a core value for any profession.

Having established what constitutes a professional approach for our plumber, we should now complete the same exercise for teachers. Sometimes, the easiest method of identifying or defining something is to consider the opposite.

REFLECTIVE TASK 8.2

Make a list of what you consider to be unprofessional behaviour whilst teaching and use it to construct a list of behaviours which would be considered to constitute a professional approach. How does your own practice compare to the list you have devised?

Your list may be lengthy, covering many different aspects of the overall teaching role. Some of your thoughts may concur with those of Tummons (2007: 5), who suggests that some of the more self-evident characteristics of a professional approach are:

- knowing your subject
- arriving on time and being fully prepared for a teaching or training session
- keeping to deadlines, for example, when marking and returning assignments to learners

- using appropriate language when talking with learners
- treating all learners the same
- modelling best practice: conducting work in a manner that learners should be willing to emulate.

BARRIERS TO PROFESSIONALISM

There is nothing contentious in the above list. We would be hard pressed to argue against any of its content and none of it makes demands beyond our expertise. Can we say, however, that we always live up to these and the other characteristics of doing a professional job that you identified in Activity 8.4? Tummons (2007) suggests not. If we aspire to do a professional job and it is within our ability to do so, why do we sometimes fall short? Nash et al. (2008: 14) suggest reasons might include the following: 'Most teachers at FE colleges in Wales work with students well beyond their timetabled hours' and 'They generally felt that the emotional labour they undertook, although draining, was part of being an FE professional'.

Although this particular piece of research was carried out within FE colleges in Wales, the statements doubtless chime with the experience of most teachers in the sector. Avis et al. (2010: 42), in quoting the results of a study he conducted in 1991, lists the following features of the 'labour processes' of teachers in FE:

- loss of control
- intensification of labour
- increased administrative loads
- the perceived marginalisation of teaching
- an emphasis on measurable performance indicators.

In quoting the work of Lucas and Unwin, Lingfield (BIS, 2012: 33) also concedes that 'too many colleges are characterised by restrictive features of job design and work organisation' which render FE lecturers into 'productive workers'.

REFLECTIVE TASK 8.3

How do you feel about the conclusions reached in the list above? It was compiled in 1991. Do you think matters have changed in the intervening years? What do you perceive to be the major constraints on you in currently performing your teaching role in the manner you would like? Are these constraints outside of your sphere of control or can you do something about them? If so, what?

MANAGERIALISM VS. PROFESSIONALISM

Avis's list uncovers some of the possible reasons for the situation described by Nash and colleagues, whilst at the same time reiterating some of the tensions existing within the role of the teacher referred to in Chapter 1. The causes stem largely from the policies of the Conservative Government of the 1990s and Margaret Thatcher's enthusiasm for a market-led approach to the economy. In the case of FE, this culminated in the process of 'incorporation', introduced during John Major's tenure as Prime Minister as part of the 1992 Further and Higher Education Act. Incorporation was meant to address the perceived skills deficit in the workforce which compared poorly with those of other countries. It was intended to make colleges more responsive to the needs of business and the economy whilst also increasing efficiency within the sector through competition, thus reducing current increases in public spending. Under the 1992 Act, colleges became independent autonomous organisations or 'corporations'. They were removed from LEA control and were funded directly by a new body (the Further Education Funding Council, later replaced under Labour by the Learning and Skills Council) set up for this purpose. Retention and achievement became the deciding factors in determining the level of funding allocated per student, unlike the situation in schools and universities where funding was still allocated on the basis of enrolment.

This new approach required a new type of management and so the practices of private sector management with their priorities of profit and 'the three E's of economy, efficiency and effectiveness' (Lea et al., 2003: 107) were adopted within the sector. This became known as 'the new managerialism'. As colleges, or corporations, now had control over their own staff, new contracts of employment were introduced in line with the 'new managerialism' ethos. The report referred to earlier describes the effect of this approach on teachers who described 'how it shapes and constrains what they do in their working lives, its impact on their private lives, and the levels of stress and anxiety which they take home'.

Randle and Brady (1997) highlight the clash of values between 'managerialism' and 'professionalism'. Managerialism emphasises student through-put and the generation of income, measures quality in terms of results rather than provision and holds up market forces and managerial decision making as the biggest influences on the curriculum.

Whilst the 'new managerialism' is no longer quite as new as it was, managerialism has become an accepted fact of life within the sector and seems to have gained a new lease of life under the new austerity measures and changes in funding brought in by the Coalition Government, and 'more for less' seems once again to be the order of the day.

PROFESSIONALISM AND REFLECTIVE PRACTICE

It is generally accepted that reflective practice underpins professionalism. Tummons (2007: 64), for instance, suggests that 'it [reflective practice] is a key component of the teacher's professional makeup' and signifies 'a state of mind, a permanent kind of behaviour'. Furthermore, Roffey-Barentsen and Malthouse (2013) explain that reflective practice contributes to maintaining 'professional standing', resulting in increased knowledge and understanding of the self as well as of teaching.

This is related to another aspect of the concept of professional autonomy discussed earlier. Schön (1987) makes a case for the relationship between reflective practice and professional autonomy in his book, *Educating the Reflective Practitioner*. He refers first to the technical rational model in which reliance is placed on experts to offer advice and guidance relating to everyday practice. This is a model which still has some application today. When I recently bought a computer, I encountered a problem with installing my internet connection. I solved the problem by phoning the technical helpline and being put in touch with someone who knew about these things – an expert. The expert talked me through a series of operations which I duly followed and – hey presto! – I could now access the internet. The following day, however, the problem recurred and I had to resort to the helpline again in order to solve it. Fortunately, my internet connection has been fine since. This particular episode provides an example of the technical rational model in action whereby I was able to solve the problem by reference to an expert. Unfortunately, this approach meant that I was unable to solve this and subsequent problems on my own, having again to rely on the expert at the end of the telephone line. I was left in a position of being reliant on the availability of this expert and with a feeling of some incompetence and embarrassment at not being able to solve problems myself. There are of course other ways I could have solved the problem. I could have experimented with different solutions based on the limited knowledge I possess, read the manual or referred to the 'help menu' – in short, I probably could have arrived at a solution myself but the helpline presented a much easier short-term fix. In this respect, although I was left with a feeling of some inadequacy and no wiser as to the mysteries of internet connection, the technical rational model worked well. Perhaps this is because it provides an example of being situated on what Schön (1987: 3) refers to as the high ground of professional practice, on which 'manageable problems lend themselves to solutions through the application of research-based theory and technique'. Problems are identifiable and solved through a systematic approach drawing on an extensive store of appropriate expertise. Do all situations fit neatly into this category?

ACTIVITY 8.3

Do you think there is a correct solution to every problem which arises within the learning environment? If so, is there someone sufficiently expert to supply this solution?

You may have concluded from the above exercise that although experts can sometimes be useful in providing solutions to our problems – we may turn to more experienced colleagues or subject mentors for advice, for instance – these are often of such a complex and unique nature that we have to generate our own solutions. Indeed, we often use conversations with colleagues as a 'sounding board' or forum for discussion rather than a request for a neat solution. During a recent Ofsted inspection of a teacher training programme, it was stipulated that all trainee teachers on the programme should have a subject mentor who is already teacher-trained and who teaches an exact match in subject. At first glance, this would seem not to be unreasonable, perhaps because it is formulated from Schön's high ground on which everything is relatively neat and tidy. The reality of finding someone willing to take on this role in a voluntary capacity, already teacher-trained and providing an exact subject match, may not be quite so straightforward in all cases and often compromises have to be made. Ofsted are good at stating requirements but reluctant to adopt the 'expert' mantle in suggesting strategies that can be used to meet those requirements. When trying to find subject mentors, we are sometimes operating in what Schön (1987: 3) refers to as the swampy ground where 'messy confusing problems defy technical solution'.

The vast majority of our practice as teachers seems to be carried out in the swampy ground. Schön (1987: 3) suggests that as professionals we must choose whether to remain on the high ground and solve relatively unimportant technical problems, or to descend into the swamp and engage with problems of greater concern that may not, however, be solvable through systematic, rigorous enquiry.

The implication is that we cannot rely on experts to provide solutions to problems but must build up our own expertise, thus becoming self-reliant in practice and, perhaps just as importantly, freeing ourselves from the sense of inadequacy that can result from a reliance and increasing dependence on experts. This is the basis of reflective practice and means that as we increasingly learn from the experiences we have, our ability to make our own professional judgements is increased. Russell and Munby (1992: 3) suggest that reflective practice involves 'the systematic and deliberate thinking back over one's actions' and that reflective practitioners are 'teachers who are thoughtful about their work'. In essence, reflective practice involves analysing and learning from current and past practice in order to make informed decisions concerning future practice.

As with most of the principles that underpin teaching and learning, you will probably find that you are currently applying these anyway, although perhaps in an intuitive rather than a deliberate manner. Consider Activity 8.4

ACTIVITY 8.4

Do you think it is possible to come up with solutions to classroom problems without perhaps being fully able to understand or explain exactly why you did what you did?

If an unexpected classroom situation arises, do you deal with it automatically/ instinctively/intuitively or do you think about/consider it before acting?

Schön considers that reflective practice takes place at three different levels:

- knowledge-in-action
- reflection-in-action
- reflection-on-action.

Refer back to your response to the first part of the above exercise. Did you manage to identify instances where you had dealt with an incident somehow, knowing it was the best course of action to take but not really knowing why you took it?

This is what Schön calls *knowing-in-action* and it is based on 'tacit' knowledge. Tacit knowledge, as described by Polanyi (1967), seems to exist at a subconscious level – it is there and we use it but cannot explain how. Polanyi (1967) quotes the example of picking out a familiar face in a crowd – it does not involve any conscious process, we cannot describe how we did it, and hence it is described as 'unspoken' or 'tacit'. It arises from repeated or skilled performance (when we have learned to drive a car, we no longer think about it) or experiences we have stored away at a subconscious level. This process can be thought of as reflective practice as it uses previous experience to inform practice but is of limited value in bringing about deliberate improvement in practice. Schön's other categories of thinking-in-action and thinking-on-action are of far greater use.

Consider your response to the second part of the exercise above. You will probably have come to the conclusion that 'it depends'. Some incidents, perhaps involving safety issues, are dealt with immediately but others are given more considered thought. It could be argued that we deal with some issues immediately because there is a prescribed or obvious solution, therefore no need for reflection, but many of the situations we encounter are not 'run of the mill' and this is where *reflection-in-action* comes into play. Schön suggests this type of reflection is initiated by surprise on our part as to what is taking place, but it can be more usefully considered as reflection 'on the hoof' as reflection is concurrent with the unfolding event. If something is not going well, it is that conscious thought process we engage in which involves answering questions such as 'What exactly is occurring here? Why is this so? What can I do about it?' For Schön (1983: 54), 'thinking on your feet, keeping your wits about you … suggest not only that we can think about doing, but we can think about something while doing it'; and 'some of the most interesting examples of this process occur in the middle of performance'. Such reflection leads to a way forward, allowing us to reshape events as they happen.

Reflection-in-action usually happens quickly, responding to the moment and, as such, can be fleeting and quickly forgotten. Often, in-depth reflection can only take place after the event. This retrospective approach is the function of Schön's third level of reflection, reflection-on-action. This is the kind of reflection with which we are most familiar, as it is the process we go through when self-evaluating sessions in an attempt to learn from what has taken place in order to make future practice more effective.

So, Schön sets out a case for reflective practice, which benefits us in that it increases our understanding of our own practice, allowing us to make informed decisions and solve our own problems without reliance on others – we become autonomous professionals.

Reflective practice can also make a significant contribution to our development as teachers by ensuring we venture outside of our comfort zone on occasions. Gregorc (1973) developed a model of teacher development which suggested that when we start teaching, we gradually move through the stages of 'becoming', 'growing' and 'maturing' before finally reaching a 'fully functioning' stage. One of the problems he sees in the 'growing' stage is that after the uncertainties of the 'becoming' stage, having now found an approach that seems to work for us, albeit at a fairly basic level, we tend to hold on to this model of teaching, leading to possible inflexibility and 'stagnation'. An active approach to reflective practice can provide the motivation and means to move on from this stage.

What Schön doesn't do, however, is give clear guidelines about how to put the process into action. Although defining practice clearly in his writings, he is rather vague on the mechanics of reflection. In a paper delivered in 2008 to the UCET Conference in Birmingham, Dr Roy Canning of the University of Stirling pointed out:

> How to be reflective remains unclear. Schön (1983) begins by claiming reflection is about 'how professionals think about what they are doing' (page 50), then goes on to associate reflection with a 'feel for' something (page 55) and an 'intuitive knowing' (page 56). Finally, reflection is then given a functional capability whereby it can 'surface and criticise our tacit understandings' and perform 'frame experiments' (page 61). There is no clarity here or explanation of how reflection encapsulates such a bewildering array of activities. (2008: 2–3)

For a guide to putting reflective practice into action, we need to turn to the work of others.

KOLB'S EXPERIENTIAL LEARNING CYCLE

Kolb's cycle of experiential learning (1984; Kolb and Fry, 1975) is represented diagrammatically in Figure 8.1.

Although the language is somewhat dense, the message it conveys is relatively simple. Kolb maintains that learning through experience only takes place if we process that experience and make sense of it. Experience alone is insufficient to lead to the development of practice, as is suggested by the phrase 'thirty years' experience can be one year's experience repeated twenty-nine more times'. Experience is what Usher (1985: 60) describes as 'raw material' and as such requires 'processing' before it can lead to real learning. Kolb's model supplies a framework to carry out the reflective processes described by Schön.

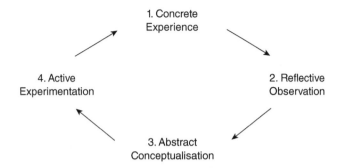

Figure 8.1   Kolb's Model of Experiential Learning Cycle (Kolb and Fry, 1975)

Consider the following sequence which might take place at the end of a teaching session (reflection-on-action):

1.   Teach the session. This is Kolb's Concrete Experience.
2.   Afterwards, you re-run the session in your mind: what were the significant features? What went particularly well? What didn't go as well as you had hoped? Did anything surprising happen? You are now engaging in what Kolb describes as Reflective Observation.
3.   You then ask the question 'why did that happen?' You would engage in some analysis of the events you had identified in stage 2, looking for the *reasons* why some things went well and others didn't. This is what Kolb calls Abstract Conceptualisation.
4.   The results of this analysis would lead you to some conclusions about how you might do things differently, and you could test out these ideas next time you encountered a similar situation. Kolb's term for this is Active Experimentation.

This process is not confined to teaching, it can follow any experience – that first date, a job interview, taking part in some kind of sporting event, etc. – but in each case finding the answer to that 'why?' question is crucial and often the most difficult part of the process. Your diploma course provides you with lots of different ways of looking at your teaching, allowing you to come to a satisfactory explanation as to why things happened the way they did.

Kolb's model of experiential learning has been criticised for its individual nature which leads to a narrow viewpoint and for its sequential approach as 'in reality, these things may be happening all at once' (Jeffs and Smith, 2005: 65). Tennant (1988: 105), however, argues that this should not stop us from using Kolb's model to inform practice, stating: 'As a rule of thumb the model provides an excellent framework for planning teaching and learning activities.' Moon (2004: 114) supports this view, claiming that 'one might say that no approach would gain so much popularity if it did not work or have some value'.

Others models such as the 'Do, review, learn, apply' approach of Dennison and Kirk (1990) have been based on Kolb's work. From Figure 8.2, it can be seen that the stages are similar, although the final stage of 'apply' suggests a more definitive action than Kolb's notion of experimentation.

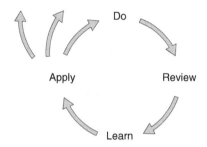

Figure 8.2   Dennison and Kirk model (1990)

GIBBS'S REFLECTIVE CYCLE

Another variant on Kolb's model is that of Gibbs (1988) who introduces a further two stages, as shown below in Figure 8.3. Together, the 'analysis' and 'conclusion' stages extend the 'abstract conceptualisation' stage of the Kolb model and its equivalent 'learn' stage in the Dennison and Kirk model, offering a potentially more rigorous process. The introduction of the 'feelings' stage provides a more holistic approach. Neither teachers nor learners are emotionally detached from the

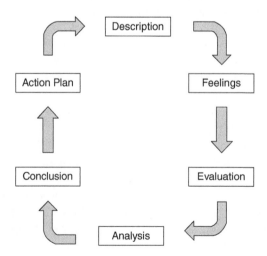

Figure 8.3   Gibbs's Reflective Cycle

experiences they share and so the 'feelings' perspective is an important consideration. Emotions and feelings affect the way in which we behave and respond to situations and should therefore be taken into account in any analysis. Our frame of mind also affects how we view and interpret events, so it is important to be aware of this during the reflective process as it may lead to a more pessimistic or optimistic view than is the case.

The kinds of questions that might be asked at each stage are:

Description – a factual account of the event:

- What happened?
- Who was involved?
- Where did it happen?

Feelings – a description of the emotions and feelings aroused by the incident:

- What were your feelings at the time?
- How did you feel afterwards?
- Were your feelings positive or negative?
- How do you think others were feeling?

Evaluation – a judgement on what happened at the time:

- What was good or bad about the situation?
- How do you think you handled the situation?
- Why do you think you did what you did?
- Are you satisfied with the outcome?

Analysis – an examination of the event to establish cause and contributory factors:

- What caused the incident to occur in the first place?
- What factors influenced the outcome?
- Which of these helped and which hindered?
- Why did the incident proceed in the way it did?
- What aspects of theory might help me make sense of it?

Conclusion – the key things learned through the reflective process are summarised:

- What have I learned from this?
- What might have been done differently?
- Could the situation have been avoided?
- Are there positives that I can build on?
- Are there specific skills or knowledge I need to further develop?

Although the Gibbs model further develops Kolb's original approach, it is open to the same criticism of taking too narrow or individual a view. In any self-initiated process, we tend to focus on those matters which are of particular personal interest and may miss important points as their significance or even existence does not occur to us at the time. This apparent lack of scope is addressed in the next model we look at.

BROOKFIELD'S LENSES

Brookfield (1995: 28) suggests that we employ four 'critical lenses' through which to view and reflect on our practice, each of which 'illuminates a different part of our teaching'. These lenses are:

- our own viewpoint (referred to as 'autobiography')
- the students' viewpoint
- the viewpoint of colleagues or other fellow professionals
- the viewpoint expressed in the educational literature.

Brookfield places high importance on self-reflection (lens 1), declaring it to be 'one of the most important sources of insight into teaching to which we have access' (1995: 31), but considers that to be effective in our teaching it is important that we venture beyond this and also try to understand the experience of our students (lens 2), as 'the most fundamental metacriterion for judging whether or not good teaching is happening is the extent to which teachers deliberately and systematically try to get inside students' heads and see classrooms and learning from their point of view' (1995: 35).

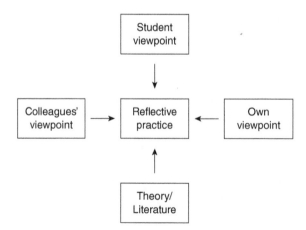

Figure 8.4   Brookfield's lenses

This can reveal, for instance, the extent to which our assumptions about teaching and learning are shared by our students. We might consider small group discussions to be a valuable activity which promotes participation and group cohesion and results in real and relevant learning. Students, on the other hand, may regard it as time-consuming and would prefer to be given the facts. More cynically, they may think we use discussion because we are unsure of our subject or see it as an easy option. We should also be asking whether or not the learning experience was a profitable one for our students, the feedback obtained allowing us to be more responsive in our teaching. Self-reflection should therefore be complemented by and interpreted in the light of what we learn from student evaluations, assessment results, student journals and possibly student focus groups.

The third lens involves looking to colleagues for mentoring advice and feedback. This may be a part of daily life for many teachers, particularly in FE, where teaching observations for internal audit or appraisal purposes are conducted on a fairly regular basis. Peer assessment arrangements are another way of formalising this process, and doubtless you will have been or will be observed teaching by your tutor and subject mentor as part of your diploma course. Others may be less (or more?) fortunate. As well as these formalised arrangements, Brookfield also had in mind far more informal approaches such as simple discussions with colleagues. He maintains that as well as examining practice, this process could lead to increased confidence through the realisation that 'our idiosyncratic failings are shared by many others who work in situations like ours' (1995: 36).

Finally, Brookfield maintains that educational literature and theory also play an important role in reflective practice as they help us understand our experiences by naming and describing them. He suggests that this can also help prevent us from believing that we are responsible for everything that happens in our teaching.

REFLECTIVE TASK 8.4

Which of the models described above appeals to you most? Do you prefer the straightforward approach of Kolb or does the additional element of 'feelings' suggested by Gibbs provide a deeper understanding of the situation? Is it essential to consider other perspectives, as suggested by Brookfield, or will this serve only to confuse? Review the questions you ask yourself when engaged in self-evaluation. Can a consideration of these models help in making your self-evaluations more effective?

Finally, David Blunkett takes us back to the original debate surrounding any claim we may make to being members of a profession and reinforces the belief that reflective practice is commensurate with this status:

Nobody expects a doctor, accountant or lawyer to rely for decades solely on the knowledge, understanding and approach which was available at the time when they began their career. Good professionals are engaged in a journey of self-improvement, always ready to reflect on their own practice in the light of other approaches and to contribute to the development of others by sharing their best practice and insights. They learn from what works. (DfEE, 2000)

We turn now to the different ways in which we might engage in reflective practice.

APPROACHES TO REFLECTION

The concept of reflective practice and subsequent professional development is not complicated. It is a natural process – we often talk of learning from our mistakes (although, interestingly, less often of learning from our successes) and frequently quote 'experience as the best teacher'. Left to our own devices, however, our approach is not usually very organised and can be rather 'hit or miss' in its outcomes. The process of reflective practice is something you will be asked to address as part of your diploma course and this can be achieved in a number of different ways, each of which is intended to provide a structure to the process, making it more systematic and ultimately more effective and useful.

SELF-EVALUATION

The most obvious and most frequently used approach to reflective practice is that of self-evaluation after a teaching session – an example of Schön's reflection-on-action. This is normally a three-stage process which corresponds roughly with Kolb's model of experiential learning, as illustrated in.

Self-evaluation questions	Kolb's experiential cycle
1. What went well? What didn't go so well?	Reflective Observation
2. Why was this the case?	Abstract Conceptualisation
3. What does this tell me about my practice?	Active Experimentation

Figure 8.5 Self-evaluation and Kolb

In the first stage, we run through and 'replay' in our minds the significant features of the session – both good and bad. It is important to obtain a balance here. When things go wrong, they tend to have a noticeable impact and so stand out more than those aspects of the session that went well, so there can be a tendency to dwell on the more negative aspects of the session. This is particularly the case when we are teaching something for the first time or something about which we feel less confident. In such instances, the session does not always go 'as planned'. There is an important distinction to be made, however, between 'what didn't go so well' and 'what didn't go as planned'. The two are not necessarily the same, and often when the session departs from the plan it is for good reason and has actually resulted in a better outcome. In order to learn from our observations, we need to make some sort of sense of them and the next stage in the process involves analysis of the events we have identified. This is where the theory from your course comes into play, as it provides you with a number of appropriate frameworks against which to compare and explore the experiences you have had, putting you in a better position to understand what took place and, more importantly, why it took place in the way it did. This leads to the third and final stage of deciding on ways in which you might modify or adapt your teaching to take advantage of what you have learned.

Self-evaluation of a particular teaching session need not be limited to 'when I teach this session again', but can lead to generalisations about practice as a whole. 'New' sessions give a fair amount of scope for identifying aspects of practice to improve on, specific to that session. When we teach something we have taught many times before, however, self-evaluations can be rather bland as successive experiences of teaching the session have led to further refinements and so generally these sessions tend to be fairly unproblematic. Perhaps the focus here might be placed more on what went particularly well and how this can be adapted and used equally successfully in other sessions or with other learners.

PERSONAL DEVELOPMENT JOURNAL

Another approach you may use is that of a personal development or reflective log, diary or journal. The term 'log' is used less frequently, as it suggests the recording of events in a descriptive rather than an analytical fashion. A diary tends to be rather personal in nature so the more general label of 'journal' is generally preferred. Wallace (2011: 6) suggests that a journal will include elements of both a log and a diary but 'will also, *and primarily*, be used to record and reflect on incidents and experiences from which something useful can be learnt that will help us to develop and enhance our professional practice'.

As the purpose of reflection is to lead to further development, the term 'personal development journal' will be used for the remainder of this chapter. You may well argue that this is a process that takes place 'in your head' anyway and question, in an otherwise busy teaching life, the need to record your reflections. Unfortunately, for assessment purposes, a more substantial body of evidence is required to demonstrate that reflection and subsequent development have taken place. Perhaps more to the point, however, the actual process of writing about, as well as thinking through, your experiences can lead to a deeper understanding and enhance your learning in a way that thought alone cannot. You also have a record of your reflections and it is a useful experience to occasionally go back and review previous entries. This can lead to a further refining of your thoughts but also reminds you of the progress that you have made and the development that has taken place. It is worth noting, at this point, that keeping a personal development journal is one of those activities in which the benefit derived is proportional to the effort that is put into it and that it is a worthwhile activity in its own right.

Generally, your personal development journal will provide you with a record of your growing understanding and development, develop your skills of self-evaluation, provide a focus for discussions with your tutor or subject mentor, and will almost certainly lead to an increase in confidence in yourself as a teacher.

Different centres will have different views on the contents of a journal. Some may contain a CV and records of tutorials with tutors and subject mentor, as well as various reflective activities, whilst others may focus solely on the latter. Included within these you may find the following.

REFLECTIVE/PERSONAL STATEMENT

At various stages throughout your course, you may be asked to write such a statement. The first time you do this, it would probably take the form of a brief review of where you thought you were with your teaching at the time and then highlight areas you felt the need to address further. Subsequent statements would build on and refer back to the previous one, reporting progress and identifying new areas for development.

INDIVIDUAL LEARNING PLAN (ILP)

The term ILP is used rather differently to the way in which it is interpreted in the online Excellence Gateway (n.d.), which defines an ILP as forming 'a "route map" of how a learner will get from their starting point on a learning journey to the desired end point'. The first thing to note about an ILP in the context used here is that it is *individual*, but it applies to you and your own personal development as a teacher rather than your route through the diploma programme. There are many decisions and skills which are common to all teachers within the sector and this allows for a course which is generic in content. Within any diploma group, however, there will be a wide range of experience and specialisms and these will give rise to individual needs, as demonstrated by the saying 'we all have the same total, but we add up differently'.

The ILP provides an opportunity for you to identify any specific concerns that you may have as a teacher, and address these as part of your experience on your diploma course. It involves, therefore, the identification of the *learning* that is specific, relevant and useful to you in your development as a teacher, as well as in meeting the requirements of this particular professional qualification. It should be seen as an opportunity to personalise the course so that it more closely fits with the way that you 'add up'. This process may happen naturally, to a certain extent, as part of any course but it will be far more effective if it is approached in a systematic manner through the devising of a *plan*. As the ILP is developmental in nature, it will involve making several entries as the course progresses and your learning needs change. Normally, entries on the ILP are agreed with your tutor before being recorded. Generally, for any planning document to be effective, it needs to be expressed in terms of SMART outcomes. The more specific you can be, the easier it will be to identify exactly what you need to do and evidence that you have achieved it. A general statement like 'I would like to improve student participation', for example, identifies a need but isn't particularly helpful in moving your practice forward. It would be better to identify an aspect of participation you think you would like to address and arrive at an actual strategy you would like to put in place. The ILP should complement the other aspects of your journal and the course in general. Your personal statement may identify a need which can be translated into an ILP entry. The strategies you use to address this need could include making it the focus of your next teaching observation, observing your subject mentor or incorporating it into any developmental project (such as a piece of action research) which may form part of your diploma. A typical ILP format is shown in.

Date	Area for development	Actions needed/Target	Intended completion date	Signed

Figure 8.6   Example ILP format used on a diploma course

CRITICAL INCIDENTS

Sometimes you may want to reflect on a situation that has made you stop and think. This is referred to as a 'critical incident'. Anything that impacts on your professional practice falls into the 'critical incident' category. Sometimes this can be a 'large' event, with a big impact. The word 'critical' in the name, however, refers to the way in which we analyse the incident rather than the event itself, and so a significant event does not necessarily have to be a 'large' event. It is an incident which has significance *for you*, regardless of size or level of severity. It is often an event which made you stop and think, or one that raised questions for you. In fact, rather than waiting for this 'big thing' to happen on which you can reflect, it is helpful to consider the mundane things, those you do on a day-to-day basis, and reflect on those. Tripp (1993: 17) refers to these things as 'routines'. He suggests that these routines enable us to expose those issues that contain 'the kind of questions about our practice which leads us to confront our professional values and judgements'. He further says that 'while the strength of routines is that they enable us to do things without consciously attending to them, that is also their danger' (1993: 13). Routines can therefore provide a fertile hunting ground for critical incidents, and Tripp suggests that it is important to explore routines as we perform these on a regular basis without questioning why or how we carry them out. We have already noted that, as human beings, we tend to focus on the 'negative' – things that have not gone as planned or wished for – when reflecting. It is just as important, however, to reflect on the positives: what has gone well and why. Analysis of all critical incidents should lead to a positive impact but need not start from consideration of a negative event. It can be seen from the above that critical incidents can be categorised into four areas, as seen in Figure 8.7.

Positive and Large	Positive and Small
Negative and Large	Negative and Small

Figure 8.7   Categories of critical incidents

In general when analysing a critical incident, it is useful to ask yourself questions such as:

- What really happened?
- Have I made any assumptions regarding the situation?
- How else could I interpret the incident?
- Why do I think it happened in the way that it did?
- What impact did it have on both myself and others?
- What other action could I have taken that might have been more helpful?
- What will I do if I am faced with a similar situation in the future?

OBSERVATION OF OTHERS

Observation and sharing of good practice can prove to be an extremely productive developmental exercise. We can become 'comfortable' in the way in which we teach, and observation of others can provide us with fresh ideas and impetus within our own teaching. We can observe for 'subject' reasons. If you have a subject concern, observation of a colleague who teaches the same subject, possibly team-teaching or even just discussing matters with your subject mentor can provide a number of insights. This is particularly useful if you are the only person in your institution who teaches your particular subject and helps relieve that feeling of isolation. We can observe for 'process' reasons. Sometimes there are general issues which we would like to explore, such as differentiation strategies, classroom management or use of particular resources. Observing within our own subject area can prove to be a distraction in such instances as we get drawn into the content of the session. Sometimes, when wider reflection is sought, it is better to observe within a different subject and even within a different environment or culture. Whatever environment you observe in, you should have a clear idea of why you are there and what you wish to gain from the exercise, although this point of focus should not close your mind (or eyes) to other unintended outcomes which may emerge unexpectedly. In a general sense, some of the points you might look out for during such an observation include:

- What kind of activities do the learners engage in?
- What kind of relationship exists between teacher and learners, and amongst learners themselves?
- How do the teachers organise sessions?
- What strategies are used to make the session inclusive in its approach?
- Is the approach used more teacher-centred or learner-centred?
- What do you notice about the physical environment? (Look at posters, pictures, furniture, equipment, room layout, etc.)
- What resources are used?
- Are you aware of any kind of assessment taking place?
- Are things different from your own working context?
- What can you take from this session to inform your own teaching?

If you were to record an observation in your journal, it would be based around your observations, thoughts and the making of any useful comparisons with your own teaching. It would not be evaluative in tone. The purpose of the observation is to learn from watching others, not to pass judgement on their practice.

PROJECTS TO DEVELOP PARTICULAR ASPECTS OF TEACHING

It may be that some time has been built into your programme which enables you to pursue the development of a particular skill or area of your teaching. The first stage in this process is to identify exactly what it is that you wish to develop. There are a number of ways of conducting an analysis of your teaching which will uncover a suitable developmental need, all of which start from a consideration of current strengths and weaknesses. The first of these is a SWOT analysis (Strengths, Weaknesses, Opportunities, Threats) but this is taken from the world of business and, although it can be used at an individual level, it is more suited to organisational analysis. More useful is the SWAIN (Strengths, Weaknesses, Aspirations, Interests, Needs) approach to analysis. As in the SWOT analysis, the first two categories concern strengths and weaknesses. These are followed by aspirations – what is the purpose of this analysis? What do you hope to gain from it? Where would you like it to take you? Interests come next on the basis that the more you find an area for development naturally of interest, the greater the commitment to pursuing it to its final conclusion and so the greater the likelihood of a successful outcome. A consideration of these four factors should lead to the identification of an appropriate developmental need. CUPA (Confident, Unsure, Priority, Action) similarly starts off by identifying areas of teaching about which the individual feels confident or unsure. The 'unsure' areas are prioritised, leading to an action plan for addressing the most pressing need. The final area for development decided on can be incorporated into the ILP and a reflective diary kept of progress towards achievement.

REFLECTIVE WRITING

The recording of any of the above in your journal needs to be done using a reflective style of writing. Put simply, this means structuring your response along the lines of:

(a) a brief description of the event:

- give the context within which events took place
- briefly describe what happened
- say why it is of interest

(b) some analysis:

- identify the key points saying why they are important
- show significant similarities or differences with comparable situations
- suggest what contribution theory might make to explaining what happened and why

(c) what has been learned:

- identify the learning that has taken place as a result of analysis
- describe how this learning might influence future practice.

Reflective writing can be considered to exist at different levels, ranging from the more superficial, descriptive type of writing which reports what happened, to the more profound, deeper levels which engage in analysis and questioning (Roffey-Barentsen and Malthouse, 2013). You may find the 'generic framework for reflective writing' developed by Moon (2004: 214) a useful guide. It identifies four categories of reflective writing. First, *descriptive writing* contains some references to emotional reactions but these are not explored and not related to behaviour. The account relates to ideas or external information. There is little attempt to focus on particular issues.

Next comes the *descriptive account with some reflection*. This is descriptive with little addition of external ideas; there is some reference to alternative viewpoints and there may be some notion of asking questions but no response or analysis. Third, *reflective writing 1* is where there is description but also some evidence of external ideas and some analysis. There is a willingness to be critical of the action, self or others and some 'standing back' from the event; different perspectives are considered. Finally, *reflective writing 2* is where description only serves to set the context. Self-questioning is evident, as is critical self-awareness. The views and motives of others are taken into account and there is a recognition that events exist in a historical or social context. Furthermore, there is a recognition that the personal frame of reference can change according to emotional state.

RESEARCH IN THE CLASSROOM OR WORKPLACE

After you reflect on your lessons, either in the classroom or in the workplace, and evaluate how the session went, you usually identify some strong areas as well as those that could be improved on. As discussed earlier, this is referred to as 'reflection-on-action'. In other words, you consider what you would do the same or differently the next time you teach that session or that group. Changes are likely to be minor ones, such as a different order of the activities planned, the use of a more up-to-date resource, different groupings of students, etc. When you notice, however, that a certain issue is recurring, you may want to take a more organised and structured approach. Such an approach is commonly referred to as 'action research': it is a 'method used for improving educational practice. It involves action, evaluation and reflection and, based on gathered evidence, changes in practice are implemented' (Koshy, 2010: 1). McGregor and Cartwright (2011: 240) suggest that teachers should 'systematically examine an aspect of their teaching; collect information and evidence about the situation; evaluate and analyse this information in order to develop and deepen their understanding of that situation; and use this new knowledge to improve their practice'. What makes action research more than a simple response to evaluation is that you will do some fairly substantial reading before you decide on what to do, and check to see if your change works by collecting evidence using appropriate methods of collecting data and analysing it.

The term action research was introduced by Kurt Lewin (1890–1947), a social researcher whose approach involved a spiral of steps, each composed of a circle of planning, action and fact-finding about the result of the action (Lewin, 1946).

THE STRUCTURE OF ACTION RESEARCH

1. Identify an area for improvement. From your self-evaluation and/or peer/student feedback, you have identified an area of your practice you would like to change.
2. Formulate a question that has arisen out of your issue which asks 'How can I...?'.
3. Read about that particular area in the literature; this is sometimes referred to as a 'literature review'. This will help in deciding what action or intervention to introduce.

4. You can combine your question and action at this stage to form a hypothesis, for example:

question: How can I get students to work harder?
answer: Reward them with gold stars.
hypothesis: Rewarding students with gold stars will cause them to work harder.

5. Decide on the type of data you need to 'measure' the problem and then select the appropriate research methods to be used in gathering this data. Typically, you might conduct interviews, send out questionnaires, look at documents, etc.
6. Collect data designed to measure the initial situation.
7. Take action.
8. Collect data to describe/measure the effects of the action/intervention.
9. Analyse the data.
10. Draw conclusions and plan for further action.

Consider the following example:

1. Identify an area for improvement.

Roger teaches a Level 1 course in Carpentry. Although generally a reasonably well behaved and well mannered group, Roger has noticed that a number of his learners regularly use inappropriate language in the workshop environment. For some, swearing seems to be almost second nature. As well as noticing this himself, the matter was also brought to his attention during a staff meeting, as some of his colleagues had noticed the language used by students when passing through the workshop.

2. Formulate a question that has arisen out of your issue.

How can the use of inappropriate language be stopped?

3. Read about that particular area in the literature.

Roger read about behaviour management and in particular about establishing ground rules within his class; about how these could be negotiated; and also about the use of rewards and sanctions. He decided to introduce a 'swear box'.

4. Formulate hypothesis.

Question: How can the use of inappropriate language in the workshop be stopped?
Answer: By introducing a swear box.
Hypothesis: The introduction of a swear box will stop inappropriate language in the workshop.

5. Decide on the data and research methods to be used.

To record the 'issue', Roger decided to keep a tally chart of every time a swear word was used in his workshop sessions with that particular group.

6. Collect data designed to measure the initial situation.

Roger kept a 'swearing tally' for five sessions, to provide a baseline.

7. Take action.

It was agreed that every time a learner used an inappropriate word in the workshop, the sanction would be for the offender to donate 50 pence to the 'swear box'. At the end of the term, the money would be donated to charity. A swear box was introduced.

8. Collect data to describe/measure the effects of the action/intervention.

Again, a tally chart of swear words was kept after the introduction of the swear box (and money counted).

9. Analyse the data.

Analysis of the data revealed that at the start of the intervention, the use of inappropriate language was quite significant, with £10 'donated' within the first hour of the session. After one week, however, learners had become much more careful in their language, often reminding each other of the consequences: a huge improvement in comparison to the first tally chart.

10. Draw conclusions and plan for further action.

It can be concluded that the introduction of a 'swear box' has reduced the use of inappropriate language with one particular group of learners. Further action could see this intervention introduced within the department as a whole.

As a researcher, you must always consider the ethics of your actions. You need to inform your learners of what you are doing by seeking informed consent. You may also need to inform your line-manager of what you are proposing. If telling the learners what you are doing will significantly influence the outcome of your data collection, you need to carefully justify not telling them, showing that they will not be harmed by this course of action. The best advice is to follow the ethical guidelines set out by the British Educational Research Association (BERA).

The advantages of conducting action research are that it is within a specific context or situation, relevant to you and your practice, and you, as researcher, are part of the process, so you feel really involved. In that sense, it is emancipatory, empowering you as a teacher. There are of course some limitations: you can only tackle issues over which you have some control and you cannot make general assumptions, as your findings are only valid for that particular project. Some therefore see action research as a 'soft' option.

ACTIVITY 8.5

What approach to action research would you propose for the following scenarios?

Scenario 1

You teach equality and diversity to radiography staff in a large hospital. You have negotiated time off for attendance at classes when they are on duty. However, you find that almost every session is interrupted by staff being 'bleeped' to return to their office.

Scenario 2

You teach a group of apprentices on a Motor Vehicle Engineering course. The course requires attendance for one day a week. Although attendance is generally good, some learners drift in anything up to three-quarters of an hour late. You consequently find yourself repeating your introduction three or four times, whilst the lesson is interrupted by late arrivals.

Scenario 3

You teach horticulture to a group of mature learners with learning difficulties. The learners enjoy the course but do not perform well in the confined space of a classroom for the theoretical aspects of the course. They cannot concentrate and find sitting at desks challenging, as, for some, it brings back bad memories.

SUMMARY OF KEY POINTS

In this chapter, we have looked at the concepts of 'profession' and 'professionalism' and how they relate to the job of teaching within the Further Education and Training sector. Reflection and continuing professional development have been identified as characteristics of both a profession and a professional approach as they contribute significantly to professional autonomy. Models of reflective practice have been reviewed, as well as the use of a number of different reflective activities.

The key points in this chapter are:

- A profession is based on a body of expert knowledge, involves a reasonably lengthy period of training and is governed by a code of practice.
- A professional approach can be thought of as the provision of a service you would be pleased to receive.
- Several writers consider that the conditions of service that teachers in the sector are subject to, provide a significant barrier to the provision of a professional service.
- Tensions can exist between managers and teachers because of the differing priorities and values each subscribe to.
- Reflective practice involves learning from past and current practice in order to improve future practice.
- Engaging in reflective practice leads to professional development and professional autonomy.
- Schön identified three levels of reflective practice: 'knowing-in-action', 'reflection-in-action' and 'reflection-on-action'.
- Experiential learning is an essential part of reflective practice.
- Kolb offers a four-stage model of experiential learning.
- Kolb's model has been adapted by others and forms the basis of Dennison and Kirk's 'do, review, learn, apply' model.
- Gibbs stresses the influence of feelings on the experiential cycle.
- Brookfield suggests that to obtain a balanced view, practice needs to be observed through the four lenses of self, students, colleagues and theory.
- A professional development journal records the results of partaking in a number of reflective activities such as self-evaluation, analysis of critical incidents and observation of teaching.
- Reflective writing involves description, analysis and identification of learning.
- Action research provides a systematic approach to examining and improving practice.

REFERENCES

Avis, J., Fisher, R. and Thompson, R. (eds) (2010) *Teaching in Lifelong Learning: A Guide to Theory and Practice*. Maidenhead: Open University Press/McGraw-Hill Education.

BIS (2012) *Professionalism in Further Education*. Available online at: www.gov.uk/government/uploads/system/uploads/attachment_data/file/34641/12-1198-professionalism-in-further-education-final.pdf (accessed 25/04/17).

Brookfield, S. (1995) *Becoming a Critically Reflective Teacher*. San Francisco: Jossey-Bass.

Canning, R. (2008) Reflecting on the reflective practitioner: Muddled thinking and poor educa-tional practices. Available online at: https://dspace.stir.ac.uk/bitstream/1893/566/2/reflective%20practice.pdf (accessed 25/04/17).

Carr, D. (1999) Professionalism and Ethics in Teaching. London: Routledge.

Dennison, B. and Kirk, R. (1990) Do, Review, Learn, Apply: A Simple Guide to Experiential Learning. Oxford: Blackwell Education.

DfEE (2000) Professional Development: Supporting for Teaching and Learning. London: DfEE.

Excellence Gateway (n.d.) Available online at: www.excellencegateway.org.uk/page.aspx?o=108288 (accessed 23/07/2013).

Gibbs, G. (1988) Learning by Doing: A Guide to Teaching and Learning Methods. Oxford: Oxford Further Education Unit.

Gregorc, A.F. (1973) Developing Plans for Professional Growth. NASSP Bulletin, pp. 1–8.

Guild Development Project Team (2013) Consultation to Establish a Guild for the Learning and Skills Sector. Available online at: www.cityandguilds.com/~/media/Documents/Consultation-Responses/FE%20Guild%20%20BIS%20consultation%20documentpdf.ashx (accessed 25/04/17).

Jeffs, T. and Smith, M. (2005) Informal Education (3rd edn). Nottingham: Educational Heretics Press.

Keeley-Browne, L. (2007) Training to Teach in the Learning and Skills Sector: From Threshold Award to QTLS. Harlow: Pearson Education.

Kolb, D. (1984) Experiential Learning: Experience as the Source of Learning and Development. Englewood Cliffs, NJ: Prentice-Hall.

Kolb, D.A. and Fry, R. (1975) Toward an applied theory of experiential learning (C. Cooper, ed.). Theories of Group Processes. London: Wiley.

Koshy, V. (2010) Action Research for Improving Educational Practice (2nd edn). London: Sage.

Lea, J., Hayes, D., Armitage, A., Lomas, L. and Markless, S. (2003) Working in Post-Compulsory Education. Maidenhead: Open University Press.

Lewin, K. (1946) Action research and minority problems. Journal of Social Issues 2: 34–46.

McGregor, D. and Cartwright, L. (2011) Developing Reflective Practice. Maidenhead: Open University Press.

Moon, J.A. (2004) A Handbook of Reflective and Experiential Learning: Theory and Practice. Oxford: Routledge.

Nash, I., Jones, S., Ecclestone, K. and Brown, A. (eds) (2008) Students Reap Benefits but Lecturers are Under Stress: Challenge and Change in Further Education. London: TLRP.

Polanyi, M. (1967) The Tacit Dimension. New York: Doubleday.

Randle, K. and Brady, N. (1997) Managerialism and professionalism in the 'Cinderella service'. Journal of Vocational Education and Training, 49(1): 121–39.

Robson, J. (2005) Teacher Professionalism in Further and Higher Education: Challenges to Culture and Practice. London: Routledge.

Roffey-Barentsen, J. and Malthouse, R. (2013) Reflective Practice in Education and Training. Exeter: Learning Matters.

Russell, T. and Munby, H. (1992) Teachers and Teaching: From Classroom to Reflection. London: Falmer Press.

Schön, D. (1983) The Reflective Practitioner. New York: Basic Books.

Schön, D. (1987) Educating the Reflective Practitioner. San Francisco: Jossey-Bass.

Tennant, M. (1988) Psychology and Adult Learning. London & New York: Routledge.

Tripp, D. (1993) Critical Incidents in Teaching: Developing Professional Judgement. London: Routledge.

Tummons, J. (2007) *Assessing Learning in the Lifelong Learning Sector* (2nd edn). Exeter: Learning Matters.

Usher, R. (1985) Beyond the anecdotal: adult learning and the use of experience. *Studies in the Education of Adults*, 17(1): 59–74.

Wallace, S. (2011) Teaching, Tutoring and Training in the Lifelong Learning Sector (4th edn). Exeter: Learning Matters.

FURTHER READING

Ashmore, L. and Robinson, D. (eds) (2015) Learning, Teaching and Development: Strategies for Action. London: Sage.

Different contributors to this book address different aspects of teaching and learning (identifying needs, objectives, choosing content, design preparation and delivery, assessment and evaluation, reflective practice, technology) and as such the book provides a good general text. Each chapter starts with a section on underpinning theory prior to examining practice and associated issues. Chapter 10 looks at reflective practice and CPD, linking theory and practice supporting the points made with a number of case studies and exercises.

Pleasance, S. (2016) Wider Professional Practice in Education and Training. London: Sage.

Chapter 2 in this book looks at both the historical and current debate around professionalism, particularly post Lingfield, from a number of different perspectives and explores the whole notion of professional identity. This theme is also addressed in Chapter 10 which looks at policy and its impact upon practice.

Rushton, I. and Souter, M. (2012) *Reflective Practice for Teaching in Lifelong Learning*. Maidenhead: Open University Press.

This book combines theory and practice, covering not only models and levels of reflective practice, but also strategies for engagement along with the pitfalls and barriers that might be encountered along the way. Useful links are established with action research and the relationship between reflective practice and CPD is explored. A useful all round text which takes a wider viewpoint.

9

CURRICULUM DEVELOPMENT AND DESIGN

Curriculum is a widely used term in the world of education at national, institutional and course level. It is important to have an understanding of curriculum in all of its forms and of the influences that shape it, as these have an impact on daily teaching life. New developments in curriculum and their resulting practical implications, particularly in the Further Education and Skills sector, are rapidly becoming a way of life. Knowledge of curriculum process and current curricular issues is therefore necessary in order to adapt to the constantly changing educational landscape. This chapter responds to the need for teachers to understand the structure of curriculum and the factors that influence both its design and implementation.

When you have completed this chapter you will be able to:

- differentiate between curriculum, syllabus and scheme of work
- distinguish between the following types of curriculum: official, actual, formal, informal, hidden
- explain how values affect the decision-making process
- recognise the role of ideologies in influencing curricular decision making
- describe the following curriculum models: content, cultural, product, process
- recognise the different approaches to curriculum planning and design arising out of the product and process models

- review the different factors which contribute to making the curriculum inclusive in nature
- explain the need for flexibility in curriculum delivery and how this can be achieved
- describe the different types and combinations of questions used in course evaluation questionnaires.

DEFINING CURRICULUM

Ideally, a chapter on curriculum would begin with a definition, providing us with a common understanding of what is involved. Curriculum, however, is a term which is notoriously difficult to pin down. It is used in a variety of different contexts and appears to mean different things to different people. Portelli in 1987 (cited in Marsh, 2009: 3) claims that more than 120 different definitions appear in curriculum-related writing. Curriculum is often equated to course content, possibly because its Latin origin means a race, a lap around the track or a course. Kelly (2009: 7) claims that such a view 'leads to a limited concept of the curriculum, defined in terms of what teaching and instruction is to be offered'. We know from Chapter 2, however, that the identification of course content is achieved through the course syllabus. The course syllabus is set by the awarding body and outlines what content must be covered and assessed in order to achieve the desired qualification. A syllabus is only a part of the curriculum as a whole. In fact, if we consider curriculum, syllabus, scheme of work and session plans as the four major levels of planning, it is evident that they exist in a hierarchical form, as illustrated in Figure 9.1.

The session plan sits at the base as it is derived from the scheme of work. The scheme of work is the document which indicates the most appropriate approach to

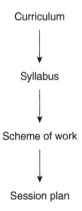

Figure 9.1   Relationship between curriculum, syllabus and scheme of work

the delivery of the subject matter it contains, taking the various practical issues into account. The scheme of work, in turn, sits below the syllabus whose content it has translated into a plan of action. Syllabus sits below curriculum and so the curriculum includes, but is more than, the syllabus itself. So what else does curriculum include? A consideration of the different contexts in which we use the term 'curriculum' may help in attaining a 'feel' for what it means.

ACTIVITY 9.1

List all the phrases you have heard which contain the word curriculum.

In your response to the above exercise, you may well have included some of the following:

1. National curriculum, vocational curriculum, A-Level curriculum – What do these have in common?

The National Curriculum, introduced in 1988, sought to standardise the subjects taught and the assessment procedures used across all state schools in England, Wales and Northern Ireland. It established a set of common aims, purposes and values across the schools system as a whole. The National Curriculum is an important element of the school curriculum which comprises all the learning and other experiences that each school plans for its pupils.

The vocational curriculum is related to the world of work and its purpose is to prepare learners to enter a given trade or industry. It gathers together all of the appropriate qualifications and training required to achieve this.

The A-Level curriculum identifies the various academic routes open to learners at that particular level.

In the above examples, the curriculum groups together a number of subjects and qualifications which have something in common or all serve to fulfil a common purpose.

2. Curriculum development – a curriculum changes over time in response to the differing needs of society and, as its name suggests, curriculum development is the process through which this change occurs. Kelly (2009: 276), in listing 'A Chronology of Curriculum Development and Change', includes such diverse events as the raising of the school leaving age (ROSLA), the replacement of Her Majesty's Inspectorate (HMI) with the Office for Standards in Education (Ofsted), the Technical and Vocational Education Initiative (TVEI) introduced into schools in 1982, the introduction of AS-Level examinations, and many others such as NVQs and GNVQs.

These examples address a wide and diverse range of educational issues. Curriculum is not just about courses and qualifications then: it also concerns itself with the bigger picture of the educational system as a whole and how it operates.

3. Curriculum innovation is related to curriculum development and refers to the introduction of new ideas into the curriculum. Your current diploma course falls into this category. Prior to 2001, awarding bodies and universities devised their own curricula for initial teacher training within the sector. In 1999, a national set of standards for teachers working in FE was published by the Further Education National Training Organisation (FENTO), and, from 2001, all teacher training programmes and awards for the sector were required to be endorsed by FENTO as conforming to these standards. These were later superseded by a new set of standards, along with a new award structure devised by Lifelong Learning UK (LLUK), which was subsequently disbanded in 2011. The latest qualification structure of Award, Certificate and Diploma in Further Education and Training is mapped to these standards, although further change is anticipated with the proposal to devise a new set of standards.

Curriculum also involves responding to change and introducing new ideas, structures and ways of working.

What is also becoming evident is that the term 'curriculum' covers a wide range of activities and applies at a number of different levels, including:

* national
* institutional
* programme.

Arguably, it even applies at an individual level. If you decide to change the way in which you teach a particular topic, you could be considered to be engaging in curriculum innovation and your actions would also fall under the heading of curriculum.

It is clear that curriculum is very much an umbrella term embracing a host of different education-related matters, which is why it is so difficult to arrive at a specific definition. Some suggested definitions include:

A curriculum is the formulation and implementation of an educational proposal to be taught and learned within a school or other institution and for which that institution accepts responsibility at three levels, its rationale, its actual implementation and its effects. (Jenkins and Shipman, 1976: 26)

A curriculum is an attempt to communicate the essential principles and features of an educational proposal in such a form that it is open to critical scrutiny and capable of effective translation into practice. (Stenhouse, 1975: 4)

The curriculum is the totality of the experiences the pupil has as a result of the provision made. (Kelly, 2009: 8)

Each of these definitions views curriculum from a different perspective. Jenkins and Shipman take an organisational viewpoint and suggest curriculum involves a planned, orderly approach, whereas Stenhouse is more concerned with the purpose and process involved. Kelly's definition is deliberately broad to encompass what he describes as the various different dimensions involved in curriculum. There are as many different definitions of curriculum as there are perspectives, leading Soltis (cited in Marsh, 2009: 5) to suggest that 'Those who look for the definition of curriculum are like a sincere but misguided centaur hunter, who even with a fully provisioned safari and a gun kept always at the ready, nonetheless will never require the services of a taxidermist'.

Although a single universal definition is seemingly unavailable to us, Quinn (2000: 133) offers a practical solution defining curriculum by its functions, suggesting that a curriculum answers the following questions:

- Who is to be taught/who will learn?
- What is to be taught and/or learned?
- Why is it to be taught and/or learned?
- How is it to be taught and/or learned?
- Where is it to be taught and/or learned?
- When is it to be taught and/or learned?

ACTIVITY 9.2

What does curriculum mean to you? Write down your own personal definition of curriculum as you understand it at this moment in time – you may like to revisit your definition when you have finished reading this chapter and see if your view of curriculum has changed.

TYPES OF CURRICULUM

Perhaps because of the lack of clarity as to the exact meaning of the term 'curriculum', it is often thought of as existing in a number of different forms or types. Some of these are:

- hidden curriculum
- official curriculum
- actual curriculum
- formal curriculum
- informal curriculum.

As you read through the list, ideas were probably forming in your head as to what each might be. The exercise below invites you to test out these ideas or work out what is meant by each type of curriculum by identifying examples of each. When you have finished, you can compare your answers to the completed table at the end of the chapter.

ACTIVITY 9.3

Using the list of types of curriculum above, match these with the examples in Table 9.1.

Table 9.1

Example	Type of curriculum
1. Course description in a college prospectus	
2. The induction programme	
3. Learning to work with others	
4. What is experienced during the taught sessions?	
5. Teaching observations by your tutor	
6. The contents of your course handbook	
7. Lunchtime pilates group	
8. The number of computers that are actually available	
9. Valuing the diversity within the group	
10. Group trip to an ICT exhibition on a Saturday morning	

THE HIDDEN CURRICULUM

The term 'hidden curriculum' derives from sociology and is used to describe the messages that learners pick up just by attending their particular institution, rather than those things which are explicitly taught. It is often said that the hidden curriculum is 'caught' rather than 'taught'. It is the institution and its cultures and how these are experienced that influence learner attitudes and behaviours. We might reasonably ask from whom the curriculum is hidden, however. One view is that it is hidden only from learners and an institution deliberately organises itself in a manner whereby learners learn to value diversity, citizenship, punctuality, authority, etc., although these may not be explicitly identified in any syllabus or curriculum document. Socialisation is considered to be one of the 'hidden curriculum' functions of schools. It is this type of control of curriculum content and values which are passed on to learners that prompted the 'de-schooling' movement, with its view of organised education as an invidious form of social and political control.

On the other hand, instances can occur in which the hidden curriculum is truly hidden from all, as in the example quoted by Phil Revell (2004) in an article in *The Guardian* newspaper on 'the hidden curriculum and hypocrisy'. He points out that lessons on sustainability are delivered in non-insulated school classrooms using worksheets printed on non-recycled paper.

In this instance, although lessons may be given on sustainability and the dangers of global warming, schools and the staff who work in them appear to be unaware of the contradictory messages given by their daily working practices. These in fact do not reflect what they teach and actually contradict the 'official' curriculum. This fact appears to be 'hidden' from all concerned. The hidden curriculum is also evident in FE establishments where exhortations to eat healthily are displayed on posters in corridors containing fizzy drink and chocolate vending machines. Examples 3 and 9 in Activity 9.3 fall into the 'hidden curriculum' category.

THE OFFICIAL CURRICULUM

When you are first thinking of applying for a course at your local college, you might look at the college website or obtain a college prospectus. At the beginning of your diploma course, you were probably given a course handbook which gave details of the content of the course procedures and protocols, the assessment requirements and generally what you could expect to do whilst on the course. What the institution or course says it offers is known as the 'official' curriculum. Examples 1 and 6 in Activity 9.3 fall into this category.

THE ACTUAL CURRICULUM

When you teach, you may well start by telling your learners the objectives of the session, the kinds of activities they will be engaging in and how you will assess their learning. This is a kind of 'official' curriculum. In most cases, this is what you will deliver in your session. Sometimes, however, for a number of different reasons, what you deliver is not quite what you thought and said it would be. Similarly, when you arrive at college and begin to take your chosen course, you may find that what you receive is not quite what you were led to expect. What you receive is known as the 'actual' (or sometimes 'received' or 'experienced') curriculum and may differ from the advertised official curriculum. In the session you delivered, it may be that an activity took much longer than you expected, but as it was well received you decide to let it run. This meant that you had to hold over one of the objectives till the next session and you used a different, shorter, assessment method. The example above illustrates a deliberate strategy but sometimes the 'slippage' between the official and actual curriculum is unintentional or is prompted by circumstance. On other occasions, a bit of 'overselling' on the part of the institution may be the cause. Examples 4 and 8 in Activity 9.3 fall into this category.

THE FORMAL AND INFORMAL CURRICULUM

The formal curriculum is the name given to all of those activities that are planned for and given space on the timetable. Other activities, often conducted on a voluntary basis, such as clubs, trips, sports teams or even fund raising activities for charity, are often called 'extra-curricular', implying that they fall outside of the curriculum. Others would argue, however, that although they do not form part of the official curriculum, these activities are still part of the overall curriculum offering and comprise the 'informal' curriculum. Examples 2 and 5 in Activity 9.3 fall into the category of formal; 7 and 10 fall into the category of informal.

THE CURRICULUM AND VALUES

Look at the words in the thought bubbles in Figure 9.2. What do they all have in common? What do they represent?

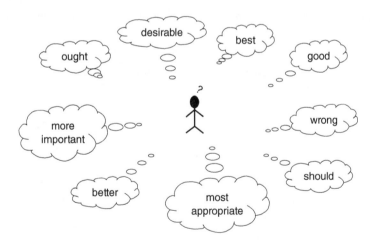

Figure 9.2   Values

The words in question are representative of values or judgements. Businesses often have sets of 'core values' which determine the way in which they operate. One core value may be that customers 'should be treated courteously, regardless of the situation'. The reason behind this would be a recognition that the business needs to maximise its customer base in order to survive and develop. Employees would therefore treat all customers in a well-mannered and considerate fashion. Any who did not might face disciplinary action or even dismissal for behaving in a manner that was not consistent with the values of the business. 'Family values' determine how family members act towards each other and as a group. An example of a family value might be 'it is important to spend time together' because the family believes that this will create a harmonious atmosphere in the home. This would affect the way in which family members organised their social life. Values, then, are the ideals or principles which guide actions and are based on what is believed or assumed to be the case at the time. As times and conditions change, so may values change accordingly.

Collectively, a set of complementary values form the basis of an outlook on the world as a whole. Typically, a political party is a group of individuals who share a particular set of values. As a party, they have a particular outlook on society and how it should be organised. This is known as an ideology. Figure 9.3 illustrates the relationship between these different factors.

At an individual level, we all possess our own sets of values, representing our beliefs and the principles by which we lead our life – how we think things ought to be. Our actions are influenced by and are in keeping with the values we hold. If respect for others is one of the values we hold, we are polite and courteous towards other people. If, however, we lose our temper and end up insulting someone, we usually feel bad about it later when we have calmed down, as we have acted in a way that does not fit with the values we hold. If honesty is one of our values but we find ourselves in a situation where for some reason we have to tell a lie, we feel uncomfortable at doing

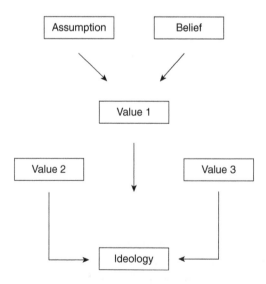

Figure 9.3   Assumptions, beliefs, values and ideologies

so as we have to act in a manner which is at odds with our values. Our general values thus determine the way we lead our lives. Similarly, the values we hold towards education exert a strong influence on the way in which we teach.

REFLECTIVE TASK 9.1

Ask a colleague or someone in your diploma group that you have not seen teach, to complete the following sentences:

1. Education should ....
2. Teachers should ....
3. Learners should ....
4. I teach because ....

From their responses, build up a picture of how they teach – the methods they use, the relationship they have with learners, their approach to classroom management, etc.

Observe them teach or check your picture with them verbally.

Repeat the exercise in reverse – invite a colleague to ask the questions of you before presenting their thumbnail sketch of you as a teacher. Do you recognise the picture they present to you? *Can you connect it to the values that you hold or is there 'slippage' between your values and actions?*

You were probably reasonably accurate in the picture you painted of your colleague's teaching as it would be in line with the values they expressed and hopefully the reverse process proved equally accurate in the conclusion it gave rise to. The exercise illustrates the way in which our values determine our priorities, intentions and actions. Values establish outcomes – in this case, behaviours.

In the same way that values operate at a personal level, they also operate at the level of curriculum. Although a definitive definition of curriculum remains elusive, a common thread which runs through all discussions around curriculum-related matters is the act of decision making.

The National Curriculum makes decisions on subject and assessment procedures in schools; the examples mentioned earlier relating to curriculum development were all concerned with making decisions relating to change; similarly, in arriving at a curriculum for your particular institution, decisions will have been made concerning the character of the institution (would it be mainly academic or vocational, for instance), and thus the range and levels of courses to be offered.

To arrive at a decision, the various pros and cons of the situation are considered and debated, and finally a judgement is made as to the most appropriate way forward. Armitage et al. (2012: 207) remind us that 'every curriculum represents a set of fundamental beliefs, assumptions and values, collectively termed "ideologies" about the nature of education and training', and so the judgement made depends in turn on the underlying values held by those who make it. The relationship between decisions, judgements and values in the context of curriculum is illustrated in Figure 9.4.

Values underpin the curriculum at whichever level we consider it.

Values set the context for decisions such as:

- what should be taught/learned
- how students should learn
- how learning is to be assessed.

Who the decision-makers are is determined by the level at which the curriculum operates. At the teaching level, we, as teachers, make curricular decisions about the sessions we will be delivering. In this case, our own values will be the major influence. At national level, we could be talking about government making curricular decisions affecting the education system as a whole, in which case the prevailing values and ideologies of whichever political party happens to be in power at the time will inform the decisions arrived at. Funding is largely dependent on compliance with these curricular decisions, and so they are readily adopted at institutional level and subsequently filter down to the teaching level. Sometimes, the values leading to specific decisions and what they demand of our practice can be at odds with our personal values – the official view of what education should be about and how it should be managed conflicts with the view that we hold. This tension between the two sets of values can show itself in a number of ways but typically results in reduced job satisfaction and a lowering of morale. In extreme cases, we may have to decide whether it is a tension we can live with or not.

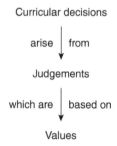

Figure 9.4   Curriculum and values

ACTIVITY 9.4

What is your institution's mission statement? Does it tell you anything about the values that inform its approach to decisions made about the curriculum it offers? Look at the aims expressed in the various curriculum documents used in your subject. Do they tell you anything about the values that inform the curriculum you follow in teaching your subject?

CLASSIFYING VALUES AND IDEOLOGIES

Values come in all shapes and sizes but share the common function of proposing what education should be about – what its purpose is, how this should be achieved and the roles that should be played. We have seen that one way of organising the values that we meet in education is to group them together in complementary sets, forming ideologies. Bartlett and Burton (2007: 77) stress the importance of ideologies: 'decisions based on ideological beliefs are made at every stage in the development and delivery of any curriculum that determine what kind of knowledge is contained in the curriculum, how it is delivered, assessed and so on'.

Ideologies themselves cover a spectrum of viewpoints. Bartlett et al. (2001: 12) suggest that to simplify matters, ideologies can be categorised through a consideration of where they place the greatest emphasis. The three categories they suggest emphasise either knowledge, society or the individual.

1. Emphasis on knowledge

Ideologies such as traditionalism, conservatism and classical humanism fall into this category. They share a view on the importance of the formal arrangement of knowledge in subjects. They ask questions about the relative importance of different subjects and who should be able to access them. These ideologies share an underlying assumption that learning starts from a simple level which is available to most people but progresses on to increasingly complex levels of knowledge which can be attained by fewer and fewer people until finally an academic elite is formed. At the lower levels, the learner is closely supervised, becoming more autonomous as she or he scales the academic ladder. Practical subjects possess a significantly lower status than academic subjects and formal assessment procedures are important in maintaining academic standards. Classical humanism is typical of this grouping of ideologies as it regards society as hierarchical in nature, and so the purpose of education is to equip people to take up their proper roles in life within these hierarchies. This can be seen with the rather elitist values associated with public schools, the more traditional universities such as Oxford and Cambridge and qualifications such as A-Levels.

In summary, education should be concerned with providing individuals with the knowledge required to take up their position in society, and the maintenance of academic standards is paramount in maintaining the status of this knowledge.

2. Emphasis on society

There are two ways of viewing the relationship between education and society. One view, expressed in the ideology of instrumentalism, is concerned with the need to develop and maintain a competitive economy. A skilled, educated workforce is required to achieve this and so the purpose of the education system is to provide such a workforce. Technical and vocational qualifications which employ a competence-based approach to assessment are used to this end. Competence, reliability and a strong work ethic are typical of the values which contribute to this ideology. A different perspective is taken by ideologies such as democratic socialism and reconstructionism, which are more concerned with the power structures that exist within society. Democratic socialism seeks to create equality of opportunity for all. Education is seen as the route to achieving this by reforming society from within. Reconstructionism takes a more extreme stance and wishes to use education to overthrow existing structures of inequality.

In summary, education should be concerned with meeting the needs of society by creating a culture of equality and/or by providing an adaptable workforce which will allow economic growth and prosperity.

3. Emphasis on the individual

Here, personal development and the individual needs and interests of the learner are considered to be of the greatest importance. Learning is seen as individual and part of a lifelong process. The development of the person is more important than formal qualifications and so formative assessment and feedback are used in preference to summative assessment. These are the values which are prized within adult and community education and are reflected in the curriculum that is offered within that sector. Progressivism, with its belief that a democratic society is strengthened through the meeting of individual needs and the encouragement of personal growth, is an ideology which is in sympathy with this view of the world, and is the ideology which lies behind learner-centred approaches.

In summary, education should be concerned with providing a structure within which people can meet their own needs and develop as individuals, leading to a strong democratic society.

CURRICULUM MODELS

Having established that curriculum is concerned with making decisions, and that values and ideologies play a fundamental role in this, it is evident that when designing any type of course, a wider view than just the syllabus content needs to be taken. Course design needs to take account of the aims and intentions of the curriculum as a whole and so includes a careful consideration of which curriculum model the course in question subscribes to.

Curriculum models reflect the underlying ethos or general approach to curriculum. They outline what is considered to be important in the bigger picture and are shaped by the context from which the curriculum is viewed. Particular curriculum models become more or less fashionable, depending on which ideology or set of values is considered important at the time.

Different viewpoints or perspectives give rise to different models of curriculum.

CONTENT MODEL

The content model arises from a philosophical perspective of the curriculum which argues that the curriculum should represent the basic structure of human knowledge. Knowledge itself can be divided into a number of categories such as the arts, humanities and sciences, each with its own particular logic, terminology and methodology. Hirst (1974) identified eight forms of knowledge which he thought accounted for 'the ways in which people experience and learn about the world' (Armitage et al., 2012: 205). The purpose of curriculum therefore is to select and provide the most appropriate range of subjects which, when studied, will impart an understanding of these essential forms of knowledge.

The aim of this approach to curriculum is the transmission of existing knowledge and the intellectual development of learners. It offers the 'traditional' approach to curriculum 'associated with the elite universities and academic "school" subjects' (Avis et al., 2010: 104).

Kelly raises objections to a curriculum based on this absolute view of knowledge, suggesting that it does not allow for debate or individual interpretation, placing the focus too firmly on 'what' is to be taught at the expense of 'how' it is to be taught. He suggests that this model of curriculum is incompatible with an inclusive approach as 'the justification for that curriculum is to be found in its content rather than in its effects' (2009: 58), labelling it as 'curriculum as content and education as transmission' (2009: 56). Avis et al. (2010: 104) support this viewpoint, stating: 'This kind of curriculum, taken to extremes, would be not much more than a list of knowledge to be passed from teacher to student.'

- Mathematics
- Physical sciences
- Human sciences
- History
- Religion
- Literature and the fine arts
- Philosophy
- Moral knowledge

Figure 9.5   Hirst's eight forms of knowledge

This model of curriculum would appear to be quite limited in that it is not that far removed from the notion of the syllabus, and because of its focus on subject seems out of step with an inclusive approach.

Other models include the cultural model which takes a sociological perspective, suggesting that the content of the curriculum is selected from the culture of the particular society. Its purpose is to transmit the key elements of a society's culture to the next generation, and, in doing this, it acts as an instrument of social control. Skilbeck's situational model of curriculum emphasises the importance of the context in which the curriculum is to operate and how internal and external factors present in this situation will impact on any proposals they make.

Perhaps the most useful curriculum models, however, arise out of an educational perspective, in which the focus is not on the content of the curriculum and the manner of its selection, or the culture or context within which it is situated, but on the type of learning that is to take place. Curriculum models arising from an educational perspective are concerned with identifying an approach to course design which is compatible with the type of learning that is looked for. Different perspectives on learning therefore give rise to different curriculum models.

PRODUCT MODEL

This approach to curriculum is derived from a behaviourist perspective on learning. You will remember from Chapter 6 that this perspective defines learning as a 'change in behaviour' and identifies the learning in the form of objectives. As a result, the product model is often referred to as the 'behavioural objectives model'. Its focus is on the end results or 'products' of learning. Using the analogy of a journey, it is the arrival at the destination which matters most.

PROCESS MODEL

The process model of curriculum is based around a cognitive perspective on learning. Reference to Chapter 6 reminds us that the cognitive view of learning is concerned with individual understanding and the derivation of personal meaning. In this particular journey, arrival at the common destination is of less importance than what each individual learns along the way.

REFLECTIVE TASK 9.2

Which of the models outlined above do you think your practice follows most closely? Why do you think that is the case – nature of subject, own views on learning, institutional pressures …?

CURRICULUM DESIGN

So, different perspectives on learning suggest different approaches to curriculum, which are identified within different curriculum models. To be of use, however, these models need to be translated into some kind of practical form. This is the task of curriculum design.

CURRICULUM DESIGN AND THE PRODUCT MODEL OF CURRICULUM

Objectives approach

The first significant approaches to curriculum design were based around the product model of curriculum. The earliest of these was that of Ralph Tyler (1949), introduced in his book *Basic Principles of Curriculum and Instruction*, and which, at the time, was considered to bring a new degree of clarity to the planning process.

For Tyler, curriculum planning was a rational process based on the answers to four fundamental questions:

1. What educational purposes should the school seek to attain?
2. What educational experiences are likely to attain the purposes?
3. How can these educational experiences be organised effectively?
4. How can we determine whether these purposes are being attained?

The answers to these questions formed the basis for a linear planning model.

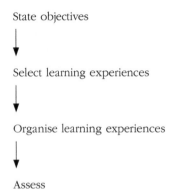

State objectives

Select learning experiences

Organise learning experiences

Assess

This was later developed into the 'Rational Curriculum Model', with the addition of the further stage of 'evaluation' creating a cyclical rather than linear process. It is more popularly known nowadays as the 'Training Cycle' (see Figure 9.6).

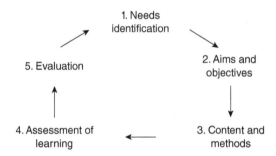

Figure 9.6   The training cycle

The main feature of Tyler's approach and its subsequent adaptations is that it provided a clear and specific statement of the learning that was to take place. This in turn made assessment a more precise process, and the use of objectives as the starting point for planning provided for a much more systematic approach than had previously been used.

The objectives model attracted much criticism. It was regarded by many as too teacher-led and overly prescriptive. Objectives were time-consuming to write, particularly in the form suggested by writers such as Mager (1975), who suggested that an objective should specify not only the sought after behaviour change but also the conditions under which it should be demonstrated and the standard of performance expected. In practice, teachers wrote a less demanding form of objective than the original behavioural objective suggested by Mager. The objectives written by teachers identified only the change in behaviour (learning) required, but expressed this in a reasonably specific manner. This type of objective is generally referred to as a 'learning objective' to distinguish it from its more prescriptive predecessor, the behavioural objective. Even so, at lower levels of learning, objectives could become too simplistic, whilst they became difficult to write for higher levels of learning.

Outcomes approach

Avis et al. (2010: 107) assert that 'despite these difficulties, the objectives model of the curriculum has been immensely influential', but, nonetheless, in the light of such criticism, there has been a move away from the objectives approach towards curriculum planning based around outcomes (Prideaux, 2000: 168). Marsh (2009: 47) suggests that 'Outcome statements concentrate on the outputs rather than the inputs of teaching. Exponents of this approach argue that objectives only concentrate on the inputs of teaching'.

Objectives specify the learning that is to take place whereas outcomes describe what can now be done as a result of that learning.

ACTIVITY 9.5

Classify the following as either objectives or outcomes:

1 Make a bouillabaisse.
2 Construct a sequential logic circuit.
3 Identify the general characteristics employers look for in an employee.
4 List the main causes of challenging behaviour in patients with dementia.
5 Complete a mock interview for a job.
6 Identify the different effects on clients of positive and negative feedback.
7 Look after a patient with dementia.
8 Describe the inputs and outputs of a J-K flip-flop.
9 List the ingredients of a bouillabaisse.
10 Conduct a feedback session with a client.

Whilst you may not recognise all of the subject specialist terminology in the above examples, you hopefully will recognise that 3, 4, 6, 8 and 9 above are all objectives: they describe the learning that will take place: they are the inputs in the given session; 5, 7, 10, 2 and 1 are the corresponding outcomes: they describe what can now be done as a result of the learning that has taken place: they are the outputs of the given session.

Outcomes Based Education (OBE) is an approach to learning which starts by determining the knowledge, competencies and qualities learners should be able to demonstrate on completion of the particular course, module or unit they have studied. The planning process then works backwards from these outcomes to determine content, teaching and learning activities, assessment and evaluation. Whilst outcomes allow for a more flexible interpretation of the curriculum, they share a common purpose with the objectives approach in that they try to express what is required of the learner in an unambiguous and measurable fashion. If you are currently registered on a university Certificate in Education programme, rather than a diploma programme with an awarding body, you will doubtless have noticed that your module specifications are laid out in this way. A module specification normally includes:

- an indication of level
- the required study time or course hours
- a series of learning outcomes
- indicative content
- an indication of how it is to be taught
- assessment requirements.

Competence approach

> A competence is a description of something which a person who works in a given occupational area should be able to do. It is a description of an action, behaviour or outcome which a person should be able to demonstrate. (Training Agency, 1988: 5)

Competence-based education and training (CBET) came into its own with the formation of the National Council for Vocational Qualifications (NCVQ) in 1986, under the White Paper 'Working Together in Education and Training' and the subsequent launch of National Vocational Qualifications (NVQs). The remit of the NCVQ was to design and implement a new framework of vocational qualifications which would establish national standards for all of the different occupational sectors. A competence-based approach was considered to be the most effective way of achieving this. Lead bodies were set up to devise appropriate sets of standards for each occupational sector. These standards are a statement of the competencies required to perform a specific job role and were arrived at through a process of functional analysis. This is a 'top-down' method of analysis which starts by identifying all of the observable activities performed within a job role. Each standard, or *unit* in NVQ terms, is broken down into a number of constituent *elements*, each containing a number of *performance criteria* which has to be demonstrated by the NVQ candidate. The performance criteria are accompanied by range statements which list the different circumstances in which the competence must be applied.

Unit 022 Reflect and develop practice (CCLD 304)

Element 22.1 Reflect on practice

PC No:	**Performance Criteria**
P1	Monitor processes, practices and outcomes from your own work
P2	Evaluate your own performance (achievements, strengths and weaknesses) using best practice benchmarks
P3	Reflect on your interactions with others
P4	Share your reflections with others and use their feedback to improve your own evaluation
P5	Use reflection to solve problems
P6	Use reflection to improve practice

Element 22.2 Take part in continuing professional development

PC No:	**Performance Criteria**
P1	Identify areas in your knowledge, understanding and skills where you could develop further
P2	Develop and negotiate a plan to develop your knowledge, skills and understanding further
P3	Seek out and access opportunities for continuing professional development as part of this plan
P4	Use continuing professional development to improve your practice

Figure 9.7 Example of a competence approach

NVQs were intended to form a system of accreditation as well as learning, and so can be delivered in a variety of ways depending on the circumstances and experience of the learners. All programmes, however, whether they focus more on accreditation for those in full-time employment, or more on learning for those entering into a vocational area, are planned and delivered around the identified competencies of the NVQ units.

NVQs have largely been replaced by certificates and diplomas in line with the old QCF awards. They will largely disappear in the RQF although some RQF qualifications may still be described as NVQs where they are based on recognised occupational standards.

The examples of curriculum design examined so far, although having different starting points of objectives, outcomes and competencies, are all based on a product model of curriculum and you will doubtless recognise the influence of this model within your own practice.

REFLECTIVE TASK 9.3

Can you identify elements of the product model within your own teaching? If so, what do you see as the particular advantages or limitations of this approach?

At course level, a product-based approach gives a degree of uniformity in provision, an important consideration if the course leads to an award which is part of a national qualification, or if a large organisation (such as the Ministry of Defence) wishes to see a consistency in practice across all of its different branches. At a planning level, a logical and systematic approach is encouraged, as in schemes of work and session plans which are based around SMART learning objectives. Perhaps a more significant factor in the widespread use of the product model in course design, however, relates to the move towards increasing accountability within the education system as a whole. There is an increasing demand to be able to adequately measure if learning has taken place, and this is a requirement which the product model of curriculum is admirably suited to accommodate. Kelly (2009: 73), for one, notes the 'emergence of a schooling system which is no longer planned with education in mind but merely as concerned with quantifiable and "measurable" learning'. A consequence of this is highlighted by Smith (1996), who notes that 'In order to measure, things have to be broken down into smaller and smaller units. The result is often long lists of trivial skills as is frequently encountered in BTEC programmes and NVQ competency assessments'.

Smith's observation is similar to the criticisms of the product model previously mentioned, but, as Stenhouse (1975: 84) suggests, 'it is idle to criticise the objectives model as a strategy for the design and development of curriculum if no orderly alternative can be found'. Stenhouse proposed the process model of curriculum as providing that alternative.

CURRICULUM DESIGN AND THE PROCESS MODEL OF CURRICULUM

Kelly (2009: 93) describes the process model as based on a concept of learning 'which sees it in terms of the development of understanding rather than the acquisition of knowledge'. It is evident from this statement that the process model is based on cognitive learning theory in which the construction of personal meaning and understanding is a central concept. Suppose the subject to be taught was an understanding of how the events prior to the First World War led to its outbreak in 1914. If this were to be expressed in terms of learning objectives, 'understanding' would have to be defined in a specific and measurable manner and the results might look something like this:

1. List the different alliances that existed in Europe prior to the outbreak of war in 1914.
2. Identify the main examples of the international tension in Europe caused by the 'scramble for Africa'.
3. State the reasons for the murder, in 1914, of Archduke Franz Ferdinand by Serbian nationalists.

Would achievement of these objectives demonstrate actual understanding, however, or rather the acquisition of a number of key points? Would learners be able to identify the relationships between these facts and show how one was dependent on or caused by another? Could they present a reasoned argument as to how these factors combined to cause war to break out? If the achievement of the above objectives was the sum total of the learning that took place, this would not be the case. This situation illustrates Smith's previously stated concern relating to a focus on the parts rather than how they relate to each other to form the 'whole'.

It would appear, then, that to establish structure in a course adopting a process-based approach, a behavioural type of objective does not provide the best solution as it is at odds with the type of learning that is to be achieved. The objectives approach also defines or prescribes the learning that is to take place in advance of it happening. Much learning, however, is spontaneous rather than prescribed and cannot be anticipated in advance. Learning can also be creative in nature, seeking to arrive at new or novel solutions to problems. In both of these cases, behavioural objectives are unsuitable as a basis for planning.

What is required is a type of objective which does not reduce learning to mechanistic behaviours and is sufficiently flexible to allow for some individual interpretation. A type of objective which fits this description, known as an 'expressive objective', has been suggested by Elliot Eisner (1969). Eisner's background was in the field of art, and the prescriptive, specific nature of behavioural, or 'instructional', objectives, as he preferred to call them, was at odds with the more spontaneous and creative approach required within his subject area. He therefore proposed a different kind of objective, called an 'expressive objective', which was 'evocative rather than prescriptive'. These objectives describe an 'educational encounter' rather than a prescription of what is to be learned: 'It [expressive objective] identifies a situation in which children are to work, a problem with which they are to cope, a task in which they are to engage; but it does not specify what from that encounter, situation, problem, or task they are to learn' (Eisner, 1969: 15–16).

This concurs with Neary's assertion (2002: 62) that in implementing a process approach 'it can be argued that prescription of learning activities provides the appropriate means of achieving the broad intentions of the curriculum'.

Eisner suggests the following as examples of expressive objectives:

- to interpret the meaning of *Paradise Lost*
- to examine and appraise the significance of *The Old Man and the Sea*
- to develop a three-dimensional form through the use of wire and wood
- to visit the zoo and discuss what was of interest there.

Planning based around expressive objectives is also in sympathy with the individuality and autonomy in learning that is characteristic of the process model, as in setting expressive objectives 'the teacher hopes to provide a situation in which meanings become personalised and in which children produce products, both theoretical and qualitative, that are as diverse as themselves' (Eisner, 1969: 16).

The role of the teacher in this model is also beginning to emerge as one which employs a more facilitative approach. Stenhouse (1975) points out that in an objectives approach the teacher is considered to be master of the subject. He questions whether this is possible, and prefers to consider the teacher to also be in a learning situation, although a 'senior' learner by virtue of their skills in 'finding out' and 'philosophical understanding' of the subject.

The main purpose of the process model of curriculum, then, is to develop the intellect by focusing on the processes involved in thinking and reasoning. Different subjects involve key concepts and principles which form a network of relationships, and, to properly understand a subject, learners need to be familiar with both the subject's structure and its particular ways of thinking and proceeding, rather than just accumulating a store of its facts and knowledge. As a result of being taught science, for instance, learners should be able to think and act in a scientific manner. They should be 'scientists' rather than individuals who know lots of science facts.

Bruner and Stenhouse were both advocates of the process approach and produced learning programmes (Bruner in 1965 – 'Man, A Course of Study'; Stenhouse in 1966 – 'The Humanities Curriculum Project') which embodied its principles. In each of these programmes, planning started not from a consideration of behavioural objectives but from the establishment of a broad aim, which led to the setting up of activities which encouraged learners to engage in enquiry, thinking and reasoning around this aim. The teacher acts as a 'senior learner' (Stenhouse) or 'problem setter' (Bruner) rather than as a 'solution giver'.

PROBLEM BASED LEARNING (PBL)

This is an approach to curriculum design where learning activities are centred on a series of problems or scenarios. Learning becomes an active process as learners have to identify the appropriate content and use it to arrive at a solution to the problem or scenario. The sequence of events is:

1. Learners are presented with a problem.
2. They are put into small groups to discuss the problem. They agree on a common understanding of the problem and share existing relevant knowledge.
3. They identify what else they need to know to solve the problem and agree on individual research tasks to be completed before they meet again.
4. Individual research tasks are completed.
5. The group reform to share the results of their research and work on a solution.
6. A solution is presented to the whole group.
7. Learners engage in individual and group reflection to establish what has been learned.

This approach fosters skills in problem solving, research techniques, critical thinking and working in teams. It equates well to a process model of curriculum as it aims for understanding and individual and collective meaning rather than the accumulation of facts and information. It is an active form of learning which promotes learning through discovery and the application of knowledge to real situations. It is used extensively in medical education but Weyers (2006) suggests how the approach can be adapted to an FE environment whilst cautioning that careful planning of a PBL task is required for it to be effective in producing the desired outcome. It is important to recognise that PBL is not the same as introducing problem-solving activities into a taught session. In the latter case, teaching of the subject normally occurs first and then the problem-solving activity is used to apply or assess what has been learned. In PBL, the problem is given at the outset and acts as the trigger for the ensuing learning. The teacher then becomes much more of a facilitator, taking on a role more in keeping with the 'senior learner' or 'problem setter' descriptions of Stenhouse and Bruner.

REFLECTIVE TASK 9.4

Can you identify elements of the process model within your own teaching? If so, what do you see as the particular advantages or limitations of this approach?

PRODUCT OR PROCESS?

The process model possesses what, in the current climate of accountability, might be considered a major flaw. It considers assessment to be a developmental rather than a judgemental activity. Stenhouse (1975: 95) states that 'the teacher ought to be a critic, not a marker' and 'assessment is about the teaching of self-assessment', and so 'It [the Process model] can never be directed towards an examination as an objective without loss of quality, since the standards of the examination then override the standards immanent in the subject'.

Take an example from Eisner's subject area of art. In a still-life class, the teacher would work their way around the group of learners, giving feedback on an individual level. The feedback would not be aimed at deciding whether the work being produced met certain criteria and was thus worth a mark of 60 or 70 per cent, but would more likely take the form of a discussion between teacher and learner. They would probably touch on areas such as the progress of the work to date, what had been learned so far from doing it, where it would go next and how it informed the bigger picture of the learner's existing knowledge and skills. This kind of approach uses the piece of work as a vehicle to further develop existing knowledge and skills (what has been learned on the journey) rather than as a means to arrive at a judgement of that knowledge and those skills (arriving at the destination). For this reason, the process model in its pure form struggles for acceptance in many instances of course design.

In reality, few courses draw exclusively on one curriculum model. You may well be able to identify some aspects of your diploma course that lean towards a more process-based, developmental approach, and others which fall much more firmly into a product-based approach. The table in Figure 9.8 illustrates the main differences between the two curriculum models.

Product	Process
1. Based on a behavioural view of learning	1. Based on a cognitive view of learning
2. Structured around behavioural objectives	2. Structured around expressive objectives or activities
3. Closed, prescriptive in nature – outcomes determined before the learning takes place	3. Open-ended, outcomes are often unknown prior to learning taking place and arise out of the learning itself
4. Outcomes largely the same for everyone	4. Outcomes can be individual
5. Focus on subject, tends to be teacher-led	5. Focus on learning, tends to be learner-led
6. Teacher considered to be expert	6. Teacher viewed as 'senior learner'
7. Assessment usually formal – summative in nature	7. Mutual evaluation rather than assessment – formative in nature
8. Tends to be associated with vocational courses	8. Tends to be associated with academic courses

Figure 9.8   Comparison of product and process curriculum models

THE NEGOTIATED CURRICULUM

Suppose you and a group of friends decide to go on a day out together. How would you decide where to go? Would one person make the decision or would you agree between you on a destination? You may have to take certain constraints into account – someone may have to be back for a certain time, someone else may want to travel by train as they get car sick – but, hopefully, you would agree on a plan for the day that everyone was comfortable with and would feel some commitment to a trip that everyone felt they would gain something from.

The above scenario illustrates the principle behind negotiation in any aspect of life – we feel more committed to any activity in which we feel we have some say. Education is no different and Kelly (1987: 61) claims negotiation is a reflection of 'the rights of the subjects to have a say in planning curricula', while Bahr and Prendergast (2005: 164) point to the benefits of a negotiated approach in that 'Research suggests that students' learning is more effective and rewarding if they have a "voice" in and ownership of aspects of the curriculum and the teaching/learning process'.

REFLECTIVE TASK 9.5

Consider the groups you teach. Do you think some form of negotiation would prove beneficial to their learning? If so, how would you carry this out? If not, what do you see as the main disadvantages or barriers to a negotiated approach?

Although we have not referred to it as such, we have already explored aspects of negotiation when looking at workshop planning in Chapter 2, ILPs and learning contracts in Chapter 4, and setting ground rules in Chapter 1. These have largely been at the individual level, however, where we have some freedom to manoeuvre. Can we negotiate with groups? This will largely depend on the flexibility of the syllabus and course, and the culture of the organisation. In adult and community education, for instance, particularly in the more leisure-oriented courses, there can be considerable freedom in determining course content and delivery approaches, and the ethos in the sector encourages an open approach. In other curricula and institutions, the constraints are far greater. For any form of negotiation to be effective, therefore, the decision must first be made as to exactly what is negotiable and what is a given and what aspects of the curriculum it is appropriate to consider. Boud et al. (1985: 159) suggest that negotiation should include 'both the "what" and "how" of the curriculum', so although the 'what' may be fairly well set in stone by an inflexible syllabus, the 'how' may offer some possibilities. The nature of the group is another factor to consider and though we may feel more confident in using this approach with some groups than others, Neary (2002) puts forward a strong case for adopting a negotiated approach with adult learners and the andragogical approach discussed in Chapter 6 bears this out. Our own attitudes and confidence levels in using this approach also play a part and will influence whether any negotiation we do undertake will be of a free and open nature or will take a more structured and controlled approach, in which 'the tutor checks things out with the group but retains the option of whether or not to modify his/her initial proposal' (Daines et al., 2006: 46). Perhaps the strongest argument for adopting some form of negotiation within the curriculum lies in the fact that if we give learners some say and choice in their learning, we are taking a significant step towards making the curriculum we offer more inclusive.

REFLECTIVE TASK 9.6

Some form of negotiation should be possible with all groups and can have a positive effect, even if conducted in a very limited fashion. Consider the groups that you teach and pick out two - the one with whom you think negotiation is most possible and the group with whom negotiation is least possible. For each, identify what can be negotiated and think about how best to organise this in each case.

THE INCLUSIVE CURRICULUM

When considering inclusion, it is tempting to fall back on the nine strands of diversity (or protected characteristics as they are now known) of the 2010 Equality Act as a basis. These are:

- age
- disability
- gender re-assignment
- race
- religion or belief (including lack of belief)
- sex
- sexual orientation
- marriage and civil partnership
- pregnancy and maternity.

Whilst these are helpful in keeping major issues of diversity at the forefront of our minds, the variety that exists within society as a whole covers a wider set of characteristics which are shared by the groups of learners with whom we come into contact on a daily basis. The inclusive curriculum provides the opportunity for learners from the full range of diverse backgrounds to access, participate and succeed in their learning. 'Inclusive FE', the Centre for Studies on Inclusive Education's (CSIE) summary of the Tomlinson report (1996), suggests inclusion means students are 'actively included' and 'fully engaged' in their learning: 'At the heart of our thinking lies the idea of match or fit between how the learner learns best, what they need and want to learn and what is required from the FE sector, the college and teachers for successful learning to take place.' Responsibility for inclusion is placed at three levels – sector, institutional and delivery.

At sector level, inclusion is given a high profile. The Excellence Gateway (formerly run by LSIS but taken over by the Education and Training Foundation in August 2013) reviews inclusion-related literature, research and policy, and gives recommendations for practice along with case studies of existing good practice. Inclusion, in the form of encouraging widening participation and managing equality and diversity issues, is high on the Ofsted agenda and 'safeguarding' is a limiting inspection grade. The occupational standards which underpin the diploma course take full account of inclusion and inclusive practice. The sector therefore raises awareness of the issues and places requirements on those working within it to follow appropriate guidelines.

When we get to institutional level, however, inclusion becomes a practical concern rather than the abstract concept which has been addressed at sector level.

ACTIVITY 9.6

Consider the particular institution in which you work. As you walk around the buildings, what physical evidence do you see of inclusive practice? What else does your institution do to promote an inclusive approach?

During your walk, you may have observed physical adjustments to the building to allow ease of access to areas such as teaching and computer rooms, canteen and library, for students with some form of physical disability. These would include lifts, ramps, automatic doors, toilets for the disabled, visual alarm systems and signage in braille and different languages. You may have walked past a crèche, a prayer room or seen hearing loops installed in classrooms. Although now subsumed into the 2010 Equality Act, the Disability and Discrimination Act (DDA) provided the impetus for a number of these features. Originally passed in 1995, the Act was updated on several occasions and included Part 4, which deals with the duties placed on providers of post-16 education and related services. One provision of Part 4 is that 'responsible bodies have a duty to make adjustments to physical features of premises where these put disabled people or students at a substantial disadvantage'. Some of the physical adjustments you noticed will have been put in place to conform to this provision. The Act also talks about making 'reasonable adjustment' for a student with a disability and not treating disabled students 'less favourably'. This widens the scope of provision far beyond that required for physical adjustments alone. The Equality Act of 2010 was introduced to combine the various previous pieces of equality legislation to provide a single more streamlined framework for the tackling of disadvantage and discrimination, and so 'reasonable adjustment' and 'less favourable' treatment are now considered to apply not just to disability but to all aspects of diversity. A crèche therefore allows those with childcare issues to access the curriculum and a prayer room allows learners to maintain their own particular religious practices as part of their curricular routine. There will be other less visible steps, however, that the institution will take to ensure its curriculum provision is inclusive that you may have noted down in your response to the above activity.

Look through your institutional prospectus and note the range, type and level of courses on offer. On what basis do you think the combination of courses which form the content of the curriculum on offer has been chosen? Do you think it is appropriate to the diversity of population the institution serves? Is there sufficient breadth and depth to allow learners to follow a course of study which is appropriate to their aspirations, needs and abilities? You may have considered level, types of course offered and progression routes in coming to a decision as to whether curriculum content can be regarded as inclusive. Are these courses offered at a time and place which allows for greatest access? Are courses offered at times (during the day, in the evening, at weekends) which allow attendance by those to whom they are appropriate, or is there some flexibility in attendance requirement? Are they offered at outreach centres or by flexible delivery methods? The way in which an institution constructs its curriculum with respect to access and suitability will have a large bearing on its level of inclusivity.

Next, turn your attention to admission procedures. An inclusive approach does not mean that anyone can sign up for any course. In some instances, such as in adult and community learning, entry to courses is quite open, but, for many courses, particularly those leading to a recognised qualification, entry requirements are put in place. These requirements spell out the prior knowledge and skills that learners need to possess in order to be able to succeed, and are the determining factor in deciding on a learner's suitability for a given course. It may be that some learners can evidence these skills through alternative qualifications to those asked for or through previous experience, and appropriate Accreditation of Prior Learning (APL) or Accreditation of Prior Experiential Learning (APEL) procedures should be in place to cater for this eventuality. The issue of inclusion relates to whether, having fulfilled the entry requirements, learners then encounter barriers to their subsequent attendance and success due to an aspect of diversity. We have already discussed the purpose and procedures of initial assessment and it is easy to see where this fits in with the bigger picture of inclusion.

The various support mechanisms that are available within an institution are also a significant factor in contributing to its inclusive nature. The levels of support on offer tend to depend on the size of an institution and so expectations need to be tempered by this factor. Bearing this in mind, identify what your institution offers learners to support them in their learning. How does your list compare with that below?

- additional learning support both inside and outside of the classroom
- counselling services
- health advice
- financial and travel advice and assistance
- computer access and assistance
- interfaith chaplaincy service
- disability officer
- career and employment advice and guidance.

The third level of the inclusive curriculum concerns the way in which it is taught.

ACTIVITY 9.7

Suppose you wanted to teach in the least inclusive manner possible. Make a list of the ways in which you could make your teaching as exclusive as possible.

You probably have quite an extensive list. Compare it with the checklist below of ways in which teaching can be made more *inclusive*:

- varying the teaching strategies used
- creating opportunities for all to contribute
- pitching questions to challenge at all levels
- using differentiated objectives or individual targets
- challenging stereotypical images and messages through the choice and design of resources used
- acknowledging and valuing all contributions equally
- ensuring the physical arrangement of the learning environment allows all to see, hear and contribute
- using varied assessment methods with alternatives available if required
- building opportunities for one-to-one contact into the session
- making extension tasks available
- using different groupings
- using inclusive language and challenging inappropriate language and behaviour
- making best use of extra support
- dividing time between learners appropriately.

THE HIDDEN CURRICULUM OF INCLUSION

There is much talk within the sector of celebrating diversity. This involves adopting a positive attitude towards diversity, viewing it as providing opportunities that can be taken advantage of rather than an additional complication. Part of an inclusive approach to curriculum involves encouraging all learners to see diversity in this way. Policies will have been laid down at sector and institutional level and statements made concerning ethos, but we have seen that more powerful influences exist. The hidden curriculum has been defined as relating to attitudes and what is learned as a consequence of 'being there'. We have also seen the importance of role modelling as a strategy in influencing attitudes and behaviour. As well as introducing policy, it is evident that our own behaviour and attitude towards issues of diversity play a significant part in establishing the attitudes and behaviours that learners are likely to adopt in regard to the same issues.

The medical and social models of disability provide useful and contrasting points of reference in this respect. The medical model sees disability as an ailment requiring treatment and so medical interventions provide the disabled person with the skills to adapt to society in as far as that is possible. Any problems experienced are seen as being rooted in the individual and their particular disability. The social model of disability makes a distinction between disability and impairment. It adopts the following definitions provided by the Union of the Physically Impaired Against Segregation (UPIAS):

Impairment – Lacking part or all of a limb or having a defective limb, organ or mechanism of the body (including psychological mechanisms)

Disability – The restrictions caused by the organisation of society which does not take into account individuals with physical or psychological impairments. (UPIAS, 1976, in Hill Country Disabled Group, n.d.)

The social model thus suggests that disability and any resulting exclusion are caused by the barriers which society places in the way of those with an impairment of some kind. These barriers can be:

- *physical* – is it the case that the disabled person cannot access the building or that the building has been constructed in such a way as to deny them access?
- *organisational* – is the curriculum implemented in such a way as to hinder access by some?
- *attitudinal* – is the disabled person unable to participate in an activity or does the teacher think that someone with an impairment is not capable of participating in the activity?

The argument is that impairment is an absolute and cannot be changed, but disability is caused by barriers created by people and that is a situation that can be changed. You will recognise that the physical adjustments to the building, previously discussed, are in tune with the social model, in that there is recognition that some learners may well have a physical impairment of some kind, but by altering the design of the building we are not allowing that impairment to become a disability. Physical barriers are relatively easy to identify and remove; organisational barriers will similarly be minimised in an institution which is sensitive to the issues. It is the barriers caused by attitudes, such as holding on to stereotypical views, which present the greatest challenge. The medical and social models of disability illustrate the way in which the effect of different attitudes on actions may be communicated to others.

The scope of the social model can be extended beyond the impairment/disability debate to cover all other aspects of diversity.

Rather than learners having to adapt to a 'medical', institutional culture, it should be the responsibility of the institution and those who work within it to adapt to and celebrate the diversity of its learners, demonstrating this commitment in their respective actions. This is the basis of the hidden curriculum of inclusion.

THE CURRICULUM IN PRACTICE

The way in which the curriculum is actually put into practice can vary depending on the nature of the subject, the qualification and the learners. The sequencing of the curriculum process, for instance, generally takes one of two forms – linear or spiral.

LINEAR CURRICULUM

As the name suggests, the content of the curriculum is approached in a step-by-step sequence, one topic being covered through to completion before progressing on to the next. The order of teaching is hierarchical, starting from the simplest form and gradually building up in complexity until the required level of understanding or performance is reached. Each topic is treated separately and is not necessarily linked to or integrated with other topics, other than to identify and point out transferrable skills or knowledge. Skills classes and language classes often adopt this type of approach.

SPIRAL CURRICULUM

In a spiral curriculum, as proposed by Bruner (1960), a topic is revisited on different occasions, each of which builds incrementally on the previous learning, taking it to a deeper and more complex level. In your diploma course, you will have encountered issues of equality and diversity. This is an area you will encounter a number of times as you progress through the various modules of the programme but, each time you do, you will achieve a deeper understanding of the issues and a wider appreciation of their implications. This is partly to do with the complexity of the topic as a whole and partly to do with what Bruner describes as a 'readiness' for learning. He argues that in order to fully understand a new idea or concept, the learner needs to have sufficient prior learning and experience, and this 'requires a continual deepening of one's understanding' and so 'a curriculum as it develops should revisit these basic ideas repeatedly, building on them until the student has grasped the full formal apparatus that goes with them' (Bruner, 1960: 13). A spiral approach to curriculum planning introduces later learning at an appropriate stage of a learner's knowledge and skill development, using earlier learning to make understanding easier by providing a general picture to which meaningful connections can be made.

ACTIVITY 9.8

How are the courses you teach sequenced? Are they linear or spiral? Why do you think this is?

FLEXIBLE APPROACHES TO CURRICULUM DELIVERY

Many courses nowadays are organised in a modular fashion. Neary (2002: 121) defines a module as 'a part or a unit of an educational programme', whilst Gray et al. (2000: 87) view modules as 'self-contained and accredited units ... of learning'. The content of the course as a whole is divided into a number of units or modules, allowing learners to study on a full-time or part-time basis, whilst building up credits towards their chosen qualification from a prescribed combination of modules. Some modules are mandatory and some are optional. There may be a set number and order in which the modules must be taken within each academic year and a minimum number of modules at defined levels will have to be completed successfully for the qualification to be awarded. Different qualifications will have different regulations determining the combination of modules and the balance between mandatory and optional modules they require. Modules are normally assessed separately. This means that rather than facing a deluge of end-of-year summative assessments, the assessment load for learners (and markers) can be more easily spread across the academic year, and more focused re-sit arrangements are possible in the event of not passing a particular module. Modularisation also opens up the opportunity to provide a variety of different assessment methods over the course as a whole, and the feedback gained from one module can have a positive effect on performance in future modules. Modularisation is particularly popular within higher education as it offers a number of advantages over the more traditional 'all-in-one' course. Benefits for learners mainly concern flexibility and include:

- the ability to self-pace – a course can be made as long or as short (within given limits) as the learner wishes, depending on the number of modules taken at one time. It is also possible to 'drop out' and return to a course within the time limits set by the providing institution
- an element of choice – in larger institutions, it is possible to choose from a list of different modules and put together a course 'pick and mix' style to suit individual needs and interests. On some courses, a mixture of core and optional modules may exist
- modules may be transferrable over different institutions
- consistency in approach – modules within a given institution follow a set arrangement, so having completed an initial module, learners will recognise the patterns and procedures of following modules and have a greater idea of what is expected of them
- short-term goals – modularisation provides short-term assessment goals which can have a positive effect on motivation.

There are also benefits for institutions as specialist courses with small numbers which would not be viable under normal circumstances can sometimes still be offered, as individual modules can be taken by groups of learners drawn from different courses. Curriculum development aimed at improvement or updating can be achieved by targeting the relevant modules rather than overhauling a whole course.

Modules are constructed by assigning them a credit point value related to the length of time required for completion. Normally, each credit equates to 10 hours of study. A 15-credit module thus requires 150 hours of study for completion, a 20-credit module, 200 hours, and so on. The word count of the module assignment is normally determined by its credit score. Your diploma course will operate on this basis although the term 'unit' is preferred to module. If your course is validated by a university or some other kind of higher education institution, the credit and module structure will differ but the underlying principle of modularisation remains.

Sometimes, an even greater degree of flexibility may be required due to factors such as the nature of the provision (e.g. work-based learning), the context (e.g. offender education) or the circumstances and lifestyle of the learners. To accommodate situations such as these, some courses are delivered on a 'roll on, roll off' or 'rolling' basis. This allows learners to begin their studies at any time during the year and finish when they are ready to do so. An individualised approach to learning is adopted, requiring a greater degree of independent study and resource-based learning than in the more conventional approaches to delivery. The teacher assumes a more facilitative role and assessment is conducted on an 'on demand' basis. Monitoring and tracking of progress are essential teaching skills to be mastered!

A more flexible approach can also have drawbacks, however, such as fragmentation or lack of coherence in learning, and a potential for the learning to become secondary to the chasing of modules. At an institutional level, there may be resource implications to be taken account of. If we are aiming towards an inclusive approach, however, a flexible approach to the delivery of the curriculum is an important consideration in responding to the needs of learners and to the wider community, particularly in the current climate of increasingly rapid technological, economic and social change.

REFLECTIVE TASK 9.7

How flexible is the organisation and delivery of your particular specialism? Can you identify any possible ways in which you can make it a more flexible offering?

CURRICULUM AND COURSE EVALUATION

Curriculum evaluation is concerned with finding out if the curriculum achieved what it set out to do. This is a relatively straightforward statement to make but less easy to implement.

The question: in judging whether the curriculum achieves what it sets out to do, do we use predetermined criteria which allow us to collect data in a rigorous and scientific manner or do we go in with an open mind and see what is to be seen, whether intended or not, and try to extract some meaning from our observations?

The answer: it depends on what we wish to find out, and this in turn depends on exactly what the curriculum was trying to achieve.

The approach taken to curriculum evaluation depends on the approach taken in devising the curriculum in the first place. An approach to evaluation based on measurement and objective data is appropriate to a product-based curriculum. A more open approach, observing the realities of what is happening without any preconceived notions, is appropriate to a process-based curriculum. Generally, at curricular level, the methods of evaluation used are considered to fall into the categories of 'goal-based' or 'goal-free'. The former employ objective measurement techniques related to a product approach whilst the latter seek to observe and uncover the different process elements of the curriculum. Evaluation models devised by Tyler and Stufflebeam are typical of the goal-based category. The 'illuminative evaluation' model of Parlett and Hamilton (so called because it shines a light into the dark and otherwise unexplored corners of the curriculum) and that of Scrivens, are typical of the goal-free category and concern themselves with description and interpretation rather than measurement and prediction.

As teachers, we tend to operate at the more practical level of course evaluation. Our purpose in doing this is to gather information that gives a measure of the effectiveness of our course. We can then use this information to put improvements in place. Effectively, course evaluation therefore consists of three stages:

1.   Gather information about the course.
2.   Make decisions based on what the information tells us.
3.   Implement these decisions to bring about improvement.

Decision making and subsequent implementation are a matter of individual judgement and so this section focuses on the first stage of the evaluative process – gathering information. Informally, we achieve this in a variety of ways, such as talking to learners, noting levels of enthusiasm and participation, reviewing statistics on enrolment, attendance, retention and achievement, and analysing the results of in-course assessments. These informal and mainly formative approaches are largely impressionistic, however, and are complemented by more formal procedures which provide a more solid evidence base. This evidence is generally gathered by asking the learners on the course for their views. This can be done either by asking directly for their opinions – spoken techniques, or by having them complete some form of evaluation questionnaire – written techniques. Before considering which of these approaches to adopt, however, we need to be clear in our minds as to what we wish to evaluate and which aspects of the course we would like to obtain information about.

ACTIVITY 9.9

Make a list of what you would like to find out about a particular course that you teach on. You might find it useful to organise the items in your list into groups to obtain a clearer picture.

As course evaluation is formative as well as summative, different aspects of the course will need to be explored at different stages along the way and this will be reflected in any evaluation undertaken at a particular time. The nature of your course and provision in general may point towards certain areas for investigation or your own informal evaluation may prompt you to probe particular issues, but in general some of the questions you may seek answers to through course evaluation will probably include:

CONTENT AND PLANNING

- Was course content up to date and relevant to learners?
- Was it sequenced in the most appropriate manner?
- Was sufficient time allocated to different areas of content?
- Did course content and materials take sufficient account of learners' previous knowledge and experience?
- How well was the course organised?
- Was it responsive to learner needs?
- Were course documentation and procedures clear?

DELIVERY

- Were the teaching strategies adopted the most appropriate?
- Was there an appropriate balance between teacher-led and learner-led activity?
- Were the level and pace of delivery appropriate to the group?
- Was sufficient opportunity given to practice what had been learned?
- How effective was the use of resources?

ASSESSMENT

- Did the assessment methods used give an accurate picture of learner achievement and progress?
- Were the most appropriate assessment methods used?

- Did learners receive sufficient and timely feedback?
- Was the workload reasonably evenly distributed over the course?
- Could better use have been made of assessment to enhance learning?
- Could more self and peer assessment techniques have been used?

CLIMATE

- What kind of relationship was established with learners?
- Were learners enthusiastic and were good levels of participation by all achieved?
- Was sufficient time allocated to providing individual and tutorial support?
- Was a sufficiently differentiated approach adopted?
- Were issues of equality and diversity handled appropriately and sensitively?

When using spoken techniques to answer the questions above, it is possible to talk to learners individually but this is generally a time-consuming process and the more likely approach is some form of group discussion. This approach has to be carefully managed to provide structure and to ensure, as far as possible, that everyone has an equal voice. The more favoured approach is a written approach using some form of questionnaire as this is less time-consuming and easier to manage. Questionnaires are relatively quick and easy to administer and can lead to more honest feedback, as learners may well feel able to commit to paper what they feel unable to tell us face to face. This is particularly the case if they can respond anonymously. Questionnaires can be open-ended or closed depending on the type of questions they contain (see Figure 9.9).

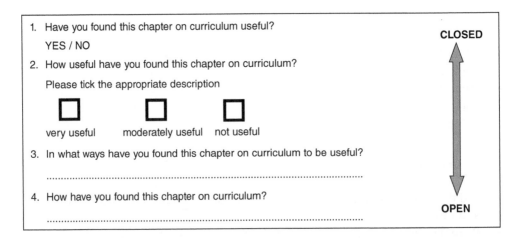

Figure 9.9   The spectrum of open/closed questions

ACTIVITY 9.10

What do you see as the particular advantages of each of the different types of question in Figure 9.9? What factors would you take into account in deciding which type of question to include in a questionnaire?

Suppose I include question 1 in my questionnaire. The result I get back is that everyone who has responded has answered 'no' to this question. I can gauge this opinion quickly by glancing through the questionnaires so I know fairly immediately that this chapter has not been received in the way I had hoped. What I do not know is *why* this is the case. Is it because it is too long, terminology is not explained properly, the level is not right? I know there is a problem, but I cannot rectify it because I don't know precisely what it is. Closed questions often take longer to devise than open questions, but produce responses which can be easily collated and presented. Open questions produce richer, more meaningful responses, but these can be difficult to collate and sometimes the diversity of response leads to difficulties in arriving at a definite conclusion. The type of question used is therefore usually influenced by the type of information we are looking for and the size of the group completing the questionnaire, as this will influence the time spent in collating responses.

Often, we try and gain the best of both worlds by using a combination of question types, the first is a closed question to elicit a simple response and the second an open question to seek further clarification if required (see Figure 9.10).

1(a)   Has this chapter on curriculum been relevant to your own teaching situation?
        YES/NO

1(b)   If not, please say why and suggest how it could have been improved.
        ....
        ....
        ....

Figure 9.10   Example of a combined open/closed question

Whatever type of question we use, the devising and writing of evaluation questionnaires requires careful thought. The following points provide some guidance:

When writing questionnaires, remember to:

- let learners know why they are completing the questionnaire and what it is trying to find out
- keep the questions simple, concise and reasonably straightforward

- keep the total number of questions asked to the minimum required to cover everything you need to know
- keep the format of the questions as consistent as possible
- ask the questions requiring least thought first
- leave sufficient space for the amount of detail you would like to see in the answers
- thank learners for taking the time to complete the questionnaire.

Course evaluation such as that described above contributes to the larger enterprise of curriculum evaluation, which at institutional level is largely concerned with quality assurance, a topic which is explored further in the next chapter.

ANSWERS TO ACTIVITY 9.3

Example	Type of curriculum
The course description in a college prospectus	Official
The induction programme	Hidden
What is experienced during the taught sessions	Actual
Teaching observations by your tutor	Formal
The contents of your course handbook	Official
A lunchtime pilates group	Informal
The number of computers that are actually available	Actual
Valuing the diversity within the group	Hidden
A group trip to an ICT exhibition on a Saturday morning	Informal

SUMMARY OF KEY POINTS

In this chapter, we have looked at the difficulties encountered in arriving at a single definition of curriculum and the different types of curriculum we recognise. The fundamental role of values in arriving at curricular decisions was discussed and the curriculum models arising out of this process were reviewed. Approaches to curriculum and course design were derived from these models and ways in which the curriculum can be organised for the purpose of delivery were discussed. The inclusive nature of the curriculum and the factors which influence this were deliberated on before the chapter ended with a consideration of how the effectiveness of the curriculum and its delivery can be determined through the process of curriculum and course evaluation.

The key points in this chapter are:

- Curriculum is difficult to limit to a single definition and can be classified as hidden, official, actual, formal and informal.
- Curricular decisions are arrived at through making judgements based on the values of decision makers or the ideologies that they subscribe to.
- Curriculum models indicate the underpinning philosophy of the curriculum.
- Product and process curriculum models emphasise the approach taken to learning.
- Approaches taken to curriculum design can be based around behavioural objectives, outcomes and competencies if based on a product model, or expressive objectives if based on a process model.
- The inclusive curriculum is informed by the attitudes and actions demonstrated at sector, institutional and individual levels.
- Inclusion forms part of the hidden curriculum as well as part of the official curriculum.
- Some aspects of the curriculum are open to negotiation with learners, increasing their sense of ownership of their own learning.
- The curriculum can be delivered in a linear or spiral form but greatest flexibility is achieved through modular and 'roll on, roll off' approaches.
- Course evaluation normally takes the form of a questionnaire-based approach which may use open or closed questions or a combination of the two.

REFERENCES

Armitage, A., Bryant, R., Dunnill, R. and Hayes, D. (2012) *Teaching and Training in Lifelong Learning* (4th edn). Maidenhead: Open University Press.

Avis, J., Fisher, R. and Thompson, R. (2010) *Teaching in Lifelong Learning: A Guide to Theory and Practice*. Maidenhead: Open University Press.

Bahr, N. and Prendergast, D. (2005) Teaching Middle Years: Rethinking Curriculum Pedagogy and Assessment. Sydney: Allen & Unwin.

Bartlett, S. and Burton, D. (2007) *Introduction to Education Studies*. London: Sage.

Bartlett, S., Burton, D. and Peim, N. (2001) *Introduction to Education Studies*. London: Paul Chapman.

Boud, D., Keogh, R. and Walker, D. (1985) *Reflection: Turning Experience into Learning*. London: Routledge.

Bruner, J. (1960) *The Process of Education*. Cambridge, MA: Harvard University Press.

Daines, J., Daines, C. and Graham, B. (2006) *Adult Learning, Adult Teaching* (4th edn). Cardiff: Welsh Academic Press.

Eisner, E. (1969) Instructional and expressive objectives: their formulation and use in curriculum, in W. Popham, E. Eisner, H. Sullivan and L. Tyler (eds), *Instructional Objectives. AERA Monograph Series on Curriculum Evaluation, No. 3*. Chicago: Rand McNally.

Gray, D., Griffin, C. and Nasta, T. (2000) *Training to Teach in Further and Adult Education* (2nd edn). Cheltenham: Nelson Thornes.

Hill Country Disabled Group (n.d.) *What is a Disability*. Available online at: http://hcdg.org/definition.htm (accessed 25/04/17).

Hirst, P.H. (1974) *Moral Education in a Secular Society*. London: University of London Press.

Jenkins, R.J. and Shipman, M.D. (1976) *Curriculum: An Introduction*. London: Open Books Publishing.

Kelly, A.V. (1987) *Education*. Oxford: Heinemann.

Kelly, A.V. (2009) *The Curriculum: Theory and Practice* (6th edn). London: Sage.

Mager, R.F. (1975) *Preparing Instructional Objectives* (2nd edn). Belmont, CA: Fearon.

Marsh, C. (2009) *Key Concepts for Understanding Curriculum* (4th edn). London: RoutledgeFalmer.

Neary, M. (2002) Curriculum Studies in Post-Compulsory and Adult Education. Cheltenham: Nelson Thornes.

Prideaux, D. (2000) The emperor's new clothes: from objectives to outcomes. *Medical Education*, 34: 168–9.

Quinn, F.M. (2000) *The Principles and Practice of Nurse Education* (4th edn). Cheltenham: Nelson Thornes.

Revell, P. (2004) *The Hidden Curriculum*. Available online at: www.theguardian.com/society/2004/apr/30/publichealth.comment (accessed 25/04/17).

Smith, M.K. (1996) What is competence? What is competency? *The Encyclopaedia of Informal Education*. Available online at: http://infed.org/mobi/what-iscompetence-and-competency/ (accessed 25/04/17).

Stenhouse, L. (1975) An Introduction to Curriculum Research and Development. London: Heinemann Educational.

Tomlinson, J. (1996) Report of the Further Education Funding Council Learning Difficulties and/or Disabilities Committee. Coventry: FEFC.

Training Agency (1988) *Development of Assessable Standards for National Certification: Guidance Note 3 – The Definition of Competence and Performance Criteria*. Sheffield: Training Agency.

Tyler, R.W. (1949) *Basic Principles of Curriculum and Instruction*. Chicago, IL: University of Chicago Press.

Weyers, M. (2006) *Teaching the FE Curriculum*. London: Continuum.

 # FURTHER READING

Armitage, A., Cogger, A., Evershed, J., Hayes, D., Lawes, S. and Renwick, M. (2016) *Teaching in Post-14 Education and Training* (5th edn). Maidenhead: Open University Press.

Chapter 7 looks at the nature of curriculum, models, ideologies and then reforms within the 14–19 sector. A good read which consolidates and extends some of the themes taken up in this chapter.

Bartlett, S. and Burton, D. (2016) *Introduction to Education Studies* **(4th edn). London: Sage.**
After exploring the nature and meaning of curriculum, Chapter 5 of this book looks at the frameworks used in curriculum design. Specific curricula, operating at different stages of the education system are subsequently analysed with specific attention given to 14–19 education from page 137 onwards.

Duckworth, V. and Tummons, J. (2010) *Contemporary Issues in Lifelong Learning.* **Maidenhead: Open University Press.**
Whilst you may find a number of chapters of interest in this book, Chapter 6 examines the concept of curriculum and its relationship to policy and subsequent impact within the sector.

Kelly, A.V. (2009) *The Curriculum: Theory and Practice* **(6th edn). London: Sage.**
Although arguably now somewhat dated, Kelly's book remains the most authoritative on the subject of curriculum. You may have to choose your chapters depending upon your particular area of interest but Chapter 1 gives a comprehensive overview of curriculum in general along with the main related issues.

10

THE WIDER CONTEXT OF PROFESSIONAL PRACTICE

As teachers in the Further Education and Skills sector, we work in an environment which is moving towards increased levels of professionalism and accountability, and in which the work we do is increasingly linked to political, economic and social agendas. We need, therefore, to be able to understand issues of policy and policymaking in a landscape of constantly changing regulatory, funding, directing and monitoring authorities. Quality assurance and quality improvement are seen by government as key processes in regulating the work of the sector, and so we need to understand their role and the contribution we are expected to make towards continuous improvement.

When you have completed this chapter you will be able to:

- define the process of lifelong learning
- identify the relationship between lifelong learning and government policy
- describe the process of policymaking, identifying the different stages involved
- explain the economic, social and political arguments that underpin policy decisions
- describe the contributions made to policy decision making by a variety of reports and policy documents
- recognise the approach to skills taken by government
- review the general principles on which the policies of recent governments are based

- name the main recent policies which apply to the sector
- recognise the ways in which government policy has shaped the regulatory and inspection systems of the lifelong learning sector
- describe the role of quality improvement in the sector
- differentiate between assessment and evaluation, and identify the role of evaluation in quality improvement systems
- identify and evaluate techniques for evaluation and the use of data to inform evaluation
- illustrate ways of applying evaluative techniques in your own professional practice.

The sector within which we work has in the past been known variously as the Post Compulsory sector and the Learning and Skills sector but was re-titled the Lifelong Learning sector with the launch of LLUK in 2005. LLUK was the Sector Skills Council (SSC) whose function was to ensure that employers within the sector could recruit, retain and develop skilled and effective staff. It represented employers in FE and HE, work-based learning, community learning and development, and libraries, archives and information services, youth work, and offender education. Although the current designation is now the Further Education and Skills sector, there is still a strong link between the policy that drives the sector and the concept of lifelong learning. This chapter therefore begins with an exploration of lifelong learning before turning to and making links to recent and current government policy.

LIFELONG LEARNING: THE CONCEPT

ACTIVITY 10.1

Do you consider yourself to be a 'lifelong learner'? What do you do that places you in that category? What are your reasons for engaging in lifelong learning?

The concept of lifelong learning is not new but was first discussed in any meaningful way by Lindeman and Yeaxlee in the 1920s. It is seen by some as a natural consequence of life, Field (2006: 1) describing it as 'a beautifully simple idea ... almost as unconscious as breathing', and Brookfield (1983: 10) suggesting that 'it would be a highly perverse individual who managed to shield himself or herself from all those circumstances and life changes which necessitate the development of new competencies'.

In its original guise, lifelong learning is considered to be a natural, ongoing process from cradle to grave which can take place in formal or informal settings for a variety of individual reasons and motivations. At a deeper level, it can be considered as a three-dimensional process (Banks et al., 2007: 12). Dimension 1, lifelong learning itself, refers to learning across time (ideally lifetime); life-wide learning, the second dimension, indicates the breadth of environments and contexts within which it can occur (formal, informal; in work, social or family situations); and, finally, dimension 3, life-deep learning, concerns the personal, developmental impact of learning which goes beyond knowledge and skills, affecting individual beliefs and values and subsequently actions. Taken at face value, however, it is simply 'all learning activity taken throughout life' (European Commission, 2002: 9).

THE SHIFT IN EMPHASIS

ACTIVITY 10.2

Consider the last 10 years – what have been the major advances in technology? Have these had any major implications for your working life? How have you kept pace with these changes?

You will probably have had no real difficulty in identifying the technological advances which have resulted in a change, either large or small, to your work practices and life in general in the last 10 years. The pace of change is fairly relentless and gives every indication of speeding up rather than slowing down, and so whilst the skills you currently possess may equip you to cope with the demands of today, how about tomorrow? At one time, study was only for those who looked for advancement in their job or career, as initial training or qualification provided all that was necessary to carry out their job role almost indefinitely. It is now an essential for everyone as skills need to be regularly updated to adapt to the changing demands of the workplace. Sometimes this may involve not just the updating of current skills but retraining and acquiring a new set of skills, as the concept of long-term stability in employment and a 'job for life' is considered to have largely disappeared. Giddens (2000) argues that we live in the age of 'reflexivity' where nothing is certain. As individuals, we accept the necessity to 'run in order to stand still' and the various CPD programmes and staff development activities in which you doubtless engage are a testament to this.

It is not just we as individuals who are affected by and need to respond to the rapid change around us. The organisations within which we work are affected and, a further level up, the effects are felt on a national scale and arise from the development and impact of globalisation which the International Monetary Fund (2002) describes as 'the process through which an increasingly free flow of ideas, people, goods, services and capital leads to the integration of economies and societies'.

Although not a new concept – tea clippers such as the *Cutty Sark* plied the trade routes between Europe and the East Indies in the 1850s, for example – advances in technology, particularly information and communications technology, have effectively 'shrunk' the world and international trade can now be carried out at the touch of a button. As a result, economies, it is argued, now require a workforce with a different set of skills in order to remain competitive. Ball (2008: 19), though critical of the notion, distinguishes between manual workers who 'work with their hands and produce *stuff*' and knowledge workers who 'work with their heads and produce or articulate ideas, knowledge and information', and points to a shift in emphasis within the economy as 'technological developments in the 20th century have transformed the majority of wealth-creating work from physically based to *knowledge-based*'.

Ball, then, alerts us to the changing nature of the economy which is now increasingly based on knowledge, information and technology. Knowledge has replaced the spanner as the tool of the worker in what is now known as the 'knowledge economy'. This suggests, of course, that learning is a constant or lifelong process and the skill of learning itself is as important as the outcomes it achieves. For this to become a reality, however, we need to recognise its value and be able to access appropriate learning through formal or informal means. We need to be part of a 'learning society'.

The Fryer report (1997) also noted that technological advances had changed working practices and there was now a need for a different type of worker who possessed a different set of skills. A new 'learning culture' was required to facilitate this. The Labour Government of the time responded to the Fryer report with the release of a Green Paper, *The Learning Age: A Renaissance for New Britain*, in which Tony Blair declared 'Education is the best economic policy we have' (DfEE, 1998: Introduction) and which contained the statement that 'learning is essential to a strong economy and an inclusive society' (DfEE, 1998: s. 2: 13).

Learning is not now just a lifelong endeavour, it also has a new emphasis and purpose underlined by the OECD view that 'Investment in education and training in pursuit of lifelong learning strategies serves to address these social and economic objectives simultaneously' (OECD, 1996: 15).

An alternative, more modern-day view of lifelong learning, then, takes a more instrumental perspective whereby learning is 'not an end in itself but is done for the economic benefits it brings' (Bartlett and Burton, 2009: 108). The emphasis has moved away from that of lifelong learning as an activity undertaken solely for individual reasons and for purposes of personal development and benefit. It is now geared to national priorities with the intention of responding to economic and social needs. Hyland and Merrill (2003: 21) sum up this shift as: 'Contemporary versions of lifelong learning – though retaining the learning through life connotations – tend to view the nature and purpose of learning primarily in terms of skill updating and the training and development needs of employees'.

This gives us a perspective that aligns with the major purpose of the sector within which we work.

LIFELONG LEARNING AND POLICY

The OECD (1996: 90) has identified what it sees as the five arguments for lifelong learning. The first two of these have already been referred to:

1. The 'learning economy' argument which recognises the extent to which OECD societies and economies have become dependent on the 'creation and manipulation of knowledge, information and ideas'.
2. The 'speed of change' argument which calls for the constant renewal of knowledge and skill, along with the provision which enables this.

The remaining three are:

3. The 'life-cycle distribution' argument which sees the working life of most people as being compressed into the middle period of life, which is sandwiched between a period of initial education which is increasing in length and an extended retirement period as life expectancy increases. The 'shrinking middle' possesses a limited ability to provide financial support for all three periods of life as recent developments concerning pensions and university fees illustrate. The OECD sees the solution to this problem arising out of a reversal of this 'compression', spreading activity more evenly over the life cycle as a whole. Lifelong learning is seen as a means of achieving this.
4. The active policies argument which has the broad aim of moving away from social policies which are passive in nature. Taking the case of unemployment as an example, rather than making unconditional payments to those out of work (a passive or 'parking' approach), payments should be linked to some form of training or education which increases the recipient's prospects of employment and of becoming a productive member of society (an active approach).
5. The 'social cohesion' argument. Some sections of society tend to be marginalised or 'excluded' because of poverty and a lack of employment prospects. Tony Blair believed that employment provided the route out of poverty and the OECD (2001: 28) found that the better educated we are, the more likely we are to be in employment. A more cohesive society with fewer socio-economic inequalities can be achieved through lifelong learning.

Compare the five points made above to the following statement in the 1999 White Paper *Learning to Succeed: A New Framework for Post-16 Learning*: 'Our vision is to build a new culture of learning which will underpin national competitiveness and personal prosperity, encourage creativity and innovation and help build a cohesive society' (DfEE, 1999: 6).

There was an evident 'fit' between a contemporary view of lifelong learning and the policy direction of New Labour. Taylor (2005: 103) confirms this, declaring 'since 1997 Labour has consistently emphasised the importance of education generally, and in the context of a transformed, globalised economy, the centrality of lifelong learning'.

This is not a purely British phenomenon and is reflected in many other countries. The EU took a similarly broad approach in the 1995 EU White Paper *Teaching and Learning: Towards the Learning Society*, in which it declared the society of the future to be a 'learning society' in which 'Education and training will increasingly become the main vehicles for self-awareness, belonging, advancement and self-fulfilment' (EU, 1995: 2).

POLICY MAKING

So, how is a debate like that above turned into government policy? A popular song from the 1960s makes a suggestion along the lines of 'you've got to have a dream, but how are you going to make a dream come true?' Governments face a similar dilemma but rather than a dream they have a 'vision' – a picture of how they think things should be. The vision 'comes true' through the process of policy making which translates the vision into some kind of programme of action which produces tangible outcomes. Policy making concludes with the passing of an Act of Parliament, but there are several stages to be negotiated before that happens and these are listed below. Each stage is illustrated by a case study of the process undergone in arriving at the Every Child Matters (ECM) legislation.

1. Issue

The process is usually initiated by some matter of concern which has gradually increased in significance or is brought to the immediate attention by an incident or event which brings it into the forefront of public consciousness.

On 25 February 2000, Victoria Climbié is pronounced dead at St Mary's Hospital, London. The Home Office pathologist who examines her body declares it to be 'the worst case of child abuse I've ever encountered'.

---

2. Report

A commission of enquiry is set up to investigate the matter, establish the salient facts and possibly make recommendations. The findings are published in a report.

In April 2001, the government announces a public inquiry into the death, to be headed by Lord Laming. Lord Laming's brief is to report on the circumstances leading to and surrounding the death of Victoria Climbié, and to make recommendations as to how the repetition of such an event can be avoided. The enquiry is split into two parts, the first involving over 230 individual interviews of connected parties, the second taking the form of a series of seminars involving experts in the field, to help Lord Laming draw his conclusions. The report of the inquiry is published on 28 January 2003.

3. Green Paper

The findings of the report are examined and the government publishes its response in a Green Paper. A Green Paper takes the form of a preliminary report of government proposals published with the intention of stimulating discussion. There is no commitment to action at this stage, the purpose being to initiate a consultation process and gauge reaction to the proposals. Anyone can respond to a Green Paper, but typically stakeholders such as think tanks and unions lead the way. In educational matters, bodies such as Centres for Excellence in Teacher Training (CETTs), the Association of Colleges (AoC), universities and professional groups are likely to contribute to the discussion.

A Green Paper, 'Every Child Matters', is published in September 2003 in response to Lord Laming's enquiry, setting out a proposal for a framework of services to be set up in England to cover children and young people from birth to 19. The five outcomes for the well-being of children and young people are proposed: being healthy, staying safe, enjoying and achieving, making a positive contribution, and economic well-being.

4. White Paper

After responses to the consultation process initiated by the Green Paper have been considered, the government lays out its policy position, often accompanied by proposals for legislative change or the introduction of new laws in a White Paper.

The White Paper, 'Every Child Matters: Next Steps', is released in 2004 (DfES, 2004). At national level, it proposes the creation of the post of Minister for Children, Young People and Families in the Department for

Education and Skills to coordinate policies across government and the establishment of a Sector Skills Council (SSC) for Children and Young People's Services. At local level, the creation of the post of Director of Children's Services, accountable for local authority education and children's social services, is proposed along with a lead council member for children. All services for children and young people (education, social services, health) are to be integrated under the Director of Children's Services as part of Children's Trusts.

5. Bill

The next stage is the drawing up of a bill. This is a draft piece of legislation, proposing a new law or a change in existing law. A bill undergoes a series of readings and is presented to both Houses of Parliament for discussion and possible amendment before being agreed in a final form.

The Children Bill is brought to the House of Lords on 4 March 2004.

6. Act

Once both Houses have agreed on the content of a Bill, it is presented to the reigning monarch for approval (known as Royal Assent). Once Royal Assent is given, a Bill becomes an Act of Parliament and is law.

The Children Act 2004 secures Royal Assent on 15 November 2004. It provides the legislation behind the reform of children's services, establishing the posts set out in the White Paper, and places a number of duties and requirements on key agencies and local councils, as well as making provisions relating to foster care, private fostering and the education of children in care. A further document, 'Every Child Matters: Change for Children', is published in December 2004 (DfES, 2004), advising how the Act is to be implemented.

REFLECTIVE TASK 10.1

What policies affect you in your everyday work? Identify five examples which impact on you the most. These might be general, or subject-specific. What have these policies meant in terms of change within your everyday practice?

POLICY TRENDS SINCE 1997

In the last 30 years or so, the sector within which we work has been subject to more governmental policy initiatives than any other area within the public sector as a whole. Norris and Adam (2017) have calculated that, 'since the early 1980s there have been 28 major pieces of legislation related to vocational, FE & skills training, six different ministerial departments ... [and] 48 secretaries of state'. Keep (2015) takes a very dim view of the effect of all these policy changes, suggesting that the sector 'is highly fragmented, complex and unstable, and has tended to oscillate between centralised command and control, and attempts at marketisation'. Hardly surprising, then, that many in the sector feel that it can be hard to keep up with all the latest policy initiatives.

In a general sense, the direction taken by policy under pre-1997 Conservative governments was largely towards de-centralisation and a relinquishing of government control, as seen in the incorporation of FE colleges and the introduction of local management in schools. Market forces were thought to raise standards. Competition was stimulated through informed freedom of choice and state intervention was seen as restricting individual freedoms. Labour traditionally tended towards a more centralised approach to government, although New Labour adopted more of a partnership view, involving individuals, employers and the unions. The main themes running through New Labour policy were:

Economic – People are the country's most valuable resource and investment in people will derive the greatest return and economic benefit. This is the concept of human capital and firmly establishes the link between lifelong learning and economic growth. This is the main concern of the Skills Strategy as 'learning develops the intellectual capital which is now at the centre of a nation's competitive strength' (DfEE, 1998: s. 2:11).

Social – The most stable society is a cohesive society. To achieve this, all members must have equal rights and access to the economic, social and political benefits of society as a whole. Social inclusion is sought rather than social exclusion. An example of social exclusion is the section of the population known as NEETs – Not in Education, Employment or Training. Social exclusion leads to isolation and potential anti-social behaviour. The legislation relating to widening participation was intended to address issues of social exclusion as 'learning contributes to social cohesion and fosters a sense of belonging, responsibility and identity' (DfEE, 1998: s. 2:12).

Political – Labour has a strong commitment to participation and a sense of community. There was a wish to avoid the situation described in Putnam's 2001 book *Bowling Alone* (once we used to bowl in leagues and social groups), which comments on the decline in civic life in America. Active citizenship is to be encouraged and is seen as one way of addressing the issues raised within a multi-cultural society as 'learning helps make ours a civilised society ... and promotes active citizenship' (DfEE, 1998: Foreword).

Humanistic – The original 'raison d'être' of lifelong learning is acknowledged and the benefits to the individual were viewed positively as 'learning offers excitement and the opportunity for discovery. It stimulates enquiring minds and nourishes our souls. It takes us in directions we never expected, sometimes changing our lives' (DfEE, 1998: s. 2:10).

REFLECTIVE TASK 10.2

Thinking about your own teaching, which of the four themes outlined above has the greatest influence and what form does that influence take? Can you see evidence of more than one of the four themes in what you do?

The volume of policy introduced over recent years is too great to list fully here and is in any case beyond the scope of this book (for a full timeline of policies, structural and personnel changes, see Norris and Adam, 2017: 6–7). However, we will focus on one area of policy – skills – to demonstrate the effect of policy within the sector.

Closing the 'skills gap' – the gap between what people can do and what employers require them to do – particularly with respect to literacy and numeracy, was a major preoccupation of New Labour. A National Skills Task Force was set up in 1998 to assist the then Secretary of State in developing a National Skills Agenda to address this issue. The Task Force produced three reports between 1998 and 2000:

1. 'Towards a National Skills Agenda' (DfEE, 1998) looked at learning in the workplace for adults already in employment.
2. 'Delivering Skills for All' (DfEE, 1999) made proposals for the education and training of young people.
3. 'Tackling the Adult Skills Gap: Up Skilling Adults and the Role of Workplace Learning' (DfEE, 2000) focused on low-skilled reluctant learners and recommended public funding for adults for qualifications up to Level 2.

These reports contributed directly to New Labour's Skills Strategy, outlined in the White Paper *21st Century Skills: Realising our Potential* (DfEE, 2003). Paragraph two of the foreword stated: 'Sustaining a competitive, productive economy which delivers prosperity for all requires an ever growing proportion of skilled, qualified people. We will not achieve a fairer, more inclusive society if we fail to narrow the gap between the skills-rich and the skills-poor'. The main purpose of the White Paper was to manage the learning of skills in a way that was more responsive to employer needs. It proposed to achieve this through a partnership approach which would 'raise ambition' in demand for skills. The White Paper identified the key partners (employer, employee/individual, government) involved in establishing a demand-led approach to skills training and sought to clarify the role which each was to play. The major elements of the White Paper were:

- an expansion of the Adult Basic Skills campaign to make ICT the third essential 'skill for life' alongside literacy and numeracy
- incentivising participation by measures such as introducing free learning for any adult who did not already have a good foundation of skills for employability, helping them achieve a full Level 2 qualification and providing new opportunities for adults to gain qualifications in technician and higher craft and trade skills, through a Level 3 qualification in skills shortage areas
- reforming the qualifications framework, making it more employer-friendly and responsive to business needs, by helping employers package units of training in different areas to form the training programme that best meets their needs
- ensuring greater employer involvement in the design and delivery of Modern Apprenticeships and boosting take-up by lifting the age cap, allowing people over the age of 25 to learn skilled trades
- expanding the Sector Skills Council network to identify, map and meet key skills needs in employment sectors.

A body to oversee progress in meeting the aims of the White Paper, the Skills Alliance, was launched to set targets and monitor progress against these. This White Paper led to the introduction of vocational GCSEs, Entry to Employment (E2E) programmes and the establishment of Centres of Vocational Excellence (CoVEs) in FE colleges.

The Skills Agenda was updated in the White Paper, *Skills: Getting on in Business, Getting on at Work* (DfEE, 2005). This White Paper came in three volumes and interestingly was sponsored by a combination of government departments – the Department for Education and Skills (DfES), HM Treasury, the Department of Trade and Industry (DTI) and the Department of Work and Pensions (DWP) – a further indication of the growing link between education, the economy and the world of work. It acknowledged the positive contributions arising out of the partnership approach, stressing the benefits of maintaining this: 'These goals cannot be met by the government acting alone. Employers, trades unions, public agencies, colleges, universities, training providers and the voluntary sector all need to play their part' (DfEE, 2005: 9).

The Skills Alliance was also perceived to be performing a valuable function. The White Paper focused on three broad areas:

1. Employer needs

    We need a new approach to the supply of skills and training. That must be shaped around the needs of employers and learners. (DfEE, 2005: 9)

Employers' needs in the design and delivery of training were prioritised through the Train to Gain (T2G) programme and the setting up of additional employer-led sector-based National Skills Academies.

2. Learner needs

    Our ambition is that we become a society in which young people and adults expect to keep learning and developing new skills, because everyone takes it for granted that you need skills to get a good job and a fulfilling life. (DfEE, 2005: 7)

Arrangements were to be made for improved information, advice and guidance. Following the successful introduction of the Educational Maintenance Allowance (EMA) in 2004, the New Deal for Skills was developed to get people from welfare to work, focusing on those people for whom a lack of skills was a barrier to employment.

3. Reforming training supply

    Over the next five years, we are investing £1.5 billion to support the long-term transformation of further education colleges and ensure they have the high quality facilities that employers demand. (DfEE, 2005: 7)

The FE sector was to be reformed, allowing FE colleges to become the 'engines of social and economic growth', providing young people and adults with the right skills to meet the demands of the economy. The principle of 'contestability' was to be applied, opening up competition and giving employers more choice over training providers. The White Paper ran in tandem with the 2005 14–19 White Paper which responded to the Tomlinson Report on 14–19 Reform, introducing the diploma framework and appointing Sir Andrew Foster to undertake a review of the future role of FE 'to establish a clear sense of purpose for colleges in the light of the two White Papers' (DfEE, 2005: 24).

Foster submitted his report Realising the Potential: A Review of the Future Role of Further Education Colleges in November 2005. Two of its recommendations were:

- General further education, tertiary and specialist colleges should see their main purpose as improving employability and supplying economically valuable skills.
- Colleges should be more responsive to specific local and regional employer needs and government should consider what it could do to improve engagement between colleges and employers.

In the meantime, in 2004, the government had commissioned an independent review of the UK's long-term skills needs. The ensuing report, *Prosperity for All in the Global Economy: World Class Skills*, better known as the Leitch Review, was published on 5 December 2006. The Report found that the UK currently ranked 12th out of 18 comparative members of the OECD and recommended that achievement in all levels of skills needed to be raised, with the intention of becoming a world leader in skills by 2020. To achieve this aim, Leitch suggested that all public funding for skills should be routed through Train to Gain and new 'Skills Accounts' by 2010 to create a demand-led system. He wanted employers to sign up to a voluntary 'pledge' to train all eligible employees to Level 2 and the creation of a new integrated employment and skills service.

In response, the government published the White Paper *World Class Skills: Implementing the Leitch Review of Skills in England* in July 2007, stating 'We accept the ambition of Lord Leitch and adopt it as our own' (DIUS, 2007: 16).

The White Paper ushered in the restructuring of government departments, the DfES being replaced by the Department for Children, Schools and Families (DCSF) dealing with children and young people up to the age of 19, and the Department for Innovation, Universities and Skills (DIUS) being responsible for learners over the age of 19.

In a series of chapters, Lord Leitch's recommendations were listed along with the way in which they would be addressed. The main outcomes of this process were:

- the creation of the UK Commission for Employment and Skills (UKCES) with a remit to assess annually UK progress towards becoming a world-class leader in employment and skills by 2020, advise government on skills-related matters and manage and fund the SSCs
- the creation of a further 12 employer-linked and employer-led Skills Academies
- phased roll-out of the first five diploma lines
- making literacy, numeracy and ICT compulsory components of GCSEs in English, maths and apprenticeships and the new diplomas
- an increase in the proportion of demand-led public funding in England.

The White Paper, *Raising Expectations: Enabling the System to Deliver* (DCSF/DIUS, 2008), set out a new set of funding arrangements, confirming that 14–19 education would be primarily under the control of local authorities, either singly or through groups of local authorities working in partnership, with a single body, the newly created Skills Funding Agency (SFA), managing funding for adult skills.

THE CONSERVATIVE–LIBERAL DEMOCRAT COALITION GOVERNMENT

GENERAL PRINCIPLES

The policy direction of the Coalition Government is seen to be strongly influenced by David Cameron's vision of the 'Big Society'. The Big Society subscribes to the notion of giving more power and responsibility to individuals and communities rather than politicians, on the basis that they will use it to create better neighbourhoods and local services. The three strands of the Big Society agenda are:

- social action whereby the government fosters a culture of voluntarism
- public service reform which removes centralised bureaucracy which wastes money and undermines morale
- community empowerment in which communities feel in charge of their own destinies and can shape the world directly around them.

The Big Society is founded on the 'three pillars' of freedom, fairness and responsibility.

Freedom is achieved through less regulation and bureaucracy and a greater responsiveness to customers and citizens. It leads to more innovation and enterprise allied to greater efficiency and reduced costs. With freedom comes more responsibility, however, and fewer answers and direction from government.

Fairness is based on the premise that those with the broadest shoulders should bear the greatest load. Its aim is widening access, participation and social mobility. Arguably, this 'pillar' is compromised because of the economic situation and subsequent need for austerity measures, particularly with respect to access. The withdrawal of the EMA (although it is claimed it has been changed to give more targeted support, rather than been withdrawn) and the new fee levels in HE would suggest this is the case.

Responsibility signals the move from state control to social responsibility, with individuals and communities finding their own solutions. Likewise, however, accountability moves in a similar direction, some observers equating this to the government 'devolving the axe' and placing the individual or community 'between the dog and the lamppost'.

POLICY

The 2010–15 government was the first coalition government since the Second World War and, therefore, its policies for education were a combination of the ideas of the two parties. Forrester and Garratt (2017) point out that the influence of the two parties can be seen in different strands of their education policy. For example, the Liberal Democrats focus on 'fairness' in education was behind the introduction of universal free school meals in Primary Schools; whilst the Conservative emphasis on diversity, choice and the importance of the market, led to the acceleration of academisation in the school sector and the increase in the range of providers for FE and HE.

However, the over-riding driver of coalition policy for education, and for all public expenditure at the time, was the perceived need to reduce the government's financial deficit. Austerity was seen as the number one government priority and the FE and skills sector, viewed as a relatively low-profile provision, experienced very significant reductions in public funding. As Allen, writing in 2015, commented 'Further education has suffered deep cuts over the course of this government, with predictably little publicity or public disapproval' (Allen, 2015: R41). The total cuts to the sector amounted to more than 25 per cent of its total funding, with a reduction of £1.1 billion in 2010 and a further £700 million in 2013 and 2015. Savings were made from direct reductions in the funds provided for adults skills provision and through the scrapping of some of the flagship educational policies of the New Labour government, including 'Train to Gain' skills provision for adults in the work place and the Education Maintenance Allowance (EMA) for young people from poorer families.

Like New Labour, the Coalition Government was no slouch in the policy field in the years between 2010 and 2015. One of Michael Gove's first acts on becoming Education Secretary was to write to all schools in England seeking views on Academy status. The generally positive response led to the Academies Act in July 2010, with the aim of making it possible for all publicly-funded schools in England to aspire to Academy status. This is in line with the underlying principles of the Big Society as, although still being funded from the public purse, the new academies would have considerable autonomy in managing both their resources and the curriculum, allowing a more liberal interpretation and, in some cases, divergence from the National Curriculum.

The focus on schools continued with the publication of the schools White Paper, *The Importance of Teaching*, in November 2010 (DfE, 2010). As suggested in the title, the White Paper set out to raise the status and profile of teachers, whilst freeing schools from many of the constraints imposed on them by central government. The four main areas covered in the White Paper were:

Teachers – emphasis was placed on the importance of good quality teaching in achieving educational success. Training was to be reformed with the introduction of 'teaching schools', similar to 'teaching hospitals', which allowed training with a greater practical component. Discipline was seen as an issue to be addressed and the proposal was for greater powers to be handed to teachers and schools to address discipline problems.

Curriculum – a less prescriptive National Curriculum was proposed with assessment at ages 6, 11 and 16 to identify progress. It was proposed that the English Baccalaureate be introduced and the Wolf Report on vocational education was commissioned. The most significant aspect of the ensuing Wolf Report for teachers within the sector was Recommendation 17 which stated:

At present teachers with QTS can teach in FE colleges; the FE equivalent – QTLS – should be recognised in schools, which is currently not the case. This will enable schools to recruit qualified professionals to teach courses at school level (rather than bussing pupils to colleges) with clear efficiency gains. (Wolf, 2011: 16)

Schools – a reduction in the burden of administration was sought to allow more energy to be diverted into teaching. The Academy programme was to be extended and support given to parents or communities wishing to set up Free Schools, particularly in areas of deprivation. The concept of the Free School is based on the Charter Schools system in the USA, and is a state-funded, all-ability school set up in response to local demand and to meet the needs of the local community.

Funding – a 'fairer' funding system was proposed, including a 'pupil premium' which allocates additional resources for pupils from deprived backgrounds. The disparity between schools and colleges in funding for pupils in the 16–18 age range was to be ended.

These proposals are generally in agreement with the Big Society concepts of freedom and responsibility, and aspects such as the pupil premium identify strongly with fairness. Aspects of the Bill affecting the Further Education and Skills sector include:

- abolition of the Young People's Learning Agency for England (YPLA), powers being transferred to the Secretary of State. The Education Funding Agency (EFA) subsequently took over responsibility for funding the 3–19 age group on 1 April 2012
- retention of legislation to raise the participation age to 17 in 2013 and 18 in 2015, but compliance measures suggested by the previous government to be scrapped
- the university tuition fees cap for full-time courses to be applied on a pro rata basis to part-time courses, and the cap on the interest rates that can be charged on new student loans to be raised.

The proposals became law with the passing of the Education Act in November 2011.

Meanwhile, in 2010, Business Secretary Vince Cable and Skills Minister John Hayes produced the strategy document, *Skills for Sustainable Growth*, setting out the government's reforms for the Further Education and Skills sector for adults aged 19 and over. In it, they stated: 'This Government's purpose is to return the economy to sustainable growth, extend social inclusion and social mobility and build the Big Society' (BIS, 2010b: 4). The issues to be addressed, however, did not seem to have changed much as skills were seen as 'not just important for our global competitiveness' but had 'the potential to transform lives by transforming life chances and driving social mobility', as well as enabling 'people to play a fuller part in society, making it more cohesive, more environmentally friendly, more tolerant and more engaged' (BIS, 2010b: 5).

The strategy document outlined a vision of a decentralised demand-led skills system. Those employers and learners who benefited from it, however, were expected to contribute to its costs. Funding was to be simplified and accessed through a single point of contact, although a reduction in funding for FE of 25 per cent by 2014–15 was also signalled. Apprenticeships were to be re-shaped, making Level 3 the level to which both employers and learners should aspire, and the number of adult apprenticeships expanded by up to 75,000 by 2014–15. Clearer progression routes would also be created. Alongside this, the importance of continuing high levels of participation and performance was stressed, with a promise to 'act decisively to tackle unacceptable performance'. The foreword of the document outlines how the above proposals are founded on the principles of freedom, fairness and responsibility.

This was closely followed by *Further Education – New Horizon: Investing in Skills for Sustainable Growth* (BIS, 2010a), which set out the government's funding strategy for the sector, prioritising young people and those with low skills, and initiating further consultation on government-backed fee loans.

In the interim, the Wolf Report on pre-19 vocational education was published in March 2011. This considered how vocational education for 14- to 19-year-olds could be made more effective in either leading to employment or progression on to higher levels of education or training. Its main findings centred on what Wolf described as 'the perverse incentives which currently encourage schools and colleges to steer young people into easy options, rather than ones which will help them progress'. Wolf concluded that curriculum provision was shaped by the chase for funding rather than vocational usefulness and relevance, and advised that qualifications should be funded on the basis of perceived value and usefulness rather than by virtue of accreditation. Apprenticeships were identified as the key route to skilled employment but evaluation of the delivery structure and content should be undertaken to ensure they deliver the most appropriate skills for the workplace.

English and Maths GCSE (at grades A*–C) were highlighted as fundamental to employment and education prospects. Recommendation 9 of the report states that 'Students who are under 19 and do not have GCSE A*–C in English and/or Maths should be required, as part of their programme, to pursue a course which either leads directly to these qualifications, or which provides significant progress towards future GCSE entry and success' (Wolf, 2011: 119). This view was later reinforced by the 2012 Richard Review of Apprenticeships, which listed 'Achieving a good level of Maths and English should be a pre-requisite for completion' (Richard, 2012: 9) as one of its recommendations.

The other major point of interest relates to the recognition of QTLS in schools, as previously mentioned. Altogether, the Wolf Report made 27 recommendations.

The government's response was both speedy and positive, immediately accepting four recommendations in May 2011:

1. To allow qualified FE lecturers to teach in school classrooms on the same basis as qualified school teachers.
2. To clarify the rules on allowing industry professionals to teach in schools.

3. To allow any vocational qualification offered by a regulated awarding body to be taken by 14–19-year-olds.
4. To allow established high-quality vocational qualifications that have not been accredited to be offered in schools and colleges in September 2011.

It was followed up with a public consultation in August 2011, *New Challenges, New Chances: Next Steps in Implementing the Further Education Reform Programme*, inviting opinions on proposals arising out of the Wolf recommendations.

These proposals were designed to promote the government's main overall aims for adult skills:

*   to promote high-quality teaching and learning at all levels of the adult education system
*   to free colleges and other skills providers from as many bureaucratic restrictions as possible, in order to allow them to respond more effectively to the needs of their local communities
*   to secure a fairer balance of investment in skills between the taxpayer, individual learners and employers.

and addressed issues such as loans for FE, removing inspection requirements on providers judged to be 'outstanding', and giving FE colleges greater validation powers.

Alongside these developments, proposals for change were being made for 16–19 learners, resulting in the introduction of new 16–19 study programmes from September 2013. These study programmes were supported by changes to post-16 funding which would no longer be linked to success rates (to encourage taking more challenging qualifications without fear of financial penalty) and also applied to 'non-qualification activity' such as work experience.

Study programmes tailored to individual needs and career aspirations are expected to be provided for all learners aged 16–19, including those with learning difficulties, in full- or part-time education. All learners who haven't achieved a C grade (or above) in GCSE maths and English by the end of Key Stage 4 have to continue to work towards this goal or other qualifications that will act as a stepping stone for achievement of these qualifications in time. The requirement for all students with a D grade in either English and/or maths to retake the GCSE created considerable controversy. So much so that the outgoing Ofsted Chief Inspector took the unprecedented step of criticising the government's policy in his Annual Report, published in December 2016 (Ofsted, 2016a).

A further series of reforms for the skills system was announced by the government's publication of *Rigour and Responsiveness in Skills* in April 2013 (DfE & BIS, 2013). Amongst the most important changes brought about through these proposals were:

*   The establishment of the 'Education & Training Foundation' (ETF) as the sector-owned professional body, charged with providing training and raising standards in FE and skills provision and launched in August 2013.

- The creation of the 'Chartered Institution for Further Education', described as a membership body for the higher performing colleges and training providers and granted its Royal Charter in October 2015. Progress for the institution in the first 18 months of operation was slow however, with only three colleges and one training provider achieving chartered status.
- Confirmation of the reform of apprenticeships, following the key recommendations of the Richards Review.
- The development of Traineeships, a programme of training with work experience, aimed at providing young people with the skills and experience they need to be able to enter the workforce.
- The ending of government funding for 'low value' vocational qualifications for adults and the introduction of loans for those over the age of 24 wanting to study courses at advanced and higher levels (Level 3, 4 and 5).

Although the FE and Skills sector is already diverse in what it offers, the government decided that, from September 2013, FE colleges would be able to enrol young people aged 14–16 for full-time college attendance. This policy shift was clearly related to the more general approach of diversifying provision within the school sector, to generate increased choice and competition. Although colleges had, for many years, provided forms of 'day release' programmes for school pupils in years 10 and 11, the decision to enable colleges to compete directly with secondary schools wasn't always welcomed within the schools sector (Ratcliffe, 2014). Due to the concerns of some schools and the challenges of taking on the teaching of the National Curriculum for school aged children, the number of colleges choosing to take full-time 14–16s remains quite low.

In March 2014 the government department responsible at that time for FE and skills summarised its plans for pushing forward the extensive policy agenda in *Getting the Job Done: The Government's Reform Plan for Vocational Qualifications* (BIS, 2014). The reform plan sought to respond to the wide range of reviews commissioned by the government into all aspects of skills provision; including the Wolf review of vocational education, the Richards review of apprenticeships, the report of the Commission on Adult Vocational Teaching and Learning, and the Whitehead review of the adult vocational qualifications system. The government's key intentions included:

- funding only high quality qualifications valued by employers
- ensuring that qualifications and Apprenticeships are relevant, rigorous and recognised by business and learners
- identifying qualifications in maths and English which best enable adult learners to progress to GCSE
- developing a clearer rationale for those qualifications to support through public funds
- moving towards more qualifications which are graded.

Thus, the reform plan clearly set out, once again, the key policy priorities for the coalition government of prioritising English and maths, ensuring employers are 'in the driving seat' for vocational qualifications, increasing rigour in assessment and rationalising the use of public funds.

THE CONSERVATIVE GOVERNMENT 2015

ACTIVITY 10.3

What changes have you noticed since the Conservative Government took office in 2015? These might be inside or outside your workplace. Can you identify any particular directions this government is taking?

GENERAL PRINCIPLES

The general election of May 2015 ended the period of coalition and established the Conservatives as the sole party of government. In many ways, the general principles of the new Conservative administration were built on similar foundations to those of the coalition. This is unsurprising, given that David Cameron entered a second term as Prime Minister and many of the established senior politicians continued in the cabinet. The key change for the new government, of course, was the removal of Liberal Democrat ministers and, consequently, the ending of their influence on policy. Indeed, so negative was the electorate's opinion on the Liberal Democrats' time in government, the party found itself reduced from 57 to 8 MPs and, thus, almost any contribution to policy formulation came to an abrupt end.

With respect to policy for the FE and skills sector, Forrester and Garratt (2017) view the early period of the new Conservative government as a time in which the enormous changes, begun under the coalition, were entrenched. The government's commitment to the operation of the market at all levels in education remained clear and policies continued to be enacted at a rapid pace. However, the direction of all government policy took an abrupt shift in direction after 23 June 2016, following the unexpected result of the referendum on the UK's membership of the European Union. As an immediate consequence of the vote, David Cameron stood down as Prime Minister and his replacement, Theresa May, took the opportunity to make significant changes to her Cabinet. As part of this reshuffle, responsibility for FE, skills and HE were all transferred back into the Department for Education; ending a nine-year experiment in which different government departments had taken responsibility for different parts of the education system.

Whilst the nature and impact of the UK's exit from the EU will not be fully under-stood for some considerable time, many commentators are highlighting the potential for significant impacts on the FE and skills sector. On the most basic level, the first and most obvious impact of an exit from the EU is a likely end to an estimated annual expenditure of £300 million pounds from the European Social Fund (ESF) by colleges and training providers. However, others are anticipating more positive effects for the sector, arguing that raising the skill level of British workers will require significant increases in the provision of education and training. 'Upskilling the domestic popula-tion to fill positions that would otherwise have been taken by EU workers will become an important agenda' (Keohane, 2017: 12).

POLICY

One of the first key policies for the sector, enacted soon after the new Conservative government took office, announced a comprehensive review of Post-16 education and training institutions (HM Government, 2015). The Area Review proposals recognised the importance of the sector to future economic prosperity, whilst also acknowledging the serious financial pressures upon many colleges. As a result, the government was overt about the need for colleges to collaborate more closely and, therefore, the 'need to move towards fewer, often larger, more resilient and efficient providers' (HM Government, 2015: 3). The reviews were planned in every area of the country, beginning in September 2015 and with an ambitious end date of November 2016. In practice, the timescale for area review had to be extended well into 2017 and, therefore, the full impacts of the review process are not yet well understood. Summarising his research on behalf of the House of Commons Library, Foster (2017) reported that around a third of the 167 col-leges in the first stages of the reviews were planning to merge. At the same time he also reported on concerns that area reviews might, ultimately, result in a lack of real change.

The system of vocational education came in for yet more scrutiny with the publica-tion of a report by the 'Independent Panel on Technical Education' in April 2016. The Panel, chaired by David Sainsbury, was set up by the then Minister for Skills in November 2015 with a remit to improve technical education and to simplify the exist-ing system. The report acknowledged that there had been failures to reform technical education successfully, stretching back over 100 years and blamed this on piecemeal solutions and a failure to learn from the successful systems in other countries. The Panel's proposals were certainly radical and included:

- the establishment of a distinct technical pathway for learners over 16, divided into 15 different occupational routes, for all qualifications from level 2 through to level 5
- the development of single technical qualifications for each occupational route at levels 2 and 3, awarded by only one Awarding Body
- the expansion of the role of the emerging 'Institute of Apprenticeships' to oversee all technical education.

The panel's report has the almost unique distinction of being published on the same day as the Government's own response to its proposals, *The Post-16 Skills Plan*, which immediately accepted all of the panel's main ideas (BIS & DfE, 2016). With the passing of the proposals into law in April 2017, immediately prior to the surprise announcement of the 2017 General Election, the government showed a clear determination to implement the radical approach of the Sainsbury Report (Technical and Further Education Act, 2017). Though the government proceeded rapidly with implementing these fundamental changes to technical qualifications, concerns were raised about key occupational sectors which appeared to have been left out of the plans. Fletcher (2017) suggests that the original Sainsbury Report failed to make clear how traditional 'craft' qualifications link to higher education and, more significantly, did not provide a clear definition of this new term 'technical and professional education' (TPE). As a result, this 'leaves whole sectors of the economy and whole groups of potential students out of consideration' (Fletcher, 2017: 3).

Whilst considering its radical overhaul to the provision of technical education, the government had been, simultaneously, working on a significant change to the nature and funding of apprenticeships. In October 2016 the DfE published the detail of its proposals to establish the Apprenticeship Levy, which would require large employers to invest 0.5 per cent of their pay bill to fund apprenticeship provision (DfE, 2016). At the same time, a complete change to the funding and organisation of apprenticeships for small and medium enterprises (SMEs) was proposed. The levy came into force in May 2017 and, therefore, represented a remarkable initiative from a Conservative government usually seeking to achieve low levels of taxation and to reduce bureaucracy for businesses.

A further policy initiative aimed at resolving problems in the delivery of higher-level technical skills was the development of the five 'National Colleges'. The drive for National Colleges, delivering training in crucial high-tech industries, began under the Liberal Democrat Minister Vince Cable in 2014, but became a firm policy commitment in May 2016 with the confirmation of £80 million of government funding. The National Colleges were planned to focus in areas considered crucial for economic growth; high speed rail, nuclear, onshore oil and gas, digital skills and the creative industries. The initiative appears to provide both an innovative approach to the delivery of specialist technical qualifications and a further contribution to the diversification of providers within the crowded FE and skills marketplace.

SO POLICIES CONTINUE TO PROLIFERATE BUT DO THEY RESULT IN MEANINGFUL CHANGE?

Norris and Adam (2017) point to the FE and skills sector as being characterised by almost constant change for 30 years and suggest that such a relentless process of change has led to instability and complexity. Lumby and Foskett (2003) question how much has really altered in the way that the sector operates, coining the phrase 'turbulence masquerading as change'. Expressing a similar thought, Hyland and Merrill (2003) refer to policy changes and the introduction and replacement of new organisations as Groundhog Day: repetition rather than innovation.

What does seem to remain a constant is the perception of the sector as the answer to servicing the needs of the economy and promoting social inclusion, the debate centring on the way in which it might best be employed in meeting these twin aims. Generally, since first surfacing in any meaningful way in the initial 2003 Skills Strategy, a partnership approach, combined with further movement towards a more demand-led system, seems now to be well established as a general policy direction. It is the mechanism to implement this in the most effective manner which remains elusive and further change can be expected, requiring the sector to be extremely flexible and adaptable in its organisation and practice.

THE QUEST FOR QUALITY

Decisions regarding policy direction need to be based on some form of information or evidence. This has led to the development of an increasing culture of monitoring and measuring performance and progress with a view to bringing about improvement. The overall approach is referred to as Quality Management and in an educational context generally encompasses the processes outlined in Figure 10.1.

Figure 10.1   Quality processes

Quality assurance and quality improvement have been and still remain important concepts in the sector and it is to these that we turn next.

As an initial guide, we can consider quality assurance as a systematic approach to the monitoring of current practice, judgements being based on feedback from the 'end-users' of the product supplied – the learners. The purpose behind quality assurance procedures is to lead to improvement in the quality of what is offered. The way in which 'quality' is interpreted is not always easy to pin down, however, and Tidball (1991: 2.5.1) describes the word 'quality' itself as 'ambiguous' and 'slippery'. On what basis, then, is quality appraised?

ACTIVITY 10.4

How do you judge the quality of the work you do or the courses you offer? Are results the most important indicator or do you place a greater importance on the way in which you work and run and organise your courses?

At one level, many of the activities that form part of your own professional work (e.g. assessing learners, reflecting on your own teaching, trying out new methods) can be described as quality assurance and improvement. You are considering the effectiveness of your own practice and looking to see how it might be improved. Other levels exist, however, where we enter the wider worlds of institutional management and national policy. These are central to the next section, which gives an overview of where the concern with quality came from, the regulatory and inspection systems in the sector, and identifies how quality issues impact on you as a teacher and/or manager of courses.

ORIGINS OF THE QUALITY MOVEMENT WITHIN THE SECTOR

There is a history to the issue of quality. A report from the Teaching and Learning Research Programme (2005: 2) said: 'Over the last 50 years there have been repeated calls for the improvement of teaching and learning in FE', arising from the previously mentioned belief that education and training would provide the solution to the country's social and economic problems. A key point in that 50-year history (though some, such as Winch and Hyland [2007] would take it back another hundred years) was a debate in the 1970s about the role of education and training, and also about its accountability and management. James Callaghan, the then Prime Minister, raised questions concerning ways in which monitoring resources and maintaining national standards might best be achieved in his Ruskin College speech.

Regulation and inspection altered and increased over the period that followed Callaghan's speech, through the Thatcher, Major and Blair governments, reaching what some would describe as excessive levels. The Foster Report (2005: 34) into Further Education, for instance, makes the point that 'the world of FE oversight is crowded. There is a galaxy of oversight, inspection and accreditation bodies'. A more recent publication, the 2011 consultation document from the Department for Business, Innovation and Skills, *New Challenges, New Chances: Next Steps in Implementing the Further Education Reform Programme*, seems to confirm that this state of affairs still exists, stating: 'Working with the sector, we have identified that the assurance processes used to monitor performance and incentivise continuous improvement are excessive' (BIS, 2011: 17).

From a government perspective, there is a desire to inspect and guide the sector, using a wide range of auditing and inspecting mechanisms and organisations in its management, and applying detailed sets of standards and criteria. Government-funded bodies speak of the need for the sector to adopt effective processes to evaluate performance and manage improvement. This was spelled out clearly in the May 2005 LSC publication, *Quality Improvement and Self-assessment*, which emphasised that the primary responsibility for improving the quality of provision rests with the provider (p. 6). The White Paper, *Learning to Succeed* (DfEE, 1999), gave an indication as to how this was to be achieved, stating that the government was looking to all providers to adopt strategies for securing continuous improvement, and that these strategies should be based on self-assessment and action planning (including target setting) and responding to and acting on learner feedback and complaints (p. 44).

REFLECTIVE TASK 10.3

How many different ways can you identify in which your teaching is monitored or inspected? What benefit have you derived from all or some of these procedures? Identify ways in which your practice may have changed as a result.

Quality assurance, as described above, is now a well established feature of the educational landscape, with its familiar routines of data collection, report completion and planning. We next explore the origins of the models for regulating, monitoring and setting standards for education and training that have been adopted by government.

MODELS OF QUALITY MANAGEMENT AND THEIR ORIGINS

The models of quality and assurance and improvement adopted within the sector are rooted in the practices of business and industry. Originally concerned with spotting faults in manufactured goods, these business models gradually evolved during the course of the 20th century into building systems and cultures whose purpose was to minimise problems and maximise performance. The new quality management techniques introduced into the sector were based on these models, with a focus on the management of people, finance and operations, and were accompanied by a new set of attitudes. This process has been described as part of the rise of the New Public Management, or managerialism, which saw private-sector values and structures introduced into education and other public sectors such as the Health Service and the Civil Service (e.g. Budge et al., 2007: 657). In line with this shift, FE colleges and other training providers developed their own internal quality systems based on a variety of approaches, including their own existing course reviews, industrial and commercial models such as ISO 9000 and Investors in People, or looser frameworks such as Total Quality Management (TQM). TQM describes an approach to the management of quality which is based on customer satisfaction. Total implies the involvement and commitment of everyone to the process and an examination of all spheres of activity. Whilst Sallis (1993: 65) declares that 'Total quality is a way of life for those organisations that live its message', he also wonders 'how to generate the passion and the pride required to generate quality in education'. Educational institutions are not factories, and so the implementation of TQM was not without its difficulties in its focus on continual improvement, however it provided a direct route to fulfilling the accountability requirements of government and funding and awarding bodies. The primacy of these requirements, however, seemed to alter priorities, leading Sallis to later comment: 'Too often today quality has become synonymous with the latest government stricture on standards, examination success, school performance, league tables or part of the latest party political pronouncements on education before an election' (2002: vi).

The basic idea of a quality system can be seen in a structure provided by the European Union (see Figure 10.2). Its general model is similar to many others. At its

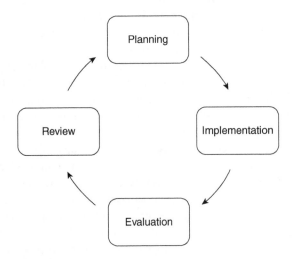

Figure 10.2   Structure of EU quality cycle

heart is a cycle of activities that can be structured around a course or institutional calendar. These activities involve planning and implementation, then gathering information, evidence and data. This leads to evaluating how well things have gone. Finally, there is an overall review and planning for improvements in the next cycle. We will return to this kind of cycle of activities later on, when we deal with your own activities in relation to quality assurance and improvement.

THE LANGUAGE AND TERMINOLOGY OF QUALITY MANAGEMENT

The words that are frequently seen in quality assurance procedures are those such as *standards, criteria, evidence, benchmarking, evaluation, review, improvement, target* and *plan*. These relate both to the cycle of activities described above, and to the methods and documentation that are used in that cycle. The BIS document, *Skills for Sustainable Growth* (2010b), laid out the new Coalition Government's plans for skills. Its executive summary identified the actions that they believed would lead to improvement. There were three main points:

1. To increase competition between training providers.
2. To empower learners by providing better information on quality.
3. To tackle poor performance.

The intended effect of these measures was to 'drive up standards', so the language of improvement in this document incorporates *competition, information, addressing poor performance* and *driving up standards*.

A further layer of language contains terms such as *excellence* and *world-class*, but as these are aspirational in nature their use tends to be limited to policy and mission statements rather than the everyday management of quality.

Quality management is, as suggested earlier, an aspect of management. Training organisations need to prove to their funding and regulating bodies that they are performing well. To do this, they need to regulate and measure their own efforts, and in particular the efforts of teaching staff. This regulation and measurement takes the form of *quality control* and *quality assurance*, and a variety of systems, roles, documents and activities are organised to ensure that this takes place. *Quality improvement* is integral to systems of quality management. The cycle of activities becomes an upward spiral. Continuous improvement irons out weaknesses, welcomes innovation and encourages performing at an ever higher or a consistently high level.

Standards form an important basis for quality management. If, for example, initial assessments are considered to be a good thing, you would plan for everyone to have an initial assessment (your organisation may already insist on this). You could specify what form the assessment should take. You now have a quality standard that specifies, for example, that every applicant will carry out a 30-minute aptitude test before being accepted onto your course. This is something that you can plan and check on. You have therefore set a measurable standard that can be monitored for compliance. The next step is to evaluate performance and take subsequent action if needed. This takes you round the quality cycle shown in Figure 10.2, from initial planning to the next round of planning. In quality assurance terms, your role in this is to ensure that the standards are complied with. In the example above, this would mean making sure that everyone took the 30-minute aptitude test and that this is recorded and monitored.

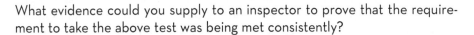

ACTIVITY 10.5

What evidence could you supply to an inspector to prove that the requirement to take the above test was being met consistently?

You could rely on learners to tell an inspector that they had taken the test. They might have forgotten it, however, or not recognised it as initial assessment, so it is useful to have evidence of a more substantial nature available. For example:

- a checklist with every applicant's name, showing that they had taken the test and what the result was
- tutorial notes or student journals showing that the test had been discussed and made use of in initial target setting
- the availability of a sample of completed tests
- records of your meetings, or your improvement plans, which might contain evaluations and decisions about initial assessments.

Some of these examples of evidence are produced through activities such as tutorials, student journals, course meetings and other forms of record keeping. In those cases, generating evidence does not require a separate activity. You will, however, need to be sure that your record keeping is accurate and up to date, so that you do not find that your picture of the initial assessments done at the start of the year is patchy and unreliable.

As well as your learners, you yourself may be monitored. Many education and training organisations make use of prescribed formats such as lesson plans or other specifications. These usually embody some of the standards of the organisation, and your compliance and performance can be measured against these.

Benchmarking is a matter of measuring yourself or your organisation against a given standard. It might be your own group's results for the previous year, or national figures for your kind of course. Whichever figures are used, the purpose of the benchmark is to provide a point of reference and comparison, for use in helping to set targets for improvement. Quality management is often based on quantitative data, numbers and measurement as these provide useful management tools. Your role in benchmarking starts with ensuring that your own figures are accurate. Simple things like registers show how many people enrolled and how many stayed on course. Data like this can raise questions and show trends, and need to be accompanied by commentary and analysis for a better understanding. Register data may therefore require an explanation of why a course has retained or lost learners. Examinations and other assessments show how well learners have achieved, though 'how well' needs to be defined (e.g. better than last year; better than the national average; worse than predicted; good in relation to their starting points).

Assessment and *evaluation* refer to different processes. In the UK, the term *assessment* is generally used to refer to the judgement of student performance, whilst *evaluation* takes a broader view, considering how well a course or system as a whole is working. That is the way that the terms are used in this book, though you will find examples of the words being used interchangeably in other contexts in the sector. Whatever the title used, these documents require some evaluative comment on the data recorded. The Self Evaluation Document (SED) that Ofsted requires from teacher training providers is an example. Ofsted complains about receiving SEDs that are not truly evaluative but are just making statements (e.g. 'Apprenticeship pass rate: 82%'), without saying if the organisation thinks that this was good or bad. Ofsted wants a judgement, or evaluation, supported by evidence and commentary, rather than a list of statistics. The gathering of evidence or data is fairly pointless unless an attempt is made to make sense of it; evaluation is the process of making sense, understanding and then making judgements, and forms the basis of plans for improvement. Your work on assessment feeds into the evaluation process. It involves you in judging and marking the performance of your learners in tests of various kinds (e.g. practical demonstration, written examination), and in the moderation of your own and colleagues' work in assessing. Assessments are often based on criteria, statements of the qualities that judgements are based on. Your assessment records throughout a course will build up a picture of how your learners are progressing, both as a cohort and as individuals. Your work in evaluation includes any aspect of making sense of course data. This includes analysing numerical and other information, making comparisons, seeking explanations and offering commentary and judgement. In some institutions, this will be done by a separate department; in others, you will be involved in discussions and meetings, and in some cases you may be the lone collector and evaluator of data. In all cases, it is useful to be prompted by the data to reflect on the progress of a course and to consider its implications.

DOCUMENTATION OF QUALITY ASSURANCE

The Self Assessment Report (SAR) sometimes known as the Self Evaluation Document or other similar variant, is probably the most significant quality document in colleges.

The process of compiling the SAR begins at course level, where teaching staff and teacher/managers get involved. It is then usually aggregated to department and finally to college level, after which it is ready to be seen by regulatory and inspection bodies. It sets out the required data and the comparisons to be made (e.g. with the previous two years' figures). The production of the SAR by colleges and providers is an established feature of the quality landscape although, interestingly, the document is no longer required by the regulatory body the Education and Skills Funding Agency (EFSA). Instead these documents are now submitted each year to Ofsted, who are responsible for inspecting all providers in the sector. Although the SAR is seen by providers as being a central part of their quality process, there is now very little guidance provided on what these reports should include, or the format that should be used. In their inspection handbook, Ofsted briefly mention how they will use the provider's SAR but are clear that there is no required format for these key documents (Ofsted, 2016b).

IMPROVEMENT

One of the most important features of self assessment processes is the related process of planning to improve quality. Provider SARs invariably conclude with a plan for the improvements that are needed; often referred to as a Quality Improvement Plan (QIP). The example in Figure 10.3 shows a typical layout, broadly following a SMART format.

Issue	Specific action to maintain strength or remedy weakness	Expected outcome and relevant success criteria	Who is responsible?	Timescale (start and end date for action)	Progress (Term 1)	Progress (Term 2)	Progress (Final)
Some lack of clarity in assignment requirements	Production of specific module handbooks outlining module structure and containing detailed assignment briefs	Students will have clearer picture of assignment requirements resulting in more focused responses to assessment tasks	Course leader and team	Booklets to be available at the start of each module	Module booklets produced and issued for Modules 1, 4, 5, 6	Module booklets being used in teaching to date. Module 5 assignment brief needs to be more closely aligned to assessment procedures in handbook	Module booklets now produced and used for every module. Reduced level of assignment queries and student evaluation indicates successful outcome

Figure 10.3   Example SAR entry

In this example, learner feedback has indicated that assignment briefs are not sufficiently specific, leading to some confusion as to what exactly will fulfil the requirements of the various assignments which form part of the overall course assessment. Following evaluation, it has been decided to take a particular action and check its outcome.

ACTIVITY 10.6

What kinds of activities can you, either alone or with colleagues, carry out in order to get ideas for improvements? Where would you look? Where would you go? What resources could you call on?

REGULATION AND INSPECTION

We looked earlier at the origins of the quality movement in the sector. This has led to the creation of a number of regulatory and inspection systems which operate within the sector.

As discussed previously, regulatory and inspection bodies are regularly reformed, abolished or reorganised by successive governments (Norris and Adam, 2017). In recent years the required levels of reporting and inspection have been reduced. This may not have been immediately apparent in the practices within some institutions, however, as significant processes of inspection, evaluation and planning were by this time embedded within the ethos and practices of the sector, and embodied in new roles, offices, data collection, reviewing mechanisms and calendars of activities.

What follows is an overview of the bodies involved in regulation and inspection. Where a provision applies only to England, there will be a parallel but separate provision in Wales, Scotland and Northern Ireland.

DEPARTMENT FOR EDUCATION

This is currently the key government department for the sector. Its functions have been reformed and realigned many times in recent years but the DfE returned to being the sole government department responsible for all parts of the education sector in 2016.

EDUCATION & SKILLS FUNDING AGENCY (ESFA)

The ESFA, whose role is to act as 'a single funding agency accountable for funding education and training for children, young people and adults' (ESFA, 2017) works to a budget, targets and priorities set by the DfE. It covers England only, and allocates funding to colleges and other skills and training organisations. It is also responsible for quality assuring colleges and post-19 providers. The ESFA is a powerful organisation as it holds the purse-strings for much of the training that takes place in the sector. Kennedy (1996: 43) reminded us of the significance of this by pointing out that 'funding is the most important lever for change'. As the funder, the ESFA monitors the performance of providers and then makes decisions about further funding of provision. The ESFA has the power to formally intervene with providers that do not meet the required standards for quality and finances.

FE CHOICES

Operational in its original format as the 'Framework for Excellence' from September 2010, FE Choices is a system which provides publicly available data on the performance of all FE providers across the country. It operates within the ESFA to compile standard data from providers and aims to provide 'clear and comparable information to help you as a learner and employer make informed choices about post-16 further education and training' (ESFA, 2017). It was originally planned rather like a comparison website so that an informed choice of training provider becomes, in theory, as easy as choosing a gas supplier or a mobile phone deal. However, austerity measures under the coalition government narrowed its scope so that it now focuses on four main areas within which data are collected; these are:

- Achievement Rates.
- Learner Destinations.
- Learner Satisfaction.
- Employer Satisfaction.

Though this data is publicly available it is not now provided in a format that is likely to be used by students and employers when making choices about where to study. Instead the information tends to be used by government bodies and providers themselves to make comparisons between different institutions.

ACTIVITY 10.7

What information do you think it would be important for a prospective student or employer to have about a provider, in order to help them decide where to study?

(Continued)

Have a look at the list of questions below, taken from the ESFA Learner Satisfaction Survey:

- How satisfied or dissatisfied are you with the teaching on your course or activity?
- How satisfied or dissatisfied are you with the way staff treat you?
- How satisfied or dissatisfied are you with the advice you have been given about what you can do after this course or activity?
- How satisfied or dissatisfied are you with the support you get on this course or activity?
- How satisfied or dissatisfied are you that the course or activity is meeting your expectations?
- How satisfied or dissatisfied are you that staff respond to the views of learners?
- Overall, how satisfied or dissatisfied are you with the college or organisation that provides your learning?
- How likely is it that you would recommend the college or organisation that provides your learning to friends or family?

REFLECTIVE TASK 10.4

Which of the questions from the survey seem most relevant to your own work? What might you do in order to receive a positive response to them? What questions might you ask to obtain a picture of learner satisfaction?

OFFICE FOR STANDARDS IN EDUCATION, CHILDREN'S SERVICES AND SKILLS (OFSTED)

External inspection for the sector is carried out by Ofsted who 'inspect adult learning and skills [and further education and skills] to provide information to providers, employers, learners and users to help promote improvement' (Ofsted, 2011: 6). In the strategic document for 2011–2015, *Raising Standards, Improving Lives* (2011), Ofsted reiterated the point that they 'focus on how standards can be raised and outcomes improved' (p. 7). It is Ofsted that provided the categories of 'inadequate, requires improvement, good, outstanding' which have become central to the language of standards and improvement in the sector. Ofsted inspections have important implications for education institutions and training organisations, many of whom will often use the same language and criteria as Ofsted in their own internal inspections. The Ofsted criteria are concerned with grading performance through their four-level system. This gives them a basic tool for comparing institutions, or the same institution on different occasions, or sectors and subjects. They thereby have a yardstick by which to require or recommend improvements.

Ofsted inspects a selected range of activities in the sector, ranging from what goes on in the way of teaching and learning, to how quality management is carried out. If you look at Ofsted inspection reports, you will find five main grades:

- Overall Effectiveness
- Effectiveness of leadership and management
- Quality of teaching, learning and assessment
- Personal development, behaviour and welfare
- Outcomes for learners.

Overall Effectiveness			Requires improvement
Effectiveness of leadership and management	**Requires improvement**	16 to 19 study programmes	**Requires improvement**
Quality of teaching, learning and assessment	**Requires improvement**	Adult learning programmes	**Requires improvement**
Personal development, behaviour and welfare	**Requires improvement**	Apprenticeships	**Good**
Outcomes for learners	**Good**	Provision for learners with high needs	**Good**
Overall Effectiveness at previous inspection			**Outstanding**

Figure 10.4   Sample entry from an Ofsted report

ACTIVITY 10.8

Look at the sample entry from an Ofsted report, Figure 10.4. How do managers in your place of work assess performance, and how much do you participate in this process (e.g. through providing statistics, feedback, reviews, evidence of learner progress, being observed)? What about plans and actions for improvement? What form do they take in your place of work? Are they useful and effective? How do you contribute at your level?

FE AND SIXTH FORM COMMISSIONERS

The separate roles of the Commissioners for FE and for Sixth Form colleges were established in April 2014, with the intention of strengthening the government's ability to intervene when providers are performing poorly. Their role is to provide advice to DfE ministers in situations where colleges have:

- an inadequate Ofsted inspection
- failed to meet national minimum standards of performance
- an inadequate assessment for financial health and/or financial management and control by the funding agencies.

In the early years of their role the Commissioners were mainly involved in interventions in colleges that were struggling with financial difficulties and then, in 2016/17, in leading the Area Review process (previously discussed).

EDUCATION AND TRAINING FOUNDATION

Formed in 2008 from the then Quality Improvement Agency (QIA), the Learning and Skills Improvement Service (LSIS) was to improve quality, increase participation and raise standards and achievement within the sector. LSIS itself was replaced in 2013 by the Education and Training Foundation (originally proposed as the FE Guild), which has taken over responsibility for areas such as training, leadership and management.

OFFICE OF QUALIFICATIONS AND EXAMINATIONS REGULATION (OFQUAL)

Ofqual replaced the Qualifications and Curriculum Authority (QCA) in 2008 as the body which regulates qualifications, examinations and assessments in England and vocational qualifications in Northern Ireland. Its primary function is to maintain standards and confidence in qualifications offered by the various awarding bodies. It achieves this through a monitoring process and the taking of appropriate action whenever it considers there is a risk to quality. Ofqual oversees the maintenance of quality of a wide range of vocational qualifications in England and Northern Ireland, as well as regulating GCSEs and A-Levels in England.

QUALITY ASSURANCE AGENCY FOR HIGHER EDUCATION (QAA)

QAA is concerned with safeguarding standards and improving the quality of teaching, learning and assessment in higher education within the UK. It achieves this through a systematic programme of peer review of HE institutions. The review process results in the production of a report which both highlights good practice and contains recommendations for improving quality. Support for standards and the promotion of quality enhancement is achieved through the publication of the UK Quality Code for Higher Education, which provide points of reference and guidance for HE providers in the areas of standards, quality and public information. QAA has also monitored higher education work carried out in FE colleges. Though the role of the QAA continues, quality assurance for higher education is changing significantly, however, with the introduction of the 'Teaching Excellence Framework' (TEF), which introduces a number of standardised measures of quality for universities and colleges who deliver HE.

ACTIVITY 10.9

What seem to you to be the most important two or three organisations listed in this section? How do they affect you and/or your organisation? Have you any way to evaluate if there are too many, too few, or if they do their job well?

FINALLY

The wider context of quality assurance provides both an everyday activity in the sector and an area of debate and disagreement over its effectiveness and purpose. Bauman (1993: 139) suggests the words 'quality' and 'improvement' each contain the elements of seduction and repression. The seductive idea is that things can get better, and the repressive one, that this is achieved through the measurement and intensification of performance. It is, however, a concept which professionals in the sector need to come to terms with and shape their practice around.

SUMMARY OF KEY POINTS

In this chapter, we have looked at the relationship between lifelong learning and government policy and the stages of the policy-making process. The chapter has reviewed the various policy drivers and current policy directions being taken. The role of quality assurance and quality improvement in regulating and inspecting the sector has been examined and consideration has been given to the form these two processes take. The various regulatory

(Continued)

bodies have been identified and the impact they have on providers and teachers has been explored.

The key points in this chapter are:

- Lifelong learning as a concept involves a natural desire to learn from 'cradle to grave'.
- The skills the country's workforce requires, in order to deal with the challenges arising out of globalisation, are those relating to knowledge, information and technology.
- Policy is made through a process which involves an initial report on a given issue, followed by the issuing of Green and White Papers, which then give rise to a bill and subsequently an Act of Parliament.
- The Skills Agenda, a major theme in New Labour policy, was designed to close the 'skills gap' – the difference between what people could do and what employers required of them.
- Coalition Government policy is based on the notion of the 'Big Society', which is founded on the 'three pillars' of freedom, fairness and responsibility.
- The Conservative Government, after 2015, continued the policy approaches established under the coalition but this changed significantly following the 2016 referendum vote to leave the EU.
- The government uses the process of quality assurance and improvement to monitor and regulate the work of the sector.
- There is a requirement to put appropriate quality assurance procedures in place on all publicly funded courses.
- The quality cycle involves planning and implementation, followed by the gathering of information, evidence and data. This leads to evaluation and review and concludes with the formulation of plans for improvement.
- Quality can be measured against devices such as standards and benchmarks.
- The key government department for the sector is the Department for Education (DfE). Its inspection arm is Ofsted.

REFERENCES

Allen, R. (2015) 'Education Policy', *National Institute Economic Review,* No. 231 February 2015: R36–R43.

Ball, S. (2008) *The Education Debate*. Bristol: The Policy Press.

Banks, J.A., Au, K.H., Ball, A.H., Bell, P., Gordon, E.W., Gutiérrez, K.D., Heath, S.B., Lee, C.D., Lee, Y., Mahiri, J., Nasir, N.S., Valdés, G. & Zhou, M. (2007) *Learning in and out of school in diverse environments: Life-Long, Life-Wide, Life-Deep*. Available online at: http://life-slc.org/docs/Banks_etal-LIFE-Diversity-Report.pdf (accessed 15/05/17).

Bartlett, S. and Burton, D. (2009) Lifelong learning, in J. Sharp, S. Ward and L. Hankin (eds), *Education Studies: An Issues-based Approach* (2nd edn). Exeter: Learning Matters.

Bauman, Z. (1993) *Postmodern Ethics*. Oxford: Blackwell.

BIS (2010a) Further Education – New Horizon: Investing in Skills for Sustainable Growth. London: BIS.

BIS (2010b) Skills for Sustainable Growth. London: BIS.

BIS (2011) New Challenges, New Chances: Next Steps in Implementing the Further Education Reform Programme. London: BIS.

BIS (2014) Getting the Job Done: The Government's Reform Plan for Vocational Qualifications. London: BIS.

BIS and DfE (2016) *The Post-16 Skills Plan*. London: DfE.

Brookfield, S. (1983) *Adult Learners, Adult Education and the Community*. Milton Keynes: Open University Press.

Budge, I., Crewe, I., McKay, D. and Newton, K. (2007) *The New British Politics* (5th edn). London: Pearson.

Department for Children, Schools and Families and Department for Innovation, Universities and Skills (DCSF/DIUS) (2008) *Raising Expectations: Enabling the System to Deliver*. Available online at: www.education.gov.uk/consultations/downloadableDocs/Raising%20 Expectations%20pdf.pdf (accessed 15/05/17).

DfE (2010) The Importance of Teaching – Schools White Paper. London: DfE.

DfE (2016) Apprenticeship Funding in England from May 2017. London: DfE.

DfE & BIS (2013) Rigour and Responsiveness in Skills. London: BIS.

DfEE (1998) The Learning Age: A Renaissance for New Britain. Sheffield: DfEE.

DfEE (1998) Towards a national skills agenda. Sudbury: DfEE.

DfEE (1999) Learning to Succeed: A New Framework for Post-16 Learning. Sheffield: DfEE.

DfEE (1999) Delivering skills for all. Sudbury: DfEE.

DfEE (2000) Tackling the adult skills gap. Sudbury: DfEE.

DfEE (2003) 21st Century Skills: Realising our Potential. Sheffield: DfEE.

DfEE (2005) Skills: Getting on in Business, Getting on at Work. Sheffield: DfEE.

DfES (2003) Every child matters. Norwich: the Stationery Office.

DfES (2004) *Every Child Matters: Next Steps*. Norwich: the Stationery Office.

DfES (2004) *Every Child Matters: Change for Children*. Norwich: the Stationery Office.

Department for Innovation, Universities and Skills (DIUS) (2007) *World Class Skills: Implementing the Leitch Review of Skills in England*. Available online at: www.gov.uk/government/uploads/ system/uploads/attachment_data/file/243202/7181.pdf (accessed 15/05/17).

European Commission (2002) *A Memorandum on Lifelong Learning*. Available online at: http:// pjp-eu.coe.int/documents/1017981/1668227/COM_Sec_2000_1832.pdf/f79d0e69-b8d3-48a7- 9d16-1a065bfe48e5 (accessed 15/05/17).

ESFA (2017) *About Us*. Available online at: www.gov.uk/government/organisations/education- and-skills-funding-agency/about (accessed 06/05/2017).

EU (1995) *Teaching and Learning: Towards the Learning Society*. Available online at: https:// publications.europa.eu/en/publication-detail/-/publication/d0a8aa7a-5311-4eee-904c- 98fa541108d8/language-en (accessed 15/05/17).

Field, J. (2006) *Lifelong Learning and the New Educational Order*. Stoke-on-Trent: Trentham Books.

Fletcher, M. (2017) Reforming Technical and Professional Education: Why should it work this time? Newcastle upon Tyne: NCFE/Campaign for Learning.

Forrester, G. and Garratt, D. (2017) *Education Policy Unravelled*. London: Bloomsbury Academic.

Foster, A. (2005) Realising the Potential: A Review of the Future of Further Education Colleges. London: DfES.

Fryer, R.H. (1997) *Learning for the 21st Century*. Available online at: www.lifelonglearning.co.uk/nagcell/index.htm (accessed 31/07/2013).

Giddens, A. (2000) *Runaway World*. London: Routledge.

HM Government (2015) Reviewing Post-16 Education & Training Institutions. London: BIS.

Hyland, T. and Merrill, B. (2003) *The Changing Face of Further Education*. Abingdon: Routledge.

IMF (2002) *Globalization: A Framework for IMF Involvement*. Available online at: www.imf.org/external/np/exr/ib/2002/031502.htm (accessed 15/05/17).

Keep, E. (2015) 'Governance in English VET: On the functioning of a fractured system'. *Research in Comparative & International Education*, 10(4): 464–75.

Keohane, N. (2017) Rising to the Challenge: The Further Education and Skills Sector Over the Next Decade. London: The Social Market Foundation.

Kennedy, H. (1996) *Learning Works*. London: FEFC.

Leitch, S. (2006) Prosperity for All in the Global Economy: World Class Skills. Norwich: The Stationery Office.

LSC (2005) Quality Improvement and Self-assessment. Coventry: LSC.

Lumby, J. and Foskett, N. (2003) *14–19 Education*. London: Sage.

Norris, E. and Adam, R. (2017) All Change: Why Britain is so prone to policy reinvention and what can be done about it. London: Institute for Government.

OECD (1996) *Lifelong Learning for All*. Paris: OECD.

OECD (2001) *The Well Being of Nations: The Role of Human and Social Capital*. Available online at: www.oecd.org/site/worldforum/33703702.pdf (accessed 15/05/17).

Ofsted (2011) Raising Standards, Improving Lives. London: HMSO.

Ofsted (2016a) The Annual Report of Her Majesty's Chief Inspector of Education, Children's Services and Skills 2015/16. London: HMSO.

Ofsted (2016b) Further Education and Skills Inspection Handbook. Manchester: Ofsted.

Putnam, R. (2001) Bowling Alone: The Collapse and Revival of American Community. New York: Simon & Schuster.

Ratcliffe, R. (2014) 'Why aren't colleges welcoming 14-year-olds?' *The Guardian*. Available online at: www.theguardian.com/education/2014/aug/26/colleges-14-year-olds-fe-institutions (accessed 28/04/17).

Richard, D. (2012) *Richard Review of Apprenticeships*. London: School for Startups.

Sallis, E. (1993) *Total Quality Management in Education*. London: Kogan Page.

Sallis, E. (2002) *Total Quality Management in Education* (3rd edn). London: Kogan Page.

Taylor, R. (2005) Lifelong learning and Labour Governments 1997–2004. *Oxford Review of Education*, 31(1): 101–118.

Teaching and Learning Research Programme (2005) *Research Briefing Number 12*. London: Learning and Skills Research Centre.

Tidball, J. (1991) The management of quality, in *Guide to College Management*, Release 6. London: Further Education Development Association.

Winch, C. and Hyland, T. (2007) *Guide to Vocational Education and Training*. London: Continuum.

Wolf, A. (2011) *Review of Vocational Education: The Wolf Report*. London: DfE. Available online at: www.gov.uk/government/uploads/system/uploads/attachment_data/file/180504/DFE-00031-2011.pdf (accessed 15/05/17).

FURTHER READING

Forrester, G. and Garratt, D. (2016) *Education Policy Unravelled* **(2nd edn). London: Bloomsbury.**
A book which does what its title suggests. Initial chapters examine the notion and purpose of policy before going on, in the following chapters, to explore its impact within various sectors of the education system. Chapter 6 is of greatest interest to those working in the Education and Training sector.

Wallace, S. (2013) *Understanding the Further Education Sector: A critical guide to policies and practices.* **Northwich: Critical Publishing.**
This book takes a historical look at the beginnings and subsequent changes that have taken place within the sector in its various different incarnations. Throughout this chronological journey, the significant features of the social, cultural and political contexts of the time are examined alongside their influence in shaping the development of the sector as a whole. Its purpose and how this determines the role of those practitioners within it is examined in a user-friendly fashion. A useful text to get a 'feel' for the bigger picture and an understanding of the factors that have made the sector what it is today.

11

SUCCESSFULLY COMPLETING YOUR DIPLOMA IN EDUCATION AND TRAINING

The previous chapters in this book have been concerned with supplementing the taught element of your diploma programme by covering topics relating to the different units. This chapter takes a different perspective, with the emphasis not on 'what you need to know' but 'what you need to do' in order to successfully complete the diploma. You will have to write assignments which satisfy the demands of a Level 5 programme, and so the chapter starts by considering ways of organising your initial reading and research, whilst developing your critical and analytical thinking skills, before going on to offer advice on ways of writing and structuring your assignments and citing and referencing the various sources you have consulted as part of this process. There are practical requirements too and the next sections of the chapter cover planning for and making the most of teaching observations and micro-teaching exercises. You will be supported in your studies not only by the core teaching team of your diploma programme but also by a subject mentor, and the next section will help you derive the maximum benefit from this relationship.

When you have completed this chapter you will be able to:

- research and read material for your assignments in an effective manner
- develop your critical and analytical thinking skills

- structure and write an assignment at a level appropriate to the Diploma in Education and Training
- cite and reference your sources accurately
- plan for and complete the necessary paperwork required for a successful teaching observation
- organise a productive pre-meeting with your teaching observation tutor
- prepare an appropriate and effective micro-teaching session
- manage the relationship with your subject mentor to best effect.

As part of your diploma qualification, you will be required to produce a number of written assignments. These assignments will demand a degree of 'scholarly process'. The first few sections in this chapter will help you refine the skills required to produce these pieces of work. The first section looks at ways of researching material and effective approaches to carrying out the wider reading necessary to give added credibility to your assignment. This is followed by an exploration of different writing styles appropriate to this level of work before introducing a recommended approach to structuring your assignment. Finally, some advice is given on citing and referencing, an essential skill in assignment writing.

READING AND RESEARCHING

Reading for assignments is of fundamental importance but can be a time-consuming task. Therefore, you need to be 'smart' in your approach and allow time to locate useful texts and publications and to actually do the reading. Your course handbook will list suggested reading for each unit you study but you will not have to read a text from cover to cover to find useful information for your assignment; more commonly, relevant quotes etc. can be found in certain chapters of the book you consult. Your best start, therefore, is to look at the contents page of the book first and select relevant chapters. To be even more specific, try looking at the index at the back, identifying key words in relation to your assignment and where these words can be found within the book.

Reading academic textbooks can be hard-going as they will probably contain subject-specific terminology or jargon. To make sense of what appears to be a complex piece of writing, it may be helpful to first look at the structure. Typically, the layout of a piece of work consists of three parts. Kirton (2011: 48) advises that if the reading you're looking at consists of five paragraphs, the layout will probably be as follows:

- introduction, or the 'topic' paragraph
- main body, paragraph two, three and four, each beginning with a topic sentence
- conclusion, or 'terminator' paragraph.

By reading the topic and terminator paragraphs, you will get a good indication of whether the piece will provide you with the information you need for your assignment. On occasion, the author of the publication you are reading may refer to some ideas or concepts which you would like to explore for your own assignment, citing from other publications. Full details of these can usually be found in the reference list or bibliography at the end of a chapter or book (see later in this chapter). Of course, the more recent publications will be the most up to date, so, when researching, consult these first. Journal articles tend to be the most current, as they are published at regular intervals during the year. They usually start with an 'abstract', which is a summary of the article, providing you with sufficient information to decide on whether or not the article is of interest to you.

A further source of information is the internet, however you have to consider its reliability. Books and academic journals are reviewed by experts in the field before publication and so can be considered a reliable source. Websites, on the other hand, can be published by anyone. You may need to consider whether they are driven by a (hidden) agenda, political viewpoint or are trying to sell something. Try not to use the internet as the sole basis for your essays or assignments, and limit yourself to the more credible websites such as those ending in .ac.uk, .org, .co(m), or government websites such as the Department for Education. In short, to organise your reading you have to be selective, which means:

- Read what is relevant to your topic.
- Start reading the most recent publications.
- Make sure your source is reliable.

The speed of your reading depends largely on the purpose of the reading. If the purpose is to get a general idea of the text, or the gist of what it is about, you can 'skim-read'. Skim-reading is a fast process which may involve reading the first and last paragraphs of a chapter or the first and last sentence of a paragraph. Scanning is used when you are looking for something specific such as a key word, date or name. How much you already know about the subject also affects your reading speed. Turner et al. (2008) recognise that the early stage of the reading process is the most thorough and slow, as your aim is to learn about the topic and maybe familiarise yourself with new terminology. Once you are more familiar with the topic, you can be more precise in your selection of texts and your reading will be faster.

There is, however, no ideal reading speed: the skill lies in being able to 'pitch your reading speed according to the purpose and the degree of challenge presented by the text' (Chambers and Northedge, 2008: 86).

READING IN DETAIL

Having decided what you are going to read, you need to make sure that you understand what you are reading. It happens to all of us: you read a paragraph but cannot remember what you have just read. There can be a number of reasons for this: you were distracted, thinking about something else, the text was difficult, etc. To improve your comprehension of what you have read, you need to be an active reader, engaging with the text. This means that you:

- scan the text first to become familiar with the material before you read, and to activate any prior knowledge
- predict, ask questions, make inferences and draw comparisons. Write down information, make notes, including a counter-argument if necessary
- explain what you have read to someone else; verbalising the material in your own words will help in activating your long-term memory. Reflect on/review what you have read. Link new ideas with what you already know (adapted from Malthouse and Roffey-Barentsen, 2013: 42).

The SQ3R system is an example of an active reading technique. Pauk and Owens (2010: 256) describe it as follows:

S: 'survey' the chapter, glancing through all the headings

Q: turn these headings into 'questions' and remember the questions as you further read

R1: 'read' actively, identifying the main points

R2: 'recall' by paraphrasing what you have just read

R3: 'review' by going back to the beginning of the chapter, answering your questions in your own words.

CRITICAL AND ANALYTICAL THINKING

(adapted from Malthouse, R. and Roffey-Barentsen, J. (2013))

Being able to think critically and analytically is a skill which you need to apply throughout your academic and professional career. As a trainee teacher you need to adopt a challenging approach, questioning what has been presented to you when listening to lectures or when reading a report, article or textbook. Further, you need to be able to identify the strengths and weaknesses in an argument and feel confident to query statements which are presented as evidence or facts. Moreover, when constructing your own argument, either in writing or in a presentation, you need to ensure that others consider your decisions and judgements to be secure and verified. Finally, it is important that you pass on those skills to your students, to enable them to become critical and analytical thinkers too.

Critical thinking was developed in the 1930s by Dewey, who defined it as 'active, persistent, and careful consideration of any belief or supposed form of knowledge in the light of the grounds that support it and the further conclusions to which it tends'

(Dewey, 1933: 118). Judge et al. (2009: 1) put it succinctly as 'a questioning, challenging approach to knowledge and perceived wisdom which involves examining ideas and information from an objective position and then questioning this information in the light of our own values, attitudes and personal philosophy'. Cottrell (2005: 2) very clearly identifies the range of skills and attitudes that constitute critical thinking:

- identifying other people's positions, arguments and conclusions
- evaluating the evidence for alternative points of view
- weighing up opposing arguments and evidence fairly
- being able to read between the lines, seeing behind surfaces, and identifying false or unfair assumptions
- recognising techniques used to make certain positions more appealing than others such as false logic and persuasive devices
- reflecting on issues in a structured way, bringing logic and insight to bear
- drawing conclusions about whether arguments are valid and justifiable, based on good evidence and sensible assumptions
- presenting a point of view in a structured, clear, well-reasoned way that convinces others.

An argument can be described as an attempt to persuade others of the validity of a conclusion, by offering at least one reason that supports that conclusion. An argument, therefore, starts with an issue, which is followed by a line of thinking or reasoning that leads to a conclusion. So, to analyse an argument, you have to find the issue and conclusion of what you have heard or read and also the reasons that lead to that conclusion. Identifying the issue can occasionally be a simple process, as sometimes the author or speaker raises the issue explicitly in the title or opening paragraph. For instance:

Barriers to learning outside the classroom.

Questioning strategies used by teachers to engage students.

Synthetic phonics and its impact on reading attainment.

However, sometimes the issue is inferred, which means you have to find a question that is addressed throughout the essay. The best way to do this is by looking at the conclusion. What does the author try to convey, what is their message? Although most of the time the conclusion is at the end of the essay, this is not always the case. It is helpful to look for clue words – such as: therefore, so, thus, in consequence, as a result, hence, shows that, indicates that, proves that – as they usually lead to what the author is trying to persuade you of. Once you have identified the issue and conclusion, you look for the reasons the author gives in order to convince you that the conclusion made is the 'right' one. There must be at least one reason for there to be an argument, however, most of the time there are more.

Consider the following: which of the following examples are arguments?:

1. More and more children leave school without appropriate reading or numeracy skills. Approximately 1 in 5 adults has the reading skills of an eleven-year-old child. Low adult literacy skills may have an impact on the economy of the country.
2. Constructive feedback enables students to improve. Marks alone do not identify strengths and weaknesses in a student's work. Therefore, teachers should write detailed comments when marking their students' work.
3. Alternative measures to discourage young people from taking drugs need to be introduced. Many young people use recreational drugs. A reclassification of drugs has had no effect on the number of young people taking drugs.

Answers:

1. This is not an argument. These are just three sentences; none of them would work as a conclusion, drawn from the other two.
2. This is an argument. The third sentence is the conclusion, supported by reasons given in the first and second sentence.
3. This is an argument. The first sentence is the conclusion drawn from the second and third sentence.

Remember, an argument has to be persuasive. Sometimes, what may look like an argument is nothing more than an explanation. Consider the following example:

> The first lesson starts at 9.00 am. Pupils come in 15 minutes earlier. Therefore, the library opens at 8.45 am.

Although it appears that the example is an argument, as there are two reasons supporting a conclusion, it is not persuasive. It is just an explanation of why the library opens at 8.45 am. Of course, explanations, or specific examples, are often used to support the conclusion. It is up to you to make a judgement as to whether or not they provide such support.

What about the following example, is this an argument?

> Teachers must have good communication skills. Their patience is often tested. Also, it helps to have a sense of humour. Therefore, to become a teacher, you must be patient, have good communication skills and a healthy sense of humour.

Again, this statement looks like an argument. However, what appears to be the conclusion is a summary of what has been stated before. The conclusion is not based on reasoning, therefore, this is not an example of an argument.

In life, we are surrounded by attempts to persuade us. Just think of politics, the media or advertising. You have to decide which (attempts) to accept and which to reject, and why you have made these decisions. Therefore, when reading a text, or listening to a speech or lecture, it is useful to ask yourself the following questions:

- Does the evidence support the conclusions; is it relevant and adequate?
- Based on the line of reasoning, would I make the same conclusions?

When evaluating the evidence, consider the following: the credibility of the author and the quality of the piece itself. With regard to the author, it may be helpful to identify whether they have a clear political stance. What hidden agendas might they have, what do they hope to gain by writing this piece? Further, do check their specialist knowledge or expertise. Are they an expert in their field? A lack of expertise, may weaken their credibility. For example, someone who does not know the rules, regulations and terminology used in cricket, may not recognise a Chinese cut (an inside edge which misses hitting the stumps by a few centimeters), and would therefore probably not comment on it. After all, it is difficult to accurately interpret evidence if you lack specialist knowledge. But how would you know if the author is an expert? To find out, it is useful to investigate if they have published any other books or articles in journals; or, do other authors, who have written on the same subject, refer to them in their publications (check the references in other authors' books!).

Browne and Keeley (2007: 112) point out that factors such as personal needs, prior expectations, general beliefs, attitudes, values, theories and ideologies can subconsciously or deliberately influence how evidence is reported. As well as being aware of your own bias and prejudice which may interfere with how you judge the presented evidence, you also have to consider bias and subjectivity in the author. For instance, if a head teacher is asked whether cuts in education, proposed by the Department of Education, are welcome, the answer would probably be 'no', followed by a list of examples of how cuts would negatively affect children's learning and national welfare. The reasoning may sound convincing but is it an un-biased, objective view? Although objectivity is at the heart of critical thinking, it is likely that there are some subjective elements or statements in the text that you are reading.

Further, look at the piece of writing itself: are there any ambiguities or inconsistencies; does the author base the evidence on facts or opinion; can you detect any flaws or errors in logic? Look carefully at the use of language. On occasion language can be ambiguous and interpreted in more than one way. For instance, when referring to 'inclusion', what is meant? When talking to someone you can ask them to explain themselves, however, in a written text it may take time to work out what is meant by careful and close reading. Keep asking if any other interpretation is possible, 'what could be meant' and 'what does it mean in this context'. Browne and Keeley (2007) advise that you cannot evaluate an essay until you know the communicator's intended meaning of key terms and phrases as well as alternative meanings. Ambiguity, however, is often intended, especially if certain meanings have emotive connotations. You are more likely to accept the author's way of thinking if they can play on your emotions. The emotional impact is quite intentional, and is carefully planned by the authors.

Next, check for consistency. This means that you consider all parts of the line of reasoning that lead to the conclusion. Are there any parts that contradict or undermine the main message? If claims are contradictory, that means at least one of them must be false. Therefore, an argument that rests on contradictory claims must rest on at least one false claim, and arguments that rest on false claims prove nothing. To dismiss the argument, you don't even have to know which of the two contradicting claims is the false one. As stated by Cottrell (2005: 65), 'inconsistencies make an argument hard to follow, leaving the audience uncertain about what the author is trying to persuade them to believe'. Therefore, inconsistencies in a text obliterate its credibility and persuasive powers.

An opinion is a personal point of view, a belief, not based on proof or evidence. Facts, on the other hand, can be checked against evidence and proven to be true, thereby adding weight to the argument. Therefore, in their efforts to convince you to accept their conclusion, authors often make factual claims. They present something as a fact, thereby discouraging you from questioning what they have said. However, when applying your critical thinking skills, your response should be 'why should I believe that?', 'what is the evidence?', 'how strong is the evidence?' etc.

One tool often used as factual evidence is 'statistics'. The numbers appear scientific and can come across as very convincing. However, they do not always provide the proof they claim to prove. You have to be careful how to interpret statistical evidence. Question who or what organisation is behind the statistics, what is their mission?

How would you question the following claim:

In the last year, pupils' achievement in science has risen by ten per cent.

Although this sounds a positive development, being critical means asking: What is meant by 'science'? Is achievement up in all three parts (biology, chemistry and physics), or has the average risen? If it is the average, then the achievement in one of the sciences could have dropped. What does ten per cent mean, is it likely to have an impact? Who made the claim, was it the Department of Education or a local newspaper? Was the rise in achievement nation-wide or in a local school? How recent is the claim and therefore the statistics? Always look for up-to-date figures and data. Are there other reports that support the claim, or claim other statistics? etc.

The main thing is that you do not just accept what you have been told but question it!

ASSIGNMENT WRITING

Once you have completed (most) of your reading, it is time to start the writing process. The structure of an assignment is nearly as important as the content. Further, it will help with your planning if you have a clear structure in mind. It may be useful to set out a timeline to plan how much time you have for drafting, editing and meeting your deadline.

The structure of an assignment is usually as follows:

- title/question
- introduction
- main body
- conclusion
- reference list/bibliography.

The first point for consideration is the assignment title. 'The worst mistake you can make in essay writing is failing to answer the question asked' (Warburton, 2006: 25). Therefore, you have to start by analysing the question: what is expected of you?

It helps to differentiate between 'content' words and 'process' words. When examining the title of an essay, Bedford and Wilson (2006: 82) advise you to 'pick out the key words'. Key words will either be content-related, referring to the subject, or process-related, referring to what to do with the subject. To meet the criteria of the assignment, it is important to understand what these process words mean. You will need to look at the title carefully, making sure you address what it asks you to do. For instance, when asked to *evaluate*, you should do more than *describe*. Remember, you will be marked down for not answering the question in the required manner, regardless of the time and effort you have put into writing a very detailed description. The table in Figure 11.1 (Malthouse and Roffey-Barentsen, 2013: 61) will help you in identifying what is required of you.

Next, it is helpful to write an outline, using a mind or concept map, if appropriate, which indicates what you already know and what you need to know. Consider the planning procedure in (adapted from Malthouse and Roffey-Barentsen, 2013: 64).

Your writing style usually needs to be 'academic'. This does not mean, however, that it has to use long sentences and difficult words. According to Kirton (2011: 128), 'academic style aims to use language precisely and objectively to express ideas'. He continues that it should be grammatically correct, avoid illogical or emotional language, and that its tone should be impersonal (p. 128). You need to avoid using slang, abbreviations and jargon, and writing is usually in the third person or passive voice: 'this essay will consider…', rather than 'in this essay, I will consider…': '"I" is sometimes thought to indicate a of lack objectivity. Phrases such as I think, I believe, I feel, risk you making assertions without offering evidence or developing a logical argument' (Warburton, 2006: 116). He continues: 'there can be a danger that personal experience will sound like bar-room philosophy, little more than unsubstantiated personal opinion; therefore avoid unless asked for' (2006: 117).

Process word	Meaning
Account for	Give reasons, explain why something happens
Analyse	Break topic into elements and examine each
Argue	Give reasons for and against, based on evidence
Assess	Make a judgement after considering in a balanced way the points for and against
Comment	State your opinions on a topic, supporting your views with evidence
Compare	Show similarities and differences
Contrast	Emphasise the differences between two or more things
Define	Give the precise meaning of something
Describe	Give a detailed account
Discuss	Consider different points of view
Evaluate	Consider and weigh the points for and against, making a judgement on which is preferable
Examine	Critically investigate
Explain	Make clear, give reasons
to what extent	Consider how far something is true or not true
Illustrate	Use examples or diagrams to make clear and explicit
Interpret	Give the meaning of other material presented
Justify	Give reasons for decisions or conclusions
Outline	Give the main features
Review	Critically examine the subject
State	Say fully and clearly
Summarise	Give a concise account of the main points

Figure 11.1   'Process words' for assignment titles

Cottrell (2008: 209) identifies four styles of academic writing:

- descriptive
- argumentative/analytical
- evaluative/analytical
- personal/experiential.

In descriptive writing, you describe the facts precisely and accurately. This type of writing is usually associated with 'report' writing. Although most assignments or essays contain some elements of descriptive writing, such as giving essential background information, you are usually asked to be 'analytical' and 'critical'. You need to examine the 'what, why and how', developing your ideas and opinions and demonstrating you can reason effectively, based on supporting evidence, which here means that your

1	Essay title	Examine and analyse the title or essay question, clarifying the task.
2	Gathering information	Write down your ideas for the essay and start selecting appropriate material from the literature such as books, journals, internet, articles, reports, etc. Be careful to record in detail where you found the information, in case you want to go back to it, or in case you want to use it directly in your writing. You can keep these notes either in alphabetical order by author, or you can arrange them in themes, or even colour-code them.
3	Organising your material and reflecting on it	Consider your notes, cluster ideas and consider a sequence for these ideas. Reflect on your findings and opinions. Keep in mind where you want to go, referring back to the title. Is the gathered evidence sufficient or do you need to go back to the sources?
4	Planning the first draft	Outline your first draft, allocating word counts to different parts of the essay. Check there is logical reasoning behind your argument, based on relevant evidence. If possible, discuss the draft with your tutor. Tutors are not always allowed to 'pre-mark' full assignments or essays but can give you feedback on work in progress. Discussing your draft with a peer or colleague also helps you to clarify your ideas. If necessary, repeat this process for subsequent drafts.
5	Final piece	Respond to the feedback given, either by tutor or peer, revising the draft. Proofread, checking spelling, grammar and punctuation; make sure all citing and referencing are accurate. Check final word count. Confirm you have met the required format of presentation for the assignment or essay (margins, line spacing, etc). Then you're ready to: SUBMIT!

Figure 11.2   Planning your assignment

statements are backed up by what you have read in the literature, or other sources, on that subject. You need to demonstrate that you have read what others say about the subject (by citing and referencing), to underpin your own thoughts and form the basis of your argument. Being 'critical' is often interpreted as being negative, however for academic writing, it means: 'making a careful judgement after balanced consideration of all aspects of the topic' (McMillan and Weyers, 2007: 75).

Cottrell (2008) suggests that good argumentative writing:

- states your position or point of view
- shows why it is valid by offering evidence or examples that support that position
- considers a counter-argument, including evidence (what would your opponents use to prove you are wrong?)
- persuades a neutral party that your position is the stronger one.

The third type of academic writing is also analytical but with an evaluative element. In evaluative writing, you almost always consider two or more theories, ideas or beliefs which you 'compare and contrast', focusing on similarities or differences respectively. When you evaluate your findings, you consider the strengths and limitations, and the implications of each theory, idea or belief. Based on this, you make a judgement as to which theory, idea or belief you think is the preferred one, justifying your opinion. Bear in mind that your essay needs to be 'balanced' with approximately the same number of words, using a similar pattern in your writing, for each theory.

Finally, as a diploma student, you will be asked to relate theory to your practice. This is where you can use some examples from your own experience: personal or experiential writing. It is useful to reflect on whether your experience supports or contradicts the theory and why. Although it can highlight certain aspects of a theory, however, personal experience does not usually form the main part of your essay.

It is now time to write your first draft. It may be helpful to show it to a colleague, friend or your tutor and get some feedback: are you on 'the right track'?

Within the introduction, you tell your reader the purpose of the essay, giving a brief explanation of the context; you next explain your intentions, how you have structured your findings and how this will answer the question.

McMillan and Weyers (2007) advise that the introduction has to be well organised and clear. It is usually a work in progress because until you complete the entire text, you cannot introduce the whole work accurately. They continue: 'some people prefer to start writing the main body, then the conclusion, then the introduction' (McMillan and Weyers, 2007: 90). Arguably, one of the most important sentences of the assignment is the opening one. Some people like to start with a catchy quote or saying, to draw the reader in right from the start, creating interest and curiosity. If you do this, you must make sure the quote you use is relevant to the subject and what you are saying about it, otherwise it will detract from your argument. In general, it is good practice to start by repeating the process word used in the assignment brief, for instance: 'This assignment will argue/demonstrate/evaluate...'.

Continuing on from the introduction, in the main body of the assignment you develop your argument by presenting your evidence. You can use the headings in your plan/outline as a guide to structuring your paragraphs. It may be helpful to check whether you can use sub-headings in your work; however, even if this is not the case, they are helpful to maintain the focus of your writing in your draft. The first sentence of a paragraph, sometimes called the 'topic sentence' (Cottrell, 2008: 192), introduces the main idea of that paragraph. Subsequent sentences develop this idea and the last sentence sums it up. Link paragraphs appropriately by making use of 'signposting' to enhance the fluency of your assignment and ensure that you guide your reader systematically through your ideas/argument.

Signposting is required when you want to:

1. add more to a point already made:
   also; moreover; furthermore; again; further; what is more; then; in addition; besides; above all; too; as well (as); either; neither ... nor; not only ... but also; similarly; correspondingly; in the same way; indeed; in fact; in reality; it is found that; as for; as to; with respect to; regarding

2. list ideas/thoughts:
    first(ly); second(ly); third(ly); another; yet another; in addition; finally; to begin with; in the second place; moreover; additionally; also; next; then; to conclude; lastly; finally
3. consider ideas from a different perspective:
    in other words; rather; alternatively; in that case; to put it (more) simply; in view of this; with this in mind; to look at this another way
4. look at examples:
    that is to say; in other words; for example; for instance; namely; an example of this is; as follows; such as; including; especially; in particular; notably; mainly; mostly.

The conclusion of your essay should summarise your argument, drawing only from the evidence you have presented, linking it to the title. It is important not to introduce any new material or evidence at this stage. In some way, the conclusion is a re-visit of the introduction. The two should be strongly connected to provide a 'rounded' essay.

Always do a final check by proofreading the assignment: does it flow coherently? Is the argument logically developed? Make sure that if you have changed the order, your links are still appropriate. Are your spelling, punctuation and grammar correct?

CITING AND REFERENCING

When you write assignments on your diploma course, you will be drawing on a variety of different sources:

1. The content of the taught sessions or, if you are on a distance learning programme, the materials that you are provided with, will give you a good overview of the topic as a whole and will serve as a springboard for further thought. If in attendance mode, you will have the opportunity to discuss the issues raised and share experiences with your fellow course members, both informally and in the more organised settings of large and small group activities, as well as receiving some formal input from the tutors on the course. In distance learning mode, you will be provided with reading to do and exercises to work through, either in paper or electronic form. This will be supplemented by meetings with your tutor and possibly other learners on an occasional basis. The purpose of the above is to introduce you to the material, giving you the bigger picture and encouraging you to think about what it means to you and the performance of your teaching role. By necessity, these activities will provide an overview rather than detailed information but will give you a structure to work from.
2. Your own experience and ideas are also an important source. Your teaching (and learning) experience gives you a context in which to make sense of the various concepts and theories you encounter. A major concern of the diploma programme is that you can relate the content of the course to your own practice and in your

assignments you will be showing that this is the case. You might use theory to analyse your practice or illustrate aspects of theory through reference to examples from your practice to demonstrate your understanding of the relationship between the two. All of your assignments will contain reference to your practice in some shape or form. In thinking about or discussing either theory or practice, you may well come up with your own ideas. These will also inform your assignment provided that you can show how they are informed, either by theory or practice, and can present some form of justification for them.

3. Whilst you may be putting your own ideas into the assignment, all assignments written at this level will use other people's thoughts and ideas from sources such as books, journals, policy documents, newspaper articles or the internet. There is no need to reinvent the wheel each time you tackle an assignment and there is an expectation that you will use other people's work to introduce new ideas or to illustrate or support your own arguments, particularly as your diploma assignments will be at QCF level 5.

4. Referring to other people's work gives your assignment added credibility and perhaps, just as importantly, provides evidence of wider reading to whoever marks your assignment. Quotes are normally included when they:

(a) make a point in a concise but original manner. Sometimes you come across a phrase or sentence in your reading which neatly sums up a point in a slightly quirky or humorous manner. It provides both understanding and a smile. For example, 'statistics can be used in much the same way as a drunk uses a lamp-post: for support rather than illumination'. The chances are that whoever reads your work will react in the same manner that you did and so you may well want to include it in your assignment, if there is an appropriate place for it to go

(b) define a bit of terminology you are introducing into your assignment; for example, Berne (1972: 20) defines a transaction as 'a single stimulus and a single response, verbal or non-verbal, [it] is the unit of social action. It is called a transaction because each party gains something from it, and that is why he engages in it'. You can give an explanation of this in your own words but sometimes it is easier and gives a more precise and accurate description if you use the words of the person who came up with the idea in the first place

(c) directly support or illustrate a point you wish to make. You may well quote from your own practice, as previously mentioned. By necessity, your experience is limited in scope, however, and you cannot assume that because that is what happens for you, the same applies to everyone else; you cannot generalise from your own experience. If, however, you can show that other people agree with what your experience tells you, your point carries a lot more weight. For example: Petty (2009: 209) agrees, stating that 'dictation is a disaster for slow writers, bad spellers, most dyslexic students – and for students whose pen has just been lost!'

PLAGIARISM

When using other people's ideas or work, it is important that you make it clear this is what you are doing. If you fail to do this, either by design or accident, you can be accused of plagiarism as you will be presenting these ideas as your own work. Plagiarism carries serious penalties and the two main causes are:

- using someone else's work without crediting it as theirs, either by design or accident
- submitting someone else's work as your own.

Plagiarism of the first kind is avoided through appropriate use of citing and referencing. Citing involves identifying to the reader any part of your assignment in which you have drawn on or used other people's ideas or work. The reader may then want to go back to the original source and read more about this particular idea. You have to supply sufficient information, therefore, to allow them to locate this source without any difficulty. The information required to do this is found in the reference list at the end of the assignment. The reference list contains only those sources you have cited in your assignment. Sometimes you may have consulted other sources but not actually used them in the assignment. If you list these as well as those you have cited, your list is now known as a bibliography. Your course regulations will tell you if you are required to provide a reference list (only sources you have cited) or a bibliography (all the sources you have consulted, but not necessarily cited).

There are a number of different systems used to carry out citing and referencing, but, in educational circles, the Harvard system is the one that is favoured. For books, this involves providing the name of the author, the year of publication and, if using a direct quote, the page number(s) of the source when citing. The author, year, title of the book and details of the publisher are included in the reference list or bibliography. The same general principles are adapted to suit sources other than books. Your centre will provide you with detailed instructions as to how to use the referencing system they prefer, but, should you wish to supplement this with further reading, try *Cite them Right: The Essential Referencing Guide* by Richard Pears and Graham Shields (Pears and Shields, 2013). Details can be found at www.citethemright.co.uk. You can also find various internet materials on citing and referencing, and Neil's toolbox at www. neilstoolbox.com/bibliography-creator/index.htm is one of the most useful.

TEACHING OBSERVATION

You will be required to complete a number of teaching observations, usually carried out by your course tutors, although a subject mentor may also be involved in this process. Observation of teaching is becoming much more commonplace within the sector as a whole, fulfilling a variety of purposes such as internal audit and informing the appraisal process. This leads Armitage et al. (2012: 52) to comment that 'being observed by others whether they be colleagues, line managers or supervising tutors, is often a stressful experience', whilst also pointing out that 'paradoxically, however, such observation of and by others can be the basis of some of the most useful professional reflection we can undertake'.

Interestingly, the above quote suggests that all teachers, regardless of experience, and regardless of the context of the observation will to some degree find the process a stressful one. This may derive from a feeling of being assessed or judged. Being 'put to the test' in any sphere of activity in life is always stressful, perhaps even more so if the person conducting the test is someone we like and respect. Another stress factor is the fear of the unknown, perhaps relating to expectations if this is a first observation, or the feeling that you do not have control of the final outcome. So how can we minimise the stress factor present in observation whilst maximising its developmental impact?

A positive view of the assessment process helps. Sir Winston Churchill attributed his limited success in school tests to the fact that he was always asked about what he *did not know* rather than what *he did know*. Try to regard the teaching observation as an opportunity to show off your skills, rather than regarding it as an exercise in looking for any weaknesses in your teaching. It may be worth considering at this point who will be conducting your observation and how they view its primary purpose. All diploma observations will include elements of both assessment and development. Where the balance between these lies may depend on a number of factors, such as the course policy and nature (pre-service, in-service, distance) or the number of observations you have had to date. The purpose of the observation may differ depending on whether it is conducted by your subject mentor or a course tutor. If you have some influence over the choice of session to be observed, you might like to consider these factors in arriving at a decision. The most tangible method of reducing stress, however, is thorough preparation before the event.

PREPARING DOCUMENTATION

Preparation of the required documents is completely in your control and a well-organised set of documents given to a tutor prior to an observation forms a good initial impression and sets a positive tone for the observation itself. Documentation will vary from institution to institution but the following is a list of paperwork you might be asked to provide:

1. Copy of the plan for the session

Exact formats will vary from institution to institution but your plan should contain:

- one or possibly two aims outlining the purpose of the session
- an appropriate number of learning objectives compatible with session aims, expressed in a SMART manner

- some kind of formal or informal assessment method for each objective built into the plan
- an indication of the differentiation strategies you will be employing
- an awareness of the functional skills requirements and opportunities within the session
- a recognisable structure of introduction, development and summary
- a variety of strategies with a good balance between teacher-led and learner-led activity
- a range of appropriate resources to support the activities to be used.

2.   Scheme of work

You may be asked for a copy of the scheme of work from which this session is taken so your tutor can see how it links with both previous and future sessions.

3.   Copy of resources to be used

In order to make a judgement about your use of resources, your tutor will find it helpful to either have a list of resources used before the session or to be included when resources are distributed to learners.

4.   Profile of the group

Rather than enter an observation 'cold', your tutor will appreciate receiving a thumbnail sketch of the group and any significant individual learners. This also gives you an opportunity to give advance notice of any particular challenges you may expect to meet and additional information such as the reasons for your particular approach – whether you are trying out something new or how you are incorporating feedback previously received. You may also highlight particular aspects of your teaching on which you would like to receive specific feedback. Even if not required, a document such as this will prove useful.

PREPARING THE LEARNERS

In the 1920s, an experiment was conducted in a factory in Chicago to examine the effects on productivity of altering the conditions in which employees worked. A surprising result emerged from this study as productivity increased not only when working conditions improved but also when they were made worse. The conclusion drawn was that it was the knowledge that they were being studied rather than the different conditions to which they were exposed that made the workers alter their behaviour. This effect, known as the Hawthorne Effect after the original Chicago factory, lies behind one of the major reservations concerning teaching observation – the presence of the observer in the room has an effect on what takes place. This affects both teachers and learners. It is likely that you will already know your observer and can minimise the personal effects of their presence through an informal meeting prior to the observation (see next section). Your learners, on the other hand, will probably not have seen your observer before and will undoubtedly wonder who they are, why they are there and what they will be doing.

The effect on learners can be minimised by a simple explanation before the observation, mentioning:

- that someone else will be present at the session in question
- that it is you that is being observed and not them
- what the observer is likely to do during the session (just observe or participate in the session and if the latter to what extent)
- whether the observer may want to talk to them, either at opportune moments during the session or after, and why.

It is not only what you say that is important, but also the way in which you say it. The message needs to be delivered in a 'by the way' manner rather than making a big issue out of it. The intention is to forewarn but also play down the significance of the event. Some teachers feel uncomfortable with their learners knowing that they are on a teaching course. If you fall into this category, you can, with your tutor's agreement, introduce the forthcoming observation to learners in a way which does not make this evident. However you broach the idea of the observation to learners, it is a practice that should not be ignored as it can make a significant contribution to reducing the impact of the observer and be less of a distraction to learners than it might otherwise be.

PREPARING YOURSELF

A number of protocols will have been established for the observation process, which are intended to make life easier both for you and your tutor by establishing set procedures you can both work to. These protocols will cover areas such as:

- procedures for arranging the observation
- timing and duration of observations
- the role of the observer
- documentation required from both parties
- allocation of grades
- arrangements for feedback
- issues of confidentiality
- procedures for dealing with disputes over grading.

You should familiarise yourself with these protocols before any observations take place. In particular, find out the criteria used in the awarding of grades, as you will want to know the basis on which you are to be judged and what you will have to do if required to achieve a particular grade in a given observation.

OBSERVATION PRE-MEETING

There is a higher likelihood of a successful observation if both parties (you and your tutor) contribute to making the experience constructive. This is the purpose of the pre-meeting, which need not be formal or lengthy but should address a number of points:

- Make a final check on the date, time and venue of the observation.
- If your tutor is an off-site visitor, make necessary arrangements for access to the premises, especially if normally a secure site (MoD, prison, etc.), and make sure they know exactly where in the building the observation is to take place. Normally, meeting at Reception or its equivalent is the best option.
- Ensure the observing tutor is aware of any requirements as far as dress is concerned – e.g. safety boots if workshop-based, soft soles for gym, warm/waterproof clothing if outdoors.
- Discuss arrangements for where the observer will place themselves, allowing for good vision and hearing whilst remaining as unobtrusive as possible, and how they will be introduced to learners.
- If the role of the tutor is not specified within the protocols, find out your tutor's preference. Armitage et al. (2012: 52) point out that some tutors 'may insist on a non-participatory role to increase their objectivity, or a participatory one to diminish the effect of the scrutinising assessor at the back of the classroom that everyone is desperately trying to pretend doesn't exist!'
- You may give your tutor the documentation you have prepared at this stage, but, if not, you need to agree when and where this will take place.
- Explain the context of the observation and check protocols.
- Agree a time and place for feedback if this cannot be carried out straight after the observed session. Feedback should be as soon as possible after the event whilst it is still relatively fresh in everyone's minds, but sometimes a short time gap can prove useful for reflection and lead to a more productive feedback session.

You are now as prepared as you can be and can perhaps relax a bit more, knowing you have done all you can in advance to 'smooth the observation path'.

FEEDBACK

After the observation, you will meet with your tutor to receive their feedback. Assuming this takes place immediately after the observation, it is probably best to arrange to carry this out somewhere where you won't be disturbed, particularly if you know that learners tend to hang around at the end of the session. Feedback practices differ from tutor to tutor, but, normally, to encourage your development as a reflective practitioner, you will be asked to start proceedings with a short self-evaluation of the session. In this, you need to focus on the process of the session. Comments such as 'I thought it went well because they all learnt what they should' or 'I thought it went well because I really knew my subject' don't do this – you need to focus on what you did, how learners responded and why.

A fairly common approach to self-evaluation suggests looking at what went well and what didn't go so well, and this provides a good starting point. Try and identify one or two strengths of the session. This may be a particular activity, a resource, an assessment method or some spontaneous event. If it was an activity, why did it go well? Did it enthuse learners, catch their interest, lead to thought-provoking discussion? Was this because of your choice of topic or the way you organised it? If a resource, why was it so effective? Did it focus attention where you wanted it, bring an explanation to life, make it easier to understand a difficult concept, counter a stereotypical image? Was this because of the way you used it or the way you had designed and presented it? Was your assessment method successful because it blended naturally into the session? Did it allow you to differentiate, provide motivation to learners, identify individual progress?

You also need to identify one or two things about the session that were less successful. Why did a particular activity not go as well as you had anticipated? Was it too long, did it exclude some learners, was it pitched at the wrong level, were the instructions not clear? If so, what have you now learned and how could you make better use of an activity such as this in the future? Did that resource actually prove to be a distraction? Was it too small to be seen by all or too quiet to be heard, did it cause confusion rather than illustrate the points you wanted to make? If so, what could you do to improve its effectiveness if used again? Did your assessment method disturb the flow of the session? Was it too easy/too difficult, did it not relate as well as you had hoped to the objectives? If so, what has been learned and how will you take this into account in choosing appropriate assessment methods in the future?

There is no set order for the remainder of the feedback session; some tutors will give the grade at the beginning so it does not become a distraction, for instance, whilst others will give it at the end on the basis that the rationale for the decision is clear, but at some stage you will be given reasonably detailed feedback on your teaching. Although it has its critics, the 'praise sandwich' is still commonly used for this purpose. The strengths are highlighted first, then areas which require further development, before finishing on a positive note. During this stage of the process, you need to use your listening skills. Try and listen to what is actually being said rather than trying to think of a defensive response or to second-guess what is coming next. Feedback is intended to take the form of a professional discussion. It is two-way and so you can ask for clarification on any points you are unsure of and offer the reasoning behind the approach you took where appropriate. Your tutor will give you a written report on the observation but you may find it useful to also make your own notes during the feedback session.

ACTION PLAN

After the feedback meeting, the final stage in the process is to sit down and make some sense of it all in a final evaluation. Ultimately, having reflected on your own thoughts and the feedback received, you need to devise some form of action plan which identifies what you have learned and how you will make use of this in your future practice. Remember that you can develop your practice through learning from the strengths of the observed session, as well as from the areas identified as requiring attention. Action plans can take different forms but a possible format can be seen in Figure 11.3.

Action plan following Teaching Observation

Name: Date:

Title of observed session: Session date:

The major points I have learned from this session are:

1.

2.

3.

4.

5.

How I will use each of these to improve my practice:

Learning point	How I will use it	Target date	Evidence of achievement
1			
2			
3			
4			
5			

I will review my progress on this action plan on .... (date)

Figure 11.3   Sample post-observation action plan

(*Adapted* from Francis and Gould, 2013: 193)

The completed action plan can be integrated within the course as a whole in a number of ways, such as complementing your ILP or providing ideas for CPD activities or a small-scale action research project. It can also form part of the documentation for your next observation, when you can demonstrate the further development of your teaching.

MICRO-TEACHING

Although not a mandatory requirement of the diploma programme, another opportunity for receiving feedback on your teaching may be presented through a micro-teaching exercise. In its original form, micro-teaching involved teaching a short session or part of a session which was videoed. The teacher and their mentor would then review the video, analysing performance and identifying ways in which it might be improved. The session would then be re-taught in light of the feedback received. Although we still use the term micro-teach (some centres call it 'peer group teaching' or a 'mini lesson'), the format and purpose have changed somewhat.

You are likely to be given guidance on the micro-teaching task and the way in which it is organised on your particular course. This will specify:

- the length of the micro-teaching session
- the paperwork that is to be completed
- where the micro-teach will be held and the range of resources that will be available
- the parts that everyone will play (teacher, audience, observer) and how these will be allocated
- guidance on how peer- and self-evaluation will be carried out.

You are now in a position to start planning what you will do. First, you will need to think about the composition and size of the group you will teach and what topic is going to be suitable. Some centres will give you an open choice whereas others may stipulate that the micro-teach should be based on the subject you teach. If your experience of teaching is limited, it may be best to choose a topic with which you are familiar and therefore confident of in your subject knowledge.

If, on the other hand, you are on an in-service programme and have substantial experience of teaching already behind you, you can use the micro-teach as an opportunity to experiment and try something new in what is a relatively safe environment – perhaps a different approach to an old topic, a new assessment method or resource, the introduction of some aspect of technology you have not used before or an opportunity to practise something that you are less confident about. Whatever you decide, the topic and approach should be appropriate to the group you will be teaching and allow them to be themselves. Asking groups to imagine they are 14 years old or have a learning difficulty of some kind, for instance, very rarely works and can distract from the more important aspects of the exercise.

When delivering the micro-teach, one of the biggest challenges you will face will be time management. By its nature, a micro-teach exercise is short in duration – it could be as short as 15 minutes and will rarely exceed 30 minutes. The first rule then is not to be over-ambitious in what you think you can achieve within the time allowed. Consider what is possible for the group to learn within that time frame rather than the amount of material you can deliver. There is little room for manoeuvre once the session starts and the likelihood is that you will run out of time, rather than finish early, particularly if you are planning to include any practical or learner-led activities. A few time checks on your plan will help with pacing and managing time in general.

Some people regard micro-teaching as a more stressful activity than a normal teaching situation with real learners. Perhaps it is felt that there is more 'face to be lost' when teaching a group containing fellow learners and possibly colleagues, or assumed that because of the nature of the exercise, the audience will be more critical. The reality is that you will, in all likelihood, be teaching a friendly supportive group of people, all of whom will be willing you to succeed, so try and engage with them from the start; make good eye contact all round and smile!

At the conclusion of the micro-teach, it is normal to give your own evaluation of the session before receiving feedback from your tutor and fellow learners. Similarly, you will undoubtedly be asked, in turn, to provide feedback on the performance of others. Giving feedback is an activity which needs to be approached with some sensitivity, particularly if the person receiving it is not very confident and their session did not go as well as they had hoped. The feedback you give should be honest but delivered in a supportive, constructive manner which allows the recipient to reflect on their performance and learn from the experience of the micro-teach. If the micro-teach was rather limited in its delivery, it is best to focus on no more than one or two areas for improvement. There is a limit to the number of issues one person can address at one time and two from you is probably sufficient as they will be receiving other feedback as well. There will also be some positive features you can comment on. Someone once claimed to have had more positive feedback from one eBay purchase than they had received in all of their school years. We would hope that whilst not afraid to address issues that arise, our feedback would be rather better balanced than this. Feedback is always more valuable and better received when it is objective, so try and describe what you saw rather than pass judgement. A comment like 'you seemed to be facing more towards the left-hand side of the group and so asked them a lot more questions' is more helpful and will receive a less defensive response than 'you totally ignored everyone on the right side of the group'. Ultimately, the purpose of the micro-teaching exercise is to help develop teaching skills and much can be learned from watching others as well as reflecting on your own performance, but in both cases the quality of feedback and the manner in which it is given are instrumental in bringing about change.

MAKING THE MOST OF YOUR SUBJECT MENTOR

As part of your diploma course, you should have access to a subject mentor. Traditionally, Initial Teacher Training (ITT) in the post-school sector has been generic in nature, based on the assumption that those coming into teaching already possess the specialist knowledge and skills required within their particular subject. However, an Ofsted review of ITT in Further Education concluded that although taught elements of courses were generally good, 'few opportunities are provided for trainees to learn how to teach their specialist subject, and there is a lack of systematic mentoring and support in the workplace' (Ofsted, 2003: 5). This theme was continued in the government White Paper of 2004, *Equipping our Teachers for the Future*, which emphasised the need for subject-specific skills and knowledge, and recommended that 'Mentoring, either by line managers, subject experts or experienced teachers in related curriculum areas, is essential' (DfES, 2004: 8).

Whilst your course tutors will be able to support you in all course-related matters and give you general feedback on your teaching, it is highly unlikely that their particular subject specialism will be an identical match with yours. Providing support when it is needed for subject-related matters is the job of a subject mentor who will ideally teach the same subject as you to similar groups of learners. Subject mentors can offer an appropriate level of advice from the background of their own subject knowledge and teaching experience and are best qualified to respond to queries such as those about useful references, resources, teaching methods which seem to work well, planning courses and lessons, devising tests, interpreting a syllabus or teaching particularly difficult concepts within the subject. Often, a few words from them can save you a lot of time and potential frustration. Observing subject mentors teaching will also prove a valuable exercise, particularly if they are using a new resource or a piece of equipment with which you are not familiar or teaching a particular bit of the syllabus that causes you some difficulty. Sometimes, you may just want someone with specialist knowledge to bounce ideas off – a subject mentor can be useful to you in any number of ways.

You need to bear in mind, however, that whoever takes on the subject mentor role will probably have a busy teaching life themselves and so opportunities to meet and talk may be difficult to come by. A lack of communication may be interpreted as not needing support or reassurance, so it is important that you and your mentor establish some kind of procedure for meeting on a reasonably regular basis. If your mentor does not propose a way of achieving this, do not be afraid to suggest that you would find it useful to meet regularly, even if only for a short period of time. To make the most of this shared time, you may well prepare by keeping a brief record of anything that happens that you would like to discuss, as it is easy to forget these things when the meeting takes place.

As well as being busy, your mentor is in all probability taking on this role on a voluntary basis and without any recognition of it on their timetable, so anything you can do to facilitate the mentoring process will help considerably. Keeping a record of meetings is a case in point. You need to keep a brief record of what was discussed and what actions arise from the discussion. This provides some structure and record of progress and will complement other personal development records you may be required to keep as part of your course. Rather than passing on this responsibility to your mentor, it would be useful if you produced some kind of template to record the results of your meetings which, when completed, your mentor could be asked to sign to confirm it as a common understanding. An example of the kind of document you might find useful for this purpose is given in Figure 11.4.

Date of meeting:

Progress since last meeting:

Topics discussed at this meeting:

Actions arising from discussion:

Date of next meeting:

Signed ....

Signed (mentor) ....

Figure 11.4   Sample record of progress

Your subject mentor may also be involved in your teaching observations. The focus will be different from that conducted by your course tutor who will be mainly concerned with areas such as:

- the quality of the planning
- the variety of learning activities and resources, and assessment methods
- the balance of teacher-led and learner-led activity
- group management.

Your subject mentor is likely to be more concerned with the way in which you teach your specialist subject. Whilst some of the above may be commented on, the main point of focus will be the way in which you teach the subject itself. Your subject mentor is more likely to consider whether:

- your subject knowledge is sound and up to date
- the resources you use achieve their purpose and are effectively used
- the technical explanations you give are clear, accurate and unambiguous
- your explanations are supported by appropriate examples and illustrations

- learners fully understand any new concepts or principles that you introduce
- the strategies you use are the most appropriate for this particular subject and involve learners
- learners are given the opportunity to put their learning into practice
- the subject matter interests, engages and challenges learners.

FINALLY

Hopefully, you now feel better equipped to meet the requirements of your diploma course. We hope it proves an interesting and challenging experience for you and wish you all the best in your future teaching career.

SUMMARY OF KEY POINTS

In this chapter, we have looked at various aspects of the organisation and requirements of the Diploma in Education and Training programme. The skills associated with producing successful assignments – researching, reading, critical and analytical thinking, writing, citing and referencing – were investigated first. The practical teaching activities associated with the course, observation and micro-teaching, were then discussed, with an emphasis on the planning procedures which make a positive outcome to these activities more likely. A subject mentor is a valuable resource and consideration was given to ways of deriving the greatest benefit from this relationship.

The key points in this chapter are:

- Books, journals, e-books and the internet provide the main sources for researching an assignment but care needs to be taken to ensure only trustworthy websites are consulted.
- An increased understanding of what you read can be achieved through using the SQ3R (survey, question, read, recall, review) technique.
- A critical and analytical approach is required to enhance your academic skills.
- Assignments normally follow the sequence of title/question, introduction, main body, conclusion, reference list/bibliography.
- Academic writing can be descriptive, argumentative/analytical, evaluative/analytical or personal/experiential in style.
- The process of citing and referencing identifies your use of the work of others and its use is essential in avoiding accusations of plagiarism.

(Continued)

- Preparation of both your learners and yourself leads to a smoother teaching observation.
- An observation pre-meeting with your tutor clarifies procedures and expectations and makes a positive contribution to a successful observation.
- A realistic view of what can be achieved in the limited time available in a micro-teaching exercise must be taken.

REFERENCES

Armitage, A., Bryant, R., Dunnill, R. and Hayes, D. (2012) *Teaching and Training in Post-compulsory Education* (4th edn). Maidenhead: Open University Press.

Bedford, D. and Wilson, E. (2006) *Study Skills for Foundation Degrees*. London: David Fulton.

Berne, E. (1972) *What Do You Say After You Say Hello?* New York: Grove Press.

Browne, M.N. and Keeley, S.M. (2007) *Asking the Right Questions, A Guide to Critical Thinking* (8th edn). New Jersey: Pearson Education, Inc.

Chambers, E. and Northedge, A. (2008) *The Arts Good Study Guide*. Milton Keynes: Open University Press.

Cottrell, S. (2005) *Critical Thinking Skills*. Basingstoke: Palgrave Macmillan

Cottrell, S. (2008) *The Study Skills Handbook*. Basingstoke: Palgrave Macmillan.

Dewey, J. (1933) How We Think: A Restatement of the Relation of Reflective Thinking to the Educational Process. Lexington, MA: D. C. Heath Publishing.

DfES (2004) Equipping our Teachers for the Future. London: DfES.

Francis, M. and Gould, J. (2013) *Achieving Your PTLLS Award* (2nd edn). London: Sage.

Judge, B., Jones, P. and McCreery, E. (2009) *Critical Thinking Skills for Education Students*. Exeter: Learning Matters

Kirton, B. (2011) Brilliant Essay: What You Need to Know and How to Do It. Harlow: Pearson.

Malthouse, R. and Roffey-Barentsen, J. (2013) *Academic Skills*. London: Thalassa Publishing (CreateSpace).

McMillan, K. and Weyers, J. (2007) *How to Write Essays and Assignments*. Harlow: Pearson.

Ofsted (2003) The Initial Training of Further Education Teachers: A Survey. London: HMSO.

Pauk, W. and Owens, R.J.Q. (2010) *How to Study in College* (10th edn). London: Wadsworth.

Pears, R. and Shields, G. (2013) *Cite Them Right: The Essential Referencing Guide* (9th edn). Basingtone: Palgrave Macmillan.

Petty, G. (2009) *Teaching Today: A Practical Guide* (4th edn). Cheltenham: Nelson Thornes.

Turner, K., Ireland, L., Krenus, B. and Pointon, L. (2008) *Essential Academic Skills*. South Melbourne: Oxford University Press.

Warburton, N. (2006) *The Basics of Essay Writing*. Abingdon: Routledge.

Appendix 1

MAPPING OF CHAPTERS AGAINST ASSESSMENT CRITERIA FOR EACH MANDATORY UNIT

Unit title: Developing teaching, learning and assessment in education and training					
1. Be able to investigate practice in own area of specialism.					
1.1	Chapter 6	1.2	Chapter 10		
2. Be able to apply theories, principles and models of learning, communication and assessment to planning inclusive teaching and learning.					
2.1	Chapter 1	2.2	Chapter 2	2.3	Chapter 2
2.4	Chapter 4	2.5	Chapter 5		
3. Be able to apply theories of behaviour management to creating and maintaining a safe, inclusive teaching and learning environment.					
3.1	Chapter 7	3.2	Chapter 7	3.3	Chapter 7
4. Be able to apply theories, principles and models of learning and communication to delivering inclusive teaching and learning.					
4.1	Chapter 3	4.2	Chapter 3	4.3	Chapter 1
4.4	Chapter 1	4.5	Chapter 5		
5. Be able to apply theories, models and principles of assessment to assessing learning in education and training.					
5.1	Chapter 4	5.2	Chapter 4	5.3	Chapter 4
5.4	Chapter 4	5.5	Chapter 4		
6. Be able to implement expectations of the Minimum Core in planning, delivering and assessing inclusive teaching and learning.					
6.1	Chapter 1	6.2	Chapter 1		

7. Be able to apply theories and models of reflection and evaluation to the evaluation of own practice in planning, delivering and assessing inclusive teaching and learning.					
7.1	Chapter 8	7.2	Chapter 8		

Unit title: Teaching, learning and assessment in education and training					
1. Understand roles, responsibilities and relationships in education and training.					
1.1	Chapter 1	1.2	Chapter 1	1.3	Chapter 1
1.4	Chapter 1				
2. Be able to use initial and diagnostic assessment to agree individual learning goals with learners.					
2.1	Chapter 1	2.2	Chapter 4	2.3	Chapter 4
2.4	Chapter 4				
3. Be able to plan inclusive teaching and learning.					
3.1	Chapter 2	3.2	Chapter 2	3.3	Chapter 2
3.4	Chapter 2	3.5	Chapter 4		
4. Be able to create and maintain a safe, inclusive teaching and learning environment.					
4.1	Chapter 7	4.2	Chapter 1	4.3	Chapter 1
5. Be able to deliver inclusive teaching and learning.					
5.1	Chapter 2	5.2	Chapter 5	5.3	Chapter 4
5.4	Chapter 4	5.5	Chapter 1	5.6	Chapter 3
5.7	Chapter 5				
6. Be able to assess learning in education and training.					
6.1	Chapter 4	6.2	Chapter 4	6.3	Chapter 4
6.4	Chapter 4	6.5	Chapter 4	6.6	Chapter 4
7. Be able to implement expectations of the Minimum Core in planning, delivering and assessing inclusive teaching and learning.					
7.1	Chapter 1	7.2	Chapter 1		
8. Be able to evaluate own practice in planning, delivering and assessing inclusive teaching and learning.					
8.1	Chapter 8	8.2	Chapter 8		

Unit title: Wider professional practice and development in education and training					
1. Understand professionalism and the influence of professional values in education and training.					
1.1	Chapter 8	1.2	Chapter 8		
2. Understand the policy context of education and training.					
2.1	Chapter 10	2.2	Chapter 10		
3. Understand the impact of accountability to stakeholders and external bodies on education and training.					
3.1	Chapter 10	3.2	Chapter 10	3.3	Chapter 10
3.4	Chapter 10				

4. Understand the organisational context of education and training.					
4.1	Chapter 10	4.2	Chapter 10		

5. Be able to contribute to the quality improvement and quality assurance arrangements of own organisation.					
5.1	Chapter 10	5.2	Chapter 10	5.3	Chapter 10
5.4	Chapter 10				

Unit title: Theories, principles and models in education and training					
1. Understand the application of theories, principles and models of learning in education and training.					
1.1	Chapter 6	1.2	Chapter 6	1.3	Chapter 1
1.4	Chapter 6				
2. Understand the application of theories, principles and models of communication in education and training.					
2.1	Chapter 5	2.2	Chapter 5		
3. Understand the application of theories, principles and models of assessment in education and training.					
3.1	Chapter 4	3.2	Chapter 4		
4. Understand the application of theories and models of curriculum development within own area of specialism.					
4.1	Chapter 9	4.2	Chapter 9		
5. Understand the application of theories and models of reflection and evaluation to reviewing own practice.					
5.1	Chapter 8	5.2	Chapter 8		

Appendix 2

EXAMPLE WHOLE-CLASS LESSON PLAN

Group: BTEC Level 2 Diploma in Public Services (18 students)	**Topic:** Organ and Blood Donation		
Date: 07.07.18	**Room:** O6		**Time:** 10.30 – 12.00

Aims: To explain the importance of blood and organ donation and blood: to discuss the procedures for donation

Specific Learning Objectives:	**Assessment:**
1. Identify the functions of blood in the human body	Through the following informal methods:
2. Name the two different types of blood donation	– Observation (LO1,5,6)
3. Recognise conditions requiring blood transfusions	– Q & A (LO2,3,5,7,8)
4. Describe the procedures in donating blood	– Responses to exercise (LO1,4,5)
5. Identify the organs of the body and their functions	– Contributions to discussion (LO7,8)
6. List risks to organs and how these relate to lifestyle	
7. Discuss how donation can make a difference	
8. State ways to get involved in organ donation	

Differentiation Strategies

Catering for mix of learning styles through explanation and discussion, use of video and practical tasks.

This is a large group, varying in ability so pairing weaker students with stronger ones in pair and small group activities.

Some learners tend to dominate; encourage quieter ones to contribute through allocation of roles in group work and through directed questioning.

Asking more open questions. Directing more demanding questions to some (LS, DR, OP etc) and less demanding questions to others (MM, GP, CN etc) particularly in final summation.

'Functions' handout graduated for differentiation.

Functional Skills Opportunities:

Use of subject specific key words. Reporting and recording results of group work

Some analysis of statistics ('Conditions' H/O). Use of interactive W/B

Time	Content	Teacher Activity	Learner Activity	Assessment	Resources
Intro 10.30	Aims and outcomes	Read out and explain and restate aims	Record aims	Observation	ILP
Dev 10.35	Functions of the blood (LO1)	Allocate learners to differentiated groups. Introduce task and take feedback	Agree roles. List functions and feed back results	Observation and responses	Flip chart sheets and pens
10.50	Distinguish between whole blood & platelet transfusion (LO2)	Explain and question	Discuss and answer	Q & A	Slides
10.55	Conditions requiring whole blood or platelet transfusion (LO3)	Distribute hand-out, explain and question	Complete hand-out in allocated pairs. Answer questions	Q & A	'Conditions' hand-out
11.00	How to donate blood (LO4)	Introduce virtual tour on interactive WB. Discuss and question	Come out in turn and 'operate' different sections. Discuss	Contributions to exercise	www.blood.co.uk / virtualsession/ index.asp
11.15	Identify organs and their functions (LO5). Function of organs	Describe organs and remove each in turn from model. Introduce matching exercise	Listen and then replace and name organs. Complete exercise in same pairings	Observation and Q & A. Observation and responses	Body model. 'Functions' handout
11.35	Lifestyle and risks to organs (LO6)	Introduce discussion task and take feedback	Discuss and feed back in same groups	Observation and responses	Discussion briefing sheet
11.50	How donation can make a difference and ways of getting involved (LO7,8)	Play video, Hand out questions. Facilitate discussion with stories, facts, discussion points	Watch video. Answer questions; contribute to discussion	Q & A, contribution to discussion	www.giveandletlive.co.uk /en/whydonate/index.html. Blood donation video. Question sheet
11.55 – 12.00 **Conc**	Summarising and checking learning	Revisit objectives and use directed questioning to summarise	Answer allocated questions	Q & A	

Self-evaluation
What went well/not so well in this session
Class started on time and all learning objectives were met. The students were very interested in the topic and participated well in the activities, which is pleasing as this group can be a handful sometimes. I was surprised at how much some of the students already knew about the topic; some volunteer with the St John's Ambulance Service or Red Cross, some others had parents or relatives who are blood donors. This meant there was a lot to talk about and share. Allocating groups and pairs worked well – productive outcome. The activities took longer than I had anticipated, so timing was a bit out. One of the strengths was the use of the video clips, although it took me some time to get the first one to work – this resulted in students talking amongst themselves and it was difficult to get them to focus again. The second clip made one of the students feel queasy and need to look away for some time. I had to 'rush' the end part of the session which had already overrun and it meant we didn't get chance to discuss the assignment properly.
What I think the reasons were for the above
This is clearly a topic the students are interested in and have some experience in. This makes it easy to teach, as all students are 'with you'. I had thought carefully about the mix of activities to use and this contributed to their levels of engagement. Assumptions – I thought I knew my students well but was surprised by the levels of knowledge they possessed on this topic, hence timing problems. I also assumed that anyone wanting to work in public services would be OK with the sight of blood, particularly on a video. The session overran because I hadn't allocated sufficient time for the conclusion and further questions. Fortunately, they didn't seem to mind too much on this occasion but that won't always be the case!
How this might inform my future teaching
Maintain a good variety of activities and continue to think about best combinations of students for exercises. Check prior experience and knowledge more thoroughly – either at end of previous session or probe a bit more with questioning at the beginning of the session.
Remember to issue warnings about sensitive or graphic materials.
Check internet connection on Smartboard before the session so video clips can be used seamlessly.
Increase time on plan for finishing the session off – need to end in a more orderly fashion and on time!

Appendix 3
EXAMPLE WORKSHOP PLAN VERSION 1

Course: First Diploma	Group: 2A	Topic: Video production workshop	
Date: 08/07/18	Room: O13	Time: 9.15–11.00	
Name:	**Outcome / target:**	**Resources needed:**	**Progress:**
Learner 1	Complete filming of project by re-shooting conversation scene (using a tripod this time) and final scene	Filming kit DV tape	Footage completed, better definition, less 'wobble' and good use of natural light. Ready to begin editing next session
Learner 2	Pre-production work – Treatment and Shooting Schedule must be written, printed off and handed in	Examples of pre-production forms Access to PC with printer	Treatment and Shooting Schedule satisfactorily completed and submitted. Discussed possible improvements to be made – first task for next session
Learner 3	Capture video footage onto Premier Pro and make rough edit, participating as part of a group	Premier Pro workstation DV tape	Worked well as member of a group and assisted in editing at least two minutes of video in a logical order. To collect various audio tracks for insertion in film during next session
Learner 4	Pre-production work – Proposal and Storyboard to be completed, printed off and handed in	Storyboard sheets and pencils Examples of pre-production forms Access to PC with printer	Proposal and storyboard completed and handed in. Although late, both pieces of work are of good standard and do not require improvement. Filming to start next session

Appendix 4
EXAMPLE WORKSHOP PLAN VERSION 2

Course: Level 1 Diploma wood occupations		Room: Carpentry workshop	Time: 9.00–12.00	
	Date: 01/07/18	Date: 03/07/18	Date: 08/07/18	Date: 10/07/18
Learner 1	Target: Mark out tenon for haunch M&T according to drawing and cut using tenon saw. Check against drawing when complete	Target: Complete cutting of tenon and mark out mortise according to drawing. Begin chiselling out mortise	Target: Complete mortise and check for fit with tenon – final adjustments. Mark out second tenon and cut using band saw if time	Target: Finish second tenon, mark up and cut second mortise using mortising machine
	Resources: Wood, tri-square, marking gauge, pencil, rule, tenon saw	Resources: Tri-square, marking gauge, pencil, rule, tenon saw, mallet, bevelled chisel, G-clamp	Resources: Mallet, bevelled chisel, G-clamp, tri-square, marking gauge, pencil, rule, access to band saw	Resources: Tri-square, marking gauge, pencil, rule, access to mortising machine
	Progress: Not finished – split wood and had to start again – to be completed next session	Progress: Tenon completed and marked off, mortise marked out and almost chiselled out – complete next session before starting second tenon	Progress: Good progress – completed mortise – good fit with tenon, all marked off. Second tenon marked out and band saw booked for beginning of next lesson	Progress: Second tenon finished and marked off, mortise marked out and had mortising machine demonstration. Had to wait for turn on machine and lesson finished before I got onto it

Appendix 5
EXTRACTS FOR MARKING EXERCISE

Produce a written report which considers the different assessment methods which can be used to check that learning is taking place and the appropriateness of each within your professional context.

EXTRACT 1

There are many types of assessment methods within the Further Education and Skills sector, and indeed in our own life if we want to have a car and drive to and from work we would at some stage have to go through a driving test, both practical and theory. However, the assessment method you use will depend on what you are assessing; you could be assessing the students' attitude during a lesson or the skills they are trying to learn within their training course, and finally you could be assessing their knowledge. The assessment method may also be set down by the governing body of that particular subject, stating which method you will need to include within the training that you are delivering. As an instructor, we need to ensure we take into account students' abilities to learn within their chosen field of education, and treat each and every student under our instruction equally and without discrimination against any individual. 'You need to treat each student as an individual, take into account equality and diversity and any particular student requirements' (Gravells, 2012: 117).

There are many assessment methods which I use as an instructor/teacher; I mainly use practical tests, question and answer sessions and written tests such as multiple choice.

EXTRACT 2

Assessment is a vital element in teaching used to monitor and record a student's progress and understanding of the subject, ensuring that learning has taken place.

Subsequently, you can use assessments to recognise specific needs of groups or individuals and tailor sessions accordingly, or identify additional tutoring needs. Depending on the purpose of the assessment, it could be formal (i.e. an exam, oral test or essay work, etc.), where the student knows they are being assessed, or informal (i.e. class debate, group discussion, observation, etc.), where the learners are not aware they are being assessed. My subject is practical in nature and so I tend to rely largely on observation as an assessment method as it is a skill I am assessing. I would normally use a checklist for this purpose. There is also a certain amount of underpinning knowledge that has to be assessed, however, and I use multiple-choice questions for the more factual elements and short case studies if comprehension and/or application need to be assessed. Page 133 in *Achieving your PTLLS Award* says that we need to be clear about what the purpose of the assessment is.

INDEX